# Violence and the German Soldier in the Great War

# Violence and the German Soldier in the Great War

## Killing, Dying, Surviving

Benjamin Ziemann

Translated by Andrew Evans

BLOOMSBURY ACADEMIC
LONDON • NEW YORK • OXFORD • NEW DELHI • SYDNEY

BLOOMSBURY ACADEMIC
Bloomsbury Publishing Plc
50 Bedford Square, London, WC1B 3DP, UK
1385 Broadway, New York, NY 10018, USA

BLOOMSBURY, BLOOMSBURY ACADEMIC and the Diana logo
are trademarks of Bloomsbury Publishing Plc

First published in German by Klartext, 2013
Paperback edition published 2019

Copyright © Benjamin Ziemann, 2013, 2017

English language translation © Andrew Evans, 2017

Benjamin Ziemann has asserted his right under the Copyright,
Designs and Patents Act, 1988, to be identified as Author of this work.

Cover image: World War I. German trench in Flanders.
Soldiers with gas masks in defensive position during a gas attack. End of 1915.
(Photo by Zennig/ullstein bild via Getty Images)

All rights reserved. No part of this publication may be reproduced or
transmitted in any form or by any means, electronic or mechanical,
including photocopying, recording, or any information storage or retrieval
system, without prior permission in writing from the publishers.

Bloomsbury Publishing Plc does not have any control over, or responsibility for,
any third-party websites referred to or in this book. All internet addresses given
in this book were correct at the time of going to press. The author and publisher
regret any inconvenience caused if addresses have changed or sites have
ceased to exist, but can accept no responsibility for any such changes.

The translation of this work was funded by Geisteswissenschaften International –
Translation Funding for Work in the Humanities and Social Sciences from Germany,
a joint initiative of the Fritz Thyssen Foundation, the German Federal Foreign Office,
the collecting society VG WORT and the Börsenverein des Deutschen Buchhandels
(German Publishers & Booksellers Association).

A catalogue record for this book is available from the British Library.

ISBN: HB: 978-1-4742-3958-5
PB: 978-1-3501-0611-6
ePDF: 978-1-4742-3960-8
ePub: 978-1-4742-3959-2

A catalog record for this book is available from the Library of Congress.

Typeset by RefineCatch Limited, Bungay, Suffolk

To find out more about our authors and books visit
www.bloomsbury.com and sign up for our newsletters.

# Contents

| | | |
|---|---|---|
| List of Figures | | vi |
| Acknowledgements | | vii |
| List of Abbreviations | | ix |
| 1 | The First World War as a Laboratory of Violence | 1 |

Part One: Practices of Violence

| 2 | Soldiers of the First World War: Killing, Surviving, Discourses of Violence | 19 |
|---|---|---|
| 3 | German Soldiers and their Conduct of War in 1914 | 41 |
| 4 | Ernst Jünger: Practitioner and Observer of Killing | 63 |

Part Two: Refusal of Violence

| 5 | Desertion in the German Army 1914–1918 | 93 |
|---|---|---|
| 6 | Disillusionment and Collective Exhaustion among German Soldiers on the Western Front: The Path to Revolution in 1918 | 121 |
| 7 | The German Army in Autumn 1918: A Hidden Military Strike? | 135 |

Part Three: Processing Violence

| 8 | The Weimar Republic: A Brutalized Society? | 159 |
|---|---|---|
| 9 | The Delayed Rejection of Violence: Hermann Schützinger's Conversion to Pacifism | 177 |
| 10 | 'Rear Area Militarism': Discussing the War in Anti-military Bestsellers in the Weimar Republic | 203 |

| | |
|---|---|
| Notes | 225 |
| Select Bibliography | 291 |
| Index | 295 |

# Figures

1. Berthold Hörhold and a friend at the Western front, 1916 (author's possession). 31
2. Photograph of Ernst Jünger in his wartime uniform, from the frontispiece of Ernst Jünger, *In Stahlgewittern. Aus dem Tagebuch eines Stoßtruppführers* (Hanover, 1920). Reproduced with the permission of Klett-Cotta, Stuttgart. 65
3. '"Nie wieder Krieg". Toten-Gedenkfeier', Munich, 31 July 1922: Münchener Stadtmuseum, Sammlung Reklamekunst, P 81/68. Reproduced with the permission of Münchener Stadtmuseum. 182
4. 'Polizeioberst a.D. Dr. Hermann Schützinger, Mitglied des Reichsausschusses' picture postcard, n.d. (1927–1930) (author's possession). 199
5. *Der Etappensumpf. Dokumente des Zusammenbruchs des deutschen Heeres aus den Jahren 1916/1918. Aus dem Kriegstagebuch eines Gemeinen* (Jena: Verlag der Volksbuchhandlung, 1920), cover image. 207
6. Heinrich Wandt, *Etappe Gent. Streiflichter zum Zusammenbruch. I. Band* (Berlin: Freie Presse, 1920), cover image. 214
7. Heinrich Wandt, *Erotik und Spionage in der Etappe Gent* (Vienna. Berlin: Agis-Verlag, 1928), cover montage by John Heartfield © The Heartfield Community of Heirs. Reproduced with the permission of Design and Artists Copyright Society. 215

Every effort has been made to trace copyright holders and to obtain their permission for the use of copyright material. The publisher apologizes for any errors or omissions in the above list and would be grateful if notified of any corrections that should be incorporated in future reprints or editions of this book.

# Acknowledgements

The First World War has long been one of my primary fields of research. Yet it was only the centenary of the war that commenced in 2014 that offered me a chance to focus more specifically on the practices of violence. The chapters in this book are driven and informed by the core idea that the practice of violence during the Great War must be considered in a differentiated manner. Violence is ultimately about killing, but it cannot be properly understood without considering those soldiers who survived, and those who refused to take part in the war machine outright. The interconnections between killing, surviving and refusing stand at the centre of this book. In addition, the repercussions and representations of wartime violence in post-war Germany during the 1920s are discussed.

Most of the chapters in this book are based on extensive archival research which I have conducted over the years. Hence, I would like to express my gratitude to the staff particularly of those archives that I have visited most often, notably the military records section of the Bayerisches Hauptstaatsarchiv in Munich, the Bundesarchiv (German Federal Archives) in Berlin-Lichterfelde, the Archiv der sozialen Demokratie in Bonn and the Bibliothek für Zeitgeschichte in Stuttgart, and here especially the archivist, Irina Renz. My research has been supported by a British Academy Small Grant and by an AHRC Fellowship Grant. I am indebted to Conny Schneider and Alrun Berger for their reliable research assistance. Professor Helmuth Kiesel of the University of Heidelberg, the foremost authority on the author Ernst Jünger, not only offered me crucial advice, but also generously provided me with copies of his important books.

This book is a translation from the German and was first published with Klartext Verlag in Essen. I would like to thank Geisteswissenschaften International, a joint initiative by the Börsenverein des Deutschen Buchhandels, the Verwertungsgesellschaft Wort, the German Foreign Office and the Fritz Thyssen Foundation, for the generous funding of the translation and the recognition that the inclusion in their programme entails. As on previous occasions, Andrew Evans has done a superb job in translating my text into English. I am very grateful for his meticulous research and attention to detail. The author and publisher gratefully acknowledge the permission granted to reproduce the copyright material in this book by the Münchener Stadtmuseum, The Heartfield Community of Heirs, and Klett-Cotta.

Over the years, I have had many opportunities to discuss the themes of this book with friends and colleagues in various countries. These include Holger Afflerbach, Sabine Behrenbeck, Benjamin Beuerle, Stuart Carroll, Kathleen Canning, Roger Chickering, Belinda Davis, Miriam Dobson, Jörg Echternkamp, Moritz Föllmer, Ewald Frie, Mike Geheran, Rüdiger Graf, Sabine Grimshaw, Wolfgang Hardtwig, Ian Kershaw, Patrick Krassnitzer, Anja Kruke, Dieter Langewiesche, Antonia Leugers, Bedrich Loewenstein, Eric Lohr, Thomas Mergel, Bob Moore, Josef Mooser, Philipp Münch, Brendan Murphy, Christoph Nübel, Nicolas Offenstadt, Lutz Raphael, Frank Reichherzer, Nadine Rossol, Dirk Schumann, Gerd Schwerhoff, Helmut Walser Smith, Nick Stargardt, Matthew Stibbe, Hew Strachan, Vanessa Ther, Jeffrey Verhey, Bernard Wilkin and Jay Winter. I would like to express my gratitude to them. The chapters in this volume are the result of an ongoing engagement with many ideas and texts by Michael Geyer, to whom I am deeply indebted. Special thanks go to Patrick Houlihan and Christian Szejnmann, who read a draft version of the introduction; to Ludger Claßen and Ernst Piper, who made the publication of the original German book possible; to Christine Brocks, who discussed these issues with me more often than she probably cared to; and finally to four friends who have fundamentally shaped not only my thinking about the First World War, but also scholarship in this field more generally: Bernd Ulrich, Thomas F. Schneider, Thomas Kühne, and Richard Bessel, who also helped me to find a home in Yorkshire.

Sheffield, October 2016

# Abbreviations

| | |
|---|---|
| AOK | Armee-Ober-Kommando (army high command) |
| AK | Armeekorps (army corps) |
| BA | Bezirksamt (district administration) |
| BA/MA | Bundesarchiv/Militärarchiv Freiburg (Federal Military Archive Freiburg) |
| BArch | Bundesarchiv Berlin-Lichterfelde (Federal Archive Berlin-Lichterfelde) |
| BHStA/lV | Bayerisches Hauptstaatsarchiv München/Abt. IV: Kriegsarchiv (Bavarian Main State Archive in Munich/Section IV: War Archive) |
| Btl. | Battalion |
| Div. | Division |
| GK | Generalkommando (general command of an army corps) |
| Inf. | Infantry |
| I.R. | Infantry regiment |
| Ldst. | Landsturm |
| Ldw. | Landwehr (units of the territorial army, made up of conscripts aged 30–45) |
| L.I.R. | Landwehr Infantry Regiment |
| NHStAH | Niedersächsisches Hauptstaatsarchiv Hannover (Main State Archive of Lower Saxony in Hanover) |
| OHL | Oberste Heeresleitung (German Army Supreme Command) |
| Res. | Reserve |

| | |
|---|---|
| Rgt. | Regiment |
| Stv. | stellvertretend/stellvertretendes (deputy) |
| Uffz. | Unteroffizier (non-commissioned officer) |
| WUA | Das Werk des Untersuchungsausschusses der Verfassunggebenden Deutschen Nationalversammlung und des Deutschen Reichstages 1919–1930, 4. Reihe, II. Abteilung |

1

# The First World War as a Laboratory of Violence

If there is any single thing that can be said to define the history of the First World War, then it is, without doubt, the perpetration of violence. This is confirmed by even the briefest consideration of the numbers of people killed, injured or left permanently disabled in the course of the conflict. German deaths alone amounted to no fewer than 2.037 million soldiers, with 4.8 million wounded, many of whom suffered multiple injuries.[1] Some 700,000 German soldiers were permanently discharged from the army as 'unfit for service', and almost 90,000 of the worst injured bore the terrible scars of war for the rest of their lives, suffering amputated limbs or grave health problems.[2] The violence of war is the product of a complex amalgam of strategies, actions and military technology, all directed at the physical destruction of the enemy. Like no other war before it, the First World War fuelled collective emotions and intensified national resentments and stereotypes, both with and without the support of government propaganda. Across Germany, industrial workers, farmers and women were mobilized for action, while writers, intellectuals and professors formulated bombastic (and in retrospect often downright ridiculous) justifications for the country's military cause. Politicians and businessmen endeavoured to secure the resources needed for war. Schools urged children to contribute to the war effort, too, by collecting materials and reciting patriotic poems.[3] This was nothing less than an attempt to mobilize an entire society for conflict and to blur the boundaries between civil society on the one hand, and the military apparatus and its organization of violence on the other: phenomena historians have come to describe as 'total war'.[4]

## I The First World War as a 'total war'

Research on all these aspects of the First World War has radically broadened our picture of the conflict. The focus no longer lies solely on the objectives of diplomats and the military, as it did during the controversy surrounding Fritz Fischer's 'grab for world power' theory in the 1960s and 70s. Nor does it rest only on the socio-economic contours of the 'class society at war' studied in the 1970s and 80s. Since the 1990s, historians have been working on a history of the mentalities and experience of the First World War,[5] building on work in literary studies by scholars such as Paul Fussell and Bernd Hüppauf. Like other authors, Fussell and Hüppauf had asked whether the shock and traumatic caesura of the First World War shaped subjectivities, and examined the symbolic forms taken by the search for a subject that was compatible with war.[6] The history of mentalities has shed light on the ways in which individuals and different social groups – front-line soldiers, for instance, or bourgeois and farming families on the home front – interpreted and came to terms with mobilization for the war effort. Attention has come to bear particularly on the forms of communication that structured and enabled this process, such as amateur photography, picture postcards and the millions of letters sent by military field post.[7] By combining these different methodologies and areas of study, it is now possible to write a history of the First World War from multiple perspectives, illustrating the profound crisis it inflicted on bourgeois society. This approach reveals how the stresses of war reshaped and eroded relationships within civil society. Roger Chickering's recent study of the city of Freiburg im Breisgau is a fascinating example.[8]

The aim of this book is not to offer a comprehensive survey of recent research on the First World War. Yet it is important to acknowledge the wave of cultural history written on a range of topics since the 1990s, giving rise to a comparative cultural history of Europe from 1914 to 1918.[9] In this volume, the focus will be on developments in Germany. It is fair to say that the practice of violence was confined for many years to the margins of German historiography of the First World War. The interwar period saw the publication of traditional military histories, which were generally commissioned by the state. These initially resumed in similar vein after 1945 and largely satisfied themselves with top-down descriptions of strategy and military policy.[10] That said, it is important to note that, even by the 1920s, such military histories were no longer limited to the perspective of officers and the army general staff. The Reichsarchiv (Reich Archive), founded in 1919 to collect military records, deserves particular mention here. Formally under the control of the Reichsinnenministerium (Reich Interior Ministry), the archive developed important approaches to archiving and analysing the personal testimony of ordinary rank-and-file soldiers. This gave rise to a 'military history from below' that engaged with the experiences of the soldiers themselves.¹¹ Popular literature on the topic included the widely read *Schlachten des Weltkrieges* (Battles of the World War) series. However, this approach limited itself to describing the action at the front, and lacked analytical depth or a focus on the practice of violence.

For many decades, the analysis of the different forms, contexts and effects of violence in the First World War was thus limited to researchers on the margins of academic historical study. Specialists in German cultural history, for example, examined the literary representation of the war. Inevitably, they encountered the writings of Ernst Jünger, who glorified the violence he saw as the dawn of a new, technologically dominated modernity (see Chapter 4).¹² Another field in which historians began to address the violence of the *Materialschlachten* (battles of *matériel*) such as the Somme or Verdun – where the warring armies targeted huge amounts of weaponry on relatively small areas – was the history of psychological trauma among soldiers and officers. A variety of terms entered the language to describe this as psychiatrists and psychoanalysts competed to offer therapy for the symptoms. These included 'shell shock' in the United Kingdom and *Kriegsneurose* (war neurosis) in Germany and Austria-Hungary. Work on this topic initially concentrated on the violence exercised by the psychiatrists themselves as they subjected their patients to electric shocks and starvation diets – more maltreatment than cure.¹³ Soon, however, attention turned to the harrowing experiences of wartime violence that manifested themselves in neurological disorders.¹⁴

From this perspective, soldiers generally appeared as the victims of overwhelming violence inflicted by long-range weaponry such as artillery or machine-gun fire. Their role as perpetrators was barely addressed. As the historian Bernd Ulrich has pointed out, one notable exception was the 'psychographic' approach of Paul Plaut (1894–1960), a Jewish physician and psychologist, and one of the outsiders of Weimar psychology, who later fled to England to escape the Nazis in 1938.¹⁵ In 1920, Plaut presented a 'psychography of the warrior'. He based this project on questionnaires he had distributed to wartime soldiers in the field until the military censors put a stop to his research. Plaut used the men's responses to discuss whether moral or political attitudes influenced soldiers' relationship to the act of killing. His conclusion was that they did not. Moral reflection, wrote Plaut, was no inhibition since 'the soldier does not perceive killing as killing in the moment of action'. Only in retrospect did some men experience 'a sort of moral hangover', which was soon overcome by force of habit. For Plaut, killing in the First World War was defined primarily by its increasingly routine nature as an everyday practice.¹⁶

## II The historical analysis of wartime violence

A direct exploration of killing thus came only late to German military history, and not via a straightforward route. In the early 1990s, some historians began to find new ways of examining the crimes of the Wehrmacht during the war of annihilation against the Soviet Union from 1941 onwards. They included Omer Bartov, for example, who pointed to the strong ideological motivations of the Wehrmacht perpetrators.[17] In 1995, as the public controversy in Germany about Wehrmacht crimes neared its climax, the US-based military historian Michael Geyer published a ground-breaking essay. He called for a 'history of war that speaks about death' and particularly about the mass killing at the centre of war. Geyer outlined a programme for a history of modern wars, conceiving them as fundamentally the 'system, act and consequences of killing and being killed'. Such a 'history of organized lethal violence', insisted Geyer, would be possible and 'acceptable only if it ascertained the conditions for surviving' war. Not least, this was for the obvious reason that every battle produced not only casualties but unharmed survivors, too. For Geyer, however, this approach was also a matter of narrative and memory. After all, it is only 'the survivors who can write the history of the dead'.[18] The history of war as a history of lethal violence, of the capacity to kill, thus also represents a work of collective memory dedicated to those who died and a debate with the survivors who told the story of those killed.

This programme for a history of war as a history of organized mass killing immediately raises two important questions. Firstly, that of the relationship between qualitative and quantitative approaches to analysing violence. Some writers limit the analysis of violence to a 'thick description' of the situations in which it is exercised. Violence is thus conceptualized as an interaction, a struggle at close quarters where the protagonists strike, stab or shoot at one another.[19] The sociologist Wolfgang Sofsky, for example, gives a particularly graphic account of the First World War, describing the reality of combat as an 'attack on the senses'. Clearly inspired by John Keegan's famous description of the first day of the Battle of the Somme, he places the reader in the midst of a military assault, describing in clinical, gruesome detail the wounds inflicted by bullets and artillery shells.[20] There is no doubt that such portrayals help us to understand the bloody reality of trench warfare and to empathise with the victims. More problematic, however, is that this approach is content to remain at the descriptive level, the casualties featuring as little more than pieces of human meat.[21] Readers gain little insight into the social forces or processes of socialization that led millions of men to perpetrate violence under these conditions for year after year of the war. Sofsky addresses these merely with the simple assertion that in war, violence becomes an 'end in itself', thus generating the 'will to kill'.[22] What is overlooked in the 'thick description' of acts of violence is the fundamental fact that wartime violence is organized violence. It is not created by the immediate interaction of the protagonists – insofar as they are in close enough proximity to perceive each other at all – but is the product of a complex military organization. This organization provides the technology, personnel and institutional resources for the perpetration of violence, and must constantly add to these so as to sustain the war effort.[23]

Other researchers take a largely quantitative approach, drawing timelines and comparisons. Harvard psychologist Steven Pinker's monumental history of violence from the beginnings of human socialization to the present is a prominent example of this approach. Pinker seeks to prove that a long-term reduction in violence has been underway since the Early Modern period: an evolutionary change representing nothing less than the sort of civilizing process put forward by sociologist Norbert Elias.[24]

A hallmark of Pinker's approach is his decision to relate the number of victims killed in violent conflict throughout history to the size of the world population in the mid-twentieth century. This, he argues, enables us to grasp the epochal scale of past wars and conflicts given the explosive demographic growth of recent decades. By this measure, the First World War occupies only thirteenth place in a list of the twenty-one wars claiming the most victims in world history. This list of the 'worst things people have done to each other', writes Pinker, 'gives the lie to the conventional wisdom that the 20th century saw a quantum leap in organized violence from a peaceful 19th'.[25] It is certainly true that, measured in terms of the percentage of the total population killed, the Thirty Years' War from 1618 to 1648 wrought even greater devastation on the societies of Central Europe than the First World War.[26] However, it must not be forgotten that the relatively small number of wars in Europe in the nineteenth century remained largely contained. The First World War, by contrast, was surrounded by a wide-ranging debate on the escalation of atrocities against civilians. Moreover, the immense losses among the young male elite of university age led many contemporaries in Britain and elsewhere to talk of a 'lost generation'.[27] Given, then, that many of those who experienced the First World War perceived the conflict to be a watershed moment in the history of violence, it is overly simplistic to relativize its significance on quantitative grounds. For all the shortcomings in the detail of Pinker's argument, however, there is nothing inherently wrong with the quantitative analysis of violence.[28] There is, in fact, much to be gained by combining qualitative and quantitative approaches. Identifying the number of people killed and the weapons that inflicted the deadly injuries is of equal importance to examining the context in which the violence took place and the question of whether the perpetrators pursued specific motives.

The second important question raised by this approach concerns the definition of violence, and is far more significant than it may first appear. In a book first published in 1986, the sociologist Heinrich Popitz proposed that violence be distinguished from other forms of power. Rather than being based on the capacity to incentivize or punish (instrumental power) or on the recognition of positions of authority (authoritative power), violence relies on the capacity to deliberately inflict injury on bodies. Thus, it is exercised in discrete actions rather than in structural patterns, and is a manifestation of *Aktionsmacht*, the exercise of power through concrete acts of human agency.[29] Crucially, this statement directs our attention to the destruction of the human body inherent in the act of killing, which marks the definitive and final boundary of all violence.[30] This focus casts a different light on other aspects of the history of violence in the First World War, such as the landscapes and urban areas laid waste by artillery fire.[31] In some cases, buildings of special cultural importance became icons of destruction, their obliteration perceived as particularly heinous acts of barbarism. Important examples include the German shelling of the gothic cathedral in Reims on 19 September 1914, and the destruction of the university library in Leuven, Flanders, set alight by German troops on the night of 25 August 1914.[32] For people around the world, both incidents quickly became vivid symbols for the brutality and lack of culture supposedly deeply ingrained in the German war effort. This despite the fact that there were no human casualties in either building, though the destruction of the Leuven library came in the midst of extensive violence against civilians by the German military, which killed 248 of the city's citizens.[33] It is certainly no coincidence that the war was only several weeks old when these two symbolic events found such broad resonance. Just a few years later in 1918, with millions of soldiers dead, the buildings' destruction must have appeared almost as a form of collateral damage. The obliteration of buildings or whole cities is an act of wanton destruction. But it ought to be distinguished categorically from those wartime actions that directly and deliberately aim to injure human bodies.

For Popitz, thus, it is important not 'to expand and to distort' the definition of violence.[34] A more recent, important study by Heather Jones on the treatment of prisoners of war in Germany, France and Britain will help us to understand why. Jones begins with a deliberately broad definition of violence, which includes not only the use but also the 'threat' of physical force. This broad definition is then quietly widened still further in the course of the book. For Jones, 'violent behaviour' includes the actions of an angry crowd in the town of Torgau, who taunted arriving French and British prisoners of war in September 1914 with insults, and those of one elderly woman who spat at the men three times.[35] It also includes an incident in Cologne, where civilians poured several buckets of cold water over British POWs.[36] There can be no doubt that such behaviour was extremely humiliating for the British and French soldiers and officers involved. It broke the code that mandated honourable treatment of prisoners of war, which was supposed to apply independently of the 1907 Hague Convention on the legal rules and boundaries of land warfare. However, it makes little sense to equate public swearing or the shouting of insults with physical attacks against the body by describing these actions as 'verbal' forms of violence.[37] Such inflationary use of the concept of violence is problematic, since what Popitz described as the *Verletzungsoffenheit* (openness to traumas) of the human body is a fundamental aspect of human life and, by implication, a key driver of human sociability.[38] Spitting and swearing, however, were in fact part of the everyday life of many people in Europe around the turn of the century, at least outside the upper classes.

Unlike being spat upon, it needs to be emphasized, a bullet to the stomach is usually fatal or at least leaves lasting injury. The unique feature of wartime was the systematic disabling of the basic mechanisms in modern society that would normally punish those deliberately inflicting harm on others. As Wolfgang Sofsky has pointed out, war is the only time when people *must* kill others in order to stay alive.[39] Moreover, treating the abuse shouted at POWs as verbal acts of violence also loses sight of another, equally important aspect of being taken captive. Taken as an average over the four years of the war, British and French prisoners, as well as German prisoners in Allied hands, had a far lower death rate (prisoner deaths were caused by illness, malnutrition and, in very rare cases, physical attack) than active soldiers over the same period. For example, around 7.5 per cent of all French soldiers held prisoner by Germany died in captivity, most of them due to the country's worsening food shortages. This compares to a death rate among active French soldiers of almost 17 per cent.[40] The protective function of captivity is revealed even more clearly if we add subjective perception to objective statistics. Notwithstanding the verbal insults and occasional mistreatment German POWs had to endure, numerous accounts by soldiers written in the final two years of the war extolled the merits of Allied captivity – a life safe from death or injury – and recommended that relatives and comrades allow themselves to be taken prisoner too.[41]

## III  Eye-catching theories and their problems

In the 1990s, with growing interest in the history of violence during the First World War, historians particularly in the English-speaking world soon began to catch the public eye with striking theories. Among them was historian Joanna Bourke and her 1999 book on *Face-to-Face-Killing in Twentieth-Century Warfare*.[42] In many respects, Bourke's text is a bold and important blueprint for a military history centred on the act of killing. Bourke analyses the thoughts and fantasies that delivered soldiers a script for their actions on the battlefield. She describes the role of military chaplains and psychiatrists, who helped soldiers to deal with the moral doubts and psychological trauma some of them experienced.[43] On the other hand, however, Bourke offers some striking but questionable claims. Using examples primarily from the British and US armies in the First and Second World Wars, she develops her core thesis that many soldiers found gratification or even enjoyment in the act of killing. According to Bourke, this 'enjoyment of killing' was an important driving force behind the destruction seen in both world wars.[44] Another problematic aspect is her focus on face-to-face combat, that is, on the direct interaction between soldiers. As we will see later in this book, face-to-face combat in fact played almost no role in the killing of enemy soldiers in the First World War. Some soldiers doubtless gave free rein to their imagination of warfare as a battle of man against man.[45] Far more of the men, however, came to the sobering realization that the act of killing was largely in the hands of military technology and dominated by artillery weapons. Not least among them was Ernst Jünger, despite the fact that his name tends to be associated with close-quarter combat (see Chapter 4).

Another historian with a tendency to make claims that are both striking and sweeping in equal measure is Harvard historian Niall Ferguson. The argument he presents in his book *The Pity of War*, published in 1998, concurs with Bourke's main thesis. Ferguson discusses the importance of positive factors in motivating soldiers to endure the war, positing among other things that 'many men simply took pleasure in killing'.[46] He also draws upon Sigmund Freud's theory of the 'death instinct' in the form that Freud initially developed during the First World War and then laid out systematically in his *Beyond the Pleasure Principle* in 1920. For Ferguson, Freud's ideas on the death instinct are well placed 'to explain the readiness of millions of men to spend four and a quarter years killing and being killed'.[47] The problem with such a sweeping conclusion is not, first and foremost, that the evidence provided consists only of a tiny number of eyewitnesses, out of all proportion to the millions of soldiers for whom they are presumed to testify. Nor is it primarily that one of the few sources indicated is *Storm of Steel*, Ernst Jünger's famous book-length account of wartime violence first published in 1920. Thanks to the much-improved availability of sources on Jünger's wartime experience, we now know this book to be far more of a literary stylization than was realized as recently as 1998.[48] In any case, however, as will be evident in Chapter 4, neither *Storm of Steel* nor his original war diaries offer adequate indications that Jünger was motivated to kill by a death instinct. Rather, the real problem of a 'death instinct' to explain the practice of killing in the First World War is that it renders historical understanding both impossible and unnecessary. Impossible, since either proving or disproving the existence of a psychodynamic, perhaps even somatic drive is beyond the powers of the historical method, that is, the critical analysis of sources in the form of texts and images. And unnecessary, since positing such an instinct renders superfluous the historian's other primary task – that of contextualizing the insights into the past which historical sources give us. Instinct functions regardless of the situation and changing contexts that limit the options of historical actors. Why, then, go to the trouble of analysing these contexts in depth by describing the battlefield or the different means of killing?

It should be clear from this brief discussion why such bold and sweeping theories on violence in the First World War hinder rather than add to our historical understanding. The same applies to the misplaced metaphors intended as a shorthand for the various forms of violence between 1914 and 1918. It is only of limited value, for example, to describe the First World War as an 'orgy of violence'.[49] The metaphor of the 'orgy' implies, after all, that the majority, if not all of those perpetrating acts of violence felt a desire to do so or obtained pleasure as a result. This assumption is not backed by empirical evidence. It ignores soldiers' well-documented disillusionment, distress, acrimony and feelings of guilt, as well as the psychological trauma and the 'stigma of violence' that later attached to those who had killed during the war.[50]

## IV A laboratory of violence

If we must find a suitable metaphor, it would be more fitting to describe the First World War as a laboratory of violence.[51] Faced with industrialized warfare, the armies of all the war's combatant nations attempted to adapt to the new conditions, experimenting with new types of weaponry such as poison gas, tanks and aerial bombardment. The practice of combat changed, too. To adjust to the reality of trench warfare, army commands tested more flexible forms of defence and new attacking techniques, such as the German army's innovative storm troop tactics (see Chapter 4).[52] Military historians have often claimed that war is 'ultimately' 'about fighting' and that the history of tactics and their application in battle should thus be a core part of any history of war.[53] Our focus on the practices of violence should allow this aspect to be accommodated in an integrative military history of the Great War.

The laboratory metaphor also emphasises the lack of fixed plans directing the course of violence between 1914 and 1918. The outcome of the military experiments was entirely open, a fact most clearly demonstrated by the end game of the German campaign. Initially, the offensives in spring 1918 brought impressive territorial gains and were welcomed by generals and ordinary soldiers alike as a change from the years of stagnation in the trenches. Just a few weeks later, however, as the advance ground to a halt and turned to retreat over the summer, the German army on the Western Front began to disintegrate. Only a few clear-sighted observers in spring 1918 foresaw what was about to happen. German soldiers abandoned the front in their hundreds of thousands and made their own way towards home, playing a major role in bringing the war to an end (see Chapters 6 and 7).

This reading, which emphasizes the contingency and openness of events before and after 1918, contrasts with other interpretations that draw a line of continuity from the First World War to the genocidal conflict of the Second World War, and thus to the Holocaust. There, the metaphor of the laboratory instead points to the ways in which the conduct of war from 1914 to 1918 anticipated certain practices and elements of the escalation of violence that would later destroy entire countries and wipe out minorities such as the Jews. Omer Bartov's work, for example, traces the imagination of violence in the age of total war, contending that the Holocaust was 'the almost perfect re-enactment of the Great War (and its own imagery of hell), with the important correction that all the perpetrators were on one side and all the victims on the other'. The other components of the Holocaust's total violence, he writes, had already been present two decades earlier: 'the barbed wire, the machine guns, the charred bodies, the gas, the uniforms, the military discipline, the barracks'.[54]

Bartov is well aware of the fundamental difference between warfare, where soldiers kill and injure each other in accordance with certain rules, and genocide, which renders its victims defenceless and strips them of all protection in law. The link between the First World War and the Holocaust, he argues, is the domination of machinery on the battlefield, which first made the killing of an entire people or ethnic group imaginable and possible.⁵⁵ In fact, however, Bartov's assumption is incorrect in several respects. The Armenian genocide in 1915–16 showed that genocide could occur without the use of complex technology. It is also barely plausible that it was the experience or imagination of the First World War battlefields that inspired the 'fantasies' of the National Socialist figures behind the Holocaust. Moreover, the focus on technical details such as barbed wire or uniforms loses sight of a more important question: to what extent did the perpetrators of violence in the First World War perceive their opponents – whether soldiers or civilians – as inferior human beings, and thus consider the war to be a justified intervention in the enemy's way of life? Only by answering this question can we determine whether and to what extent the morality of the perpetrators in the Second World War was founded upon or bore similarities to the views and resentments of First World War soldiers (see Chapters 3 and 4).⁵⁶ Chapter 8 of this book will discuss whether there were possible continuities in a glorification of violence after 1918.⁵⁷

## V  The structure of this volume

This book does not offer a sweeping theory which sums up the history of violence in the First World War, nor does it contain a comprehensive explanation for the escalation of violence from 1914 to 1918.⁵⁸ Instead, the core idea that runs through the following chapters is the attempt to differentiate, both with regard to forms of violence and the willingness to perpetrate it. The book will look, for example, at how these phenomena differed over time as the war progressed. It will examine how they differed along class and social lines, comparing officers, on the one hand, and soldiers performing military service from a range of social backgrounds on the other.⁵⁹ We will also tackle the spatial differences, including the contrast in the intensity of killing between the Western Front and the Eastern Front.⁶⁰

While the focus in this book is on the Western front, it is important to note some distinguishing features of violence in the East that have been highlighted by recent research. In Central Eastern, Eastern and South-Eastern Europe, the First World War ushered in the demise of four multi-national empires (the German, Austrian, Russian and Ottoman), turning large swathes of land into a 'shatterzone' of violent ethnic and national conflicts that continued to blight these territories in civil wars until 1921, long after fighting in the West had ended. In addition, the front line in Eastern Europe was 'not static: twice, in 1914/15, and again from 1917 onwards, it swept across large parts of Central and Eastern

Europe like a giant windshield wiper, leaving the indigenous population at the mercy of retreating or advancing armies and turning millions into refugees'.[61]

Another aspect of our analysis of violence in this book follows on from Michael Geyer's insistence that historians should explore not only what led soldiers to kill, but also what enabled them to survive. After all, the soldiers of the First World War did not take part in kamikaze missions designed to end in inevitable self-destruction. Instead, they based their participation on expectations as to whether and when their involvement in the struggle would further their own survival. In the First World War, as in every war, there were those who either participated only reluctantly in the killing, or who took advantage of opportunities, when these arose, to avoid combat. At the other end of the spectrum were the young men who felt driven, particularly in summer and autumn 1914, to volunteer themselves for military service.[62] The history of soldiers who avoided active involvement in the machinery of violence, whether briefly or for an extended period, remains at best a marginal issue in the historiography and public perception of the First World War.[63] There are two mains reasons for this. Firstly, the fact that soldiers' resistance during the Great War seldom took the spectacular form of outright mutiny. It was a rare exception for an entire regiment or division to turn against their superiors and issue political or military demands. Of the major warring powers in Central and Eastern Europe, only the French army was significantly affected by mutiny. This occurred in spring 1917.[64] In most cases, then, those who sought to avoid the fighting were not a clearly defined group making 'heroic acts' of defiance, but were rather acting on their own initiative. Taking advantage of the blind spots of a bureaucratic apparatus tasked with mass mobilization, they outwitted the military and disappeared, drawing as little attention to themselves as possible.[65] If we were to use a literary metaphor, we could describe these unwilling soldiers and shirkers as German equivalents to the 'Good Soldier Švejk', who was immortalized in the 1923 novel of the same title by the Czech author Jaroslav Hašek.[66] Secondly, individuals resisting violence often belonged to the marginalized groups in Europe's nation states: small farmers, who were often poorly integrated, or national minorities (see Chapter 5). From the outset, then, theirs was already a fractured relationship to the 'language of national obligation' that governed the public practice and symbolic representation of military service during the war.[67] This also explains why remembrances of the war, which were always centred on the nation state, largely neglected such individuals in the years after 1918. There can be no clearer illustration of this than the fate of the wartime memoirs of Dominik Richert, son of a farmer in the Alsace region. Richert was reluctant to participate in the German war effort from the start, and his recollections culminate in a detailed description of his eventual defection to the French in the summer of 1918. Yet the manuscript lay neglected in a German military archive for decades, until historian Bernd Ulrich finally edited and published it in 1989.[68] Only then was one of the most detailed and substantial First World War accounts of killing, dying and surviving in the German army from the perspective of an ordinary soldier made available to the reading public.

The current book aims to present a nuanced analysis of the practices of violence and to explore the connections between killing, surviving and refusal in the German army. The first part discusses the practices of violence, beginning with a broad overview of the contexts in which soldiers in the First World War died or survived (Chapter 2). This chapter takes a comparative approach including the other major combatant nations in Europe. As well as national differences, this reveals the similarities in the willingness to go to war and in semantic representations of violence, for example among soldiers from farming backgrounds or the socialist working class in different countries. Chapter 3 focuses on the willingness of German soldiers to go to war in the summer of 1914 and their many ambivalent experiences as they first encountered the reality of killing in mechanized warfare. Here, important differences emerge between East and West in the perception of the enemy and potential victims of violence. The first part concludes in Chapter 4 with a biographical case study of Ernst Jünger, a volunteer and storm troop lieutenant. Jünger is often cited as a key witness by many First World War histories centred on the radicalization of violence. These base their conclusions on his literary texts, and particularly *Storm of Steel*. Following publication of Jünger's original war diaries, it is now possible to offer a much more nuanced view of how Jünger actually exercised and observed lethal violence.

The second part of this volume focuses on the ways in which soldiers refused to exercise violence. This begins with an analysis of the contexts, motives and practical obstacles of the most important form of refusal in the German wartime army: desertion (Chapter 5). Although it is impossible to determine the extent of desertion with precision, the figures available reveal that it was anything but a marginal phenomenon. At the same time, an important source – discussed in detail in Chapter 5 – highlights the fact that refusal to perpetrate violence also provoked counter-violence by the military apparatus. In the context of the execution of an Alsatian deserter in 1917, an officer revealed that such executions were a frequent occurrence intended to dissuade potential deserters. Chapter 6 concentrates on the pivotal moment on the Western Front in 1918 when willingness to perpetrate violence switched to mass refusal. With their high expectations of the German spring offensive having been disappointed, the mood among German troops shifted with dramatic consequences. Now, only a rapid peace mattered. This wave of disappointment triggered a hidden military strike in which mass 'shirking' hollowed out the German army from within. This interpretation of events in the final months of the war, first suggested by historian Wilhelm Deist, has recently been contested by some scholars. On the basis of new source material, I therefore seek to clarify controversial issues and reaffirm the significance of this military strike. It remains a fundamentally important outcome of the war – which influenced German military thinking and practice long into the interwar period – that the mighty German military machine collapsed in late 1918 as hundreds of thousands of soldiers decided that they would no longer run the risk of being killed (Chapter 7).[69]

The final part looks at the problem of coming to terms with violence. These chapters explore how the experience of violence in the First World War shaped German society after 1918. We begin with an extremely contentious issue: the 'brutalization' of German veterans in the Weimar Republic (Chapter 8). This topic links the practice of violence during the war with its after-effects on veterans as they attempted to reintegrate into civil society. The 'brutalization' of Weimar society and culture is a controversial topic, not least because it is linked to questions about the origins and course of National Socialism.[70] Political violence was a constant feature of the Nazi regime, and historians have repeatedly asked whether this can be traced back to the experiences of 1914–18. Here, too, it is important to take a nuanced approach, avoiding sweeping theories about an entire generation of soldiers supposedly brutalized during the war. A considerable number of German war veterans in fact pursued pacifist objectives after 1918. However, this was not simply a direct consequence of what they had experienced on the front, but also stemmed from post-war events and learning processes. We examine this issue in Chapter 9 with a biographical case study on Hermann Schützinger. Familiar only to a small number of experts today, Schützinger was such a well-known figure in late 1920s Germany that his image even appeared on postcards. Schützinger's rejection of violence and commitment to the pacifist cause was a particularly protracted and complex process given his role as a professional officer in the Bavarian army contingent before and during the war, as Schützinger continued to climb the military career ladder until shortly before the armistice in 1918.

The book's final chapter draws attention to a largely forgotten aspect of Weimar Germany's attempt to come to terms with the legacy of the First World War. It presents two literary bestsellers of the 1920s, both of which took a pacifist and critical stance towards the military and the phenomenon of *Etappenmilitarismus* (rear area militarism), that is, the corruption and moral degradation of the

German occupation in Belgium and northern France. Their authors, Heinrich Wandt and Wilhelm Appens were, each in their own ways, committed socialists, whose critical interventions were met with sanctions or open repression even in the democratic Weimar Republic. Our purpose in analysing and contextualizing these texts is not to discover how accurately they represented the reality of German rule in the rear area (this is a task that must be left to research on German occupation policy in Belgium and northern France, which is now finally gathering steam).[71] In line with the overall topic of this book, we will instead look at how Appens and Wandt portray the rear area as a scene of violence. This contrasts with the perspective of front-line soldiers at the time, for whom the rear area was defined precisely by the absence of violence, as a place where they did not need to fear for their lives. By shifting the focus of attention to the rear area, it is also likely that Appens and Wandt were seeking to evade the issue of German soldiers' culpability for the violence on the front.

In closing this introduction, it is necessary to state that some important aspects of the topic are not covered by this book. One of them is the war in the German colonies. In recent years, historians have intensively discussed the dramatic radicalization of violence in the German colonial wars of the early twentieth century. In German East Africa, for example, a small contingent of the German *Schutztruppe* under Paul von Lettow-Vorbeck held out against the Allies until 1918, assisted by a much larger number of indigenous support troops and soldiers. The guerrilla war this entailed destroyed the colonial order that had taken decades to establish, and thus unleashed new violence.[72] Another topic beyond the scope of this book is the portrayal and memory of the First World War in the media and arts in the 1920s and even beyond 1945. Novels, poems and films were already becoming increasingly important during the interwar period in symbolizing and interpreting the practice of violence.[73] There is room in this book to cast only a cursory glance at the gendering of violence in the Great War. Ideas of masculinity and the practice of violence have increasingly come into focus in recent years (see Chapter 4). In contrast to the British army, however, research on the German army in this regard remains in its infancy.[74]

More than in any other country, the centenary of the Great War in Germany in 2014 was marked by the question of how the violence of those years fits into Europe's turbulent history up to 1945. This question includes not only the direct social practice of violence itself, but also its political and cultural aftershocks. This is now bringing the practice of violence, for so long a marginal topic of First World War research, fully into focus. The aim of this book is to contribute to the systematic analysis of that phenomenon.

Part One

# Practices of Violence

2

# Soldiers of the First World War: Killing, Surviving, Discourses of Violence

So hostile were the conditions on the front line in the First World War that they have raised an obvious question for historians: why did the violence continue for so long? How can we comprehend the mental resources that enabled soldiers to continue fighting despite the high probability that they themselves would fall victim to the bloodshed? The German sociologist Heinrich Popitz defined violence as a form of power 'exercised through action', where perpetrators inflict pain on their victims as a means of gaining self-affirmation or other advantage. Yet this particular dimension of agency through violence appears of only limited relevance to explaining the violence of the First World War, where the prospect of immediate gratification was slim and a general stalemate persisted. Some historians have tended to use binary alternatives in framing the question as to why millions of men were prepared to continue the slaughter. Perhaps the most fundamental and controversial of these: did the perseverance of front-line soldiers stem from compulsion or from general consensus on the war's purpose? Often discussed in the English-speaking world in recent years, it was in fact the French who were first to debate this question. For one side of the argument, which has raged since the 1990s, the resilience of the *poilus* (French infantrymen) reflected the men's authentic nationalist convictions. The French soldiers fought for France, it is argued, because they believed their nation was the embodiment of freedom and civilization. They were motivated by a nationalist culture of war and a hatred of Imperial Germany, which they regarded as the principal threat to the values they held dear. Meanwhile, those historians on the other side of the debate instead emphasize the army's firm discipline. Its military courts, they point out, were brutally effective in punishing the mutinies of spring 1917. The *poilus* continued to fight, runs this counter-argument, because the repressive military apparatus simply left the men with no other choice.[1] Within the terms of this binary debate, it is not difficult to see why those in the second camp have the better cards. Proponents of the 'culture of war' theory must generally resort to the writings of intellectuals to find evidence for the motivational power of nationalist passions. Moreover, from what we know of the First World War military apparatus in the various combatant nations, it is highly plausible that soldiers were forced into a disciplinary straitjacket that dramatically limited their options.

Yet this second interpretation is by no means sufficient to paint a complete picture of events on the battlefield, nor indeed are such binary alternatives in general. On its own, the question of compulsion versus conviction cannot fully explain why soldiers used their weapons to such deadly effect, or why even previously injured men were willing to return to the front. A historical understanding of these cycles of violence and commitment requires an understanding of the contradictions that shaped soldiers' lives. This chapter therefore begins by analysing the practice of killing itself, along with the casualties that resulted. Our knowledge of this is based largely on the testimony of survivors. The chapter will also examine the myriad ways that soldiers could survive the war. After all, soldiers' willingness to continue participating in the killing depended in no small measure on their own chances of living to tell the tale. Finally, the chapter will explore how the practice of killing fitted into soldiers' long-held world views and how they attempted to make sense of the conflict. Did soldiers' willingness to perpetrate acts of violence develop before the outbreak of war, or was it a new phenomenon? Was it exceptionally high between 1914 and 1918, or characterized more by continuity with the years before and after? Much of the quantitative data and many of the examples in this chapter relate to the German army. Where space permits, however, we also take a comparative look at the forces of the other major combatant nations.

## I Killing and dying

In order to obtain a clear picture of the number of casualties on the front line in the First World War and the troops who inflicted them, it is important to begin with some hard data on the numbers of dead, wounded and sick. These figures also show us which forms of violence were most effective and which men were most likely to fall victim to them.[2] They therefore not only give us a deeper understanding of the demographic consequences of going to war, but also provide some initial indications as to why individual soldiers' experiences of the front line were so different. First and foremost, however, the data reveals that there was a clear spatial, temporal and social structure to the exercise of lethal violence during the First World War. At the most banal level, this means that not all soldiers who died in the war were killed in the same place at the same time; a basic insight, yet one that even the most well-respected sociologists and social historians of the war have sometimes struggled to take to heart. Many accounts of the First World War still focus overwhelmingly on those killed in the battles of *matériel* from 1916 onwards, at Verdun or the Somme for example. Though the statistics cited on the human cost of these battles provide a vivid picture, which some historians use to encapsulate the horrors of the First World War as a whole, they often do little to promote sober analysis. The figures quoted by the renowned German sociologist Wolfgang Sofsky are a case in point. Sofsky claims that approximately 420,000 soldiers were killed at Verdun.[3] In fact, however, the German 5th Army that fought at Verdun reported *only* (if that is the right word) 81,668 soldiers killed or missing in action during the battle from February to December 1916.[4] Losses among French troops over the same period were of a similar order of magnitude. Even assuming that there were further deaths at Verdun before the end of the war, the figure of 420,000 is therefore more than a twofold exaggeration. Had some 200,000 German soldiers really fallen at Verdun, this one battlefield would have accounted, impossibly, for almost one in ten of the German war dead.

This is not to deny the usefulness of aggregate figures for examining the nature and scale of killing in the First World War. If it is to aid meaningful analysis, however, data must reliably indicate the changes throughout the duration of the war and enable us to draw comparisons with other conflicts. The killing during the First World War was spread highly unevenly in temporal, spatial and demographic terms. The first three months of mobile warfare brought loss of life on a scale that not even the battles of 1916 would come close to repeating along the Western Front as a whole. This was true for the German and French forces alike.[5] Official German statistics show monthly loss rates ('total losses' or 'total wastage', the rather detached term used by the German statisticians). These were calculated by adding together all soldiers reported killed or missing in action and those suffering long-term illness or injury, and subtracting the number of recovered men returning fit for duty to their units. In 1914, the loss rate for German soldiers on the Western Front was 12.4 per cent in August, rising to 16.8 per cent in September. This compares to a rate of just 3.5 per cent on the same Western Front over the duration of the war up to July 1918. A return to anything like the casualty rates seen in the first months of the war came only in the final year of the conflict. During its spring offensive of 1918, the

German Western Army suffered loss rates of 6.0 per cent in March and 6.8 per cent in April. The German retreat in the war's final months led to much higher losses, though the lack of data for this period makes these difficult to quantify precisely.

The figures clearly show that there were also dramatic differences between the two fronts. In the period 1916–17, German units on the Eastern Front reported total losses that amounted to little more than a third of those experienced by their counterparts in the West. The following year, in the wake of the ceasefire with Russia from 7 December 1917, this number then fell to less than a tenth of that reported in the West. In terms of the analysis of violence, then, historians' primary focus on the Western Front is certainly justifiable. Soldiers were killed in the West both more frequently and over a longer period of time than in the East. In addition to these temporal and geographical differences, there were also enormous variations in loss rates between different demographic groups. Almost half the fatalities in the German and British armies involved men aged from nineteen to twenty-four. Soldiers aged over thirty-five made up just over 30 per cent of the troops, but accounted for only around 10 per cent of the deaths.[6] The death rate skewed further towards younger men as the war progressed. By the two final years of conflict, the small group of soldiers aged from eighteen to twenty made up almost a quarter of all deaths. This meant that those newly conscripted into military service during the war were at extremely high risk.

Some of the trends summed up in these dry figures warrant closer examination here. With respect to men's willingness to fight, it is significant that the rate of losses was particularly high at the outset of war – a time when many of the men heading to the front were still exuberant or at least enthusiastic about their role in the conflict (see Chapter 3). Accounts by the youngest soldiers without ties to wives or children show that these men were, in large part, extremely positive about their role as soldiers and the opportunity to prove themselves in battle. Particularly in the infantry, these younger men experienced the most intense battles and had the greatest involvement in the exercise of violence and killing of enemy soldiers. It was also they who were most likely to be on the receiving end of such deadly force. By contrast, many fathers aged from thirty to forty-five served in units and functions that, though essential to the war effort, were only sporadically involved in active battle. For all the physical hardships the war involved for these men, their obligation to participate in killing enemy soldiers was thus often only symbolic, and their risk of death considerably lower.

We can infer who killed the most enemy soldiers from statistics showing which weapons inflicted the most casualties. These reveal that artillery fire was the deadliest weapon, especially as the war progressed. It was the cause of injury for no fewer than 76 per cent of French soldiers wounded between the end of 1914 and the end of 1917. Data for British troops puts the corresponding figure at 58.5 per cent, although it is unclear whether this statistic is based on a fully representative sample.[7] For German troops, figures from the official medical report, the *Sanitätsbericht*, provide further detail. Of the injuries to some two million German soldiers treated in field hospitals between 2 August 1914 and the end of January 1917, 43 per cent were attributable to artillery fire and just under 51 per cent to rifle or pistol fire. If we look at the numbers *killed* over the same period, the balance shifts in favour of the artillery, though the sample size in this case is considerably smaller. The German medical report puts the proportion of deaths inflicted by artillery fire in the period up to the beginning of 1917 at almost 55 per cent, compared with a figure of just 39 per cent for small arms. This indicates that when it came to artillery shells, even shrapnel wounds were highly lethal. The importance of artillery becomes even clearer when we look at the second half of the war in isolation. Figures for one German army on the Western Front in spring 1917 show that small arms and machine guns caused just under 18 per cent, artillery fire 76 per cent and hand grenades around 1 per cent of injuries. Melee weapons such as sabres, swords, daggers and bayonets accounted for just 0.1 per cent.[8] The proportion of soldiers who fell victim to poison gas is likely to have stood at around 3 per cent of the wounded.[9] Although encountering poison gas was thus relatively unlikely, the unpredictability and invisibility of this weapon were enough in themselves to trigger panic. Despite its limited use, gas therefore maintained a powerful hold on soldiers' imaginations.[10] The mortality rate of soldiers affected by gas was comparatively low in relation to the terrible injuries that it inflicted. For this reason, the use of gas has been described as a form of 'torture', and as a 'terror weapon' that was not intended to defeat the enemy, but rather to maximize their suffering. That is a helpful distinction. However, it should be noted that this terminology is not entirely analytical, as it clearly echoes the expressions of revulsion and moral outrage used by British newspapers after the Germans first deployed poison gas at Ypres on 22 April 1915, in a clear breach of international law.[11]

Listing the numbers of injuries caused by the various weapons of industrialized warfare does not give a complete picture of the war's casualties. For all the improvements in medical provision since earlier conflicts, almost a tenth of German soldiers, around a sixth of Austro-Hungarian soldiers and some one in five French soldiers killed in the First World War fell victim not to the destructive power of military weaponry, but rather to disease.[12] The enormous number of soldiers who fell sick reveals the devastating impact of the war's long duration, the weather conditions and, above all, the rapidly worsening food supplies. Soldiers' living conditions were so poor that German military doctors treated just as many diarrhoea cases as injuries over the cause of the war.[13] As the global influenza pandemic reached the exhausted armies along the front in summer and autumn 1918, it quickly revealed the extent to which food shortages had sapped the physical strength of soldiers on both sides.

The statistics on the effectiveness of different weapons make it clear that both the most traditional – handheld weapons – and the most recent means of killing – such as poison gas – were of only marginal importance. War novels and other popular portrayals of the conflict tell countless stories of soldiers who unleashed their aggression in horrific fashion during military assaults, driving their bayonets into enemy bodies. In reality, however, this form of close-combat killing, whether out of violent impulse or self-defence, was a rare exception, at least in the main theatres of war. In this respect, the First World War contrasted sharply with the War of 1870–71, the last conflict German troops had fought in Europe. There, one injury by melee weapon was inflicted for every fifty-four caused by firearms. In the years from 1914 to 1917, it was just one for every 174.[14] However, the figures of the German medical authorities also allow another interesting comparison. They show that the number of *fatal* injuries caused by firearms for each death by melee weapon had barely increased between the 1870–71 and 1914–18 wars. In the Franco-German war, the ratio of deaths by melee weapon to firearms stood at 1:319, compared with 1:359 in the First World War. This suggests that the mechanized weaponry of the First World War had not necessarily made the army more efficient at killing enemy soldiers. Used with skill in close combat, the bayonet was almost as deadly as the rifle or machine gun. What was new in the First World War, however, was the sheer scale on which the armies deployed deadly weaponry. It was not primarily the precision of the gunners, but rather the enormous deployment of armaments that made the new technology such a formidable killing machine. A statistic based on documents from a German reserve division dating from March and April 1916 illustrates this phenomenon clearly. The records show that the enemy on this section of the front required no fewer than 329 artillery shells to kill or injure a single German soldier.[15]

The dominance of artillery fire in the destructive power of the First World War deeply unsettled not only those in the line of fire, but also those tasked with operating this fearsome weaponry. The professor of Romance literature Victor Klemperer, for example, described his astonishment upon finding the atmosphere at his artillery battery in France as quiet as that on the training ground in

Lechfeld, Bavaria. Klemperer, a Protestant of Jewish descent, who would later become a well-known figure following publication of his diaries of the Third Reich, was already an astute chronicler of destruction in 1914–18. He was struck by the remoteness of the artillery firing positions from the enemy soldiers.[16] This distance, which meant that artillerymen were not immediately confronted with the consequences of their work, was a typical and important example of the 'Promethean gap' – a term coined by the philosopher Günther Anders with regard to the atomic bomb – induced by modern weaponry. The intensity with which the artilleryman could inflict violence far exceeded his moral capacity to absorb the outcome of his actions. If he perceived the death of his victims at all, it was only upon later confrontation with their already lifeless bodies. This technologically dictated form of violence therefore certainly did *not* have to rely on a 'death instinct'.[17]

The blanket destruction wrought by the artillery was, of course, even more disturbing to its potential victims. Though positioned deep in the dugouts, the infantry were tormented by the howl of artillery shells (see Chapter 4). They could do little but wait helplessly, at the mercy of a force beyond their control. In the imaginations of soldiers, the artillery weapons thus took on a life of their own, becoming a powerful military actor in their own right. Machines rather than people did the killing, or 'claimed victims' as soldiers often described it in their war letters.[18] On both sides of the front, killing and being killed in artillery warfare was an essentially anonymous process. Soldiers largely regarded themselves as victims of this technological war. Their accounts describe with savage precision the charred wastelands it left behind: churned-up landscapes, animal corpses, mangled bodies and settlements that had been razed to the ground.[19] However, the artillery left behind not only physical destruction, but psychological damage, too. This is an aspect of the First World War that even the most detailed 'body counts' can tell us nothing about, but which is essential to understanding what set this war apart from previous conflicts. The sudden experience of a weapon of such overwhelming power broke soldiers' 'coherent sense of self' as its violent force completely overcame them.[20] This triggered psychological disturbances, which manifested themselves in anxiety, nervous collapse and twitching limbs. More important for our purposes than exploring the medical debate over 'shell shock' or 'war neurosis' is to note the simple fact that the violence of 1914–18 destroyed not only the physical, but also the mental integrity of soldiers.

Paradoxically, the trench warfare ordered by the military authorities tended to limit the scope of violence provided both sides sought only to maintain the status quo. Attempting to break this stalemate required specialist troops. The British military leadership in particular relied on snipers, who were placed ready to fire at anyone careless or unfortunate enough to extend a limb beyond the trench parapet. The German and Austrian armies used *Stoßtruppkämpfer* (assault detachments or 'storm troops'), whose job was to work in small groups to clear the path for the regular infantry. Ordinary soldiers greeted the storm troops with serious animosity, realizing the escalation of the conflict that their presence entailed. Both snipers and assault detachments shared a strong motivation for battle, and many emphatically identified with their role as perpetrators of violence.[21] It is no coincidence that a direct line of continuity can be drawn from these German storm troops and the elite Italian Arditi units to the fascist aestheticization of violence in the interwar period.[22] This, however, does not imply that the storm troops' methods were a form of fundamentalist violence that anticipated the wanton destructiveness perpetrated by the Wehrmacht in the Second World War. While many academics have cited the writer Ernst Jünger as the embodiment of such a supposed continuity, Chapter 4 will show that his newly available war diaries give the lie to this suggestion.

This throws up the question of whether the German army was particularly efficient in terms of killing as many enemy soldiers as possible while minimizing its own losses, and whether this efficiency was deeply ingrained in the organizational culture of the German army and its preference for 'absolute destruction'.[23] The 'body counts' of the dead and injured give us an important indication. The average annual injury rate of 376 per thousand soldiers in the German field army on the Western Front was below the equivalent figure for the Allies (482 injured men per thousand soldiers, taking the British and French armies together). A similar discrepancy is found in the number of soldiers killed per year.[24] Yet even for the German army, these figures are still remarkably high. They show that in each year of the war, enormous numbers of soldiers returned to battle after overcoming often serious injuries in military hospitals. It is thus clear that in order to kill enemy soldiers, the men had to accept the strong possibility of becoming casualties themselves. What made German soldiers willing to take that risk and kill with such efficiency?

Three factors likely came into play here. Firstly, we should note that the German army was largely in defensive mode from 1916 to 1917, which had the effect of somewhat reducing the risk of further injury. Secondly, we must consider the tactical innovations in the German army from 1916 onwards. Instead of holding a rigid line in the first set of trenches, the strategy now shifted to providing a more mobile defence in depth, allowing temporary retreat before small groups gathered to recapture the first line of defence. Michael Geyer has cited this 'aggressive defence', which offered a measure of independence to individual soldiers, as a reason why German troops remained motivated to fight.²⁵ This is certainly an important point, but it is also one that can be overstated. In summer and autumn 1918, German soldiers often used the principle of flexible defence merely as a pretext for retreating hundreds of metres before the enemy and giving up positions entirely. As fear of punishment declined, defence in depth also lost its ability to motivate soldiers to kill. Finally, many German (and British) soldiers were industrial workers. These men associated skilled handling of machinery with strong self-discipline, which also appears to explain why they fought so efficiently.

While the nature of the conflict, and particularly the dominance of the artillery, was often similar on the Western and Eastern Fronts, there was one arena of the conflict where violence took a more irregular course. A 'wild war' raged in the Balkans, creating a trail of destruction that ended in the expulsion and hostage-taking of civilians. The Austrian military committed a series of violent excesses against enemy soldiers and non-combatants alike.²⁶ The stage for this wild war was Serbia, which paid a higher price in blood between 1914 and 1918 than any other country in Europe. The extreme violence began in August 1914, when the Austro-Hungarian army made its first failed attempt to conquer Serbia. Officers and soldiers of the Habsburg army pushed into the country, firm in the belief of their moral superiority and convinced that Serbian guerrillas (*Komitadjis*) were lying in wait for them behind every corner. Austrian officers' persistent suspicion that even civilians were ready to commit atrocities against their troops lay rooted in a conviction that they were dealing with a fundamentally inferior culture. The Austrians' primary aim was the conservation of the Austro-Hungarian empire. They sought to prevent a *levée en masse*, a nationalist people's war that they believed would be led by Serbian civilians. This, the army was convinced, justified measures including hostage-taking and summary executions of men, women and children. For August 1914 alone, reliable estimates put the number of Serbian civilians killed at approximately 3,500.²⁷

This form of warfare, which made a civilian population the target of military aggression, differed substantially from that seen in the other arenas of the First World War. However, it probably did not constitute a 'war of annihilation' against Serbia. The Austrian campaign therefore cannot be said to have foreshadowed the Second World War in seeking the total destruction of a state and society.²⁸ Having almost fully occupied the country following a second offensive in autumn 1915, the Austrian army resumed its reprisals and violence against the civilian population, including hostage taking and the destruction of entire villages. It now also had the support of Bulgaria as a new ally of the Central Powers. Following a major uprising by the *Komitadjis* in the territory occupied by Bulgaria in March 1917, German aircraft also intervened, dropping incendiary bombs over the town of Prokuplje. The conflict in Serbia was a guerrilla war, conducted with hatred and bitter intensity on both sides. However, when the Austrians noticed that the *Komitadjis* increasingly lacked support among the civilian population, and that the conflict was becoming a simmering civil war between rival groups and gangs, they changed their strategy. They now began to rely on intelligence gathering and police operations, thus de-escalating the violence. Preventing mobilization for nationalist causes was the Austrian army's primary objective given the threat posed by nationalist sentiments from within its own ranks.[29] In this sense, its campaign in Serbia was the final act of nineteenth-century punitive imperialism rather than the twentieth century's first war of annihilation against civilians.

## II Survival

The story of death for some was also one of survival for others. Soldiers had the best prospects of survival wherever they were out of range of artillery fire. There were various means of reaching such places, and a range of factors that determined the extent to which men did so. These included differences in soldiers' functional roles, the locations in which they served and their various national backgrounds. The military's organizational structure in industrialized warfare meant that some soldiers' roles exposed them to much lower risk of death than others. Many men worked at a safe distance from the front, including all those soldiers in front-line units who were charged with maintaining the logistics of war, whether they were transporting ammunition to the front, staffing field kitchens or taking care of the uniforms of their officer as a batman. In artillery regiments, they also included the considerable number of men whose job was to feed and look after the numerous horses needed to transport cannon. For front-line soldiers, developments in weapons technology necessitated countless training courses, which kept them away from the action for weeks at a time. The increasing intensity of bombardments and long duration of the war meant that the men needed regular short breaks and, particularly after major battles, extended rest periods. These took entire regiments or divisions out of action for several weeks. Each spell in the trenches was followed by a short rest period. Soldiers in one British battalion therefore spent, on average, 42 per cent of their time directly on the front line, 38 per cent in the reserve immediately to the rear and 20 per cent in 'rest areas'.[30] Soldiers in the other armies on the Western Front apportioned their time in a similar manner.

These rest periods were precious. Aside from training and leave, they were front-line soldiers' only relief from the hardships of the trenches. It is thus no coincidence that one of the most frequent complaints heard from troops in all the wartime armies was that officers were unnecessarily interrupting rest periods with pointless drills. And it is perhaps no surprise in this context that the British army's only incidence of large-scale mutiny during the First World War was triggered not by the hardships of the front line, but by conditions in one of its training camps: the British Expeditionary Force's infamous 'Bull Ring' camp in Étaples, a small French town close to the English Channel.[31] From spring 1915 onwards, somewhere between 3 and 7 per cent of front-line soldiers were on home leave at any one time. Both the German and French armies allocated farmers longer, more frequent leave periods, such was the importance of the harvest. This perhaps unspectacular, but highly emotionally charged privilege, made farmers the target of verbal aggression from their comrades. The French army deliberately used the granting of leave as a safety valve in an attempt to relieve the pressures and hardships of the front. It redoubled this practice after the mutinies in spring 1917, for which complaints about the unfair allocation of leave had been an important trigger.[32]

Meanwhile, others posted away from the line of fire had little need to fear for their lives. They included the men attached to the supply trains replenishing munitions and food, as well as *Armierungssoldaten*, the usually older men known as *Schipper* (shovellers), who dug trenches and fortified positions. In the German army, these two groups alone numbered in the hundreds of thousands. The many soldiers in the rear area formations on occupied territory were even further from the danger on the front line. Given its relative safety and the opportunities it offered for sexual relationships, the rear area acquired a reputation as a hotbed of corruption and moral debauchery. Injury or illness also afforded at least a temporary respite from the conflict. Over the course of the war, 3.2 million injured German soldiers spent a long spell in hospital in Germany before they were fit to return to the front. Two other groups were away from the front for long periods or even the entire duration of the war: firstly, soldiers recalled to work in the war industry or armaments factories. And secondly, those stationed in the garrisons of the replacement army on home soil. Both of these accounted for substantial numbers of men. The replacement army based in Germany made up no less than a third of army personnel.

To picture only Verdun and other major battles of *matériel* when we think of the First World War is to ignore these many functional differences in the armed forces. These arose partly because of the 'invisible fronts' that kept the war machine running, requiring an unprecedented level of specialization and a multitude of different tasks.[33] The million-strong armies of the First World War and the sheer size of their bureaucratic structures also resulted in organizational gaps and countless niches, where soldiers were able to evade front-line fighting. These included units, offices and activities of little functional benefit, for instance, where soldiers could escape danger, often with the tacit approval of their immediate superiors. Even outside such 'unofficial' niches, some soldiers avoided the front line by reporting to a certain troop unit or training course, through sheer luck, or thanks to their professional qualifications. Resourceful soldiers like Dominik Richert, son of a farmer from Alsace, made full use of these small-scale opportunities for escape.[34] And the German-Jewish sociologist Norbert Elias (1897-1990) owed his survival in the First World War to his family's (correct) advice that volunteering for a radio unit would spare him from dangerous operations on the front line.[35] It must also be remembered, however, that First World War weaponry injured far more people than it killed, such was the imprecision of its destructive force. An estimated eight million soldiers in Europe survived with permanent physical and psychological damage.[36] Many of these injuries were horrific, and required extensive medical care and the provision of welfare state agencies. But nevertheless, these soldiers had survived.

Geographical differences in survival rates among front-line troops were an inevitable consequence of the enormous length of the front, with troops facing each other along hundreds of miles of trenches. Supplies of artillery munitions dwindled as the war progressed, making it impossible to fire with equal intensity at every location. There were thus many opportunities to 'live and let live'.[37] The troops on both sides tacitly agreed to keep fire to a minimum, to shoot into the air instead of at each other, and sometimes to refrain from firing entirely. Soldiers were thus able to gain a degree of control over their immediate environment and reduce the level of violence. The infantry would respond to a reduction in enemy fire by holding fire themselves, and it also proved possible to agree temporary ceasefires. In extreme cases, these could last for several weeks at a time.

Such tacit agreements were most commonplace on the parts of the front line furthest removed from the main offensives. In the Vosges mountains, for example, the same trench divisions, populated by large numbers of 35-to-45-year-old

**Figure 1** A survivor. Berthold Hörhold (on the right), the grandfather of the author's mother, is pictured here with a friend in 1916. Due to an injury he sustained to his left hand, he was transferred to the navy and spent the remainder of the war in Wilhelmshaven, repairing the telegraphy equipment of U-boats. After the war, he returned to his hometown of Halberstadt, where he ran a *Kolonialwarenhandlung*, a grocery store selling overseas produce. Hörhold died in 1935.

men, faced off against each for months or years at a time. Mutual aggression was already reduced to a minimum as troops performed only the most essential patrols to gather intelligence on the strength and intentions of the enemy forces. Officers in the trenches and, in all likelihood, the commanders of these generally undermanned units, had an interest in minimizing losses as far as possible. It often took intense artillery bombardment or the work of snipers to tip these places of survival back into scenes of destruction.

The analysis of national differences in survival rates should give special attention to soldiers who evaded military service by 'shirking' duty, deserting, defecting or deliberately mutilating themselves. Turning this analysis into a search for certain personality types that might explain such behaviour, however, is not a fruitful methodology. This was the approach taken by military judges, who were responsible for sentencing 'shirkers' and deserters and who remained wedded to an ideal of absolute discipline – right up to functionally irrelevant details such as maintaining flawless uniforms – even in the extraordinary conditions of trench warfare. In both the German and Austrian armies, industrial workers were far more likely than peasants to defect. Approximately three-quarters of deserters were unmarried and therefore had relatively few family ties. In the armies of the Western Allies and Central Powers, deserters were outsiders who generally acted alone in planning and realizing their escape, distancing themselves from their comrades in the process. However, not all deserters planned the act in detail. In a sense, many of those who took their survival into their own hands and violated military law were simply taking advantage of the small-scale opportunities for escape that presented themselves, just like their contemporaries who evaded front-line service altogether. As we will see in Chapter 5, the actual trigger to desert was often something rather coincidental. The motives behind such actions were diverse and not always clear.[38]

Nationality was a major influence on desertion. In the British and German armies, a disproportionate number of deserters came from national minorities seeking self-determination: Irishmen (in the latter half of the war), Danes, Poles and Alsace-Lorrainers.[39] Until the German army began to collapse in autumn 1918, however, the German, British and French armies all displayed a high degree of internal cohesion. The same could not be said for the armies of countries with more serious conflicts between different ethnic groups, or of those where the majority of soldiers from peasant backgrounds were poorly integrated into the symbolic order of the nation state. The former category applied especially to the Austro-Hungarian army, where national antagonisms involving the German-speaking troop leaders began to cause mass desertions in majority Czech units from as early as 1915. In 1916, there were increasing reports of desertions among soldiers of Italian, Ruthenian and Serbian nationality. As with the Alsatians and Poles in the German army, the deserters included not only soldiers and NCOs, but also officers. From 1917, the Slovenes and Croats – nationalities the army had previously regarded as reliable – began to desert too. The year 1918 saw widespread disturbances and mutinies, particularly in the rear area and at home.[40] In the summer and autumn, gangs of deserters and local peasants roamed the Dual Monarchy's southern tip in Croatia and Bosnia-Herzegovina, outraged at the continued requisitioning of agricultural products.[41]

Meanwhile, the second problem – lack of national integration – was to shake the Italian army to its foundations. At least half of the men serving in the Italian military were peasants and labourers. Deeply rooted in their families and local villages, their lives had, until the war, remained untouched by questions of national politics. Around a third of Italian soldiers were unable to read or write. A social and cultural chasm separated these peasant soldiers from the officer class. This estrangement between the officers and their men was reflected in the disciplinary measures pursued by the army leadership under General Luigi Cadorna. Their harshness was unparalleled in any other European army during the First World War. In March 1917, an incident in the Ravenna Brigade, stationed on the front line, illustrated the extreme consequences. Here, an entire regiment refused one afternoon to return to the line. The demoralized men and many of their junior officers sat down and initially refused to move, some drunk, others simply belligerent. After patient persuasion by the brigade commander, the soldiers agreed to end their mutiny, and by evening the regiment was in position. The urgently summoned divisional commander, however, was unwilling to show lenience, and instead asked the brigade commander how many men had been shot. Slightly hard of hearing, the latter misunderstood the question and replied that no shots had been fired. That was not what the general had meant. Now, the divisional commander ordered his accompanying military policemen to shoot two of the regiment's soldiers who had not even been involved in the mutiny. While inspecting the regiment on the front line the following day, he selected five more men by lot and had them shot directly in the trench. This was the infamous practice of 'decimation', which was unique to the Italian army and took place in a legal grey area, entirely subject to the arbitrary decisions of commanders. The Ravenna incident led to further court-martial proceedings and executions, which cost the lives of thirty-nine of the regiment's soldiers.[42]

Even this uniquely brutal regime of decimation, summary executions and court-martial sentences proved unable to stem the mutinies and indiscipline on the part of Italian peasant soldiers. At 729, the official number of death sentences carried out was higher in proportional terms, given the Italian army's total strength of 5.6 million men, than in any other country. Yet even this figure is incomplete. It ignores at least 200 summary executions, which usually killed several soldiers at once. Despite the intended deterrent effect of 'decimation', there were countless cases of self-mutilation and desertion, with exponential growth in both crimes recorded from 1914. The approximately 10,000 court-martial convictions for self-mutilation and 101,000 for desertion give only a partial picture of the scale of troops' refusal to fight. September 1917 alone saw some 100,000 Italian soldiers abscond, either by leaving their units or after refusing their call-up.[43] And this was before the catastrophic defeat at the Battle of Caporetto in November that year, which marked the absolute disciplinary low point in the Italian army's history during the First World War.

The opportunity for soldiers to save their lives by defecting or giving themselves up to the enemy has been a topic of intense debate among historians. Given the stigma of betraying one's country that attached to soldiers, and especially to their relatives left behind, the number of those deliberately planning to defect was probably relatively low. Soldiers were far more likely to end up on the enemy side of the lines having been taken prisoner. Many of these men may have spontaneously grasped the opportunity to surrender and save their lives rather than opening fire or fighting to the end. It has often been claimed that the French and especially the British frequently killed defenceless prisoners on the spot, and that this deterred many German soldiers from giving themselves up without resistance.[44] However, the sparse source material on which this claim is based does not withstand critical examination (see Chapter 4). In practice, the distinction between voluntarily and involuntarily being taken prisoner was fluid, and many soldiers used this grey area to survive. They could be sure of the approval of most of their comrades, in whose eyes the advantages of captivity far outweighed the risks.[45] Only the most battle-hardened officers like Charles de Gaulle, held captive in Ingolstadt, found life away from the front 'unbearable'.[46]

Over the course of the First World War, at least seven million, and probably nearer eight million soldiers ended up as POWs, almost one in seven of all the men called up.[47] This figure alone gives the lie to the idea that it was routine practice to kill surrendering troops. Larger numbers of POWs were taken in the midst of offensives during periods of mobile warfare, which explains why there were far more prisoners on the Eastern Front, in Italy and in the Balkans than there were in the West. The Allies on the Western Front only began taking a larger number of prisoners in the final weeks and months of the war, when hundreds of thousands of German soldiers participated in a 'hidden military strike' largely unbeknown to the public. As Chapter 7 will show, soldiers' primary motivation for striking was to protect their own lives. The enormous numbers of prisoners created acute logistical problems. For the Central Powers, these were aggravated by poor food supplies, resulting in a rising death toll among the men held captive. Despite cases of malnutrition, however, the survival rates of both German and Allied POWs remained higher than those of active soldiers. Some nationalities were less fortunate: among Romanian prisoners in German captivity, the death rate was an exceptionally high 29 per cent.[48] Italians held captive by the Austro-Hungarian army were also subjected to extreme hardships. Some 100,000 of the approximately 600,000 Italian POWs did not survive the war. This was likely the result of a deliberate policy by Austria-Hungary, which sought revenge for the 'betrayal' of Italy's entry into the war on the side of the *Entente*. In POW camps like Mauthausen and Theresienstadt – later used by the Nazis for other purposes – the Italians thus not only went hungry but were often victims of brutal treatment.[49]

## III Discourses on violence and victimhood

As they attempted to interpret what was going on around them and find meaning in the upheaval of war, soldiers sought ways to express the experience of death and the emotional demands imposed on them by violent conflict. In so doing, they relied heavily on two important media of communication that provided them with meaning. The first were the letters to and from their relatives at home, in which the unfolding war was translated into terms more compatible with family intimacy. This communication drew extensively on semantic traditions long provided by public discourses on the fatherland, on victimhood and heroic death.[50] Soldiers' other source of meaning was their continual conversation with comrades in the trenches and barracks, which helped the men to consolidate their own ideas about the war and their role in the conflict. Though such discussions are extremely difficult to analyse given the lack of source material, they were enormously important to soldiers in shaping their collective opinions.[51]

The mass publication of field post letters, whether they were immediate expressions of soldiers' sentiments or edited to conform with a register of acceptable patriotic discourse, already moulded the popular image of the war during the years from 1914 to 1918. The 'voice' of the front was widely requisitioned to justify cultural values and political decisions.[52] It has taken considerable time for researchers to free themselves from the suggestive power of these published, nationalist representations of the war and make way for a more differentiated approach based on archival sources. French historiography in particular has set the benchmark in this regard.[53] While there is much still to research on this topic, it is clear that soldiers drew upon a variety of languages, or discourses, to interpret the war.[54] Socio-cultural similarities were far more important to the inner structure and coherence of these than national differences. After all, troops from all combatant nations faced the same problem of how to make sense of the mass killing and their part in it.

Perhaps the most important language was that of religion, despite the unmistakeable slow erosion of its persuasiveness as the war progressed. Its specific form was, of course, determined to a large degree by confessional differences. Yet there were many commonalities in the religious answers to the questions raised by war. Religion lent a non-verbal, symbolic and ritual dimension to soldiers' attempts to assimilate their experiences on the front. The most obvious manifestations of this were the attendance of mass, the praying of the rosary and the popularity of Sacred Heart of Jesus prayers among pious Catholics. The theme of atonement in the veneration of the Sacred Heart promoted the view that the war was the judgement of God, thereby turning this contingent historical event into something with a far deeper personal meaning for individual soldiers.[55] Yet even soldiers without confessional ties seized superstitiously on amulets, chain letters containing prayers, and other devotional objects in the hope of their magic power. The language of religion was by no means confined to those soldiers with long-standing religious convictions. The Christian message of salvation had a broad appeal, which lay in the established and sophisticated language it offered to help soldiers deal with the ever-present and indiscriminate threat of death. Its particular strength was its ability to address three closely related aspects of the horrors of war. A soldier could address his fear of death in his prayers and in the Holy Communion or Eucharist. He could express his grief over the injury or death of friends and comrades in the language of Christian charity and devotion. And his remembrance of the fallen could draw on a host of forms, symbols and social practices specific to the Church.[56]

However, there were inherent limits to the effectiveness of religious language, which meant that, for many soldiers, its persuasiveness diminished over time. One of the problems lay in the need to translate the faith into the everyday lives of the troops, to ease their individual suffering by collectively drawing upon religious values. This was traditionally the role of the clergy. During the First

World War, however, military chaplains were in a poor position to perform this task with credibility, such was their integral role in patriotic war theology and its instrumentalization for propaganda purposes by the military authorities. This was true for Anglican and Protestant military chaplains[57] as well as for their Catholic counterparts in Germany and France. In these countries, Catholics used their war effort in a bid to gain recognition in national politics.[58] A second problem lay in the issue of theodicy, that is, the question why an almighty God might want to tolerate extended human suffering. Wartime sermons preached that the conflict was an opportunity for purification and moral renewal. Religious discourse thus initially offered an interpretation not only of the consequences of war, but also of its causes: war had to come, this suggested, because 'people' had become too 'wicked'. The moral abandon of life in the rear area and of the munitions workers at home soon undermined this argument, as did the actions of war profiteers. Over time, the lengthening duration of the conflict shook the belief that the war could offer any form of moral purification. It also rendered increasingly problematic the idea of a redeeming justice guaranteed by divine providence. While it still offered comfort to individual soldiers, religious language thus lost much of its power to shape any form of universal interpretation of the war.

Another important discourse was that of nationhood and nationalism. During the conflict, this was charged more than ever with religious pathos. The language of nationhood placed the soldier in a wider social context, signalling loyalty to the crown or republic, depending on his nationality. German loyalty to the monarchy proved far more fragile amid the stresses of war than the much stronger republican ties of the French soldiers. Paradoxically, the latter were most evident in the mutinies that shook the French army in spring 1917. A close examination of the political language of the mutineers reveals that their objective was not to bring about political revolution or peace at any price, but rather to restore the balance between their expectations of peace and the real pressures on the front line. The mutineers did not reject military service outright. Rather, their mutiny was a way to renegotiate the terms of this service, which they understood as a duty of every male citizen. In directing their call for negotiations to the parliament, these citizen soldiers effectively reaffirmed the Republic's legitimacy in spite of their ostensibly socialist rhetoric.[59]

The most important function of the language of nationhood, and one which was strongly infused with religious connotations, was to elevate soldiers' suffering into a sacrifice for their community. Yet this was also a function it performed with rapidly diminishing effectiveness. It offered few words even to describe, let alone justify, the enormous losses of men. Death thus remained an empty semantic space in descriptions of the war by middle-class soldiers, among whom the language of nationalism was most widespread. Nationalist language was far more effective in codifying a canon of soldierly virtues: duty, obedience and fighting spirit. In this form, it greatly influenced all the other wartime discourses, and particularly the language used by supporters of socialist movements. The language of nationhood was reflected in real social practice, its proponents believed, in the form of a comradeship that transcended class and rank. However, this ideal was so romantically exaggerated as to soon prove largely empty, existing only in basic forms of solidarity among soldiers.[60]

Injecting political content into the language of nationhood proved largely ineffectual in all combatant countries. Far from identifying with detailed plans for agreeing peace or with specific territorial objectives, soldiers responded with growing aversion. The nation was far more useful as a broader symbol for all the reasons why it was worth holding out for victory. Differing in specific form from country to country, the discourse drew on both national traditions and developments on the ground. The intense defensive patriotism of the *poilus*, for example, stemmed in no small part from the fact that ten French *départements* were occupied by foreign troops. Meanwhile, the German soldiers' national sense of mission drew on a long tradition of inwardness: the notion that self-formation through engagement with highbrow culture would align the individual with the nation. This notion, however, proved far harder to adapt to the war at hand, and survived only among soldiers from bourgeois families.[61] Finally, the language of nationhood was also a means of legitimizing the violent conduct of the war. National hatreds escalated on all sides as nationalist discourse depicted other countries as enemies of civilization, demonizing them as 'Huns' (Germans) or 'barbarians' (Russians), for example.

As the war progressed, the language of nationhood proved even more fragile than the language of religion. Meanwhile, socialist discourse became increasingly attractive in Germany, Italy, France and, to a lesser extent, Great Britain. Though particularly widespread among industrial workers, its appeal during the second half of the war reached a far wider group of soldiers.[62] For those at home in the socialist movement, its language performed a similar function to that of religion. The suffering of war was a necessary martyrdom, which would be followed by revolution and thus the promise of earthly happiness. Unlike religious language, however, the socialist discourse had little to offer those coming to terms with the immediate proximity of death. Remaining indifferent to soldiers' individual problems, the socialist alternative concentrated instead on the big picture. Its ability to address actual social practice in the army by highlighting the conflict and segregation between officers and troops was a notable exception.

Soldiers whose interest in socialism developed only in the course of the war had little interest in its eschatology and universalist doctrine. However, fragments of socialist theory offered them an explanation as to why they were still at war after years of struggle, despite the fact that neither they nor other ordinary people had any interest in the conflict's continuation. Many of these men attributed the war to the 'big capitalists' and 'war profiteers', and placed their hopes for peace in the Second International. The language of socialism was thus syncretic in nature, allowing soldiers to combine it with aspects of other languages: those of religion, nationhood and the agrarian milieu.

The language of soldiers from peasant backgrounds was entirely tailored to the living conditions and worldview of this social group, whose impact on the internal structure of the wartime armies is often overlooked.[63] Its special nature lay in the way it combined elements of the languages of religion and victimization with its narrow field of view. It was a litany of complaint about the misery and hardship at the front, as well as mistreatment by 'comrades' and officers alike. The peasant soldiers combined this with an idealized opposite image of life and work on their own farm. The seasonal rhythms of farming had a material presence even among the soldiers at the front. They remained the men's preoccupation, indeed their obsession. Focusing on their own mental universe of sowing, harvesting and looking after livestock, peasants were detached from the group culture of their units and the often rowdy off-duty pastimes of their comrades. At the heart of this language was the desire to return to the family home and familiar seasonal work on the farm. A basic form of religious language lent an inner structure to the peasant soldiers' suffering and prevented it from drifting into outright despair. The language of nationhood, meanwhile, was only embraced by the peasants where it presented the soldier's personal respectability and sense of duty as unquestionable values. Such was the importance of the peasants' own discourse that the languages of modernism, so prevalent in the art and literature of the time, found far less foothold among soldiers than has been suggested.[64]

A final language of the First World War, or rather a pattern present in all the other wartime discourses discussed here, was that of victimhood. Soldiers used the socialist language to describe themselves as the victims of the capitalists and army leadership, which had them fight on behalf of economic interests. In religious language, meanwhile, it was God who sat idly by as the troops were sacrificed. And for the peasant soldiers, it was a multitude of factors that forced them to hold out on the front line and suffer the hardships of war. This latter group lacked any notion of how collective action could improve their situation. Their feelings of victimhood thus took on a far stronger air of resignation. The language of nationhood, by contrast, most strongly expressed the feeling that soldiers were actively and willingly making a sacrifice for the greater good of the nation. This was particularly the case in Britain and France. In Germany, meanwhile, the growing crisis of the language of nationhood consisted in no small part of a switch in perspective: the feeling that soldiers were *being sacrificed* in the name of the fatherland.

It was nothing new for soldiers to feel like cogs in an all-powerful military machine. In the 1914–18 war, however, soldiers' descriptions of themselves as victims were reflected in the specific nature of the new and decisive artillery weapons, which subjected the infantrymen to a largely passive role. This distinguished the Great War from earlier conflicts, which were characterized to a far greater extent by close-quarter combat and the initiative in battle of the infantry soldiers. The extent to which soldiers described themselves as having been 'sacrificed' has also influenced popular memory of the front line. Amid this general narrative of victimhood, it has taken tenacious work to draw attention to the fate of a particular group of victims. In France, pacifist and socialist war veterans (including Robert Jospin (1899–1990), father of former French Prime Minister Lionel Jospin) have worked devotedly to seek recognition and an official pardon for the some 600 *fusillés de la Grande Guerre* – soldiers executed for desertion or their part in the mutinies of 1917.[65]

3

# German Soldiers and their Conduct of War in 1914

The general mobilization of the German army on 1 August 1914 set in motion an enormous military machine. The field army mobilized a total of 2.08 million men, divided into 40 army corps. Another 3.8 million men were called up to serve in the replacement army stationed in Germany.[1] Perhaps even more extraordinary than these enormous troop numbers themselves was the fact that the army achieved this level of mobilization in the space of just four days. The Bavarian army, which made up only one contingent of the German army as a whole, had already surpassed its planned wartime strength of approximately 407,000 NCOs and ordinary soldiers by 20 August.[2] This was only the beginning of a historically unparalleled military mobilization of 18-to-45-year-old men. Over the course of the First World War, some 13.3 million men served in the German armed forces, and 10.5 million of them spent at least part of the war in the field army.[3] By no means all of these men were directly involved in operating weaponry or killing enemy soldiers. Many instead had the enormous logistical task of supplying materials, food and munitions to the front, a mission that tied up huge numbers of personnel throughout the war.

## I Emotional mobilization

This vast physical mobilization of manpower was only half of the story, however. The authorities were also faced with the task of uniting the populace emotionally in support of the war machine. The commencement of hostilities unleashed a wave of different individual and collective sentiments that it is impossible to encapsulate within a singular definition. The oft-cited 'war enthusiasm' or *Kriegsbegeisterung*, for example, overlooks the concern, shock and depression felt by many at the outset of the conflict. A series of studies on the German civilian population have already explored this issue,[4] and this chapter will therefore turn to a slightly different question: what were the perceptions and emotions that accompanied the readiness of German soldiers for war in the initial weeks and months of the conflict? On the one hand, their period of compulsory military service in the standing army had already trained many of the men in the use of weapons and familiarized them with the army's structures of command and discipline. This military service had also instilled a sense of duty to the state, which contributed to the smooth unfolding of the mobilization in 1914.[5] On the other hand, however, little in the soldiers' two-year military service can have prepared them for the reality of mechanized warfare that they encountered in 1914. In this sense, their position was not dissimilar to that of the mainly young men, many though by no means all of them from the bourgeois middle classes, who signed up voluntarily in the initial weeks and months of the war.[6] These volunteers were soon forced to acquaint themselves with the military's rigid social hierarchy and group culture only too familiar to those who had already completed military service. As will be seen below, many volunteers developed an often deep sense of disillusionment about their wartime service from the early stages of the conflict.[7]

This chapter will examine the contradictory expectations and experiences of the soldiers advancing into hostile territory in the initial weeks and months of the war. It will explore their ambivalence between excitement about the anticipated swift victory and disillusionment about the realities of life at the front. It will also look at how the men reflected on the violence they experienced as both victims and perpetrators. Finally, the chapter will examine how ordinary German soldiers regarded the civilian population in the territories they had conquered. There have been only a few systematic studies on this topic to date. The majority of these have concentrated on German atrocities in Belgium and France, which will also be briefly examined here.[8] Using three case studies and extended excerpts from war diaries and field post letters, the chapter begins by attempting to explore the chaotic events and contradictory impressions of the early weeks of the war from the perspective of ordinary soldiers.

## II  Extreme losses

Much has been written about the enormous human cost of the battles in these early weeks of the war. This may stem in part from a desire to underline the brutality and bloody reality of war that suddenly confronted many of the men. However, it also reflects a simple truth: the first weeks of the conflict, and particularly the month of September 1914, were indeed the deadliest of the entire war for the German army. The German authorities recorded a monthly figure for 'total losses', which added together all soldiers reported killed or missing in action or as suffering long-term sickness or injury, and subtracted the number of men returning fit for duty. On the Western Front, total losses in September reached 16.8 per cent, or more than a sixth of the total troop strength. In October, they declined somewhat to a still exceptionally high 10.1 per cent. The army would not come close to repeating these figures at any other point in the war, even during the intensive battles of *matériel* in 1916. As the battles of the Somme and Verdun raged in July and August 1916, for example, the rate of total losses on the Western Front was 'only' (if that is the appropriate word) 5.9 per cent and 6.1 per cent. Death rates showed a similar picture. In September 1914, the number of soldiers killed in action reached its absolute peak: 2 per cent of the total 'actual strength' of the Western Army. This compared to 0.8 per cent in July 1916.[9]

The soldiers had obvious trouble finding words to express the deadly reality of the first phase of mobile warfare. Even for historians, translating these abstract numbers into an appropriate account of the war is fraught with difficulty. To put the voices from the front which feature in this chapter into context: the months from August to October 1914 were a time of mass killing and mass death on all sides; the 'singular peak' in the First World War's long 'history of death'.[10]

## III  The voice of the soldiers: Georg Schenk

The diary of Georg Schenk, a journeyman carpenter from Nuremberg, is our first source. Schenk, born in 1888, was drafted into the 21st Bavarian Infantry Regiment on 4 August 1914 and experienced the German advance in Lorraine and northern France. Like many other men, he began keeping a diary to document his own experiences during the frenetic early days of the war. The diary entries begin with the announcement of the German mobilization on 1 August.

> Finally, on 1 August at 6.00 pm, it was announced that the general mobilization had been ordered and now everything came to a climax. Many a tear was shed and many an eye that had been dry for ten years became moist. It was particularly the women and girls who were crying, for many men and young lads had to leave home to fight for the fatherland, which was threatened by Russia and France. Few slept well during the first night, since the anxiety for the husband, the wife, the groom, and the bride was greater than ever, as people knew that a very grave war was coming.

[20 August:] We got nothing to eat on 20 August, not even coffee in some cases. I still had bread and a bit of bacon, which was all I had to sustain me. We were happy to escape with our lives, for it was a hard day and we had our baptism of fire. Trust in God, he will help in the hour of need – that was my consolation. I wasn't that scared of the infantry fire, but when the shells exploded close behind us, some of us got frightened and everyone jumped forward as fast as he could. When I was lying in the firing line I was thinking of my Gretl [Margarete Popp, Schenk's bride-to-be] and what would she do and what would she think. And some thoughts flashed through my mind. What might she say if I got injured or dropped dead? I kept thinking, you promised you'd come back, and I had no doubt at all that I would get wounded. Well, thank God, this battle is over. We have no idea how many more there will be.

[25 August:] after heavy fighting near the village of Serres] We'll remember the 25 August for as long as we live. It cost many lives on both sides, without even considering the wounded. I promised that I would pray the rosary in my family or get a prayer said every day if I came back safely from this campaign.

[31 August:] On the 31st, we cleaned our weapons and then manned the trench. As this was too small, we had to dig until lunchtime. After lunch we had a rest and lay in the cover trench. On the 30th, the foot artillery fired across, but the French couldn't shoot that far and had to leave it be. A tethered balloon was sent up to observe our fire and scan the area. Life at war is quite nice when there aren't any battles going on, but we have an officer who should have stayed at home because he's made our life even more difficult than it should be. Life would be fine if it was just the battles, but we don't get a minute's rest, because nobody can stand to see us unoccupied.

[3 September:] This afternoon I was on patrol with Lieutenant Merz, but we didn't see anything. Then we got some more rest. Our First Lieutenant completely bricks himself whenever he hears anything from the enemy. Then, when he knows the enemy isn't close by, he's terribly harsh and boneheaded. We've ended up with a company leader who knows less than a recruit and is as frightened as a rabbit.

[7 September:] Digging till nine o'clock, then we had to lie in the trench in the boiling heat and weren't allowed out. The shrapnel fire was often very high on both sides, then it dropped off a bit until four in the afternoon. The water patrol went off at three o'clock. At four o'clock, the infantry fire began and there was an attack. The 8th Company were up front and were so shot to bits by our own artillery that not a single man in the first column could hold his position and anyone who wasn't dead or injured pulled back of his own accord. It was terrible to see the wounded coming back, often three, four or five together.... Shots kept flying over our trench but we didn't show ourselves and didn't fire either. The French infantry withdrew. We could see it clearly and it looked like only weak detachments remained. In the night from 6th to 7th [September], Remereville was ablaze. Four other villages had been set on fire and the whole area was illuminated. Remereville is a place of devastation now; there is hardly a single house left standing. On the evening of the 7th, the water patrol brought wine with them and we had something else in our bellies again at last. The food was barely edible; on the 7th it was too salty and the meat already smelled. We got bread again after four days and had to make do with it.... I haven't received post for five days, otherwise I'd have written back, so I had nothing to do in the trenches apart from write my notes and talk to my colleagues. Anyone who really thinks about it has to admit that there can be nothing more terrible than war. Yesterday's dead are lying about 300 metres in front of us, most of them killed by our own artillery.[11]

These notes by Schenk cover little more than the first four weeks of a war that was to last another fifty-one months. Yet even in this short time frame, it is clear that he had a series of rapidly changing and contradictory impressions to process, beginning from the very outset of the conflict. For Schenk, it was unquestionable that Germany was going to war to defend itself. He thus considered it self-evident that men like him had a duty to fight for the fatherland. The first diary entry also provides a vivid insight into the dejected mood in cities and rural areas alike when the time came to say goodbye to loved ones. Schenk's somewhat stylized account emphasizes the despondency of the women in deliberate contrast to the composure of the men. A few weeks later, on 20 August, Schenk and his regiment experienced their 'baptism of fire'. This immediately led Schenk to reflect on his closest personal relationship: his engagement to Gretl, whom he would go on to marry almost two years later on 1 January 1916. In his diary, Schenk writes that he was certain he would be injured – a conviction based less on superstitious premonition than on a sober consideration of his impressions of the war so far.

In the costly battles on 25 August, Schenk drew on a traditional response to personal problems that was provided by his deep Catholic faith. The fact that Schenk had already sought consolation in God several days before the battle suggests that, as for many Catholic soldiers, this pattern of religious behaviour was well-rooted in his personal make-up.[12] It is also obvious that the battle was not the first crisis in which he had turned to the rosary. Up to this point, Schenk's impressions of his wartime service had been largely positive. Although he appears to have lacked fervently nationalist motivations for his role in the conflict, his diary describes life at war, at least between the fighting, as 'quite nice'. He experienced the campaign – a rapid advance into a foreign country – as an adventure: a journey of discovery to far-away places. Only the bullying and cowardly behaviour of his company leader dampened Schenk's enthusiasm somewhat. Fear was, of course, a constant companion for all front-line soldiers; but being 'as frightened as a rabbit', as Schenk describes his company leader in dramatic terms, was, he believed, unfair, unsoldierly and unmanly. Schenk was evidently convinced that there was no room for such cowardice in times of war.

## IV The destruction of Réméréville

The battles on 6 and 7 September would rapidly change Schenk's attitude to the war. His regiment was deployed near Réméréville, a small town close to Nancy. There, German soldiers apparently received an allegation that the local 'priest had signalled to French troops from the church tower'.[13] This rumour – if it really was circulating among the troops in the town – may have resonated with expectations in the German army of a 'people's war', in which Catholic priests and other members of the civilian population would rise up and resist the Germans. The suspicion was supposedly the trigger for the wholesale destruction of the town by German troops and the killing of a number of civilians remaining there.[14] This atrocity was just one of 484 incidents where German soldiers committed deadly attacks on civilians in Belgium and northern France between 5 August and 21 October 1914. In 129 of these gross breaches of international law, German troops killed ten or more civilians, contributing to a total death toll of close to 6,400. The Germans also destroyed at least 15,000 houses, largely by setting fires. The events in Réméréville came relatively late in this series of atrocities, which mostly took place in the first ten days after the major German offensive began on 18 August. Unlike the incidents in the initial days of the war, however, these later attacks in the second half of August did not occur spontaneously, but resulted from orders by German regimental or brigade commanders.[15]

There is no indication that such orders were given in Réméréville, which was a far smaller incident in terms of the numbers killed. In this case, it appears that soldiers were acting on their own initiative having heard the rumours against the clergy, if indeed these were the true cause of what took place in the town. This was certainly how the French committee that investigated the German atrocities in December 1914 interpreted the events. And historians John Horne and Alan Kramer, authors of an important study of the German atrocities, have followed them.[16] However, it is notable that Schenk's diary mentions neither the killing of civilians nor the rumours about the priest sending signals to the French troops. The latter omission seems particularly surprising given that Schenk clearly spent considerable time discussing the events of the war with other soldiers in his company. The allegations against the priest would certainly have been of interest to the pious Schenk. While the available sources cannot explain this omission with any certainty, Schenk's diary indicates something that may in fact have influenced the actions of German troops to a far greater extent than anti-Catholic rumours. As is clear from Schenk's account, the French infantry were retreating at the time of the battle at Réméréville. This meant that the majority of casualties were inflicted by the Germans' own Bavarian artillery. It is likely that these deaths from so-called friendly fire contributed to a sense of confusion and frustration among the German troops, which may have triggered their violence towards the town and its civilian population.[17]

## V Collective learning processes

Whatever the true motivation for the attack, Schenk himself gives only brief mention to the scenes in the town, describing Réméréville as a 'place of devastation'. He appears, however, to have been far more disturbed by the 'terrible' sight of the deaths and injuries from friendly fire. It seems likely that this experience left Schenk with persistent doubts about the claim that Germany was simply conducting a defensive war. In the aftermath of the incident in Réméréville, Schenk appears to have been unable to draw on the emotional support of his family or on religious ritual. Yet he was not forced to reflect on events alone, despite technical problems that prevented the exchange of field post letters with friends and relatives during these days.[18] Instead, he found an abundance of opportunities to talk over his experiences with other soldiers. Such conversations were a collective learning process, in which soldiers subjectively constructed their front-line experience, interpreting events through interaction. They rarely found their way into written sources, however.

Schenk's discussions with his 'colleagues' – he evidently preferred this neutral term to the more loaded 'comrades' – left him with what he considered the undeniable conclusion 'that there can be nothing more terrible than war'. This assertion had clearly emerged as the lowest common denominator of soldiers' individual learning processes in the Bavarian 21st Infantry Regiment. It was the product of just four weeks' experience of the reality of mobile warfare on the Western Front. This judgement of the conflict stood diametrically opposed to the theology of the 'just war' espoused by prominent figures in the Catholic Church – the very institution in whose forms of prayer Schenk had sought and found consolation barely two weeks earlier. Just one week earlier, he had described life at war as 'quite nice'.

Schenk's diary does not reveal how his views on the war changed in the subsequent years of conflict until his death on 24 October 1917. He ceased writing his diary after 7 October 1914. This may indicate that, after the contradictory experiences of the initial weeks of the war, he had now emerged with an interpretation of the conflict he found satisfactory. Only in 1917 did he resume his diary for a time. These later entries reveal that he held a nuanced view of the French enemy soldiers. On a patrol in April 1917, the French unit opposite that of Schenk took a prisoner who was unpopular in Schenk's company. Schenk considered it 'very decent' that the French did not open fire when the German patrol advanced.[19]

Despite his conclusion that 'there can be nothing more terrible than war', there is nothing to indicate that Schenk's willingness to participate in the conflict had diminished. Nor does he reflect on how or by whom this 'terrible' war could be brought to an end. Schenk evidently lacked the keen political convictions that might have led him to interpret the wider picture. Some soldiers who had been members of the Social Democratic Party (SPD) members before the war were already drawing much deeper conclusions by the end of 1914. They were encouraged by the actions of Karl Liebknecht, a Reichstag deputy on the left wing of the SPD. On 2 December 1914, Liebknecht spoke out against further war loans at a parliamentary vote. The only member of the Reichstag to vote against further loans, he soon began to receive large numbers of letters of support from the soldiers in the field, commending his courageous stand. Many of these letters reveal that their writers regarded the war as a faceless cruelty and blamed its continuation on the actions and commercial interests of the 'big capitalists'. Even at this early stage of the conflict, such soldiers expressed their conviction that only determined and united action by the people as a whole could bring an end to the war.[20]

## VI The voice of the soldiers: David Pfaff

A second eyewitness whose diary entries give us an insight into the soldiers' readiness for war was David Pfaff, a 24-year-old volunteer. Pfaff made a series of brief diary entries during the German advance through Belgium and France until his death on 4 November 1914:

11 August / Digging out trenches and drill.

12 August / Drill exercises.

14 August / Drill and night-time training. Lots of bullying by the superiors. Everybody wants to approach the enemy at last. In the morning, artillery was shooting at an aeroplane. Later on, it turned out that the plane was one of ours.

15 August / Drill. In the afternoon, swimming pool in the city of Luxembourg. Fantastic pool. Haven't seen a pool as terrific as that in all my life . . . .

16 August / . . . In the afternoon, drill. . . . Square-bashing is getting so bad that one comrade who feels like me said that only the Germans with their inborn patriotism could put up with these monotonous drills without grumbling . . . .

23 August / Civilians were shooting at us. They were all killed.

30 August / Field service at 11 in the morning in stifling heat. We sang: 'We stand in prayer before God the Almighty'. It deeply affected us. Many who had turned away from God have found their saviour again, as have I.

8 October / In the trench, standing to. I have been very poorly. But the doctor hasn't helped me.

2 November / The Battalion Lieutenant hit Jakob and Paul, because they were about to fetch firewood and entrenchment material without their rifles. It seems to be becoming a habit to behave as if we were in Russia. It is disgraceful when an extremely young lieutenant hits an old soldier and reservist who is fighting for his fatherland. Of course, there is huge exasperation. These sad incidents are as regrettable as those situations when young officers use their pistols to force their soldiers to advance while they themselves remain under cover. Unfortunately, I witnessed that again on 1 October.

3 November / We stay in the trenches. Artillery fire on both sides.[21]

It is immediately apparent that Pfaff's attitude to the war differed from Georg Schenk's in a variety of ways. For the Protestant volunteer Pfaff, the 'fatherland' appears to have been a far more important vessel of moral and political values than it was for the Catholic Schenk. This is evident from the different ways they describe officers' bullying behaviour towards subordinates, which clearly upset both men. Schenk personalized these incidents, interpreting them as the product of individual officers' lack of character. Pfaff, meanwhile, attached a deeper significance to the conduct of such men, regarding them as a threat to soldiers' readiness to defend the fatherland. It was, he writes, 'as if we were in Russia'. For Pfaff, the use of physical force against older soldiers threatened the Teutonic moral standards on which he believed the idea of the German nation was founded. In his eyes, the war had essentially put these moral values on trial. The young volunteer's renewed faith in God charged this belief in the fatherland's moral virtue with further emotion.[22] Unlike Schenk's Christian faith, Pfaff's was thus more than simply a comfort in his hour of need.

On 22 August, Pfaff's 80th Hessian Fusilier Regiment was involved in heavy fighting against French troops near Neufchâteau in the Ardennes. German troops perpetrated extreme acts of violence against Belgian civilians and initially took a number of them prisoner. They later killed seventeen of the town's inhabitants, alleging that these men had joined the fighting as *francs-tireurs* (free shooters).[23] Pfaff notes these events in the briefest conceivable form: 'Civilians were shooting at us. They were all killed.' He evidently saw no cause to doubt the objectivity or accuracy of the German allegations against the Belgian civilians, nor does he respond in his diary with any expression of sympathy. For Pfaff, *Kriegsnotwendigkeit* (the 'necessities of war') – the term used by the German military elites to justify such atrocities – appears to have warranted no further mention, let alone any reflection.[24] This attitude contrasts sharply with the moral tone of his diary entry just a few weeks later, when he denounces an officer's physical bullying of two older soldiers as nothing less than a descent into Russian standards of behaviour. In this respect, the diary clearly reveals the self-centred moral compass of Pfaff's vision of German nationhood. His entries show that his idea of the fatherland, which developed hand in hand with his rediscovered Protestant piety in the early days of the war, was a cause he firmly believed worth fighting for. At the same time, however, Pfaff also notes that some men had to be forced into action by officers wielding pistols.

## VII The voice of the soldiers: Stefan Schimmer

A final account of the experience of ordinary soldiers in the early days of the war comes from Stefan Schimmer, a farmer, born in 1876, who served in a Landwehr regiment. From 6 August 1914 onwards, Schimmer sent almost daily letters by field post to his wife Katharina at home on their farm in Oellingen, Lower Franconia.[25] Schimmer's first letters came from the village of Herxheim in the Bavarian Palatinate, where his regiment was billeted. On 2 October, he then crossed the border into France and was stationed over the following weeks in the town of Senones in the Vosges mountains.

11 August 1914: I would like it best if we had an armistice now.

24 August 1914: Four villages in Lorraine were set on fire because they attacked the German troops. On the German side, every battle has been won up till now. The Bavarian army are fighting like fury; anyone spared by the bullets is slaughtered with the bayonet or rifle butt.

25 August 1914: Had to go to church. After that our captain read the war history [*Kriegsgeschichte*] to us [Schimmer may have meant the *Kriegsartikel*, a list of soldierly duties and of the punishment for the most common disciplinary offences]. We took an enormous number of prisoners, more than 150 cannon, a lot of machine guns and a vast array of rifles and munitions. The war will and must be won by the Germans. The French haven't won even the tiniest engagement so far.... On 25 August, my birthday, I went to confession again early because we were off duty. After all, it's the last chance for this year. Maybe even for my whole life, for nobody knows where we will be going to. If I should not return, you will marry Michael. You will come out of the whole thing all right. As I mentioned before, Germany will win the war; there is no doubt about it. The Belgian fortress of Liège has been in German hands for fourteen days and is besieged by German troops. But the war costs lives and it may last until spring. The Germans will be finished with the French by winter. They run away if the Germans go after them, or they surrender.

1 September 1914: Paris will be encircled in a few days. The poor people there are having to leave already.

3 September 1914: Leuven is a town in France of 7,000 people. It has been battered, too, because the inhabitants shot at the German troops.

4 September 1914: The German cavalry is at the gates of Paris. The Bavarian army is in battle in the Vosges. We can assume Paris will have capitulated within eight days.

27 September 1914: Please celebrate two masses on the divine providence. Today I went to confession again and heard two masses and one High Mass.

2 October 1914: Letting you know that we crossed the border on 2 October at 7.00 pm. Roaring cannon were the first thing we heard of course. We could see bombed carriages there as well, a destroyed customs house. The air smells of gunpowder from the bombarded villages. We have just been resting in a French village. It's basically deserted. All one can see is the sky and the soldiers.

9 October 1914: Write to tell me how the war is going. We don't know anything. Isn't there going to be a peace agreement soon?

14 October 1914: Is there no news of the war coming to an end soon? Please don't stop praying for me.... It doesn't look nice around here, for a battle has taken place. Many soldiers' graves are to be seen.

18 October 1914: Often I don't sleep more than two hours a day because I'm in fear of my life. I only hope because of you and the children that I won't be killed.... The area where we are positioned has already been a battlefield. It's a place of terrible devastation.

20 October 1914: We don't believe what the *Kaiser* says here. There's really no sign of peace negotiations after all.

17 December 1914: There's no point thinking about peace before March. This is now siege warfare. The country whose money and food holds out the longest is going to win.[26]

These passages reveal a striking shift in Schimmer's expectations after leaving German soil. While still in Herxheim, Schimmer was eager to believe the countless rumours and biased pronouncements on the quick and decisive victories of the German troops. He heard stories about the Bavarian 'lions' – dispatching their enemies using a bayonet with their typical heroism – and was keen to relate these to his wife. Only too aware of the human cost of any war, however, he was far from euphoric. Fearing the worst for his own life from the outset, he advised his wife to marry again and secure the farm's future if he should die. Schimmer's confidence of a quick German victory persisted into September. Even when the truth emerged about the propaganda reports of German successes (as was the case with the report that Paris had fallen, which later had to be corrected and finally dropped), this was unable to seriously shake his belief in such news.[27]

All this suddenly changed even before Schimmer reached the front. Having crossed the border into France in early October, he now saw at first hand the devastation the war had left behind. After the speculation of the previous weeks, his diary entries began to concentrate on his immediate impressions: the sights, sounds and smells of destruction. Seeing for the first time the real consequences of the conflict, his confidence that he was sufficiently informed of the war's progress now vanished. Schimmer's seemingly commanding perspective on events made way for the worm's-eye view of the ordinary soldier. And along with that sense of overview disappeared his willingness to pronounce on the further course of the war. Instead, he began to ask his wife to pass on news of developments at the front. The practical objectives behind the military command's official reporting on the conflict were soon apparent to him, too. Expectations of imminent victory were replaced by the urgent desire for peace. As the year neared its end, it is notable that Schimmer clearly understood that the war had reached a stalemate. The victor would now be the state that could best mobilize its economic resources. Schimmer's learning process was based, like Schenk's, on talking to other soldiers. His interest in Confession and Holy Mass confirms the importance of popular religion, also evident in Schenk's diary, for Catholic soldiers trying to assimilate the experiences of war.

## VIII  German atrocities

Like Schenk and Pfaff, Schimmer also addresses the German atrocities against civilians in Belgium and France. In his case, however, there was an important difference in perspective. Schimmer's unit had not been directly involved in the killing of civilians nor in setting buildings or entire towns ablaze. This greater distance largely explains the factual inaccuracies in his diary notes. His entry for 24 August mentions the fires almost simultaneously with the popular mythology of the brave and belligerent 'lions', as Bavarian soldiers were often referred to. His notes on the atrocities in Leuven were incorrect in every respect. The town is situated in Belgium, not France. As today, it numbered considerably more people in 1914 than the 7,000 Schimmer claims. Furthermore, the people of Leuven had not attacked the German soldiers. It appears instead that friendly fire between different German units confused the troops and left them convinced that they had been under attack from *francs-tireurs*. Schimmer gives no mention of the fact that the German troops destroyed a sixth of the city's buildings and killed 248 civilians,[28] nor does he express any sympathy for the fate of the town's inhabitants. His empathy – albeit rather sparingly expressed – is reserved for the citizens of Paris. Later in the occupation of northern France, and probably also of Belgium, shared faith created 'bonds of Catholic solidarity' between occupiers and the occupied, based especially on gestures by German chaplains within the caritas network.[29] For the period immediately surrounding the atrocities, Schimmer's diary is one piece of evidence that this was not yet the case.

This observation leads us back to an issue of some contention in historical research, and one already touched upon in relation to Georg Schenk's war diaries. John Horne and Alan Kramer, to whom we owe the first substantial study of the Germans' violent excesses against civilians in Belgium and France in 1914, have concluded that anti-Catholic resentments formed an important component of a particular complex of myths. They argue that these beliefs were widespread among the German troops and provided the cultural context in which the atrocities took place. The animosity against Catholics, claim Horne and Kramer, centred on a particular German stereotype of the Belgians, with which German commanders explained the supposed ability of the country's Catholic clergy to manipulate their flock at will. The 'priests' domination' (*Pfaffenherrschaft*) in Belgium, as General Hans Hartwig von Beseler described it in a letter to his wife on 16 August, had apparently enabled the clergy to incite civilians to take up armed resistance.[30] Such perceptions and resentments, argue Horne and Kramer, fed into the *francs-tireurs* myths that were widespread among German troops and built on memories of the Franco-German War of 1870/71, when irregulars had fought on the French side. The cultivation of these memories meant that German troops and officers were fully expecting to be confronted with the activities of *francs-tireurs* as they advanced through Belgium and France.[31]

As soon as fears of *francs-tireurs* began to be accompanied by rumours of their presence, the German troops thus had a motive for the extreme violence they were about to perpetrate. But while Horne and Kramer highlight the *francs-tireurs* myths as an essential factor behind the atrocities, they also emphasize that it did not fully explain the treatment of civilians. Another crucial component of the atrocities lay in the German understanding of the rules of war, which was diametrically opposed to the provisions of international law. In the eyes of the German military, civilians who took up arms were illegal combatants, whom they could treat as fair game.[32]

For Horne and Kramer, then, anti-Catholic resentments were not the direct cause for the killing of civilians so much as a cultural framework that contributed to soldiers' extreme reactions on the battlefield. This interpretation has recently met with criticism, however. In his book on Adolf Hitler and the soldiers of the List Regiment, in which Hitler served in the First World War, Thomas Weber rightly points out that the atrocities cannot be laid entirely at the door of Protestants. In fact, units comprised partially or even wholly of Catholic officers and troops also committed acts of extreme violence against Belgian and French civilians. It is simply implausible to suggest that these men were motivated by anti-Catholic sentiments. Moreover, the supposedly enduring cultural factors are ill-placed to explain why the atrocities came to an end after little more than two months.[33] Weber's explanation for these violent incidents therefore places greater emphasis on the frenetic fighting in the early weeks of the war.

The Germans, Weber notes, had encountered unexpectedly strong Belgian resistance from soldiers of the Garde Civique. The uniforms of this defence force, if the men wore any at all, were 'unusual', thus reinforcing German anxieties about guerrilla combatants. Other factors included the poor military training of many soldiers from reserve regiments before their deployment on the front, which made it difficult for them to understand the battlefield adequately, as well as the numerous cases of 'friendly fire that was perceived as enemy fire'.[34] This tallies with the testimony of our two Catholic soldiers' diaries. Schimmer was convinced that Leuven had been the scene of an unlawful attack on the German army, but did not mention possible *francs-tireurs* in his letter. Schenk's diary omits the alleged provocation by the local priest and focuses on the shock of friendly fire. It is entirely possible that such experiences of friendly fire were enough in themselves to trigger knee-jerk reactions by soldiers, even without the myth of the *francs-tireurs*. Clearly neither Schenk nor Schimmer held any resentments against Catholics.

In another study, published in 2016, the German amateur historian Gunter Spraul has levelled even more substantial criticism at Horne and Kramer. According to his interpretation, the two historians have overlooked German evidence suggesting that there was in fact armed resistance by Belgian civilians against German troops in August 1914, who thus had a legitimate reason to retaliate with lethal force.[35] This line of argument does not seem especially plausible, particularly since Spraul's main sources are regimental histories. These texts, published during the 1920s, were written by nationalist officers in the clear knowledge of the tremendous weight of the atrocity issue for post-war politics vis-à-vis the Western Allies. Yet Spraul's book serves at least as a helpful reminder that the empirical and the conceptual basis of Horne and Kramer's argument is somewhat shaky. Spraul demonstrates in substantial detail that many of their claims about the presence of certain units or officers at documented atrocities are incorrect. This is due to their misreading and misinterpretation of unit codes and names, and their failure to properly corroborate information.[36]

It is more important, however, to reiterate and emphasize the key conceptual weakness of the book by Horne and Kramer. Long-held ideological beliefs or cultural perceptions do not offer a convincing explanation for acts of collective violence, either with regard to German atrocities in 1914 or more generally. This is not least because Horne and Kramer largely fail to demonstrate that social Darwinism or anti-Catholicism drove atrocities as they happened on the ground. Collective violence, a more plausible line of argument reasons, is furthered and enabled in the specific spaces where perpetrators and victims meet: in this case, the chaotic circumstances of a fast-paced advance of inexperienced troops through foreign territory.[37]

## IX The limits and ambivalence of empathy with the victims

It remains an astonishing fact that neither Georg Schenk nor Stefan Schimmer felt the need to express any empathy with the French civilian population, particularly since at least one of the two men had witnessed the suffering at close hand. Other voices in the German army did in fact condemn the mistreatment and killing of civilians as a fundamental breach of the ethical rules of war. The majority of these objections appear to have been raised by members or supporters of the Social Democrats.[38] This is perhaps no surprise given that denouncing the abuses and excesses of 'Prussian' militarism had already been an important intellectual and political position of the Social Democrats prior to 1914.[39] However, even the emphatic solidarity of the Social Democrats with the embattled civilian population in Belgium had its limits (see also Chapter 10). This is illustrated by the following letter written by Otto Rümmler, a member of the Social Democratic miners' union, Alter Verband. On 7 October, Rümmler reported to the head office of the Alter Verband in Bochum on his impressions of the advance through Belgium. He addressed, relatively openly, the rape of Belgian women by German soldiers. Other sources confirm the occurrence of many such incidents, particularly in the early months of the war:[40]

> Dear Comrades, Some experiences among the organized and unorganized workers, or yellows [*Gelben*, referring to the German name for company unions that openly collaborated with employers] and *Hintzegardists*.... Before we left the garrison, some were saying they wanted to go pillaging when they arrived on enemy territory. But they could not wait that long and started before they even left their own country, taking grapes and fruit from the trees, even though there was enough to eat. Once on enemy territory, they were even more mischievous. They did not ask if a family had anything to eat or not. I cannot list every incident, for it would take too much time and space, I would have to write a whole book. Instead, I just want to flag up a few cases. Unfortunately, I do not know the culprits' names.... Some of them (Landsturm men) went to a family with seven children (indeed a rare kind of family) and literally took the bread off the table. The husband, or rather the family father, wants to keep the bread for his children and explains that it is all they have and that the family haven't eaten for three days. Our *Hintzegardists* are unmoved. They place a rifle on the man's chest and tell him to shut up and go hungry with the rest of his family. Others have an even better idea. They go into a family home and ask for whatever they want, all very calmly. Then one of them starts feeling frisky, but the husband is in the way. That problem is solved, too – one of the men holds his loaded rifle against the man's chest, while the other has his way with the wife, then they swap places and the husband has to

watch on silently. These were *Wehrmänner* [Rümmler is emphasizing here that these were just ordinary soldiers].... If anyone says anything about the Germans in this regard, then it should be clear that it is only the capitalists who are to blame, for they first created the brutal gang [*rohe Sekte*].[41]

The letter offers a sense of Rümmler's moral outrage as an eyewitness to the rape of Belgian civilians and looting of family homes. However, it is also clear that the incidents did not raise the question of the perpetrators' individual moral culpability in Rümmler's eyes. Rümmler understood these acts as the work of 'Hintzegardists'. This was a derogatory term used among Social Democrats for the supporters of the 'yellow', business-friendly union associations used by a number of companies after 1900 to contain the influence of Social Democratic unions. He therefore suggests that it was not the individual German soldiers but the capitalists who were ultimately the culprit for the attacks on Belgian civilians.

## X Killing and fighting on the Eastern Front

Unlike Belgium and France, which witnessed many atrocities, the territories along the Eastern Front experienced just one major German war crime against civilians. This took place during the German capture of Kalisz, a city in the voivodeship of Lodz. Then part of the Russian Empire, Kalisz had 25,000 mainly Polish and Jewish inhabitants and was located close to the Prussian border. Unable to effectively defend the city, Russian troops pulled out on 2 August, though not before setting a number of buildings on fire. An official Russian investigation later in the war found that Kalisz 'was left to its fate' by the departing army.[42] When the Germans arrived on 3 August, the city remained quiet for a time. Then, for reasons that are not entirely clear, panic broke out. German troops responded with a barrage of artillery and rifle fire, and set numerous buildings alight. Random hostage-taking and shooting of civilians in full public view followed, before a deceptive, short-lived peace returned. When units from Saxony moved in on 7 and 8 August, there was a further outbreak of extreme violence against the city's residents. As in various atrocities against civilians in Belgium, it appears that the confusion caused by friendly fire was the most likely trigger for the panic among German soldiers.[43]

On the Eastern Front, a large majority of German soldiers had a clear mental picture of their enemy. The image of a barbarian Russia, against which Germany had to be defended, was widespread even among Social Democrats. These expectations were soon confirmed in the eyes of the advancing troops by their first impressions of the towns and villages they encountered. The sight of the 'miserable hamlets' and 'squalor' in Russian Poland reinforced the Germans' perception that they were in a country far less civilized than their own. Anti-Semitic prejudices against the 'Jewish scoundrels' in Galicia also came into play.[44] Soldiers on the Eastern Front wrote letters that aggressively implored victory, deliberately highlighting the escalating intensity of their own violence. A teacher from Hesse, for example, wrote the following letter to his fiancée on 16 September:

> We have been here in East Prussia for fourteen days now. We encountered the enemy near Allenstein [Polish: Olsztyn] on 8 September. The battle lasted from Tuesday until Friday. I can't tell you what we had to endure over those days. There was no chance of sleep, the kitchen cars couldn't follow us and food ran short. On top of all that, there were those huge marches! But we were victorious. We chased the hordes of bandits back to their country in a wild stampede. 120,000 prisoners, an immense amount of ammunition and wagons and horses fell into our hands. The Russians ravaged here in a cruel manner. They spared nothing. The Huns could not have behaved worse.... You can imagine how ferociously we went at those fellows. In a village near Gumbinnen [Gusev], 500 Russians and 30 Germans were buried; that seems to be the general proportion.... We don't get any newspapers and we hear very little. Now they tell us that the Germans are in Paris. France will be finished soon at any rate and then it's Russia's turn. I don't think the war will last much longer. In fact, it must not last much longer.[45]

To put this letter into context, it is important to note that its author was fighting on a section of the Eastern Front lying on Germany's own soil in 1914. Russian troops had advanced into East Prussia in mid-August and occupied the eastern part of the province. It took two battles near Neidenburg [Polish: Nidzica] (22–31 August) and the Masurian Lakes (8–15 September) to defeat the Russians and force them to withdraw from East Prussia. The first of these two battles, which became known as the Battle of Tannenberg, would enter both the region's nationalist culture of remembrance and German folklore, instrumentalized as a celebration of German strength by the nationalist political right in the Weimar Republic.[46] Paul von Hindenburg drew upon the mythology of Tannenberg to win popularity initially in military circles and later in his political life. The brief Russian occupation was important in a more immediate respect, too. News of wanton destruction, pillaging and atrocities against civilians by Russian troops spread rapidly among the German population and was highly emotionally charged.[47] In reality, an official German report put the number of civilians killed at no more than 101 and showed that these were largely victims of indiscipline by individual soldiers rather than of any deliberate policy ordered from above.[48] Nevertheless, the occupation meant that the Germans fighting the Russians in East Prussia were motivated by more than just long-standing national resentments and stereotypes about the Russian culture and nation. Amid the wave of nationalistic hatred intensified by the press, these men saw their mission as the liberation of Germany from the horror of war in its most immediate form: enemy occupation.

## XI War against Russia as social engineering

The German soldiers' willingness to fight on the Eastern Front, which fed on the experience of occupation, was directed not simply against Russia's military, but also its entire culture and society. This was to have consequences long after autumn 1914. Combined with received ideas about Russian barbarism, the conflict shaped a German lens which in many respects would also filter Wehrmacht soldiers' perceptions of the Soviet Union nearly thirty years later in 1941. Russia's supposed backwardness and the self-confidence with which Germans perceived their civilizing mission proved a powerful combination for Social Democrats, too. This is revealed in a letter by August Balke, a member of the Alter Verband union. On 8 August 1915, he wrote to the union chairman, Hermann Sachse:

Dear Hermann!
    Sitting here in Russia – I happen to be at rest – with a glass of Schultheiß [beer]. By chance I had the opportunity to see the devastated landscape of East Prussia. You have certainly heard and read about this, so it is unnecessary to write a lot about it. It looks bad.
    But a different story: It is well known that one's first impression about any matter is almost always right. And here I must say: the impression I have gained here in Russian Lithuania and Russian Poland of the local culture serves nothing more than to strengthen my view of the war, of which you are already well aware. I have witnessed a great deal of squalor in my life, but what I have seen here beggars all description. If one judges the level of a culture by the level of their housing – and I have found that this is nearly always the best benchmark – then one will come here to an almost horrifying conclusion. Old wooden huts, not good enough to be cattle sheds, poor furniture and vermin are the possessions of the lower classes. I claim: there is not one German who still lives in similar conditions. Only by coming here does one start to realize what a blessing our

unions are and actually to appreciate the activities of the labour movement. These conditions must have a terribly demoralizing effect on the Russian army.

A people living in such circumstances can only be driven to fight by force; against a people who love their fatherland – although it is self-evident that there is still a lot to improve – the former is always at a disadvantage. Russia can harm us, but it will never be victorious . . . .

There is just one thing to be done: ensure against a Russian invasion. And therefore you have to grant whatever it takes to continue the war. The Russians have to be deterred from returning to Germany forever. Every German who has seen the situation here, however cursorily, will and must support this wish.[49]

Balke's letter clearly shows that the perception of Russia's 'squalor' was based on a prior expectation. It took no more than a cursory glance to confirm and further reinforce this 'first impression'. The radical objectives that Balke associated with Germany's civilizing mission, which he believed the German workers and soldiers were fulfilling on the Eastern Front, are striking. In his view, the German troops were not in Russia simply to fulfil an instrumentally defined, short-term war objective. Instead, their aim was nothing less than to put a stop to Russian aggression 'forever'. Whatever the practicalities of achieving such an objective, it is clear that this vision of war amounted not only to a military struggle, but also to an aggressive form of 'social engineering' intended to radically transform the social order of an enemy country. It is important to note, however, that Balke does not define this reshaping of society in racist terms, as would be the case in 1941.[50]

## XII  Conclusion

Diaries and letters of German soldiers written in the early weeks and months of the war reveal that these men experienced a maelstrom of often contradictory impressions and emotions. On the one hand, some soldiers expressed serious doubts about the legitimacy and purpose of the war, including men who had volunteered for the war effort with patriotic élan. On the other hand, the very same men also experienced the war as an exciting, self-affirming journey to unfamiliar lands. While the numbers of dead and injured were higher during the initial months than at any other stage of the war, this did little to lessen soldiers' motivation for battle and willingness to kill. On the contrary, it was precisely the shock of sudden fire and losses of men that led to the killing of civilians in Belgium and France. This breach of international law was only to some extent attributable to the mythology surrounding supposed *francs-tireurs*. In many cases, it was death by 'friendly fire' that triggered violent excesses against civilians. More generally, situational factors that were present in the very moment of the atrocity played a much bigger role than any long-term cultural predispositions. At any rate, it is misleading to explain the German atrocities in Belgium in 1914 as a manifestation of an organizational tendency towards 'absolute destruction' in the German military, thus effectively postulating a German *Sonderweg* or special path towards a totalization of warfare.[51] Finally, though soldiers killed and died on both the Eastern and Western Fronts, the sources reveal differences between east and west that require further research. In the case of the Eastern Front, there are clear indications that some German soldiers regarded the war not only as an instrument for achieving political and military objectives, but also as a project to reform a Russian society perceived as backward and barbaric.

# 4

# Ernst Jünger: Practitioner and Observer of Killing

If there is one German author of war literature who appears emblematic for the brutality of the First World War, the glorification of violence and the fascist reading of the wartime experience from 1914 to 1918, it is without doubt Ernst Jünger. His knowledge of life on the front line was virtually unparalleled among German writers. Jünger joined the army as a volunteer in 1914 before advancing up the ranks to serve as a lieutenant and storm troop commander. From spring 1915 to August 1918, he fought on the very front line. Like almost no other German-language author, Jünger has come to stand for the affirmation and acclamation of First World War violence. His ambivalence and, at times, sympathy towards the National Socialists in the run-up to 1933 have been well documented. As early as 1923, Jünger wrote a stinging attack on the Weimar Republic in the *Völkischer Beobachter* – the NSDAP's party newspaper.[1] More important for our purposes than these overt political views, however, are the texts in which he appears as a militant representative of a literary current known as 'soldierly nationalism'. For the writers of this genre, the enduring lesson of the First World War was the necessity for renewed military mobilization and the creation of a 'New Man'.[2] The hardening experience of the war of attrition, they believed, would enable this New Man to raise the German nation up again from the humiliation – felt most intensely by the far right – at the defeat and subsequent disarmament under the Treaty of Versailles. The symbiosis of man and machine created by new technology would assist him in this quest.

## I  *In Stahlgewittern* as male fundamentalism

Historians have frequently drawn upon two of Jünger's texts in particular. The first is *In Stahlgewittern. Aus dem Tagebuch eines Stosstruppführers*, published in 1920 and repeatedly revised for later editions. The first English translation – *The*

*Storm of Steel: From the Diary of a German Storm-Troop Officer on the Western Front* – appeared in 1929. A more recent translation by Michael Hofmann in 2004 shortened the title to *Storm of Steel*, a metaphor that evokes the violence of industrialized warfare and the toughness needed to endure it.³ The second, an essay entitled *Kampf als inneres Erlebnis* (Battle as an Inner Experience), was first published in book format in 1922.⁴ The literary interpretations of both texts are legion. In his *Männerphantasien* (Male Fantasies) first published in 1977, for example, Klaus Theweleit interpreted Jünger's books as an example of the autobiographical construction of a specific personality type: that of the soldierly, proto-fascist men moulded by the cadet schools of the Wilhelmine military, for whom the battlefields of the First World War presented an opportunity to prove themselves. Such soldiers created a body armour of manliness to protect themselves against the supposed danger of effeminacy emanating from the home front.⁵

For the historian Bernd Weisbrod, writing in the year 2000, *Storm of Steel* essentially has only one central theme: the ecstatic self-affirmation that Jünger derived from the exercise of violence and the feeling of becoming a real man. The emotional highpoint of this manliness, writes Weisbrod, was 'the duel of bold masculinity', or 'the destructive union with the enemy in battle', which relied upon what Jünger described as a 'colossal will to destruction'. Jünger's detailed description of his pleasure at the destruction of the enemy, Weisbrod argues, reveals that he only came 'into his own in these extreme states of killing frenzy'.⁶ Weisbrod interprets this mentality as a form of 'male fundamentalism', a quasi-religious bearing based on the idea of redemption through military violence. For Weisbrod, Jünger is a propagandist of a masculine decisionism or lust for action, which treats the act of violence as its highest value and regards it as intrinsic to the salvation of the German nation. It was his contribution to establishing this male fundamentalism as a political identity, rather than his literary abilities, argues Weisbrod, that made Jünger such a relevant figure in German history between 1914 and 1933.⁷

Like many before him, Weisbrod draws upon *Storm of Steel* and *Battle as an Inner Experience* for his close reading. His approach warrants two observations here. First, it is evident that many of Weisbrod's arguments are already to be found in literary studies works of the late 1970s, particularly those of Klaus Theweleit.⁸ Second, and perhaps more important, a consideration of Weisbrod's analysis raises the question of the textual basis of Jünger's autobiographical writing. Weisbrod reads *Storm of Steel* as a 'historical ego-document'. Jünger wrote the book using material from his wartime diary entries, leading Weisbrod

**Figure 2** This photograph was the frontispiece to Ernst Jünger's *Storm of Steel*, which he self-published in 1920. It shows Jünger in his fur-embellished uniform coat, with his decorations clearly visible. The *Pour le Mérite* (Order of Merit) sits beneath the collar, in the shape of a blue enamelled Maltese Cross. The *Pour le Mérite* was the highest military decoration awarded in Prussia.

to regard *Storm of Steel* as a historical testimony, or a piece of 'self-examination', in which Jünger seeks to develop and reflect upon his identity as a writer and as a man.[9] This is a legitimate reading given that a blurring of the boundaries between literary genres characterized the war literature of the 1920s. Remarque's *All Quiet on the Western Front* is likewise more than simply a novel about the war. The works of both men – Jünger and Remarque – lack a clearly defined boundary between the fictional narrative and the writer's real experiences that serve to authenticate it. Contemporary readers sought the 'truth' of texts about the war experience precisely in the authenticity of the author's own wartime service.[10]

## II Jünger's original war diaries

Since Weisbrod published his article, there has been a radical change in the material available for researching Jünger's personal experiences on the front line. Jünger kept a diary throughout his entire wartime service, beginning when his regiment, stationed in Hanover, moved to the front line in December 1914, and ending in August 1918 as he was about to be taken back to Germany to recuperate from injury. The German Literature Archive in Marbach has housed these handwritten diaries since 1995 following a premortem bequest. Since 2010, they have been available in German in a complete edition compiled by the Jünger expert Helmuth Kiesel.[11] The diaries provide us with a new perspective on Jünger's attitudes to wartime violence. Jünger appears here not as a protofascist ideologue of a male fundamentalism, but rather as a far more sober observer with a keen interest in chronicling in detail the mental and physical traumas wrought by violence. Jünger was, of course, no mere passive observer of violence, but also an active participant, who was often involved in the killing and himself suffered multiple injuries. A close reading of his war diaries offers us important insights into the nature of killing and survival in the trench warfare of 1914–18. This chapter is a first attempt at such a historical interpretation and contextualization of Jünger's war diaries with respect to the practice of violence.[12] It joins the work by Helmuth Kiesel, who has provided a literary comparison of Jünger's writings to other wartime diaries.[13] The British scholar of German literature, John King, who was the first to have access to the full corpus of diaries, has presented a subtle analysis. This, however, focuses primarily on the way Jünger uses the diary as a medium to relate 'the epic project of a heroic, autonomous subject'.[14]

This chapter begins with some observations on the nature of the diaries and their textual characteristics. Like many other soldiers and officers in the First World War, it is likely that Jünger began keeping a diary to 'lend permanence to the ephemerality of life by chronicling it'.[15] This was soon joined by a second motivation, which emerged at the time of his promotion to lieutenant in November 1915 or perhaps even earlier: the desire to comprehensively document his own achievements as a soldier. Jünger therefore tends to give little more than a cursory account of the time spent at the rear, in rest areas or in military hospitals. The focus of the diaries instead lies emphatically on the days of combat and descriptions of battle. In this sense, the war diary is already a *Heldenbuch* (book of heroism), as Kiesel has rightly described it.[16] This is not to suggest that the diaries describe only moments of glory, ignoring those of depression, grief and emotional shock. Rather, it is to point out that we should not assume that Jünger sought in *Storm of Steel* to achieve a literary stylization entirely absent in the war diaries. Whether Jünger intended in the diaries to stylize his account of the war to the same degree as in *Storm of Steel* is a question best examined on a case-by-case basis and will therefore remain unanswered here for now.[17]

A crucial difference between the notes Jünger made during the war and the literary version published in 1920 is apparent from the title alone. With the 'storm of steel', Jünger employs a refined metaphorical language to help readers grasp the terrible destructive force of the war.[18] We can illustrate the contrast with the diaries in quantitative terms, too. A lexicometric comparison of the two texts has shown that Jünger uses more than 1,000 metaphors in *Storm of Steel*, compared to the 500 that feature in the diaries, despite the fact that the former is only around half the diaries' length.[19] The metaphors that do occur in the war diaries therefore warrant special attention.

## III Killing in the artillery war

What aspects of the forms of violence encountered on the front line does Jünger emphasize? How does he describe the practice of killing and the realities of death and survival in trench warfare? Does he indicate the existence of possible informal rules, under which some captured enemy soldiers were killed and others spared? And finally, how did Jünger's position as a lieutenant and, later, his leadership of a storm troop, shape his perspective of the physical violence unfolding on the Western Front?[20] In seeking to answer these questions using the war diaries, one thing is immediately apparent: for long stretches of his time at the front, Jünger was confronted with the overwhelming firepower of the artillery. In this respect, his everyday experience of the Western Front was just like that of all the other infantry troops deployed in the trenches there. Jünger's first direct encounter with enemy fire came on 2 January 1915, when nine men in his company were killed by shellfire. He had already heard the 'rumbling of cannon' a day earlier (8). Jünger spent his entire wartime service in the (Prussian) 73rd Fusilier Regiment, whose home garrison was in Hanover. In early 1915 he was stationed in Orainville north of Reims. The war still a fresh new experience, he noted to his amusement that someone had affixed a sign reading 'Ordnance this way' on the château serving as the military headquarters, pointing to the spot where a shell had impacted (8). As he soon discovered, however, trench warfare routinely meant nothing more than sitting tight under cover in a 'hole in the ground' and listening to the 'French battery [firing] at the German one' and vice versa. With the artillery dominating the action on the front line, Jünger noted that he was unable to see 'any Frenchies' from his hiding place (9). For Jünger like many other infantrymen, the almost literal emptiness of the battlefield was one of the dominant features of the static phase of the war that began in late 1914.[21]

The fire from the enemy artillery thus forced passivity upon the infantry, leaving the men confined to the smallest of spaces for often days and weeks at a time, broken by rest periods behind the front. During bombardments, soldiers had to seek cover in the dugouts and tunnels of the trench system if they did not want to recklessly put their lives at even greater risk. In October 1915, Jünger described his company's reaction when British troops bombarded the neighbouring sector with 'heavy artillery': 'With every whoosh we ran into the tunnels like rabbits into their burrows' (48), his diary reads, the metaphor emphasizing the infantry's extreme helplessness and vulnerability when confronted with the faceless firepower of the enemy artillery.[22]

As Jünger had quickly realized, the action on the Western Front was dominated by the artillery. Any man who wanted to survive its onslaught was well advised to keep his ears pricked and familiarize himself with the different sounds caused by the various types of artillery projectile. The soldiers could hear the approaching shells and mortars before they came into view. In January 1916, Jünger devoted a special diary entry to the 'sounds of projectiles' (75–8).[23] 'Experience is important in this regard', he notes here by way of explanation for his extensive reflections on the different noises, which all sounded alike to the unpractised ear. The loud vehicle-like 'rattles' and 'rumbles' produced by heavy shells prompted soldiers to call them 'hearses'. Light shells, by contrast, announced themselves with a brief 'flash' or 'bang'. Given this lack of warning, these projectiles often left soldiers shocked and bewildered even if they 'got away safely' (76–7). Shell detonators 'whistled all sorts of notes up to a C' and were therefore dubbed 'canaries' (77).

The violence of the Western Front was thus audible to Jünger as a series of 'roaring and crashing' sounds interspersed with the whistle of flying detonators (35). Even before the consequences of violence were visible in the churned earth and the blood of the wounded, the trained ear registered the approaching danger. Given how artillery fire dominated the battlefield with its deafening noise, devastating physical impact and uniquely high death toll, it is little wonder that Jünger found numerous powerful metaphors to describe this aspect of the war. In April 1915, he noted that a 'wild dance' began once the first projectile exploded and 'shells of all kinds' began to 'pepper' the position 'from three directions' at once (35). In July 1917, he chose another metaphor to capture the overwhelming presence of the artillery. It is no accident that this also conveyed the devastating effects on the men's hearing:

> As the platoons were standing there and I was just about to fall in, a hellish artillery fire broke out, aimed at the field, the concrete blocks and the Art Wood. Towering columns of dust rose into the sky all around us and the crack of heavy explosive shells almost burst our eardrums. (287)

Only once this 'hellish' fire had 'subsided somewhat' was Jünger able to bring the infantry back into the battle and order his company to fall in (ibid.). This was not the only time that Jünger depicted the power of the shelling as a hellish inferno. In an entry dated 25 August 1918, he describes his final battle, where he received the injury that would send him home from the war. The bullets of shrapnel shells, he writes, 'flew between us with a hellish hissing sound' (424; cf. 223). Yet this was not the most powerful metaphor with which Jünger sought to capture the shells' impact. In January 1916, reflecting on his twelve months at the front and the sounds of artillery fire, Jünger described an imaginary hit by a heavy shell: 'a terrible bang and the world ends' (76).

Towards the end of the war, Jünger had cause to return to this metaphor. Significantly, he was referring this time not to enemy fire but to the artillery of his own side. Early in the morning of 21 March 1918, the Germans began a major offensive on the Western Front with concentrated artillery fire against the Allied positions. To his great displeasure, Jünger was again forced to wait out the bombardment hiding with his company in a deep tunnel. Eventually, he could bear the confinement no more and leapt out into the trench. However, he soon had to put his gas mask on as the wind blew the gas deployed by the German batteries back towards their own men. This long period of passive waiting appears to have done little to dent Jünger's 'delight' at the 'great artillery preparation' for the German attack. Nevertheless, his diary entry describes the power of this artillery fire as a form of apocalypse: 'It was a thunder like nothing I had ever heard in battle before. The noise was absolutely incredible, as if the world was ending' (375–6).

In Jünger's eyes (and ears), the ceaseless shellfire remained a hellish, apocalyptic force even when it was supporting the spring 1918 German offensive, in which he and his compatriots had placed their hopes of victory. Artillery bombardments forced the soldiers to sit tight in dugouts and deep tunnels. And when the roar and thunder of enemy fire took them by surprise in the trenches, they had to scurry back under cover like 'rabbits'. Jünger's metaphors emphasize the brutal force and inferno of destruction wrought by this weaponry. Unlike soldiers more critical of the war, however, he did not use the infantrymen's helplessness in the face of enemy shelling to emphasize their victimhood. War letters from the front, particularly by soldiers on the political left, often used the metaphor of 'cannon fodder' to hammer home this sense of victimization, as did critical remembrance literature in the Weimar era. The slaughter of troops by a war machine controlled 'from above' appears here as the defining feature of front-line action.[24] Ernst Jünger was certainly no proponent of this victimization theory. By contrast, he regarded it as his mission, both as a soldier and a writer, to restore the agency of infantrymen in the midst of a mechanized warfare dominated by the artillery. Despite this, even he turned to the 'cannon fodder' metaphor in one diary entry in July 1918. In this instance, he was not referring primarily to enemy shelling, but to the danger of 'friendly fire' from the German artillery:

> Today we saw both our artillery and heavy mortars repeatedly firing into our own trenches. I reported back ceaselessly but nothing changed. The fellows behind couldn't tell the difference between the two sides anymore. One starts to feel like cannon fodder that must be finished off at any cost. (417–18)

Burying himself deep in the ground to escape sustained fire from all manner of shells and projectiles: this was certainly not how Jünger had originally pictured his role in the war. On 1 September 1916, Jünger spent the day with his group in the cellar of a brewery near Combles, a location with which he was already familiar. His diary notes his 'indifference to the shells exploding above', at least as far the 'bang of the light' shells was concerned (181). That evening, near the cellar entrance, he was hit in the lower leg by a 'shrapnel bullet' (182). The wound was bandaged as Jünger continued to smoke his pipe. Then, amid enemy fire, he was transported across a road to a casualty assembly point near Fins. On 4 September, two days before boarding a hospital train to Germany, Jünger heard the news of the heavy losses inflicted on his battalion in an attack by British troops just a day after his injury. The news of the loss of his comrades left Jünger 'quite dejected', particularly since this 'chance hit' in the lower leg had saved him 'as if by miracle' from the devastating attack and the 'fate' of death (185). In this uncharacteristically melancholy mood, Jünger noted how his experiences at the front so far contrasted with the expectations he had held upon signing up as a volunteer:

> I have experienced a great deal in this greatest of wars, but I've so far been denied the experience I've been aiming for: the charge and clash of the infantry. To zero in on the enemy, to face him man on man; that is quite different to this perpetual artillery war. (185)

After twenty months on the front line, this was a sobering conclusion. Jünger had sought the thrill of offensive combat and the struggle of man against man. In a war dominated by artillery, this was nowhere to be found, as he himself was only too aware. What alternatives were open to him? On two occasions – first in April 1916 and again in July 1917 – Jünger had applied to join the Fliegertruppe, the nascent German Air Force. On the second of these, he even underwent a comprehensive assessment to test whether he had the physical fitness and mental aptitude to become a pilot (96, 277ff.). Yet it seems unlikely that it was boredom with trench warfare that motivated his first application in spring 1916.[25] In fact, on his twenty-first birthday, just a few days before applying to become a pilot, Jünger had expressed his hope that one day he would be the 'first in the platoon to encounter the enemy'. This was a moment he was happy to 'patiently await' (96).

## IV Patrols

A diversion from the monotony of sentry duty and trench digging came in the form of patrols. These took place on a regular basis in order to gather information on the locations, nature and weaponry of the enemy positions on the other side of the trench system. Such patrols also offered the opportunity to take prisoners, who could provide valuable information. In October 1915, Jünger expressed his hope, so far unfulfilled, that a 'few good patrols' could soon be among his 'best memories of the war' (52–3). Later the following month, in a move that increased his chances of leading such an undertaking, Jünger received a promotion to lieutenant. In June 1916, he also took part in several days' training for troop officers (118). Soon afterwards, Jünger wrote a lengthy diary entry, describing the process of leading a patrol for the first time (119ff., 122ff.). Further such missions quickly followed. Then, on the third patrol, which took place on 28 July, Jünger finally experienced the direct confrontation with the enemy that he had so long desired. Having discovered a group of British soldiers in no-man's land, Jünger first instructed one of his men to throw a hand grenade, then launched himself at the enemy with a shout: 'You are prisoners!'. In the space of 'fractions of seconds', there now unfolded a 'desperate scene', a battle to the death at close quarters: 'I fired off my pistol right in the middle of a fellow's face. He went down with a ghastly cry "Wah!"' (159–60). Jünger and his men were soon forced to rush back to the German trenches when the magazine clicked out of his pistol and machine gun fire began. The experience was a positive start nevertheless. All participants, he wrote, agreed that it had been a 'good patrol', presumably as there had been no German casualties (160).

Immediately after this mission, Jünger meticulously noted in his diaries the most important requirements for a successful patrol. Only the 'best men' should be chosen, the entry reads, and it is important that the patrol should 'awaken a sporting instinct'. One participant should be able to speak English and the men should bring 'weapons for close combat such as clubs, truncheons and sharpened spades'. Everyone in the team of ten soldiers should know exactly what job they are to do, he adds. For example: 'You seven kill everyone except for the Englishman furthest to the right. I'll take him prisoner with the other three' (161). Taking an enemy soldier captive was the primary mission of such patrols, and every part of the strategy was based on achieving it. This included quickly killing all enemy soldiers who might stand in the way of fulfilling that main objective. But there was another aim, too, as Jünger noted in August 1917. Jünger's regiment had been instructed to hold a position near the town of Regniéville for a period of two months. At 730 metres in extent, the section of the front that his company now occupied was 'very long', which indicated that the military command was not expecting heavy fire from the enemy or an attempt to break through the German line at this location. Nevertheless, it was important to give the appearance of activity from time to time. Jünger's diary recounts that the divisional command found the position 'too quiet again' and therefore requested the individual sections to suggest patrols that could be performed without artillery preparation (306).

Patrols thus served to simulate readiness for attack on quiet sections of the front as well as to capture prisoners. What do Jünger's diaries tell us about the killing of enemy soldiers in the course of such patrols? How did troops react to enemy soldiers who were prepared to surrender or had already done so? British historians have provided rather strident, one-sided answers on the issue of prisoner-taking, which is a further reason to re-examine it with the benefit of Jünger's diaries. Joanna Bourke, for example, has claimed in her history of 'face-to-face killing' that the British army routinely killed German prisoners in the First World War and that this was 'an important part of military expediency'.[26] In his book, *The Pity of War*, Niall Ferguson claims that 'on numerous occasions on both sides men were killed not only as they tried to surrender but after they had surrendered'. Ferguson describes these widespread incidents as 'the forgotten atrocities of the First World War'.[27]

## V  The killing of prisoners of war?

Ferguson points out that it was German troops 'who started the irrational practice of taking no prisoners'.[28] This was indeed the case in the sense that the German atrocities in Belgium in August 1914 included orders from some commanders for soldiers to kill prisoners on the spot. One well-documented case is that of the 58th Infantry Brigade from the Baden region, whose commander, Major General Karl Stenger, issued just such an order on 26 August 1914: 'No prisoners will be taken today. Frenchmen wounded or captured are to be finished off'. The Alsatian solider Dominik Richert, who recalled this order from memory, noted, however, that it provoked moral disgust among most of the soldiers.[29] Even after August 1914, writes Ferguson, there were cases 'throughout the war' in which German troops 'killed enemy soldiers who had already surrendered'.[30] Yet Ferguson offers no empirical evidence to support this theory. He points to a single passage in Jünger's *Storm of Steel*, which describes how a soldier in a neighbouring company slaughtered a dozen British prisoners with pistol fire in March 1918.[31] This passage does not feature in Jünger's original diaries, however, and is therefore nothing more than a piece of literary fiction.[32] Ferguson's supposed evidence for the equivalent practices by French and British troops against surrendering German soldiers is similarly problematic.[33] Alan Kramer, one of the foremost experts in the history of violence in the First World War, has likewise pointed to the lack of adequate sources behind such claims. Kramer argues convincingly that the killing of soldiers who surrendered took place at most 'episodically' and 'opportunistically' rather than as a routine or even 'systematic' practice.[34]

The legal situation with regard to such acts of violence against surrendering soldiers was clear. All nations at war were bound by the Hague Convention of 1907, which governed the treatment of non-combatants, civilians abroad, the wounded and prisoners of war in land warfare. Imperial Germany had accepted the Convention in law in 1911. A dedicated section covered the humane treatment of prisoners of war. Article 23(c) prohibited the killing of enemy soldiers who had surrendered or had no means of defence. Article 23(d) expressly prohibited commanders from declaring that no mercy would be given.[35] This was the article breached by Major General Stenger, leading French authorities to begin an investigation against him even before the war had ended. After the war, Stenger was accused of war crimes at the Leipzig Trials in 1921 by a German government pre-empting his extradition to the Allies.[36]

The legal position thus could not be clearer. The situation on the battlefield, however, was far more complex. Soldiers had just split seconds to decide whether the enemy really were laying down their weapons and should be given mercy. It may well be true that a form of instrumental rationality came into play, as Niall Ferguson has argued, where troops weighed up the value of prisoners in providing information and manpower against the possibility that the enemy was only feigning surrender. There were also practical problems in taking prisoners, whom soldiers had to escort rearwards through the chaos of battle, weakening the manpower available for attack.[37]

Such rational considerations may in some cases have led soldiers to kill surrendering enemy troops. Particularly where the notoriously complex issue of surrender is concerned, however, it is questionable whether rational calculation can offer an adequate explanation of wartime violence. As in other conflicts, violence in the First World War was not reducible to the weighing up of means and ends. Violence is better understood as an act of overstepping boundaries; a process in which protagonists can lose control of themselves, leaving rational consideration behind. The role of emotions also demands consideration. Soldiers in combat can become enraged, act out their anger and enter a state of frenzy, a phenomenon that a model based on the sober analysis of risks and objectives cannot comprehend.[38]

This raises important broad questions for the historical analysis of violence that are beyond the scope of this book. We will instead turn here to the narrower empirical question of how German front-line soldiers in the First World War decided whether to take prisoners alive. The war diaries of Ernst Jünger cannot be the last word on this issue, of course, as they represent the views of just one man. Nevertheless, it should not be forgotten that Jünger was willing like almost no other front-line soldier to explore in writing the ambivalences and problematic dimensions of the practice of violence. The length of his time on the front also meant that he was frequently confronted by these questions. What insights can we gain from Jünger's notes on violence against prisoners between 1915 and 1918?

## VI Rationality and emotions

It is clear from the very first of Jünger's comments on prisoner-taking that considerations of expedience were closely intertwined with soldiers' emotions and experiences. In late August 1916, Jünger reflected in his diary on his experiences in the Battle of the Somme. Given the confusion on the battlefield, he writes here, 'getting lost' was one of the 'greatest dangers' the soldiers faced. One could easily 'bump into the English' unexpectedly:

> And if you end up in the enemy's hands, you cannot expect mercy. Everyone here knows it's crunch time and there is huge animosity. Why take prisoners only to have to drag them back through a barrage of fire? The enemy is even more inconvenient when wounded. (177)

In this passage, Jünger points out the logistical and practical difficulties in taking prisoners at the Somme. In addition to these considerations of instrumental rationality, however, he also mentions the general 'animosity' felt by the German troops. This had arisen from the special nature of what was one of the war's longest-running battles. The Somme Offensive had begun almost two months earlier with an attack by British troops on 1 July.[39] In this entry in August 1916, Jünger writes in abstract terms and does not recall specific incidents. Elsewhere in the diaries, however, he clearly describes how prisoners were easier to handle in everyday patrols and skirmishes than in the midst of an intensive battle like the Somme. On 5 March 1917, for example, a patrol of seven British soldiers reached the position held by Jünger's company. As the Germans threw hand grenades from close range, five of the men beat a rapid retreat. Two of them became stuck on the barbed wire, 'apparently hit by the hand grenades. They were grabbed immediately and dragged to our trench.' One of the pair died straight away, while the other badly wounded soldier was 'tied up and taken away to the rear' (219–20).

The following day, 6 March, saw another foray by British troops. Of a group of some fifty men, just one reached the trench system held by Jünger's regiment: 'At the second line [i.e. the second German trench located some distance behind the first trench line], he was asked to surrender, and as he resisted he was shot dead.' (221) These two contrasting cases point to a general pattern. If it was relatively straightforward to take a prisoner and transport him away from the scene, a surrendering soldier could usually expect proper treatment. If, however, he put up a fight, he effectively forfeited his life. As is clear from various entries in Jünger's diaries, the logic behind this handling of prisoners rested on soldiers' consideration of objectives and practicalities. It took into account the aim of taking enemy soldiers captive and the hope that respect and good treatment would be reciprocated by Allied soldiers capturing Germans. The first motivation is evident in Jünger's notes from January 1917. On 13 January, Jünger spontaneously joined a patrol from another company as what he called, with a touch of irony, a 'travelling supporter'. The Germans had spotted British troops digging and set off with the clear objective of 'taking a prisoner'. On this occasion the patrol was unsuccessful and Jünger returned to his sentry post (262).

That same night, however, saw a foray by the British, which resulted in a chaotic skirmish in wooded terrain. Spotting a line of enemy skirmishers, Jünger ordered his men to stop firing and shouted, 'Come here, you are prisoners, hands up!' One man split from the group of enemy soldiers and approached. As Jünger shouted at the man, he retreated again, and Jünger issued an order to his men: 'Shoot him down!' Shortly afterwards, Jünger along with some other men from his company found several wounded Indian colonial soldiers 'begging us for mercy'. Three of the wounded were dragged back to the German position (264–5). The conclusion of this episode, which inflicted heavy losses on the enemy, evidently filled Jünger with pride. The diary entry records his delight at presenting the Indians as 'living testimony' to the two-hour battle. In this instance, then, the prisoners were a form of human trophy. They bore witness to the fact that Jünger had 'successfully' proven himself in leading a dangerous mission (265). The primary objective behind such missions was the usefulness of enemy prisoners in providing intelligence (318). However, soldiers choosing to take enemy men prisoner rather than killing them often had another, less immediate consideration in mind: that of reciprocity. In April 1917, Jünger noted his disappointment that one of his 'war comrades' had ended up in British captivity. Nevertheless, the diary entry adds, it was a consolation that he had 'at least escaped with his life' (249). Whatever the overblown claims of some historians that British troops regularly killed German prisoners, it is clear that Jünger rightly expected the enemy generally to respect the lives of those they took captive.[40] This provided a strong motivation not to engage in the mindless killing of surrendering British soldiers.

Ernst Jünger's diaries are evidence that, alongside rational considerations, anger, resentment and other emotions determined the treatment of surrendering enemy soldiers. Moreover, the rational considerations at play were not so much those of the commanders, who generally hoped that prisoners would provide useful information and labour, but rather a product of the individual expectations of soldiers and officers. These men were motivated to take prisoners not only by the hope that the enemy would reciprocate in its treatment of German soldiers, but by a desire to bring back captives alive as a trophy of the patrol's success. It is notable, however, that such rational motives were particularly evident in the context of 'normal' trench warfare, that is, in the patrols and skirmishes that broke the monotony of artillery fire and dominated the action on the front line away from the major battles. In larger battles such as the Somme, soldiers' emotions played a much greater role without, however, completely overruling other considerations. This is evident from Ernst Jünger's highly detailed account of the first day of the major German offensive on 21 March 1918 (375–87). In the 'heat of battle', to quote a much-used metaphor, knee-jerk reactions could occur.[41]

## VII  The heat of battle: 21 March 1918

Jünger's company were due to launch their assault at 9.40 am as soon as the 'wave' of German artillery fire moved forwards. Jünger's diary records the 'mixture of feelings' coursing through him and his men at that moment: 'excitement, bloodthirstiness, anger' and the effects of 'alcohol consumption' (378). This cocktail of emotions intensified further for Jünger in the initial minutes of the assault. 'Against all expectation', his unit came under machine gun fire from the second British trench despite the intensive German artillery preparation. 'Enraged', he continued to advance, and in this emotional state had his first direct encounter with the foe:

> There I saw the first enemy soldier. An Englishman crouched wounded in the defile, which had been hammered by shelling. Raising my pistol, I approached him. He held out a card to me imploringly. I saw a photograph of a woman and at least half a dozen children. I'm relieved now that I suppressed my insane anger and stepped past him. (379)

In the heat of the moment, it took an extreme act of willpower for Jünger to bring his emotions under control and prevent himself from crossing an ethical line by killing a defenceless, injured man. In the next situation, which took place shortly after this first incident, Jünger again followed the routine, and perhaps also his instinct, rather than his emotions. On suddenly encountering an 'older fellow' who was 'in the way', Jünger sent him to be taken prisoner with the words, 'Go back, you English son of a bitch'. This was less an insult than a courtesy given that at that very moment, a major's head appeared and shouted at Jünger, 'Kill the bastard!' (380). Jünger did not follow this order to kill a prisoner, but instead turned his fire on enemy soldiers attempting to flee the German assault.

The advance of the German troops made rapid progress. Only a short time later, Jünger was again confronted with British soldiers attempting to surrender. Two machine gun positions were resisting the German troops. While the Germans managed to put one of them out of action relatively quickly with a few targeted shots, the other gun continued to fire. Jünger attempted to bring the captured British machine gun into play, but to no avail. There ensued a scene that Jünger's diary describes as follows:

> A light machine gun operator was better able to bring his weapon into position. Now, the men to the right of us ran straight at the [British] machine gun nest and the defile behind, whose occupants only now put their hands up. But this did not stop the angry German troops from firing into their midst. You could see the English with their hands raised running as quickly as possible through our first lines, as they probably knew that the fury of the men further behind would not have reached such boiling point. But you can't blame men who have just been shot at from as little as five metres away for wanting to wipe the enemy out. (382)

This description reveals several insights. With the 'boiling point' metaphor, Jünger aims to illustrate how emotion could overpower other rational objectives in such moments of combat. He also points to the specific circumstances that had stirred such intense anger in the first place. The face-to-face nature of the battle appears to have been instrumental. Anyone still attempting to return fire from as little as a few metres away could not reckon with mercy. This was a crucial difference from the incident at the beginning of the day's assault. Earlier, Jünger's proximity to the wounded Englishman and the sight of his family photograph had enabled him to control his anger in a moment of empathy. Whereas that soldier had begged for his life, these men continued to resist from close range. Jünger's description also shows that it was here, close to the first line of German soldiers, that the surrendering British were most at risk. Once beyond this point, they were safe from further harm. Whether any of the men who surrendered were killed in this instance is unclear from Jünger's diary.

This incident was still not the end of the fighting on 21 March 1918. Later that same day, Jünger's unit combed through enemy dugouts. The entry in Jünger's diary makes it clear once again that it was possible to take prisoners even amidst vicious fighting. Hand grenades 'made short shrift' of the occupants of several dugouts. The Germans called other 'Tommies' out from their shelters and, having taken their cigarettes, showed them the way back behind the German lines (384). On 25 August 1918, a day which would turn out to be his last on the front line, Jünger encountered the practice of taking prisoners for a final time. By now, like many German soldiers, he knew that 'final victory' for Germany was no longer achievable. The Allies' 'crushing' superiority would bring the war to a 'bitter end' for the German army (422). Jünger's exasperation at this looming defeat may explain his reaction to the scene that now unfolded before his eyes. Wounded early on by a shot to the chest, Jünger was condemned to watch the rest of the battle as a spectator. From a narrow trench, Jünger saw German soldiers moving from the rear towards the enemy line with their hands up. The British had clearly outmanoeuvred his unit. 'Meanwhile, ever more men [German soldiers] came from behind, calling on us to surrender' (428). This collective call to capitulate was an important aspect of the military strike that undermined the German army on the Western Front long before the armistice on 11 November (see Chapter 7). While other soldiers gave themselves up in large numbers, Jünger was appalled. His fury erupted as he witnessed another 'bunch of Germans' approaching the enemy line, 'waving their hands' and accompanied by only two rather casual-looking British soldiers. Jünger was seized by a desire to 'blow the whole miserable rabble to bits', including the German men. Had it not been for his injury, it is plausible that he would have done exactly that (428).

## VIII  Killing and survival from Jünger's perspective

Ernst Jünger's diaries provide a somewhat ambivalent picture of the killing of enemy soldiers. In large part, strategic considerations came into play when soldiers encountered the enemy. If the encounter came during a patrol, the aim was to take prisoners, even if doing so meant killing other men who posed a threat to that mission. With reciprocity in mind, it was advisable to spare the lives of men who surrendered. After all, the Allies were also holding large numbers of men captive. It was a different story on days of intense fighting and in the battles of matériel from 1916 onwards. With soldiers experiencing a maelstrom of conflicting emotions, including anger and resentment at the resistance put up by the enemy, it was inevitable that men would be killed if they did not surrender clearly or quickly enough. Even in the heat of battle, however, Jünger was able to keep his emotions in check when he encountered men who had already laid down their weapons. This does not mean, of course, that all German soldiers necessarily behaved in the same way in all circumstances. However, it appears to confirm Alan Kramer's theory that the killing of surrendering, defenceless soldiers was the exception rather than the rule.[42]

How did Jünger describe his own involvement in the practice of killing under the conditions of trench warfare? What do his diaries tell us about the killing of enemy combatants and the emotions that came into play? And in what form did Jünger reflect on his own survival? As an infantryman in an 'artillery war', Jünger in fact had relatively little occasion to reflect on killing soldiers himself. Artillery fire, rather than the infantry, was responsible for the majority of casualties. Far longer parts of Jünger's diary therefore chronicle the deaths and injuries that enemy bombardment inflicted on his own position.[43] Jünger leaves no doubt that he was prepared to give his own life. After completing training for company leaders, an entry in February 1917 describes how he expected that 'fate' should take its course: 'I ask that it [fate] take me during the sensation of battle, in an assault on enemy lines', he writes, with the pathos of the professional soldier (213). Nearly a year earlier in April 1916, the anniversary of his first serious injury, he had written in similar vein: 'I want to have another go at the enemy, whatever the cost' (102).

It would be wrong to assume from such remarks that Jünger felt no emotion in the face of death. This is evident from his reaction to the events described above on 5 March 1917, when Jünger's company seriously injured two English attackers with hand grenades. The diary entry records that one of the men was taken prisoner, but the other, a Lieutenant Stokes, died shortly afterwards. 'I felt sorry for the poor fellow lying there', writes Jünger, noting that the man's face was 'contorted by death' (220). Jünger regarded it as his 'comradely duty' to give the fallen officer a proper burial. He prepared a wooden cross, which he sketched in his diary. However, this feeling of a last duty of respect for a fellow professional soldier had no impact on Jünger's motivation to fight or his willingness to exercise violence. The next day, he wrote with evident satisfaction, he had a 'fine success' (221). On spotting a British soldier who had broken cover in the third trench on the other side of no man's land, Jünger grabbed a rifle and fired, killing the man from considerable range and prompting congratulations from a major on this 'excellent shot'. In the same diary entry, Jünger notes that such incidents were extremely rare in trench warfare: 'I had never had a man so clearly in my sights in my two-and-a-quarter years of war (222). Face-to-face killing, even through the sights of a rifle, was the rare exception rather than the rule in the First World War.

The British soldier posed no threat to Jünger or his men at that moment. The shot to the head was thus essentially an execution rather than an act performed in the heat of battle. Commenting on this episode, Helmuth Kiesel argues that 'Jünger almost automatically followed the rules of warfare'. These 'required him to kill every enemy soldier who came into view'.[44] Kiesel's interpretation is problematic. As we noted in Chapter 2, front-line soldiers in the First World War had various opportunities to control, at least on occasion, the scale of violence in their immediate environment. These included, first and foremost, the principle of 'live and let live'. Infantrymen choosing to live and let live avoided opening fire on visible enemy soldiers, provided this tacit ceasefire was reciprocated by the other side and officers gave no direct orders to the contrary. Jünger describes such an episode in December 1915, and his ambivalent reaction to the situation shows clearly that he did not believe in the universal 'rules of warfare' posited by Kiesel:

> Today when I left the dugout I was greeted by a strange picture outside. Our men had climbed onto the parapet and were talking to the English across the barbed wire. I climbed up on the parapet and looked around. A peculiar sight for an old trench warrior! The dreadful mud of the trenches seemed to bring both sides closer to one another. Everyone was standing up on the trenches and not a shot was fired. A new, unfamiliar feeling crept over me. Peace? (65)

The feeling was only momentary. The officer's instinct clicked in straightaway and Jünger ordered his men to take cover in front of the German machine gun. The tacit agreement held, however, with only a single shot from the enemy line. This gave Jünger himself the opportunity to walk forward for a 'friendly' conversation with a British officer. The discussion took place partly in English and partly in French, and ended with a 'solemn declaration of war', which Jünger reinforced with a single shot from his rifle. The soldiers in Jünger's platoon made it clear that 'they much preferred' the informal ceasefire (65–6). As on many other occasions, the decision to 'live and let live' appears to have resulted from the state of the terrain. The horrendous 'mud' that filled the trenches made it difficult to work without breaking cover.[45] Jünger himself, who had been promoted to a lieutenant just a few weeks earlier, was only too aware of the fundamental ambivalence of the situation. On the one hand, he was clear that 'of course nothing like this should happen again'. In this, he agreed with the company leader, who was enraged by the incident and threatened to shoot anyone revealing themselves above the parapet again, including his own men. Jünger intended to 'keep lookout' for a few hours the next day to spot any such transgressions. On the other hand, he admitted to himself, 'the men have a point. They sense that the English are only people too.' (66)

There were thus no 'rules of warfare' that forced Jünger and other soldiers to kill enemy soldiers. The act of violence was instead a social phenomenon shaped first and foremost by the context of the military organization. This offered praise or even military accolades to reward conformist behaviour and particularly keenness for action, such as that demonstrated by Jünger's rifle shot at the lone soldier. Yet non-conformist behaviour such as the principle of 'live and let live' was tolerated at least on occasion, particularly since immediate prevention was not always possible. And even the most hardened fighters like Ernst Jünger knew that the purpose of war – the violent suppression of the enemy – did not negate the combatants' shared humanity. The soldiers Jünger wanted to kill on the other side of no-man's land were fellow men with every right to attempt to kill Jünger. This anthropological premise sharply differentiated the violence on the Western Front between 1914 and 1918 from the Wehrmacht's war against the Soviet Union from 1941. There, the Germans regarded the enemy not as an equal, but as an *Untermensch*, a subhuman being. This mindset resulted in the systematic killing of women, children and other non-combatants,[46] giving the war on the Eastern Front from 1941 a genocidal dimension not witnessed on the Western Front in the First World War.

## IX Violence as social practice

The military organization provided the structures for the social relationships where the practice of violence took shape. This was true not only in respect of the army's praise and reward for conformist behaviour, such as Jünger's 'excellent shot' in executing a British soldier, but also with regard to the military's efforts to exercise violence more efficiently by increasing the level of specialization. The stalemate of the First World War trenches called for specialists to break the deadlock. The German army responded by adapting its storm troop tactics. From September 1915, Captain Willy Rohr and his 'Storm Battalion Rohr' developed new techniques for overcoming the fortification systems on which trench warfare relied. His approach was to enable storm troops to infiltrate and capture enemy trenches by combining large quantities of hand grenades, machine guns, flamethrowers and mortars.[47] The successful trials of this new tactic encouraged the Army Supreme Command to instruct the divisions to set up their own storm troop units for special attack missions.[48] The military selected unmarried volunteers aged under twenty-five with particularly high levels of physical fitness. It exempted these men from normal sentry duty in the trenches and provided them with special rations.[49] Soldiers serving in the storm troops thus escaped the monotony of static warfare, and this special treatment ensured that there were more than enough volunteers. In general, each battalion created a storm troop consisting of approximately a dozen soldiers commanded by a single officer.[50]

Research has not yet fully explained how the storm troops fitted into the German army's tactical approach. It remains to be clarified whether the military used them merely to reconnoitre the terrain or involved them systematically in attack missions. It seems clear that the initiative to introduce storm troop tactics emanated not only from the Army Supreme Command, but also from experiments in attacking techniques that various units on the Western Front conducted independently.[51] There is no doubt that the specialist training involved in creating storm troops changed these participants' perception of the war. This was certainly the case for Ernst Jünger, who noted in his diary on 5 April 1917 that he was now serving his regiment as the 1st Battalion's 'storm troop leader'. The regiment had spent the day on an exercise in a mock-up trench system near Cambrai. There they had practised strategies combining various weapons and performed a trial counter-attack (275). As a storm troop leader, Jünger was aware that there would be good opportunities to 'get stuck in' on his return to the front. Such enemy encounters were what made the war 'interesting' for him (ibid.).

Jünger's involvement in regular patrols from summer 1916 and his leadership of a storm troop from spring 1917 gave him repeated opportunities for face-to-face combat for the first time. During his period on the front line, he was hit and wounded fourteen times. On three occasions, his injuries were inflicted by blanket artillery fire: shell splinters and a shrapnel bullet. The other incidents involved rifle bullets or shrapnel from hand grenades aimed directly at Jünger. Helmuth Kiesel has suggested that this gives the lie to the 'much-cited anonymity' of the killing in the First World War.[52] However, this seeming contradiction is resolved immediately when we consider that as a platoon commander, Jünger was routinely deployed on precisely those missions that exponentially increased the risk of close-quarter combat with the enemy.

## X Close-quarter combat

These attacking missions involving close-quarter combat with the enemy saw Jünger immersed in a frenzy of killing and destruction. On two occasions, at least, he not only described these incidents in vivid detail but reflected more deeply on their significance. The first of these entries relates to an attack on 1 December 1917 and comprises copious notes under the title 'Special day for the seventh company' (344–52). The day began with the successful rolling-up of an enemy trench. Jünger's men used hand grenades to force a group of British soldiers to surrender. As the men capitulated with their 'hands raised', there followed a sudden and 'curious' change in the mood:

> Just moments earlier we had been throwing deadly weapons at each other. Now, everyone was laughing and joking peacefully. Our men handled the prisoners very respectfully and only took their weapons. (345)

In a surprise attack, Jünger's company had taken no fewer than 102 British soldiers and three officers. Jünger himself talked at length with the wounded British captain and made sure to part with a handshake having ensured the prisoners' safe passage back to the German position. One could interpret this gesture as a typical expression of a traditional code of honour that required officers to treat their captive counterparts with respect. As various diary excerpts in this chapter have shown, however, the respectful treatment of prisoners did not lessen the intensity with which Jünger fought and killed enemy troops at the next opportunity that presented itself. This time, he did not have long to wait. When the German advance met fierce resistance, Jünger was forced to erect a barricade as an improvised defensive position (347).

The improvised defence was followed just a few hours later by a further 'improvised attack' (349). In the maze of trenches, which formed a particularly dense and extensive system around the Siegfried Position, or Hindenburg Line as it was known by the British, Jünger's company eventually encountered a group of British soldiers in a section of trench running almost parallel and in close proximity to that of the Germans. Jünger's diary entry describes the scene that unfolded as follows:

> The hand grenades flew in their dozens like snowballs, cloaking everything in white smoke. Two men kept passing me unscrewed hand grenades, which I threw assuredly among the Tommies. I wished I had a hundred hands, but caused enough havoc anyway. Yells of commotion from a hundred throats on both sides. In the heat of the moment I saw and heard nothing but the men I wanted to exterminate. (351)

The 'indescribable' bang of hand grenades, the bellowing voices of combatants and the staccato of the flying weaponry created the 'heat of the moment' when wiping out the enemy was all that mattered. In this moment of intense emotion, Jünger forgot everything else around him. It is no coincidence that it was the use of hand grenades in particular that generated this 'heat of the moment'. There is considerable evidence that training with and using hand grenades afforded infantrymen an especially strong feeling of agency in exercising deadly violence. This overcame the feeling of 'impotence' felt by soldiers forced to rely largely on the bayonet in close-quarter combat. The intensive and universal training of infantrymen in the use of hand grenades (at the start of the war, these weapons were primarily the preserve of the engineer troops) had disadvantages, too. Fatal accidents happened occasionally. Nevertheless, the benefits outweighed the risks and a typical German division engaged in a major battle used some 30,000 hand grenades on average.[53]

Jünger was only too aware, however, of the rarity of such moments of direct combat, even for an experienced troop officer and storm troop leader. On a small, separate piece of paper attached to the diary page, he added the following thoughts:

> It is without doubt the most exciting moment of war when you see the enemy right in front of you. In that instant, the soldier feels the fever, the passion of the hunter. But it is a passion that grips the soldier even more strongly than the hunter can ever experience. (ibid.)

Jünger's reflections indicate that this 'most exciting' moment only seldom occurred. Jünger first noted his deep desire to fight the enemy man-to-man in September 1916 (185). He would have to wait for more than another year to experience the intoxicating 'heat' of close-quarter combat. How should we interpret Jünger's comments on the different emotional experiences of the hunter and the soldier in battle? In essence, the remarks are a further reflection on the anthropological premise of First World War violence that distinguished it from the war of annihilation on the Eastern Front from 1941. The difference between a hunter and a front-line First World War soldier was that the latter did not shoot at defenceless prey. The same could not be said of the Wehrmacht troops, who killed large numbers of defenceless civilians. In the First World War, the soldier encountered fellow soldiers, who were themselves capable of inflicting injury or death. The special 'passion' that Jünger describes thus arose from the fundamental fact that a soldier in close-quarter combat was both the hunter and the hunted. Jünger's metaphor is instructive for our understanding of the dialectic that shaped the practice of violence encountered from autumn 1914 onwards: the tension between the desire to limit violence by concentrating it on the enemy soldiers alone (with the notable exception of the German atrocities of August 1914) and the potential for violence to spiral out of control in the maelstrom of emotions induced by close-quarter combat.

On 21 March 1918, the first day of the German spring offensive, Jünger found further occasion to reflect upon the intoxicating nature of killing. This chapter has already introduced and analysed other important aspects of the day's complex series of events. The present section will therefore confine itself to a moment of the battle particularly relevant with respect to close-quarter killing. Jünger noted the sight of a group of British soldiers who were 'shot down' like defenceless 'rabbits' as they fled across open ground (379). It was not these men who triggered Jünger's urge for violence, but another group, who, rather than fleeing, 'fought back in the trenches' (379–80). Jünger fired his pistol at them at short range, then, feeling an 'irrepressible need' to 'shoot something to bits', grabbed an NCO's rifle (380). He first shot dead a British soldier standing close to one of the Germans, then turned his fire on the fleeing men. 'Probably very few of them got away with their lives', states the diary entry. This, Jünger concludes, was 'good work'. The incident had 'brought out the fighting spirit and bravado in everyone' (ibid.). It was rare, however, for such fighting spirit to be targeted at fleeing soldiers. Soon thereafter, he and his men were confronted with the fire of enemy machine guns. Now, he summed up, 'it was about life or death' (381).

## XI Explaining the readiness for self-destruction

In this situation, then, Jünger was fully aware that attempting to kill the enemy brought the risk of being wounded or losing his own life. How can we explain his willingness to accept such dangers time and again, year after year, despite incurring serious injuries on several occasions? In an essay focusing on tactical innovation in the German First World War army, the military historian Michael Geyer argues that soldiers' repeated willingness to fight and kill relied ultimately upon their readiness for 'self-destruction', whether this was self-willed or otherwise. Without this, it would not have been possible to 'annihilate the enemy' over the duration of the war.[54] The great advantage of Geyer's approach is that it spares us the false binary choice between two theories typically cited to explain soldiers' willingness to kill. This is the choice between an explanation based on 'ideology and fighting motivation' and one based on troops' 'group solidarity' and comradeship.[55]

In truth, it is not possible to isolate either of these factors for the German army in the First World War and demonstrate convincingly that it provided a substantial motivation for soldiers to fight. Only a vanishingly small minority of German soldiers on compulsory military service possessed such an authentic fighting motivation. In this respect, Ernst Jünger was one of the rare exceptions that proves the rule, not least as he had volunteered in 1914. At the micro level of the company or battalion, the social capital of group solidarity or comradeship was certainly an important contributor to the cohesion of small groups, although the significance of some of the evidence presented to prove this is somewhat doubtful.[56] It should not be overlooked, however, that the social and cultural practices of comradeship were accompanied, as the war progressed, by permanent competition for ever declining resources such as leave, food and clothing. The conflicts surrounding these scarce goods hollowed out and counteracted the cultural ideal of comradeship from within.[57]

The most in-depth study to date on comradeship in the First World War has shown that although it functioned as social capital, it did not provide substantial motivation for exercising lethal violence. Even in the 1920s, the term had largely 'bourgeois connotations' and had been 'absorbed into Christian ethics'. This bourgeois-national mythology of comradeship differed substantially from the soldierly nationalism embodied by Jünger's war literature, which regarded the 'morality of killing' as the decisive act of comradeship. In this respect, too, the Imperial Army up to 1918 differed fundamentally from the Wehrmacht in the Second World War, for whom the mythologized comradeship of the *Landser* (as German soldiers called themselves) was an important source of motivation in their genocidal warfare.[58]

Michael Geyer is therefore correct to argue that German soldiers' willingness to continue risking their lives on the First World War battlefields is best explained by the tactical changes introduced from 1916 onwards. The Army Supreme Command pushed the new storm troop tactics and the strategy of flexible defence. This new form of combat training gave soldiers a sense of certainty that they were entering the battlefield well prepared and that the risks they were taking were reasonable or at least calculable. Less convincing is Geyer's theory that the thorough training of the elite storm troops led to a kind of 'hubris'. This arose, Geyer claims, from a 'feeling of invincibility' that gripped soldiers who had survived several battles.[59] Geyer's explicit point of reference for this theory is none other than Ernst Jünger.[60] Geyer cites a much-quoted passage of *Storm of Steel*, which describes the moment of the German attack on 21 March 1918. In a passage rich in metaphors, Jünger celebrates the 'unstoppable' advance of the

German troops towards the enemy line, protected by the wave of fire from the German artillery: 'It was as though nothing could hurt them anymore.'[61] The description of the same moment in the war diary is, as one might expect, considerably more prosaic. Significantly, it makes no mention of the feeling of invincibility that Jünger later added in the 1920 version of the book. In the diary, Jünger notes merely a 'mixture of feelings' – 'excitement, bloodthirstiness, anger' – but no hunch, let alone certainty, that he would emerge from the battle unscathed (378). Jünger was a highly experienced soldier, who clearly moved with great care on the battlefield. Even for him, however, the reality of war also included moments when he did not believe 'in a safe return' as his 'subconscious' was in 'constant expectation of being hit' (269–70). Jünger's experience as a soldier and troop officer had taught him only too well that the chances of a serious or deadly injury were substantial. This forced him to acknowledge that the fact of his survival was something to cherish in itself given the dangers soldiers faced. He noted his ambiguous feelings in August 1917 after a particularly costly defensive battle:

> All in all, the experience of that day was that life is better than one had realized after all and that one is glad to still be alive. Or is it that surviving danger makes life worth living? In that case, danger would be something to seek out. (303)

In his twelve months of action that followed this diary entry, Jünger never eschewed the risk of death. However, there is nothing in his diaries to suggest that he actively sought this risk out. Towards the end of the war, Jünger began to feel a degree of 'indifference' towards his own mortality. However, this was not an emotion he was willing to share with others (379–80). The diaries provide no evidence that Jünger confronted violence with a feeling of invincibility. In fact, Jünger repeatedly describes it as a 'miracle' when he or his men survived enemy fire unscathed (175, 378).

## XII  Conclusion

The new insights offered into Ernst Jünger's wartime experience by his diaries give us cause to re-evaluate the many interpretations of the war literature he published from 1920 onwards, beginning with *Storm of Steel*. This literature is commonly held to have created the model for a certain type of warrior: a 'steely figure who directly combined experience and technology, passion and discipline, excess and order'.[62] The blueprint of 'fundamentalist masculinity' featured in these texts has come to be read, with some justification, as a protofascist programme. This, it is claimed, set out to transform the soldier's body into a fighting machine compatible with mechanized warfare.[63] Yet this fighting machine is not the same lieutenant and storm troop commander whom we encounter in the war diaries written between 1914 and 1918. It is clear that the warrior who features in *Storm of Steel* and Jünger's other war books was in fact a literary figure created out of repeated revisions of the diaries post-1918. The war diaries, which we have examined here with regard to Jünger's relationship to violence, are a repository of his wartime experiences. The texts published after 1918, and particularly *Storm of Steel*, reflect upon and stylize this wartime experience in the light of events since the German defeat on 11 November 1918. Jünger himself wrote of his realization of what the Germans had 'lost' with the outcome of the war: 'a great deal, perhaps everything' and especially their 'honour'. He considered it his essential duty to counter the 'age of renegadism' triggered by defeat and revolution with the 'honourable remembrance' of the 'struggle' of war (434). This was the mission Jünger set for himself in an extended note at the end of his diaries, explaining his motives for turning them into the publication that later appeared as *Storm of Steel*. The version of his wartime experience that appeared in his books was thus not the essence of Jünger's experiences on the front, but a reflection of his political and social radicalization during the inter-war period.

As for his experiences prior to 1918, which should provide the framework for our interpretation of the war diaries, Jünger writes clearly of his wartime motivation in the same diary entry: 'I was raised in the spirit of the Prussian officer corps and am a soldier with all my body and soul. I have fought for four years as a rifleman and commander, have been wounded seven times and hold many decorations and medals' (433). With these words, Jünger outlines the traditional expectations of a war volunteer and professional soldier, whose idea of war centred on the hope of proving himself in one-on-one combat and on the fabled sense of duty of the Prussian officer. The same ethos motivated his actions on the battlefield and led him repeatedly to threaten to shoot men in his own unit fleeing rearwards to escape heavy fire. 'Undisciplined running away' greatly offended Jünger (296, cf. 298). It is also clear that Wilhelmine right-wing nationalism, which regarded the *Kaiser* as a potent symbol to unite the nation, did nothing to motivate Ernst Jünger or shape his identity.[64] Jünger was certain that, as he put it, he had 'more national feeling than some who had tanked themselves up on alcohol every 27 January [to celebrate the birthday of Wilhelm II] and came back "down to earth" on 9 November [1918, the proclamation of the republic] without so much as drawing a dagger' (433).

It may seem surprising that after four years on the front line, Jünger continued to affirm the traditional values of the Prussian officer corps.[65] This contradicts the many theories suggesting that the experience of mechanized warfare radically debased their currency.[66] It is also inconsistent with the idea that 'a new type of officer' emerged at the end of the war: a 'charismatic military leader' who was both 'technocrat and fanatic in equal measure'.[67] There is no disputing that such men existed in the armed forces of the Weimar Republic.[68] At least with a view to Ernst Jünger, however, it can be argued that this charismatic type of officer was less a product of the war itself than of the anti-revolutionary and anti-republican mobilization that occurred after the armistice.

The Jünger we encounter in his war diaries is neither a protofascist fighting machine nor a prophet of the amalgamation of man and military technology. Jünger appears here first and foremost as a detailed chronicler of the destruction to life and – though beyond the scope of this chapter – to landscapes and settlements. He notes the enormous discrepancy between his hopes of man-to-man combat and the reality of an artillery-dominated war. At the moment of close-quarter combat, Jünger is intoxicated by killing. He knows, however, that such moments are rare exceptions. Even in the 'heat of battle', Jünger never loses sight of the instrumental nature of the battle. Fighting remains a means to an end, as is evidenced by the practice of taking prisoners. Jünger fought throughout the war with the ethos of a professional soldier. However, in December 1915, even he wrote that killing in war was an act of 'murder' (62). The following year, he also acknowledged the psychological consequences of violence: the growing inurement to killing. It is no coincidence that it was the opportunity to wield a new type of hand grenade that triggered these thoughts. Jünger was well aware of the 'brutalizing influence of war'. In his case, this was evident less in the rare moments when he noted the intoxicating pleasure of killing than in the cold-bloodedness with which he registered the death of his own men (277).

Up until the moment of his final injury in August 1918, Jünger regarded the business of war not as an end in itself, but as a means to German victory. In December 1915, for instance, he noted that the war had 'awakened his longing for the blessings of peace' (63). As a professional soldier, Jünger also knew that war could provide a sense of moral order to a soldier's life, especially since the conflict also had 'its peaceful moods' (158). Yet the sight of green fields in May 1917 prompted even the 'once gung-ho' Jünger to ask: 'When is this crap war [Scheißkrieg] going to end?' (258). It is precisely this awareness of how closely violence and normality were intertwined, of how war and the hope for peace were bound together, that make Jünger's diaries such an important and insightful historical document for our understanding of the practice of violence in the First World War.

# Part Two

# Refusal of Violence

5

# Desertion in the German Army 1914–1918

Soldiers in the German First World War army had a variety of options for escaping the violence of the conflict. These ranged from self-mutilation to feigning illness, and going absent without leave for hours or days at a time. Of all the ways the men refused to fight, however, there was one – desertion – that had a greater impact than any other on both the military as a whole and the individual soldiers who chose this route. In Germany, studies on this topic have so far concentrated on the Wehrmacht, discussing the controversial question of whether desertion constituted a form of resistance against the Nazi regime.[1] In the case of the German army in the First World War, the most relevant question is a somewhat different one: On what scale did such desertion take place and did it escalate into mass 'shirking' (see Chapter 7) and a 'hidden military strike' in the final months of the war?

Before attempting to quantify the number of soldiers deserting the German army, this chapter begins by examining when and where desertion was possible. This analysis will include a look at the measures taken by the military authorities in an attempt to prevent desertion spiralling out of control. In a sense, it will also present a topography of survival in the First World War. The places and functions in which soldiers stood the best chances of surviving the war also created opportunities for desertion. The chapter will then examine the scale of the phenomenon (II) before shedding light on the deserters' motives, despite the many difficulties this raises (III). Finally, it will look at the specific backgrounds to the numerous cases of desertion involving soldiers from national minorities within Imperial Germany (IV).

## I Places of survival: Escape routes for deserters

The options for an ordinary soldier or NCO seeking to escape military service by deserting the army depended first and foremost on his location. For those on the front line intending to defect to the enemy, the topography of the battlefield and intensity of fire were the most important factors. From autumn 1914, the entire Western Front was comprised of a series of positions and trenches. These were arranged in lines at staggered distances back from no-man's land. Each was secured by barbed wire, making it useful for defectors to carry wire cutters.[2] The armies positioned listening posts on the foremost line, making good local knowledge essential if soldiers were to choose the best path to the enemy. Studying a map, for example, helped a defector gain a mental picture of the fortifications and of precisely where he could expect to encounter troops.[3] Soldiers already positioned in the trenches closest to the enemy or at a listening post had the best opportunities to escape across no-man's land and accounted for the majority of such defections.[4] In isolated cases where two soldiers occupied a listening post and only one of the men was minded to desert, the defector could use physical force against his comrade to make good his escape.[5] Patrols heading to the enemy trenches offered another good opportunity for defection, provided soldiers could abscond unnoticed from the group.[6] Meanwhile, would-be defectors who were not posted on the foremost line first had to seek authorization to move forward under other pretexts or risk inconvenient questions by the officers patrolling the trenches.[7]

These practical considerations make it easy to understand why soldiers normally defected to the enemy individually or with no more than one or two close comrades.[8] Only soldiers from national minorities frequently did so together in larger groups or in quick succession. One such recorded incident involved every single occupant of a German saphead positioned close to enemy lines.[9] In the 73rd Infantry Regiment, which was stationed in Flanders, no fewer than sixty-seven Poles and Alsatians escaped in the space of a single day on 28 September 1917. And in Russia, in a period from August to October 1917, the 224th Reserve Infantry Regiment reported some 3,100 soldiers missing. Allied information shows that the majority of these men were from Alsace-Lorraine.[10] As well as a good knowledge of the terrain, low intensity of enemy fire also improved the chances of success. Sudden heavy fire could scupper escape attempts and force would-be defectors back to their own lines.[11] On the other hand, heavy shooting in the midst of battle could sometimes create opportunities for spontaneous defection. One such incident took place in the 206th Infantry Division in August 1917, when 119 soldiers from two separate regiments, including an entire platoon, defected to the French. They had dodged heavy mortar fire by moving forwards and, having virtually been catapulted towards the enemy, took advantage of the fortuitous circumstances.[12]

Depending on the section of the front on which soldiers were posted, the level of fire was often sufficiently low to enable men to make their escape. Intense exchanges such as those seen in the battles of *matériel* in 1916 were the exception rather than the rule. On quiet sections of the front, such as those occupied by Landwehr and Reserve divisions in the Vosges mountains, troops generally faced only low-intensity artillery activity. This often consisted merely of a ritualized exchange of fire at the same time each day.[13] Areas where the opposing sides had reached such 'tacit agreements' provided particularly favourable ground for defection. Here, the exchange of fire was reduced to a minimum, or sometimes suspended altogether, for hours or even days at a time. Such agreements often resulted in direct contact with the 'enemy' soldiers as the men waved and called to one another or exchanged newspapers, food and tobacco.

Though it is impossible to determine exactly how often such unofficial ceasefires took place, they were certainly not entirely out of the ordinary. These occurrences repeatedly presented individual soldiers with the opportunity to defect in safety. In one incident recorded in September 1916, for example, a sapper by the name of Bamberger, deployed in a *Minenwerfer* (short-range mortar) company found his way to his division's furthest advanced trench. There he began talking to an NCO of the reserve and a fusilier. After a short time, Bamberger told the two men that, as an Alsatian, he spoke fluent French and wanted to see if he could obtain bread and wine from the enemy. He called across no-man's land, from where a small group of soldiers soon appeared. Other German soldiers and the NCO would later claim that they had ordered Bamberger to leave the trench's raised parapet. However, all watched passively as the sapper from Alsace engaged in a brief conversation with the French, climbed over the barbed wire and defected.[14]

In this case, the NCO in charge attempted at first to cover up the incident and instructed the fusiliers who had witnessed the defection not to report what they had seen.[15] Later, the authorities initiated proceedings against all the eyewitnesses. The men had failed to follow an existing order requiring them to shoot at any unarmed man leaving the German trench in the direction of the enemy.[16] In the case of other units, such an order was only issued once a number of defections had already occurred.[17] Deserters therefore faced potential danger from their own ranks even when tacit agreements existed between troops on both sides.[18] Nevertheless, tacit arrangements still presented a good opportunity to defect. The direct interaction and lack of fire during these informal ceasefires at least meant that there was relatively little danger of defecting Germans being shot by the British or French.

In other circumstances, and particularly in the midst of battle, soldiers could not be certain whether the enemy would be willing or able to take a surrendering soldier prisoner. Soldiers usually surrendered by throwing down their weapon, calling or making hand signals, or by waving a white cloth.[19] This was an unsettling prospect for the potential defector. From 1916, the French and British attempted to assuage such concerns by dropping leaflets on German troops. Some emphasized the strict instructions issued to their own men on the treatment of surrendering Germans. Others called directly on soldiers to defect using the password 'republic'.[20] German soldiers also took the initiative in informing the opposing side of their intentions and requested that the troops hold fire so as to assist them. In September 1915, for example, a patrol by the 7th West Prussian Infantry Regiment found a letter tied to a stone lying between the enemy trenches. It had been thrown there by Polish soldiers from their own unit:

> To the French soldiers. Our esteemed half-brothers! It is very saddening, and displeases God, that brother is fighting brother. Let us unite and spill no more of our shared blood. May your children and our children cry needlessly no more. Tell us tonight between 1–4 or 4–7 in the morning, or in the afternoon, whether we can come to you through the valley of the Flabas-Hammont forest towards the forest's leftmost tip. Tell your comrades in the Hammont forest so that they don't shoot at us. Write down the words in French that we should call to you. We want to join you in the days from the 18th to the 22nd of this month. Let the four who came to you here these days tell you the rest. One of many. Please reply.[21]

Though the risks involved in attempting to defect to the enemy were high, we should not overstate them. Large numbers of men succeeded. However, for soldiers on the front line or in the rear area, as well as those in garrisons at home in Germany, another means of escape was often far more promising and straightforward. This involved crossing into neighbouring neutral countries: the Netherlands, Denmark and Switzerland. Germany's extensive land border with Denmark proved impossible to secure. This escape route was used largely by conscripts with Danish origins who hailed from North Schleswig.[22] In return for a small payment, members of the Landsturm battalions posted on the border allowed conscripts to cross on an almost daily basis.[23] Home leave in Schleswig-Holstein thus presented a relatively straightforward opportunity for desertion.[24]

Switzerland was reachable by a vigorous swim across the Rhine or even Lake Constance, and growing numbers of men appear to have chosen this route in 1917.[25] For a 'strong swimmer' determined to reach Switzerland, wrote one deserter to a friend in 1918, immediately upon reaching the neutral country, there was 'no river too wide'.[26] In a letter dating from September 1917, a woman from the Swiss town of Aarau described the influx into Switzerland. Escaped French and Russian prisoners of war and even greater numbers of 'young 25-to-35-year-old deserters' were reaching Swiss villages along the Rhine 'every day'. The arriving men told the locals that they had 'suffered enough' and would rather 'take a bullet to the head on the Swiss border than go back to that misery'.[27] Some had a less arduous escape, such as Rolf Reventlow, son of the author Countess Franziska zu Reventlow. Having been granted leave to meet his mother for a holiday in the town of Konstanz in summer 1917, Reventlow rowed across Lake Constance to the Swiss side with his mother's blessing.[28] This was an embarrassing incident for the German military authorities. Franziska zu Reventlow was the sister of Count Ernst von Reventlow, a well-known publicist and member of the Alldeutscher Verband, famed during the war for his tirades against Britain and the US. The desertion therefore attracted wide attention in the international press.[29]

For those soldiers who had resided in Switzerland prior to the war – the majority of whom served in Bavarian and Württemberg units – desertion was more straightforward. These men could simply choose not to return from home leave.[30] A Landwehr regiment recruited in Upper Swabia in Württemberg had conscripted 725 Swiss-resident men in the mobilization of 1914. In the period up to early 1918, the regiment recorded only one case of defection. However, twenty-one of the 'Swiss' had deserted following a period of leave: thirteen of them from leave on German territory and eight from leave in Switzerland itself.[31] The 3rd Army High Command reported that of forty-four soldiers who went on leave in Switzerland between November 1917 and January 1918, sixteen had so far failed to return. In nine of these cases the leave period had not yet expired and there was therefore no certainty that the men had in fact deserted the army.[32]

In many cases, such desertions were clearly not planned in advance, but resulted from encouragement by the Swiss and pressure exerted by family members during the visit home. Soldiers often requested an extension to their leave. If the army refused to grant this, some men felt 'duty bound to their family' not to return to their military service.[33] The 16th Army Corps, which was particularly affected by such desertions, eventually responded in January 1918 with a general ban on leave to visit Switzerland. Prior to this order, a number of its regiments and divisions had evidently continued to grant such leave despite their bad experiences.[34]

Men without official permission to go on leave used counterfeit or manipulated leave permits to reach border regions undetected. Trade in such papers burgeoned in 1917 and 1918.³⁵ Escaping soldiers travelled on military leave trains, where checks were minimal. Major interchange stations were favoured locations for deserters seeking to blend into the crowd, and police raids on these locations always turned up large numbers of such men.³⁶ Some deserters completed their journey across the border on freight trains.³⁷ Others used the services of people smugglers, who offered to take deserters, escaped prisoners of war and civilian prisoners safely across the frontier. A 1917 memorandum by the Deputy General Staff stated, probably in reference primarily to the Dutch border, that it was 'barely possible' to 'secure the frontier more effectively' with the resources available. The 'people smugglers', it added, had good knowledge of the conditions and controls along the border thanks to their experience in smuggling food. In return for good money – allegedly up to several hundred marks – they were more than willing to help deserters. Unable to seal the border effectively and with the number of escapes reaching 'an incredible level' by autumn 1917, the authorities hoped that tackling this trade would at least provide an indirect means of controlling the situation. They therefore began imposing harsher punishments for treason on 'people smugglers'.³⁸

German deserters in the Netherlands had to choose whether to take up work or to be sent to various camps in Bergen, Alkmar and elsewhere following a brief medical observation. After a temporary stay, even those who opted for the camps were permitted to leave in order to seek work. They were obliged to return to the camp if unsuccessful.³⁹ In Switzerland, a Federal Council resolution on 30 June 1916 officially entitled deserters or conscientious objectors from foreign countries to remain for the duration of the war. This policy changed radically on 1 May 1918, when the Council decided that such men should in future be sent back at the border. In reality, however, treatment was more lenient. The government reinstated the original practice of accepting deserters following pressure from the labour movement and churches.⁴⁰

Another option for deserters was to remain within the rear area. One Bavarian infantryman, for example, successfully found shelter in a series of Belgian communes before he was finally arrested in Brussels. He survived off leftovers from soldiers at various canteens and later worked for several weeks on a Belgian farm.⁴¹ The number of men hiding out in the rear area in northern France and Belgium is likely to have remained relatively low until late 1917. By the early days of the 'hidden military strike' in mid-1918, however, it had reached an estimated 30,000.⁴² In the part of the rear area under the Commander Ober-Ost, soldiers began to seek shelter in the forests of Lithuania from as early as 1915. Their numbers grew continually up to 1917, by which time reports of such cases were arriving 'almost every day'. Some of the German soldiers even joined Lithuanian partisan groups.[43]

Finally, a deserter could attempt to find a safe place in Germany itself. Returning to one's own home was to be avoided at all costs, since the military investigation would usually notify the relevant local authorities of the desertion. Police searches and interrogation of relatives were the norm.[44] Violent incidents could result, such as the exchange of fire seen in a Lower Bavarian village in September 1918 when the police arrested a deserter. The miller's son, who was hiding out at his parents' house having fled the army, sustained serious injuries.[45] Given the severe shortage of labourers, farmers were sometimes willing to provide a deserter with work and a roof over his head without asking difficult questions. Police checks on cattle markets in the 10th Army Corps district in Hanover caught up to eighty deserters in some cases.[46] Another option was to join groups of wandering gypsies.[47] In summer and autumn 1918, with the end of the war imminent, many deserters and 'shirkers' found shelter with friends or relatives in major German cities for the final weeks and months. Military authorities – perhaps exaggerating – estimated the numbers of such men in Cologne and Berlin at 30,000 and 20,000 respectively.[48] Neutral countries, the rear area and home soil thus provided potential deserters with destinations that were easier to reach than the enemy lines and offered adequate protection from rapid discovery.

For all soldiers considering desertion, whether to neutral countries or across enemy lines, there was a psychological barrier to be overcome. This is likely to have been most significant for older, married men and especially those with children. All soldiers in the field army were granted leave to visit home at least once a year. Along with food rations, these trips remained foremost in the minds of wartime soldiers. They not only meant a temporary escape from danger, but also reunited the men with their families.[49] A potential deserter, meanwhile, had to be prepared to spend several years in a foreign country, usually one where he could not yet speak the national language, and to endure an indefinite separation from his family. By late 1914, most soldiers understood that the war had reached a stalemate. Though not everyone went as far as one Bavarian unit, where the men began to speak of the '1914–20 world war', there appeared little prospect of a military victory for either side for the foreseeable future. Nevertheless, many soldiers clung repeatedly to the hope that the latest military offensive or diplomatic efforts would bring an imminent end to the conflict.[50] It is therefore reasonable to assume that the majority of those who deserted were more convinced than their comrades that such hopes were in vain. On 29 May 1917, a decree issued by the Prussian War Ministry brought the dilemma faced by many deserters to a head. This assured deserters (but not men who had defected to the enemy) that they would be offered a reprieve, spared pre-trial detention and given the prospect of a pardon if they turned themselves in at a German border post by 15 July 1917.[51] A 42-year-old factory worker from Saxony told his interrogators that he had decided to return to Germany from the Netherlands after receiving a letter from his wife. She had enclosed a newspaper cutting announcing the decree and told him to come back to her.[52] In another case, a soldier from the Chemnitz area had written to his wife, asking her to join him in Tilburg in the Netherlands, the city to which he had fled from Belgium in September 1916. For reasons that are unrecorded, she declined to do so. In a letter full of bitterness at the long separation, her husband replied that he might have returned to Germany had he not already missed the deadline set by the military authorities.[53]

The majority of defectors were placed in the same enemy camps as the 'normal' prisoners of war. This implies that those who chose to defect considered the poor treatment, bad food and other potential drawbacks of the camps to be preferable to the dangers of life at the front and the other grievances they experienced in the German army.[54] By the second half of the war, propaganda on the perils of enemy captivity had largely lost its deterrent effect. Only a minority of soldiers continued to believe that 'being a prisoner of war is no solution'.[55] Evidence from the ranks of those who fled to the enemy shows that fear of captivity did not pose a major barrier to desertion. In early 1917, the military authorities found that some of the letters arriving in Germany from 'un-German' defectors and prisoners of war were describing 'their lives on enemy territory in favourable terms, sometimes including photographs of themselves in civilian clothing or French uniform'.[56] Two fusiliers attached the following letter to a post in one of the foremost German trenches just a few hours after their defection to the French. The message was addressed to their comrades:

> 6 June 1915 My dear friend Robert! Kariger and I left our trench this morning at quarter to three and have had a friendly reception from the French so far. They are not as bad as you always told us; that's just the fear and imagination of the others talking. On the contrary, we have been given bread, sausage, cigarettes and wine. As you can see, one must try everything first before one can make a fair judgement. Greetings to Rößler [a superior] and tell him we're happy to have been freed from the devil's claw. He should watch out for us or else he'll be picking his bones up off the floor. . . . Hope to see you soon, Robert Kupka and Wilhelm Kariger. We ask for your moral support.[57]

In soldiers' eyes, then, the opportunities for desertion or defection were manifold, though the risks could vary greatly depending on the specific means of escape. For the military leadership, meanwhile, discipline and the preservation of the army's fighting strength depended on keeping the number of deserters as low as possible. Available countermeasures included use of preventive deterrents as well as disrupting and monitoring potential escape routes and the flow of information.[58]

The first means of deterrence came in the form of the *Kriegsartikel* (Articles of War). Officers in each unit regularly read these Articles aloud in a ritual designed to intimidate the men.[59] The *Kriegsartikel* contained a list of soldierly duties and punishments for the most common disciplinary offences, including desertion.[60] In addition to the general deterrent effect this provided, the army issued further warnings to units from which soldiers had already deserted. The commander of one infantry regiment, for example, responded to the disappearance of three defectors by ordering that 'each battalion leader should gather his entire battalion together and discuss the three men's criminal actions in the strongest possible terms, emphasizing sections 73 and 77 of the Military Penal Code', which covered desertion.[61] In another case, the troops were informed that 'a deserter or defector can never expect mercy and shall face the strictest legal penalty or be barred for life from returning to Germany'.[62] In June 1918, shortly before the onset of mass refusal among the troops to play any further part in the war effort, the Army Supreme Command called on front-line units to 'again point out in the clearest terms the reprehensible nature' of defection and give the men a 'sharp reminder' of the punishments.[63] The very fact that such warnings had to be repeated, however, suggests that they probably had little impact on potential deserters. Soldiers spontaneously deserting were unlikely to have thought through all the possible consequences. And where a desertion had been long in the planning, it was improbable that the threat of punishment would sway the final decision given all the other obstacles and risks the soldier was determined to overcome.

Monitoring of possible escape routes began in the foremost line. Officers and NCOs serving in the trenches conducted regular inspections of listening posts. Their aim was partly to update commanders on the military situation, but also to deter defection by the occupants. Given that these visits were highly predictable, however, they were not especially effective. Additional unannounced inspections by the company leader in the middle of the night also proved unable to solve the problem of defection.[64] Company leaders were required to choose the occupants of the listening posts carefully. Some officers deliberately avoided posting unreliable soldiers to the foremost line altogether.[65]

The boundaries of the rear area in Flanders were sealed far more effectively than Germany's borders with Denmark, the Netherlands and Switzerland. Minefields, dog patrols and a high-voltage electric fence were intended to prevent soldiers from fleeing directly from the Belgian rear area to the Netherlands.[66] Gaps in the fence were protected by gates, to which only officers had the keys. Deserters were, however, able to break the gates down using sheer force.[67] From 1916, the field police carried out patrols to inspect reserve positions and accommodation. Soldiers returning from the battle line were required to show that they were either wounded or carrying out a specific mission. This measure may have led to the capture of deserters in some cases. Its primary aim, however, was to counter the rapidly multiplying cases of 'absence without leave' and 'cowardice' since the major battles of 1916.[68] As hundreds of thousands of soldiers streamed back towards the rear area and home to Germany in late summer and autumn 1918 (see Chapter 7), the establishment of *Versprengten-Sammelstellen* (assembly points for scattered soldiers, or 'stragglers') and blockades in the rear area of operations proved unable to stem the flow.

The Prussian War Ministry advised the deputy general commands in as early as summer 1915 to patrol domestic passenger trains. Police officers in civilian clothing performed such operations throughout Germany from 1917 onwards. Their purpose was partly to monitor the mood among the general population. However, the police also checked military and identity documents, enabling them to arrest soldiers wanted for desertion or other offences.[69] There are two statistical indications of the level of success this measure achieved. The first is provided by data from five local police stations and the *Zentralpolizeistelle Mitte* in Berlin, established in late 1915 for the coordination of counter-espionage. Over various periods around the last three months of 1917, these arrested a total of 396 deserters. The second relates to the districts covered by five central and four local surveillance units, whose records show that checks on the railways resulted in the arrest of 360 deserters between 1 January and 28 February 1918. The arrested deserters were joined by a 'considerable' number of young men who had evaded the draft altogether.[70]

The authorities also monitored soldiers' letters to reduce cases of desertion. From late April 1916, postal surveillance offices at divisional and army high command level began censoring post. This served to monitor the general mood and punish 'damage' to military interests and 'serious breaches of discipline'.[71] The latter generally involved complaints about inadequate rations or unfair treatment by superiors. Statements such as these often resulted in punishment for defamation of an officer. So delegitimized was the military apparatus in soldiers' eyes by autumn 1918, and so deep the sense of war weariness, that some letters even described plans for serious acts of disobedience. A postal surveillance report from October 1918 stated succinctly: 'Where an intention to desert was identified, the unit has been informed directly.'[72] In the case of soldiers belonging to national minorities within Imperial Germany, the authorities adopted additional postal censorship measures to root out deserters. Special postal surveillance offices on the Danish border inspected letters by soldiers from North Schleswig to their relatives in Denmark. At one stage in 1917, the authorities even checked all correspondence to and from Alsace-Lorrainian troops.[73]

In January 1917, the Deputy General Staff sent a notification to the deputy general commands and war ministries. There was information to suggest that the Allies were persuading deserters in neutral countries to write letters to individual German soldiers, enticing them to follow suit. The postal surveillance offices responsible for monitoring international correspondence were therefore instructed wherever possible to stop post to and from deserters living in other countries. They were also to regard with suspicion any letters from abroad addressed to soldiers.[74] The Deputy General Command in Münster responded by setting up a 'postal surveillance card index of deserters', which contained the names of all deserters reported by the replacement units.[75] The Deputy General Staff, intervening again in this process in June 1917, pointed to its intention to create a 'central office to answer all queries relating to cases of desertion and defection to the enemy'.[76] There appears to be no other evidence of this plan, which was not pursued further. Nevertheless, the very fact that it was mentioned indicates a problem faced by the military authorities. In their view, the division of powers between the war ministries of the German states, the deputy general commands, the Army Supreme Command and the authorities in the field was making it unduly difficult to combat desertion.

## II  Desertion as a mass phenomenon

To determine the scale of desertion in the German wartime army, this section begins by adopting the approach of the military authorities attempting to identify and sentence deserters. Like other court-martial procedures, this involved four steps. The soldier's superior, usually the company leader, reported the absence – or, if witnessed, the act of desertion itself – to the battalion or regiment, who in turn reported to the division's *Gerichtsrat* (court officer – the trained jurist in charge of court-martial procedures at the divisional level). If sufficient evidence was available, the court officer then initiated an investigation. This involved questioning witnesses and examining and securing evidence such as the suspect's equipment. If the culprit was caught, the third step was to bring charges and arrange for the case to be heard in court. A guilty verdict formed the fourth and final step in reaching an official finding of desertion.

In response to a 'lack of clarity' about the official process, the Army Supreme Command and Prussian War Ministry again informed the units in 1917 and 1918 as to how to proceed in cases where the authorities were unable to apprehend deserters.[77] In such instances, as the authorities had already explained in May 1916, the official declaration of desertion had to wait until after the demobilization. Where soldiers were missing and suspected to have deserted, however, preparatory investigations for the court case were to begin immediately. Only if suspicions proved sufficiently grounded could the division immediately declare that the soldier had deserted. A declaration of desertion resulted in termination of financial support to the suspect's relatives. After two years had elapsed, the authorities could begin a process to strip deserters of their citizenship and confiscate their assets.[78] The objective of this approach to desertion cases was clearly to prepare the documents that would be required to secure a conviction after the war, while also enabling immediate deterrent measures depending on the decision of the judges and the disciplinary situation in the relevant unit.

In the event of a possible defection, the soldier's unit had to describe as precisely as possible what had happened and gather potential evidence. Individual cases reveal the difficulties this created and show that soldiers were sometimes accused of desertion despite a lack of substantive proof. This was the case for a Polish lance-corporal who went missing on 24 February 1916. His regiment never established how he had left his position or where he had gone. It treated one suspected escape route as plausible simply because 'single infantry shots' had been heard from that direction. The 'urgent suspicion' was clearly based solely on two factors: first, the fact that the man was a Pole and, second, that on the 'evening before his desertion', he had complained about the strict postal censorship. This came after the authorities had intercepted and returned one of his letters.[79] In another case, witness statements were insufficient to provide conclusive proof of defection. The two suspects had only been with the unit for a few weeks and were therefore unknown to the company leader. This did not stop the regiment claiming in its report that the men may have defected out of fear of a further deployment in the Battle of the Somme. The brigade reported this motivation on to the General Command, noting that it was a 'very likely' explanation.[80]

Footprints leading towards enemy lines in the snow, the disappearance of the suspect's freshly washed clothes, blankets, letters or iron rations, and the discovery of equipment on the suspected escape route, were all generally considered strong evidence of defection. Soldiers who had once remarked to comrades that they would abscond were considered probable deserters, as were those who virtually said their farewells to other men immediately before their disappearance.[81] The same applied to those who told their relatives not to expect 'any more post for a while'.[82] The most reliable evidence, of course, came from officers or comrades who witnessed the act itself.

The greatest difficulty facing court martials was the legal position concerning desertion. The Military Penal Code of the German Empire, which dated from 1872, stipulated that a soldier was guilty of desertion if he was found to have absented himself 'with the intention of permanently withdrawing from his legal obligation to serve in the army'.[83] The Code thus emphasized both the permanent nature of the offence, which distinguished desertion from simple absence without leave, and the 'intent' behind it. This definition put the onus on the military to prove that every single defendant had taken the deliberate decision to desert. This burden of proof was forced upon the army by verdicts of the Reichsmilitärgericht (Imperial Military Court) and reaffirmed by meetings of military judges during the war. If a soldier left his unit to travel to the rear area or back home, his conviction for desertion therefore relied upon an admission that he had done so with no intention of returning to the army before the end of the war.[84] In the case of one sapper who failed to return from leave in June 1918, for example, the military secured only a conviction for absence without leave. The man had been working in Munich until his arrest. For the prosecution, the fact that he wore civilian clothing during his time in the city was a clear indication that he had no intention to return to the army. The defendant successfully countered this, arguing that without civilian clothing, he would have been unable to find work.[85]

These legal difficulties mean that statistics on desertion probably exclude a considerable number of cases where soldiers did in fact deliberately withdraw themselves from the remainder of the conflict. In some cases, the military brought charges of desertion but secured only a conviction for absence without leave. Particularly in cases involving national minorities, the military courts took a selective and inconsistent approach.[86] A further problem lay in the lengthy processes within the military jurisdiction. The number of offences to be tried by court martial grew dramatically from the beginning of 1918 and exploded in the summer of that year. The military courts were soon unable to handle such volumes with the available personnel. In the 33rd Infantry Division, for example, there were 500 pending charge sheets for absence without leave in August 1918.[87] In the various Bavarian infantry divisions for which figures are available, the court-martial proceedings reached a verdict in only a fraction of cases in 1918. In the 3rd Bavarian Infantry Division, there were verdicts in just 183 of 671 cases, and in the 14th Infantry Division as few as 120 of 856 cases.[88]

The following figures on convictions for desertion and absence without leave therefore do not provide a complete picture of the number of soldiers hauled before the military courts for desertion. In four Bavarian divisions for which separate figures on both crimes are available, there were a total of thirty convictions for desertion over the course of the war. For each conviction for desertion, there were another eighteen for absence without leave.[89] These figures can be compared with those for other divisions, whose statistics made no such differentiation. For ten Bavarian divisions, lists of criminal proceedings are available for the entire duration of the war. These show that convictions for desertion and absence without leave in each year of the war were as follows: 1914: 78; 1915: 292; 1916: 359; 1917: 827; 1918: 561.[90] This data reveals a sharp increase in the course of 1917. The years 1917 and 1918 therefore differed markedly from the rest of the war, both in terms of the number of such convictions and, in all likelihood, the real number of deserters.

We can extrapolate from the figures for the above-mentioned four Bavarian divisions to estimate the total numbers for the German army's 251 divisions in early 1918.[91] This calculation yields a total of approximately 1,900 convictions for desertion in the field army. In a 1942 estimate, however, the Kriegsgeschichtliche Forschungsanstalt des Heeres (Army Research Institute for Military History) put the figure at 1,000 convictions in the first half of 1918 alone.[92] While this makes the total of 1,900 for the war as a whole appear somewhat on the low side, it also constitutes further evidence that cases of desertion in the field army increased especially in the final year of the war. In the Bavarian replacement army, meanwhile, convictions for desertion and absence without leave were spread more evenly over the course of the conflict. The number of convicted deserters in the home army was four times that in the field army. This reflected the fact that it was considerably easier for soldiers in the garrisons to find escape routes and safe places than for those on the front.[93] Extrapolating the Bavarian figures yields a total of 8,000 to 10,000 convictions for desertion in the German army as a whole.[94] This suggests that some 10,000 German soldiers and NCOs (deserting officers were a great exception and usually from Alsace-Lorraine[95]) were convicted for desertion during the First World War.[96] However, this figure should be treated as a possible underestimate. The national minorities, who were by far most likely to desert, were extremely underrepresented in the Bavarian army.[97]

To estimate the total number of actual desertions, we must combine a variety of different figures.[98] Most important are the statistics on the numbers fleeing to neutral countries, especially Switzerland and the Netherlands. In 1925, Karl von Roeder, a former major, put the number of German deserters in August 1918 at 9,000 men in Switzerland and 15,000 men in the Netherlands. His figures were based on German intelligence.[99] They probably did not include the considerable number of men who reported to German border posts in response to the amnesty of May 1917. At the Reichstag's parliamentary subcommittee on the 'Causes of the German Collapse in 1918', Dr Ludwig Herz put on record that some 4,000 German soldiers had been registered in the Netherlands between September and December 1918.[100] The Landsturm Inspectorate in Schleswig wrote in late 1915 that 328 men from the Danish minority in North Schleswig had already escaped military service by fleeing to Denmark, in some cases probably before receiving their draft notice.[101] By May 1917, the number of deserters had reached approximately 7,000.[102] In the final months of the war, the military authorities registered another 'enormous rise in the number of deserters' heading to Denmark.[103] All in all, it is therefore likely that more than 30,000 German soldiers fled to neutral countries.[104]

There are no total figures showing how many men defected on the fronts in Russia, France, Italy, Serbia and Romania. One source of information is the number of defectors and deserters to neutral countries recorded in the court files of the 2nd Bavarian Infantry Division. These document three defections. Another five soldiers successfully escaped to Switzerland or the Netherlands.[105] This example suggests that the numbers of defectors in the field army did not come close to those fleeing to neutral countries. However, it is little help in quantifying defection across the German army as a whole. Given that this division had the lowest number of convictions for desertion and absence without leave in the entire Bavarian army (ninety-three cases compared with 361 in the 4th Bavarian Infantry Division), it seems likely that the division's rate of defections was also at the bottom of the scale.[106] The 2nd Division, like others in Bavaria, had few Alsatians and Poles among its ranks. However, there is another explanation for the low rate. In the view of the Allies, the Bavarian 2nd Infantry Division was 'one of the very best German shock divisions', which had proven its mettle in heavy fighting in various arenas of the war.[107] Divisions such as these received large numbers of young replacement soldiers aged no more than twenty-five, who were considerably more motivated to fight and thus less likely to defect than older troops.[108]

While there is good evidence that the number of defectors on the Western Front remained low into the summer of 1918,[109] it is likely to have been a different story on the Eastern Front, as will be discussed below. Defections appear to have risen sharply in the final weeks and months of the war, once the hopeless inferiority of the German troops was plain for every soldier to see.[110] The various sources cited here do not enable us to put a figure on total defections. For the period prior to the summer of 1918, however, it is unlikely that they exceeded a few thousand.[111]

As for the number of soldiers who successfully found shelter in the rear area, or back at home in Germany, where they remained undetected, there is little basis for even a rough estimate. Relatively reliable data is available on the soldiers for whom the director of the field police in the West received a manhunt request between 1 January and 18 July 1918. Their number was put at around 43,000, a figure which doubtless included soldiers wanted for crimes other than desertion. There were also indeterminable numbers of soldiers who were caught or surrendered themselves voluntarily during this period.[112] Though the figure of 43,000 is therefore somewhat problematic, it would be unwise to disregard it altogether. In the broader context of the changing mood on the Western Front, it suggests, plausibly, that the number of soldiers refusing to continue fighting started to increase dramatically even before the beginning of the 'hidden military strike' of July and August 1918 (see Chapters 6 and 7). There is little sense in attempting to calculate the number of deserters during the 'hidden military strike'. Few of the many 'shirkers' are likely to have intended to return to their units before the armistice, even if exhaustion or lack of food compelled them to report to the assembly points established by the military authorities.[113] Though many 'shirkers' who succeeded in absenting themselves until the end of the war may have met the formal criteria to be considered deserters, the mass scale on which soldiers now left the ranks blurred the boundaries between desertion, 'shirking' and absence without leave.

A calculation based on the analysis in this chapter shows that the number of soldiers defecting to the enemy, of conscientious objectors and deserters who reached neutral countries, of deserters convicted by court martial and, finally, of men escaping to the rear area or home to Germany with no intention to return, probably amounted in total to approximately 90,000 or perhaps even 100,000 men.[114] Desertion was the most significant form of disobedience and refusal in the German wartime army, and by some margin, both given the number of soldiers involved and the attention the military authorities paid to it. It grew to become a mass phenomenon even before the summer of 1918. Relative to the lower number of soldiers called up to serve in the First World War, the total number of deserters was higher than that recorded by the German Wehrmacht between 1939 and 1945.[115]

## III The motives for desertion

Drawing reliable conclusions on the specific motivations for desertion is an extremely difficult undertaking. There are few available sources describing the reasons why soldiers chose to desert. In the case of defectors, the authorities often had to rely on suspicions or vague indications. These were obtained by asking the defector's comrades to recall their conversations with the perpetrator in the days before the act. Court martials did not always explore the defendant's motives in detail. There were also good reasons for the defendant not to divulge them if possible. This was especially true if the soldier had deserted under heavy fire in the midst of battle. In such cases, a tougher sentence for 'cowardice' could result.[116] Publications by military psychiatrists, who were introduced to deserters prior to court martials in order to prepare a medical report, offer the historian a number of insights.[117] The psychiatrists' job was to identify possible unsoundness of mind, which could provide grounds for a more lenient sentence under section 51 of the Imperial Penal Code. However, the medical categories used to assess deserters distorted the motivations. Men with 'war neuroses' fell all too easily into suspicion of being 'weak-willed psychopaths' who had deserted the army solely because of an unhealthy mental disposition.[118]

In analysing deserters' motives, military psychiatrists rarely distinguished between desertion and absence without leave. They instead assumed that both crimes had similar causes.[119] This partly reflected the legal position, which made differentiation difficult. However, it also suggests that, with the exception of soldiers from national minorities, the motivations for desertion were the same as those behind other forms of refusal. When analysing the reasons why soldiers refused to participate in the war, it is often informative to differentiate between three determining factors: relatively low-risk opportunities, gradually emerging underlying motivations and sudden triggers.

The example of self-mutilation illustrates these three dimensions. It is straightforward to identify a desire to escape the deadly risks on the front as the broad underlying motivation, which was sometimes accompanied by other factors rooted in the personal circumstances of the individual. Inflicting injury on oneself (usually in the form of a gunshot wound to the left hand), however, took considerable willpower. The act of self-mutilation itself was therefore often a response to a more immediate trigger, such as a soldier's first experience of front-line fighting. Soldiers in the trenches or at listening posts had no shortage of opportunities to inflict injuries on themselves. It was extremely difficult for the courts to demonstrate that they had done so deliberately. Medical diagnostics at the time was unable to disprove the soldier's claim that he had been hit by enemy fire or accidentally triggered his weapon while cleaning it. For the men who chose this means of escaping military service – primarily farmers' sons and agrarian labourers – self-mutilation was often an impulsive act, a painful but relatively safe form of refusal with few legal risks.[120]

If deserters had the same underlying motive as the men who chose self-mutilation – to escape the dangers of wartime service – why did they choose such a radically different solution? The answer to this question must lie in the different ways in which soldiers connected their underlying motive to the immediate trigger, that is, how they took the decision to act. A deserter had to be far more conscious of the finality of his decision, and of the risks, fears and obstacles awaiting him even after a successful escape, than a soldier deciding to self-mutilate or go absent without leave. Desertion required substantial reserves of courage and self-assurance and was easier for those without a wife and children at home. These suppositions are corroborated by the available data on the age and social profile of deserters in the Bavarian army. Farmers – who were much less well versed in the individual and collective pursuit of their interests than industrial workers, and tended to be more deferential soldiers – were greatly underrepresented among deserters. They opted instead for self-mutilation as a means to escape military service. It is also notable that 85 per cent of the men charged with desertion were single. This clearly demonstrates that family ties were a major obstacle to desertion.[121]

The military psychiatrists did, however, cite one motive that was specific to desertion and fits into the pattern described here. They write that soldiers already facing punishment for a lesser transgression, such as overstaying their leave or absenting themselves for a short time, were particularly likely to desert.[122] Disciplinary measures or looming court-martial proceedings evidently encouraged soldiers to contemplate the next step – desertion – with its more dramatic consequences.[123] Other factors, too, either prompted or contributed to the decision to desert. Homesickness figured as a motive for Alsatian defectors in particular. For Dominik Richert, it provided the final trigger for his desertion in July 1918 – an idea he had been pondering since the end of 1917.[124] In many cases, the dreadful quality of food and shortages of supplies appears to have prompted desertion.[125] A further motive came in the ever more apparent class injustices of wartime society. The burdens and spoils of war were divided highly unevenly. The resentment this could create is illustrated by the self-assured letter of farewell written by the infantryman Adolf Armbrust. The letter, written shortly before Armbrust escaped to the Netherlands in late 1917, is a rare testimony from a soldier for whom desertion was an overt civic act, a termination of the social contract on which military service was based.

> According to these words [by Wilhelm II], parties no longer exist, only Germans. But has that been the case during this war? The cleavage among the people has never been greater nor more ruthlessly apparent than precisely during the war. Has not every poor man the same right to exist as the members of the financially better-off circles? This is certainly true from a so-called humanitarian view. But where is a sense of humanity and equal rights to be found among the upper strata of the people? Nowhere, from my point of view. If the working people in particular were in possession of their undisputed right to maintain their existence and livelihood, the differences between the classes would be much diminished. Most pronounced is the difference between rich and poor in the army. Does an ordinary soldier here have any right which he is capable of defending? No, there are only duties and more duties. And why is that? And for what reasons are all the rights of the common soldier disregarded? There will probably never be a clear answer to this question, which I am not the only one to ask. Why did they impose such terrible sacrifices and heavy burdens on the humbler people during the war? The answer will certainly be: on the grounds of defending the fatherland. But have all the countless blood sacrifices really been necessary to come to the point we have reached today? Is the success that has been achieved substantial enough to ease the sufferings and privations, not to mention all the losses? We, the members of the working people, are supposed to be happy with the explanations they have given to us. Hopefully, this futile murdering will come to an end soon: Hence, I personally did only what every 'free German citizen' is entitled to do. I took the justified liberty of doing what I did and will remain at liberty in future. When somebody asks me: 'But what if everybody acted like that, what would happen with Germany?' I answer: Why don't they stop the murdering, which is so futile and such a great offence against the lower strata of the people? According to the official army regulations I have committed a criminal offence; according to my own consideration I have not. I have thrown off oppression and freed myself. I will also take care that I stay free.

By the time you receive these lines, I will be over the Dutch border and will remain there after the war, too. I do not feel like receiving a severe punishment after the long years in which they have already violently taken away my rights. Sincerely, Adolf Armbrust.[126]

The small number of soldiers who deserted for overtly political reasons were a final special case. These were radical left-wing USPD members and supporters of the Spartacus Group. From 1917, Spartacus Group members began to support a variety of initiatives against the war, including fraternization with enemy soldiers. In 1915, Karl Liebknecht, the co-founder of the left-radical Spartacus Group, had still rejected desertion as a means of pursuing anti-militarist ends.[127] In Braunschweig, the Spartacus Youth assisted deserters by providing falsified papers. Members of the Spartacus Group found hiding places with their comrades in Berlin and other cities or, like Wilhelm Pieck (1876–1960), who later became the first president of the GDR in 1949, fled to the Netherlands.[128] It was in that country that the radical left-wing USPD politician Carl Minster came into contact with an association named Freie Arbeiter (Free Workers), whose aim was to revolutionize the German workers by organizing deserters. Working from Amsterdam, Minster began to publish *Der Kampf* (The Struggle), a weekly newspaper. The publication was smuggled into Germany with other texts and distributed among soldiers.[129]

## IV The desertion of Alsace-Lorrainers and Poles

With the rate of desertion running particularly high among the national minorities, the military authorities responded with vigorous attempts to bring the situation under control. This chain of action and reaction emerged from the very outset of the war as men with Polish ancestry (mainly from West Prussia) sought to evade the draft. Meanwhile, a publication in Alsace reported that as many as 3,000 Alsace-Lorrainers had fled to France. At the start of the conflict, the Deputy General Command of the 15th Army Corps in Strasburg counted 6,292 Alsatian conscientious objectors in its area alone.[130] From the very first weeks of the campaign, army commands began to receive numerous reports of defections by soldiers from Alsace-Lorraine, often en masse. Therefore, on 15 March 1915, the Prussian War Ministry issued a secret order. All army high commands were to transfer Alsace-Lorrainers who appeared 'dangerously unreliable' to four specified deputy general commands in Germany. These would then arrange for the men to be redeployed on the Eastern Front. The army soon extended the measure to other men who, though not from Alsace-Lorraine, were considered untrustworthy 'on account of their business or family ties to France'.[131] These policies meant that from spring 1915, most Alsatians fought on the Eastern Front against Russia. A series of army corps initially refrained from implementing the measure, but soon relented after further incidents of defection by Alsace-Lorrainers.[132]

However, these measures still did not enable the military authorities to solve the problem of Alsatian deserters. In fact, the redeployment to the east appears to have made matters worse. With its greater length and lower intensity of fire, soldiers found the Eastern Front an easier place to defect.[133] The Catholic military chaplain Karl Lang, who was posted to the 11th Bavarian Infantry Division, recalls in his war memoirs that an Evangelical divisional clergyman requested he visit a regiment in Koworsk in February 1917. There, he was to stand in for the absent Catholic priest and provide pastoral support to an Alsatian soldier. Philipp – or Philippe, Lang's spelling varies – had been sentenced to death for desertion. Lang writes a perceptive and moving description of the ritual of execution, which deserves quoting in full:

> The officer reads the sentence by lamplight. I watch the scene from outside through the low window. At the end, he is asked to sign the verdict. He refuses. Crying and broken, he stammers: 'I don't deserve that.' Then back to the dugout. We make the final arrangements. I dictate him a farewell letter to his parents. He gives me 80 Reichsmarks in gold to send to his parents. Then we pray before the Blessed Sacrament [the consecrated host in the monstrance], which I had rested against a ledge inside a folder. This is the altar.... Then they bring him civilian clothes to put on. Only his soldier's cap remains. At 6.15 [am] we leave the dugout.... Into the wagon. I climb in first, Philipp after me. A soldier with a loaded rifle on the box with the driver.... Driving snow, we travel at a gallop. Philipp rests his head on my lap like a child. I sit him up as best I can. We drive like this for half an hour. Then, stop! We get out. A whole company of soldiers is standing there, as if on a field march. All of them from Alsace. The idea is to deter them [from deserting]. As soon as I get out with the poor man, a loud voice shouts: 'Here comes the traitor!' It is the regiment commander. As I walk past him with Philippe, the commander whispers in my ear: 'Be quick, Father! One has children oneself, you know!' 'As far as I am concerned, it will be quick.' There on the railway embankment, a freshly peeled pole stuck in the ground. Behind it the coffin. They tie him to the pole. He does not want to be tied. I cajole him to let them tie him for Christ's sake. Now he lets it happen.... They remove his cap to make him look like a man without honour.... Now I hear the commander of the execution squad counting quietly – 1, 2, 3. The crack of eight shots, eight

bullets fell the man to the ground. I say a few words, we say the Lord's Prayer; then, on behalf of the executed man, I have to tell his superiors that he repented his deeds and asked for forgiveness. On the way back to the cemetery, the court officer tells me: We know that 10 per cent of the men we execute are in fact innocent, but we have to be this strict because otherwise we could not continue the war. Philipp was buried away from the soldiers' graves. His final words were: 'My poor parents.'[134]

Lang's description is insightful in several respects. It is notable that the commander ordered that the execution should take place in the presence of an entire company of Alsatians so as to deter other potential deserters. This was not for want of alternative measures to combat desertion. The army's attempts to control the problem included restricting the deployment of Alsatians to the rear area, permitting them to act as sentries or join patrols only in the company of 'German' soldiers, and ultimately removing Alsatian troops from sentry duty altogether. Lang's testimony is therefore an important indication that some units in the east believed these alternatives to be insufficiently effective.[135]

Even more significant is the indication that it was routine practice in this division to execute Alsatian deserters convicted by court martial. Research on the numbers of death sentences in the German wartime army typically cites a 1929 report prepared for the Reichstag's parliamentary committee of investigation by Erich Otto Volkmann, a former major employed by the Reich Archive. Lang compiled his memoirs in 1935, probably on the basis of notes made during the war. There is no reason to doubt the credibility of his account. His description of the execution suggests that it is time for a fundamental reappraisal of Volkmann's figures. According to Volkmann, only 150 death sentences were passed in the German army, of which forty-eight were carried out. Volkmann attributed just forty-nine death sentences and eighteen actual executions to cases of desertion.[136] However, he had a clear motive for understating the number of death sentences carried out. In so doing, he made the German military justice system appear far more humane than its British counterpart. Historians, too, have repeatedly contrasted the German military's relatively lenient handling of the death penalty with the practice in the British Expeditionary Force. The latter executed no fewer than 269 deserters in an army only half the size.[137] However, if the testimony of the Catholic priest is correct, this comparison lacks all basis.[138]

Finally, Karl Lang's testimony offers us a third important insight into the way the German wartime army carried out death sentences. Lang writes that Philipp was buried 'away from the soldiers' graves'. The execution of the deserter in the name of *raison d'état*, the good of the state, was thus followed by his symbolic exclusion from the community of soldiers. In this respect, too, the practice of execution in the German army appears to have been much closer to that of the British army than research has so far acknowledged. Britain sometimes used anonymous graves to bury men executed for desertion.[139] In Germany, however, it seems that the army limited this symbolic exclusion to soldiers from national minorities.

However, there is no dispute about the lack of success of all efforts to deter desertion by Alsatian soldiers in the east. In January 1918, the authorities reversed all the previous decrees and transferred the men back to the 'difficult fighting conditions' on the Western Front. This decision was prompted by the concern that the Alsace-Lorrainers on the quieter Eastern Front were effectively being 'rewarded' for their treacherous nature.[140] Cases of defection and desertion continued to occur in large numbers following the soldiers' return to the west.[141] Of the 800 soldiers from Alsace-Lorraine in the 77th Reserve Division, twenty-three defected to the enemy in the course of the summer. In the 10th Landwehr Division, seventeen Alsatians who had been transferred from the east openly stated that they did not want to fight French troops.[142]

The military authorities did not take such decisive action in the case of soldiers of Polish or Danish stock as they had with the Alsace-Lorrainers.[143] In as early as 1915, various command staffs in the field registered their concern that Polish troops were often defecting to the French, sometimes in large groups. They attributed this to specially targeted French propaganda material designed to encourage Poles to desert. A number of deserters with Polish backgrounds also joined the French army.[144] Allied intelligence units held information dating from 1915–18 on various divisions on the Western Front with a high proportion of Polish soldiers, 'who were generally ready to desert when they had a chance'. These included the 3rd, 12th and 19th Reserve Divisions.[145]

The General Command of the 5th Army Corps, which was severely affected by such incidents and had between 500 and 950 Polish soldiers in each of its regiments, requested that, insofar as possible, the recruiting authorities in Germany should 'no longer send soldiers of Polish nationality'. Initially, the request was met. Two decrees by the Prussian War Ministry in January and February 1915 had evidently ruled out transferring Poles to the Eastern Front. Following the army's intake of recruits in 1915, however, it was no longer considered possible to exempt certain units from receiving Polish soldiers. The units on the Western Front were therefore to exchange Poles between one another to achieve a more even distribution.[146] Various divisions took up this proposal over the following year.[147] In addition to these measures, the Prussian

War Ministry began in late 1915 to train Polish recruits in garrisons outside their home province. This served to remove them from their familiar environment. The policy was repealed for troops from Upper Silesia following an intervention by the Prussian Interior Ministry. This followed various reports suggesting that Poles from Upper Silesia had largely proven their loyalty, unlike those from Poznan and West Prussia.[148]

In the case of the Alsace-Lorrainers, the military authorities' reports were steeped in mistrust. Erich Otto Volkmann, who served as a divisional General Staff Officer during the war, later admitted that officers' unjustified mistrust of the Alsatians in peacetime turned into an 'extraordinary irritation' in the initial months of the war. It is likely that in many cases – it is impossible today to know how many – commanders swiftly deemed missing Alsace-Lorrainers to be defectors despite a lack of further evidence.[149] Such assumptions were not entirely without foundation, however. Reliable Allied intelligence reports confirm that soldiers from national minorities were indeed proportionately far more likely to defect to the enemy than other troops.[150]

In the case of the Poles, the army saw 'two highly confident nationalisms collide'. This conflict was a product of the Prussian army's long-standing 'ruthless and arrogant' policy towards this particular national minority.[151] A letter written in July 1915 by the Deputy Commanding General in Stettin, Hermann von Vietinghoff, provides an insight into senior Prussian officers' perception of the Poles. Writing to pass on news of the unreliability of Polish troops, to whose 'cowardice' he attributed the death of 'good German NCOs and soldiers', he concluded with the following assessment:

> The seriousness of the situation is unmistakable, as is the fact that it holds great danger for Germanness (*Deutschtum*) and the fatherland. However, the greatest danger lies not in the matter itself so much as in the way the government treats it. Weakness and indulging Polishness will never win gratitude, but simply heighten the danger.[152]

The willingness of soldiers from national minorities to desert resulted primarily from Germany's aggressive policy towards its national minorities and minority languages. The state's approach compromised the willingness felt, particularly by Alsatians, to integrate into German society and normalize their position within Imperial Germany. The arrogance towards minorities shown particularly by the Prussian military was capable of destroying any feelings of loyalty that may have arisen towards the Prussian-German nation state. The Zabern Affair at the end of 1913, in which a young army lieutenant in the garrison town of Zabern in

Alsace had verbally abused civilians and was subsequently protected by the army leadership, demonstrated this clearly.[153]

The discrimination and bullying of Alsace-Lorrainers followed seamlessly from the tendencies that the Zabern Affair had revealed. It meant that the Alsace-Lorrainers developed an even greater war-weariness than the army at large, making them more willing to desert. Calling Alsatians by defamatory names such as 'Wackes', assigning them the most unpopular tasks, and engaging in other forms of everyday discrimination was the norm in both the field and replacement armies.[154] Many lower-ranking commanding officers saw the censorship directed at Alsatians' letters as a vindication of such behaviour and carte blanche for it to continue. Eventually, in August 1917, the Prussian War Ministry felt compelled to issue a decree to rein in the worst excesses of its own policy.[155] Polish troops, too, were on the receiving end of discriminatory remarks.[156]

In March 1915, the Prussian War Ministry issued a particularly oppressive directive. It suggested that the military authorities ban soldiers from speaking French, not only when on duty, as had evidently already been the case, but even in private conversations, too.[157] Some units used the same measures against soldiers of Polish origin. Reading the order aloud to his men, one officer added, 'We are the German military; we are Prussians, not Polaks'.[158] This measure, along with rules forbidding the use of Polish in soldiers' letters to their relatives, was the subject of an interpellation in the Reichstag.[159]

The military authorities also issued decrees that banned Alsace-Lorrainers from positions of trust, such as batman or headquarters orderly, and restricted home leave. This followed incidents in 1916, when troops on leave in the district of Ober-Elsass had fled to Switzerland. A series of cases in which soldiers had defected immediately after taking in leave in Alsace-Lorraine fed the suspicions of the Supreme Commander in the East and of the Army Supreme Command that many desertions could be 'traced back to systematic manipulation at home'.[160] In February 1917, Erich Ludendorff responded by returning to an idea that had already been considered two months earlier. He called on the Imperial Chancellor to take the relatives of defectors from Alsace-Lorraine into protective custody. The State Secretary of the Reich Interior Karl Helfferich and the Prussian War Ministry both rejected this proposal, however. Given the 'already agitated mood concerning the imposition of protective custody' in Alsace-Lorraine, Helfferich feared the impact 'domestically and abroad of highly unwelcome discussions in the Reichstag'. He also believed it misguided to apply this measure only against Alsace-Lorrainers. A recent report had suggested that the Danes and Poles, who were deserting just as frequently, had probably also responded to persuasion from their relatives.¹⁶¹ Despite its failure, this plan by the Army Supreme Command reveals that the influential military cited the links – both new and historical – between the Alsace-Lorrainers and the French army so as to justify particularly harsh measures.

Continuing discrimination by the military only increased the willingness of Alsatian and Polish soldiers to desert.¹⁶² It is likely that the majority of them were also seeking to escape the dangers on the front, as a letter from November 1916 suggests:

> I am doing what I can to save my life, just like you. What should I care about Germany? We aren't Germans and we are treated as French; if only our homeland stays as it is now then everything will be fine.¹⁶³

A minority of the Poles and Alsace-Lorrainers defected to the enemy with motives other than to escape the violence of war. These were deserters who, like some regular POWs, were willing to join the French army. The French gave them privileged status, housing them in special prison camps with better treatment and food. They also paid the men a wage.¹⁶⁴ For the German military authorities, who kept detailed lists of the 'preferential' or 'traitors' camps' established in France for all three national minorities, being assigned to such an institution was sufficient grounds for suspicion of treason and an investigation.¹⁶⁵

After reporting for duty in the French army – a process that was usually voluntary but sometimes involved compulsion – the men were handed new names and identity papers and assured that they would not have to fight against German troops. These soldiers initially served only in the rear area, in Africa and at Gallipoli. However, they were soon forced to fight on the Western Front in the French offensives in Champagne and especially at Verdun.¹⁶⁶ Alsatian defectors and prisoners in the hands of the Russians were also transported to France, provided they declared themselves willing. The alternative was to end up in a camp far to the east in Asian Russia.¹⁶⁷ The Russian authorities handed over 2,639 Alsatian-Lorrainers in the period up to September 1917 alone. It is impossible to say how many were defectors and how many regular POWs. By the end of the war, the number exceeded 5,000.¹⁶⁸

Defectors were no ordinary deserters in the eyes of the German military authorities. They were excluded from the amnesty of 1917 and emphatically denied any prospect of a pardon after the war. This was all the more so for those defectors who went on to serve in the French army. The Deputy General Command of the 10th Army Corps established a special central unit – the Obere Leitung in Sachen der Ermittlung deutscher Fahnenflüchtiger unter den

Kriegsgefangenen – to identify German defectors among French prisoners of war. It worked with painstaking precision and a sophisticated methodology to track down defectors who had served in the French army and ended up in German captivity. Its methods included monitoring all post and identifying soldiers with poor French language skills. Detective work in *Arbeitskommandos* (work details) caught soldiers arranging for their comrades to write letters for them in French. The unit identified fifty-six such defectors between the end of September 1917 and March 1918. It was aided in its mission by the French army's practice of clustering groups of these defectors in some of its regiments.[169]

## V  Conclusion

The men who deserted the German army in the First World War lacked any special qualities that would have marked them out as the heroes in a story about the subversion of power and violence. Deserters were in many respects completely 'ordinary soldiers'.[170] And yet it is also misleading to describe them as such, since this ignores their distinctiveness. They certainly lacked a shared social background. The deserters covered a wide variety of ages and professions. Most, however, were single. Many deserters were neither especially brave nor inventive in planning their escape. Some stumbled into desertion out of anger at an affront from a superior. Others simply took advantage of the easy opportunity to 'extend' their home leave in Switzerland. Nevertheless, the deserters of the First World War were individuals with a distinctive profile.

First of all, many of them belonged to the national minorities of Imperial Germany. The military authorities labelled the Alsace-Lorrainers and, to a lesser extent, the soldiers of Polish origin, as outsiders. This provided these troops with a sense of otherness that they shared with all deserters. The Alsace-Lorrainers comprised a substantial minority among the deserters. Precise figures as to their numbers are not available for the army as a whole. In the Albrecht Army Group, the proportion of Alsace-Lorrainers fluctuated between a fifth and a half of all deserters over the period from December 1917 to June 1918.[171] This despite the fact that they made up just 2 per cent of the total troop strength. Yet even deserters who did not belong to a national minority were also outsiders in the sense that they planned their desertion alone, keeping their intentions secret from their comrades. This did not change until the beginning of the 'hidden military strike' in July/August 1918. The Poles and Alsace-Lorrainers were only a small minority among the many shirkers and deserters in the final months of the war. By now, desertion was such a widespread, collective phenomenon that soldiers were prepared to speak openly about it.[172] In the final weeks of the war, deserters thus turned from outsiders into a mainstream current. In the focus on these final weeks, it should not be forgotten that the sharp rise in desertion had already triggered drastic action from the military authorities before June 1918. This included far higher numbers of executions than historians have previously assumed. Faced with the deserters' refusal to fight, the military, at least on the Eastern Front, sometimes saw no other solution than the violence of the execution squads.

6

# Disillusionment and Collective Exhaustion among German Soldiers on the Western Front: The Path to Revolution in 1918

1918 was a year of trauma for the Prussian-German officer corps. This stemmed not only from the military defeat itself, but also from another reality its members had never thought possible, at least not on such a massive scale: the shocking realization in the war's closing months that they were increasingly commanding an 'officer corps without troops'. Seeking to end the war on their own initiative, large numbers of ordinary soldiers had simply left the ranks. This was a trauma that would permeate the discussions of the interwar period on the shape and possibilities of future warfare. Like the immediate operational consequences of soldiers' 'hidden military strike' in 1918, these debates make it vividly clear that the attitudes, expectations and objectives of the German rank and file, and officers' ability to mobilize these troops during the final year of the war, had a significant influence on the military outcome.[1]

Alongside the initial military consequences, however, the perceptions and expectations of soldiers in 1918 also continued to shape events long after the armistice. Veterans of the front line entered the interwar period armed with a vast knowledge of warfare and wartime society that they had gathered during their time at the front and particularly during the final year of the conflict. This had, firstly, an impact on the ability of political and paramilitary groups to mobilize former soldiers after the war. Two manifestations of this were the sometimes difficult attempts to recruit volunteers for the Freikorps and the largely failed efforts to turn the Bavarian *Einwohnerwehren* (citizens' militias) into a counter-revolutionary intervention force.[2] A thread of continuity ran from soldiers' refusal to fight in the final months of the war to veterans' rejection of paramilitary violence in 1919. Moreover, the impressions of soldiers in the final months of the war had major implications for the various myths and legends that emerged from the war. The stab-in-the-back legend was a case in point. Particularly among former front-line soldiers, it by no means found unreserved acceptance.³

The primary source materials for analysing the opinions and attitudes of ordinary German soldiers on the Western Front in 1918 are the personal accounts of the men themselves, handed down mainly in the form of war diaries and field post letters. Private collections and government archives hold large numbers of such documents, many of which are still awaiting systematic study.⁴ Based on such material, we can draw relatively reliable conclusions about the soldiers' morale and their views on political and military matters. The reports of the military postal surveillance offices, which operated from spring 1916 at divisional and army high command level, are another useful source.⁵ These surveillance offices examined samples of the accumulating post and prepared summaries of the soldiers' views, citing numerous letters in the process. Their task was to provide a representative picture of opinion and inform the upper echelons of the military command of the troops' morale.⁶ The field post surveillance reports give us at least a rudimentary view of the prevalence of certain views within the army, to the extent that soldiers aired them openly. The consistency of the reports themselves and comparison with letters from the front held in major collections support the view that the reports' authors generally sought to give an objective portrayal.⁷

We can broadly distinguish two lines of argument in the historical analysis of German soldiers' changing attitudes during the final year of the war. The first goes back to a report presented by Martin Hobohm in 1929 to the Reichstag's parliamentary subcommittee on the 'causes of the German collapse in 1918'. This pioneering report is still of considerable historiographical interest today. Hobohm was a committed republican and pupil of the renowned Berlin military historian Hans Delbrück. Based on the records of the Prussian army still available at that time, his report described the rapidly growing resentment of the rank and file at the privileges enjoyed by officers, as well as the many other sources of grievance in the Wilhelmine 'class army', which he called a 'travesty [*Zerrbild*] of the class state'. Hobohm emphasized that the delegitimization of the state apparatus that followed from such moral acrimony also had repercussions for the military power apparatus.⁸ Expanding upon Hobohm's ideas, historians have emphasized how this mood was strongly infused in the minds of the majority of soldiers with criticism of the war and support for the political objectives of the Majority Social Democrats, especially from 1916 onwards. The rapidly increasing politicization of front-line soldiers and their active contribution to the November revolution is central to this perspective.⁹

Another reading centres, from the perspective of a history of experience, on the interplay between experiences and expectations, emphasizing the shifting and short-term nature of front-line soldiers' expectations. According to this view, expectations were rapidly superseded by experiences on the front line that either confirmed or negated them. The interplay between expectation and experience was therefore decisive in determining soldiers' morale.[10] This interpretation puts particular emphasis in the final year of the war on the rapid succession of events and soldiers' responses to them. It aims to gain as precise an understanding as possible of the changing objectives of the rank and file. The violent reality of war and the grievances accumulated over several years of life in the army still needed to be framed in the minds of soldiers. If collective action to bring an end to the war was envisaged, it had to be guided by clear expectations as to the outcome of the war.[11]

These two interpretative approaches are not mutually exclusive, but can in fact complement one another in helping us to understand the events of 1918. They are each able in different ways to unravel the tangle of contradictory motives and the conditions that constrained the course of soldiers' actions on the Western Front. However, their power to explain the events of the final year of the war depends crucially on a careful balance between both interpretative approaches. This chapter attempts to achieve this balance in exploring three important periods in January, March and July/August 1918, each of which saw radical changes in the expectations and attitudes of German soldiers on the Western Front.

In 1917, war weariness and the longing for peace reached an intensity and clarity unprecedented in the conflict which, up to that point, had lasted for three years. This manifested itself in soldiers' broad acceptance for the call by the Majority Social Democrats for an immediate peace 'without annexations and contributions'.[12] It was clear by the beginning of the peace negotiations on 22 December 1917 that Russia could no longer be counted among the opponents of the Central Powers. Among the soldiers hoping for imminent peace, this had far-reaching implications, altering their expectations as to which groups and events were most likely to bring the war to an end. This shift in outlook was fully revealed for the first time by the reaction of front-line soldiers to the January strike.

In late January 1918, almost a million German industrial workers – primarily in Berlin and other industrial heartlands – took part in an enormous strike movement. The mass industrial action was a severe blow for the Wilhelmine system of rule and, in many respects, a dress rehearsal for the November revolution.[13] On the front, however, the voices decisively rejecting the January strike far outweighed those in favour. This was true even among soldiers who agreed, in principle, with the strikers' calls for peace and their objective of reshaping and democratizing the government of the *Reich*. There were various reasons for the relatively unanimous rejection of the strike by those on the front line, which contrasted with the more sympathetic views of the replacement army stationed in Germany.[14] Soldiers compared their own material situation and food shortages with the conditions enjoyed by the workers recalled to the factories in Germany, which they believed to be much better. They also feared that the authorities would meet the strikers' demand for increased bread rations by making cuts at the front. Troops therefore responded by demanding that the authorities conscript all recalled workers into front-line service immediately. They extended this call to all members of the annexationist Vaterlandspartei, which soldiers had regarded as the party of the *Reklamierten* (the recalled workers) since its founding in 1917.[15] More important than the concerns about rations, however, was the conviction that, far from shortening the war, the strike would significantly prolong it by as much as six months. This expectation arose partly from the fear that the sheer size of the protest movement would strengthen the confidence of the Entente Powers and their determination to defeat Germany. It was also driven by a growing certainty among soldiers from late autumn 1917 that the resolution on the Eastern Front in the spring would be followed by a German attack on the Western Front, aiming to end the war with a rapid, definitive victory. At this point, the majority of front-line soldiers thus no longer placed their hopes for peace in social democrats, but in a successful offensive in the West.[16]

In the soldiers' view, the strike action now threatened this objective. A determined antipathy towards the *Radaubrüder* (rowdy yobs) at home – as the strikers were usually called by soldiers on the front – therefore emerged, expressed by one soldier as follows:

> There's one thing we have to thank these bastards in Berlin for: the war will go on for half a year longer at least. You can't imagine the furious rage here from all and sundry about these rascals and womenfolk, for that's exactly what they are. If we'd been put there with our heavy artillery, I reckon our lads would have fired at them with pleasure.[17]

Soldiers who read about the strike in letters from their wives replied with somewhat more restrained criticism of the industrial action. By contrast, another letter commented that the troops on the front would simply 'gun the red brothers down in cold blood' given the chance.[18] In the words of one soldier:

I think it will be quite a spectacle when it [the spring offensive] starts. This time Michel will make a good job of it and will smash everything that stands in the way. If only the idiots at home hadn't stabbed us in the back with the strike. Such a\*\*holes![19]

In soldiers' war letters in the wake of the January strike, then, we already encounter the aggressive imagery that would form part of the repertoire of the stab-in-the-back myth's proponents after the war. Significantly, the stab in the back was closely associated in popular perception with the home front, a place that connoted weakness and femininity. This was a development prefigured by some soldiers' perceptions of women's participation in the industrial workforce during the war and by the measures taken by civil and military authorities against 'whining letters' from soldiers' wives.[20] While the deep emotional chasm now opening between soldiers at the front and workers at home did not maintain the same form and intensity right through to the end of the war, the responses to the January strike show that soldiers were, on the whole, no more willing to endorse revolutionary sentiments in the army than they were to express a fundamental opposition to war. The soldiers who openly declared their allegiance to the USPD, the Independent Social Democrats who had split from the majority wing in April 1917, were a significant exception to this. Meanwhile, in the wake of the strike, supporters of the Majority Social Democrats even expressed support for the arrest of USPD Reichstag deputy Wilhelm Dittmann for attempted treason, arguing that before the fight for people's rights at home, the 'external enemies of our fatherland' first had to be vanquished.[21]

In their reactions to the January strike, soldiers metaphorically contrasted the qualities of decisiveness, strong will and order on the front line with the supposed dissolution, chaos and moral decline at home. Some letters went even further, already indicating a desire, which would become prevalent among many Germans during the Weimar Republic, for the intervention of a strong leader, a longing for decisive action to tackle mounting social and political problems unhindered by rules of procedure, the instituted order or party strife:[22]

> After four years of war, people can think of nothing better to do each day than set up new parties or arrange strike meetings. The madness of social democracy, this terrible global disease, is sprouting new buds – although hardly anyone knows what they want. Discord, hate and weakness everywhere. Nothing is missing more than a strong hand that acts ruthlessly and determinedly, a Bismarck. Don't think I'm ranting about it; no, at most I just regret it. Maybe it's

good that this is the way things are, so that people can see and realize how beautiful life is, how pathetic they are themselves, ready for bankruptcy.[23]

Although a large majority of front-line soldiers sided with those opposing the war in 1918, it should not be overlooked that the January strike and, later, the looming defeat, also triggered a radicalization of the language and views of those soldiers who fundamentally supported the war or at least felt an emotional duty to the Wilhelmine nation state.

Many of the rank and file had a relatively clear idea of the impending campaign in the West, which was generally regarded as the best way to bring a rapid end to the war. Troop movements, the suspension of postal services and cancellation of leave were a clear indication that larger-scale operations were planned. Among some soldiers, there was even detailed speculation about the probable time and place.[24] This further raised the optimism with which troops awaited the attacks. Among a significant proportion of the men, the expectation that Germany would soon be on the offensive again unleashed aggressive demonstrations of enmity towards the French and British even before the action began. The jingoism with which soldiers expressed their readiness for the coming 'battle of the titans' reached a scale and intensity rarely seen since 1915. Organizational preparations for the campaign instilled the troops with 'boundless confidence'. All this meant that hopes for a rapid German victory were widespread.[25] On the other hand, as Martin Hobohm has rightly pointed out, the optimistic mood of these days and weeks of preparation, and the military campaign that followed, already carried an air of desperation.[26] 'It will and must succeed', commented one soldier, capturing the tension and awareness that what followed would be decisive.[27]

The second important turning point of 1918 was the beginning of the German offensive on 21 March. This had a substantial impact in terms of troop motivation. The days immediately before and after its launch saw soldiers display an unusual enthusiasm for battle, and comparisons with the 'spirit of 1914' were frequently drawn. At least in the initial days and weeks of the attack, this boost in morale appears to have also reached those troops not directly involved in 'Operation Michael' of the 2nd, 17th and 18th Armies.[28] The soldiers' widespread determination and willingness to go on the attack was a major factor behind the considerable initial successes of the German troops, and one that cannot be relativized as merely a product of the army command's propaganda efforts. In any case, soldiers' collective rejection of military propaganda – the so-called *Vaterländischer Unterricht* (patriotic instruction) – relented for a time in the course of the campaign, making way for a degree of acceptance.[29]

This 'enthusiasm for war', which was commonplace at the front in March and April 1918, but soon began steadily to decline again in the weeks and months that followed, was an authentic expression of the widespread hope among soldiers that the final push would see them 'return home soon'.[30] The powerful mobilizing effect of peace, which now seemed achievable, is especially striking given soldiers' broad disenchantment with the war as recently as 1917. Anticipation of an imminent end to the conflict unleashed new energy. It also encouraged soldiers to repress thoughts of the grievances of army life that had accumulated over the past three and a half years. As one lance corporal remarked on 7 March, a few days before the campaign began, 'all the hardships suffered in the last two years of the war were forgotten', since 'everyone' had 'just one objective in mind: get the job done first, then rest'.[31]

At least two other important factors bolstered soldiers' optimism over these weeks and months. First, the much-improved food rations received by the troops involved in the offensive.[32] These were supplemented by the substantial Allied food supplies that fell into the troops' hands during the initial days and weeks of the offensive, lending the campaign the air of full-scale organized looting. Given the importance of food to soldiers' morale and the experiences of hunger that pervaded wartime society, this was a considerable contrast to the previous years of the war. On the other hand, plundering Allied supplies also provided a sobering insight into the material superiority of the enemy troops.[33]

Second, the switch to mobile warfare after years of stalemate in the trenches also had a motivating effect. Given the high turnover and considerable losses of rank-and-file soldiers since autumn 1914, the majority of the men were experiencing this form of fighting for the first time. Over the years, soldiers had adapted to the oppressive conditions of trench warfare as far as humanly possible. They had done their best to improve the situation, for example with the widespread practice of informal ceasefires and ritualized shooting. Compared with the stagnation of the trenches, which had made any thoughts of an imminent end to the war appear absurdly unrealistic, the offensive strategy now initially seemed a far more acceptable form of warfare and unleashed new energies:

> This 'forward' every day has an encouraging and stimulating effect on the soldier's mind, dulled by the all-too-long years of trench warfare, for it raises new hopes that the return to mobile warfare could bring the final decision, the much-longed for return to one's *Heimat* [homeland], to one's dear family, to familiar, peaceful work. And this wonderful award, beckoning full of promise from far away, strengthens body and soul and makes the unsettled and disorderly life here with the perennial images of hardship, sorrow and worry easier to bear.[34]

It is also notable that the war diaries of the young lieutenant Ernst Jünger (see Chapter 4) describe his feelings of bloodlust precisely in the context of the 1918 March offensive. With his extreme readiness for violence, Jünger was certainly no average soldier, still less so in the final year of the war. However, he was not the only soldier in spring 1918 to reflect on how his weapons gave him *Aktionsmacht* (Popitz), the ability to exercise power through concrete acts of human agency. The machine gunners, whose weaponry 'most effectively embodied the industrialized and engineered means of killing', were especially prone to such thoughts. Firing up to 600 shots a minute, these devices could not only take aim at individual soldiers, but were capable of blanketing entire combat zones with fire.[35] This particular form of *Aktionsmacht* also involved a degree of ambivalence, as the following excerpt from a machine gunner's letter reveals. As well as offering an effective means of killing enemy soldiers, the machine guns made the troops operating them vulnerable to concentrated enemy fire:

> It can all easily go wrong, for when they discover a machine gun position, they let loose on us with all their weapons, since the machine guns are really terrible weapons. One wouldn't know until experiencing the impact of such a weapon working at full power while lying behind it. The whole work takes place on the ground – mainly these thirty seconds of the most fabulous work and rushing until the machine gun is in position and ready to fire – and then the handicraft of murder starts. It must be a very strange feeling to lie behind a machine gun shooting at infantry troops moving forward. One can see them coming and directs this terrible hail against them.[36]

The flipside of soldiers' high expectations soon revealed itself, however, when the phase of mobile warfare came to an end 'as if it were a dream' and the German advance became bogged down.[37] The initial German offensive was abandoned as early as 4 April 1918. It was followed by further German attacks, which ultimately turned into a retreat from early August until the end of the war.[38] This switch from the offensive to the defensive from August onwards rapidly changed the attitudes of German soldiers.

Only a small number of far-sighted observers of the morale among the troops had foreseen the likelihood that such widespread hopes of a quick and decisive victory would be disappointed, or the dramatic consequences such disillusionment could bring. Heinrich Aufderstrasse, a Social Democrat and member of the Alter Verband, the Social Democratic miners' 'Free Trade Union' (Freigewerkschaftlicher Bergarbeiterverband), was one of them. In a letter from the Western Front on 1 May 1918, he predicted the events of the final months of the war with a lucidity and precision worth quoting at length:

> Now this is how I imagine peace, if nothing unexpected turns up: Ludendorff and Co. have done a great service to these developments, but in terms of their own plans a very dubious service in bringing the army and the people over the last months to believe confidently in a great unconditional victory. Today, 80 per cent count on the 'certain and complete success of our weapons in the West'. The present victory frenzy is almost comparable with that during the first months of the war. That is the case here and that will probably be the case at home, too, as far as I can see from the newspapers.... Ludendorff and Co. cannot do otherwise. If they do not force through a victory, what then??? Let us assume the following: the next offensive operations will bring success but not a resolution. After some months, everybody is out of breath and it all stops, stops. But as sure as fate there will be a hangover as big as Michel's current victory frenzy, which has been artificially stimulated to the highest degree. The realization will follow that one cannot force through a complete victory. Then – in July or August, maybe a bit earlier or later – the time will come for the supporters of a negotiated peace. Even today, only patriotic airheads believe in the success of the submarine war. How do Ludendorff and Co. then plan to reassure people, when all believable options to achieve victory are gone? Then Scheidemann and Erzberger will have the most fertile ground.... As far as I am concerned, there is still a slight possibility of Ludendorf[f] succeeding, but I rather reckon there will be a dead spot after some months.... I understand and have accepted that I have to wait here for the rest of the war. But I am not disheartened, for by my calculation the slaughtering will be over in the foreseeable future, in autumn at the latest.[39]

Aufderstrasse's predictions were to come true, right down to the imagined time frame. The beginning of the retreat in August robbed the overwhelming majority of soldiers of their 'last hope' of a successful end to the war. From this time on, they were convinced that defeat was inevitable. At various points along the Western Front, the rank and file had already stopped believing even some weeks before August that the ongoing offensives could force victory.[40] Now, in the final months of the war from August 1918, the large majority of soldiers came to terms with the impending defeat. In many cases, this was not only because they were forced to do so, but because they were convinced of the historical justification for this outcome. Only defeat, they believed, could bring the longed-for peace.[41] This sudden swing in opinion was a direct consequence of the great faith invested in the offensive, which had now proven misplaced.

From this point on, the majority of soldiers were no longer interested in the terms of the armistice, that is, the territorial or political conditions on which it would be based. Instead, their main concern was simply the timing. The troops hoped to see the war end as quickly as possible and to escape injury in the final months of the conflict. Many thus came to terms with the loss of Alsace-Lorraine as an essential condition for peace.[42] Alongside voices that decisively rejected the American 'dictate', many others placed their hopes for a quick peace in US President Wilson.[43] Meanwhile, few reacted with positive expectations to the pronouncements of the Central Powers. This is evident from the comments on the Austrian peace note of 14 September, for example, which the majority of German troops dismissed as a crude manoeuvre to support the publicity for the ninth war loan. 'Peace at any price' is now being 'vehemently demanded' noted a report by the 5th Army's postal surveillance office as its most important observation.[44]

After a year of extreme swings in morale and rapidly changing expectations, German soldiers had largely come to terms with the military defeat by the autumn. As we have seen, there is substantial evidence to suggest that the force of this shift from high expectation to grave disappointment was a major factor in the mobilization and subsequent demobilization of German soldiers on the Western Front in the final year of the war. This was also the conclusion reached by the army doctor Eugen Neter, who described the 'mental collapse of the German battle front' in a detailed 1925 study.[45] Awareness of the social inequality and continuing injustices of the military and wartime society was an essential contributing factor to the actions of soldiers who submitted passively to defeat in autumn 1918 or actively absconded from the front line. But it did not fully explain them. It is also questionable whether the 'revolutionary politicization' of a majority of front-line soldiers really was the driving force behind their political objectives and strategies for refusing to fight in the final months of the war.[46] At least five other factors also played a part.

First, a hope that Prussian-German society would change once the war was over. Although it only found rather limited and imprecise expression, this was a desire that nevertheless carried identifiable political implications. The most important of these was the widespread conviction that the German monarchies in the *Reich* and individual states, including the Emperor himself, had squandered all entitlement to power, not least with their endorsement of overambitious war objectives. The form of government that the majority of soldiers on the Western and Eastern Fronts were hoping for in autumn 1918 was, without doubt, a republic.[47] Many also certainly desired steps towards democratization and greater participation for large swathes of the population, for example through the abolition of the Prussian three-class franchise.[48] This attitude gained credence not least from a deep disillusionment with the vested interests of Imperial Germany's civilian and military elites and particularly with the annexationist positions pursued by them. In autumn 1918, soldiers with otherwise very different (party-)political affinities could identify with the view that the Germans were a 'poor people, wrongly led by a military caste without conscience' and that the 'dominance of the Alldeutschen' – the ultra-nationalist Pan-German League – had to be broken. It should not be overlooked that some on the front welcomed the parliamentarization of the *Reich* government under Prince Max von Baden as an important step in the right direction. This development may in fact have held some soldiers back from developing more radical expectations.[49]

A second genuinely political desire was the general longing for a return to the peaceful norms of civil society. This was in no small part a product of the various ways in which the military had deprived soldiers of their basic rights and liberties such as free speech during the war.[50] The strength of this desire is particularly evident from letters sent by soldiers in the final months of the war, which do not hold back in their descriptions of grievances and hopes for peace, despite the oppressive censorship regime. One soldier even declared his yearning to be freed from this 'Prussian prison'.[51] It is no coincidence that this hope was often tied to social democracy, the only party political movement to have preserved at least remnants of a critical discourse on the war. In August 1918, for example, one soldier wrote:

> For me, there is only one thing that could come to the rescue now: the war ends this year and one can speak freely again, for as long as one is dressed as a slave, one may not speak the truth; although even everybody who is not a soldier knows how people are oppressed, the war has turned everyone into a social democrat.[52]

It must, however, be emphasized, that these expectations were not usually linked explicitly to Social Democratic political objectives or even shaped by them in any identifiable way.[53] Social Democratic demands in the form of the Scheidemann peace had found a high degree of acceptance among the troops in 1917, which reached far beyond the supporters and voters of the SPD themselves. By 1918, however, this had become irrelevant. Peace was now expected to emerge not from the initiatives of political players in the Central Powers, but primarily from the destruction of the *Reich*'s military capacities. Where radical left-wing positions found resonance in autumn 1918, it is likely that this also represented an endorsement of those who had long warned against placing too much hope in a military resolution to the conflict.[54] Large social groups among the troops did not share the social democratic viewpoint familiar to workers since before the onset of war, which interpreted the social grievances and injustices of the military apparatus in terms of the division and opposition of different social classes. Soldiers from rural farming backgrounds in the Catholic regions of the *Reich*, for instance, tended instead to interpret the social order and disorder within the army in line with Catholic social teaching. For them, excessive social inequality was first and foremost a symptom of moral decay.[55]

Thirdly, it should not be overlooked that it was precisely the organized supporters of the Majority Social Democrats who often strongly advocated military discipline, vehemently opposing spontaneous moves by soldiers to abscond from front-line troops. This was a position they continued to uphold even in the final days of the war. One soldier and union member wrote on 1 November 1918 of his hope that an armistice would come 'before the army collapses'.[56] This was an attitude rooted in the strict organizational discipline long instilled in Social Democrats by their party. From this perspective, fulfilling one's duty was a virtue in itself, and spontaneous insubordination could not be condoned. This applied to Social Democrats at home in Germany and those on the front in equal measure.[57] A politically aware, active contribution to the revolutionizing of troops on the Western Front thus probably came only from the minority of soldiers who were USPD supporters.

The fourth factor influencing many soldiers' expectations of the future in summer and autumn 1918 was the vague sense that the prevailing moral, political and economic values that had seemed so unshakeable in the pre-war era were now crumbling away. It is almost impossible to compare the prevalence of this viewpoint across soldiers from different social backgrounds with any degree of certainty. However, there is good reason to suspect that such pessimism was most likely to reside among those from bourgeois and petit-bourgeois families. In their letters, these soldiers often emphasized the rising inflation and immense public spending of the war effort, highlighting the impending bankruptcy of the state and the risks to their own financial means:

> In the space of five years, the Prussians have got me to the point that I'm completely indifferent as to the terms on which we have to make peace. Just so long as it happens soon. As far as I'm concerned, they can declare national bankruptcy, too. That way we'll all just start again from scratch.

> Difficult times are coming for Germany as it's doubtful whether peace will still take hold now. Honour is lost, everything is lost. If only I knew how I could rescue my fortune, for hard cash will probably be lost.[58]

Remarks such as these were certainly not the product of pro-revolutionary attitudes in the German army, even though the soldiers making them were convinced, just like the political left, that military defeat was inevitable. By emphasizing the devaluation of the existing order across broad spheres of society, they instead reflected a sense of confusion at a world that seemed to have been turned upside down, upended by the failure of the monarchical state and the erosion of the value of money.[59] In the pessimism and resignation that reigned in the war's closing months, the 'many victories' achieved and 'sacrifices' made by the German army in four years of war now appeared 'worthless'. For the soldiers repelled by the extreme positions of annexationist nationalism, nothing positive could now result from the war. The exhausted troops simply wanted it to end:

> We don't care how it happens. It only matters to the Vaterlandspartei and the Alldeutschen.
> The people just want out of this misery; it doesn't matter what happens, just peace. I don't know what to do apart from throw it all in; I just can't take any more.[60]

This brings us to the fifth and final consideration: the physical and psychological state of German troops on the Western Front in the final months of the war. This is crucially important to any assessment of soldiers' morale and motivations during this period. From summer 1918 onwards, soldiers wrote of 'war weariness' that had reached 'a degree that can hardly be increased any further' and of a 'feeling of absolute impotence faced with all these events'.[61] The physical exhaustion of the troops worn down by continuous fighting since the spring also had enormous psychological consequences that revealed themselves in resigned and fatalistic comments of this nature. From August, increasing numbers of officers recognized their troops' desperate need for rest, describing soldiers in realistic terms as 'jaded', 'battle weary' and 'run down'.[62] Flu infections had been rife since the summer, rendering the hundreds of thousands of soldiers affected 'completely apathetic'.[63]

The fatigue of rank-and-file soldiers, the growing losses and especially the high numbers of lightly wounded men, the lack of supplies for the retreating troops and the perceptible superiority of the enemy in terms of equipment and manpower all reinforced the fatalism and hopelessness of many soldiers and their willingness to resign themselves to defeat. This, too, suggests that soldiers' efforts to keep themselves alive were a far more important motivation for their actions in the final weeks of the war than any active revolutionary movement among the field army.[64] For the most part, then, it was not revolutionary politics so much as disappointed expectations and collective exhaustion that drove the collapse of the German army's system of command on the Western Front in autumn 1918. The mass movement of front-line soldiers was first and foremost a 'peace movement', whose attitudes were comparable with those prevalent among large spheres of the population outside the industrial working class. The declaration of armistice – and thus the achievement of a goal that constituted the lowest common denominator of all the tendencies and views within the field army – was already sufficient to throw the movement's internal coherence back into question. From then on, the 'diverging domestic political and social demands returned to the fore'.[65] It remains for future research to throw further light on how the expectations and mentality of front-line soldiers responded to the process of demobilization and partial radicalization in the revolutionary transition phase that lasted into spring 1919.[66] This is an issue only touched upon by studies in the 1970s, which rightly concentrated first of all on the political make-up and decisions of the *Rätebewegung* (movement of soldiers and workers councils). It would be valuable to more closely examine the views and expectations of soldiers in the replacement army, whom we can correctly regard as the real drivers of the uprising in the military in autumn 1918. As we have seen, soldiers' willingness to escalate violence – which was evident in their response to the January strike and later during the March offensive – was just as prevalent in the final year of war as their refusal to continue the violent combat. Although the latter phenomenon far outweighed the former in autumn 1918, we should not ignore the differences and ambivalences in soldiers' expectations for the future or the often rather diffuse sentiments that characterized their outlook.

7

# The German Army in Autumn 1918: A Hidden Military Strike?

In 1986, the military historian Wilhelm Deist (1930–2003), one of the foremost authorities on German military history in the Wilhelmine era, wrote an article entitled 'The military collapse of the German Empire: The Reality Behind the Stab-in-the-Back Myth'.[1] In this short text originally published in a relatively obscure volume, Deist put forward a completely new interpretation of events in the German army on the Western Front in the weeks and months leading up to the armistice on 11 November 1918.[2] Deist's core thesis, indicated in the second part of his title, tackled the infamous stab-in-the-back legend of the 1920s, which claimed that the socialist workers at home had betrayed the army on the front, preventing what would have been certain victory. For Deist, the stab-in-the-back was not so much a legend as a deliberate falsification of history that held no 'reality' at all, a myth propagated primarily by former officers of the wartime army to obscure their own responsibility for the defeat.[3]

Deist's reinterpretation of the events of 1918 focuses on the mass absconding of rank-and-file soldiers. This began to have an impact by mid-July 1918, and, once autumn came, had entirely undermined the Western Army's fighting power. Deist describes soldiers' efforts to avoid front-line action from July 1918 as a 'covert strike', drawing an analogy to the mass movements of workers who took industrial action in their hundreds of thousands in April 1917 and again in January 1918 to improve their material circumstances and bring a swift end to the war. Just like the strike by the industrial workers at home, writes Deist, this hidden strike by the soldiers of the field army 'began with the far-reaching loss of authority by the established powers'. Unlike in the factories, however, the 'rules of military discipline kept spontaneous action within narrow bounds'.[4] Deist himself thus indicates that his 'strike' metaphor is primarily intended for heuristic purposes and is not necessarily to be understood in a literal sense. After all, the 'striking' troops on the Western Front never followed self-pronounced ringleaders, let alone official strike committees or representatives.⁵ Deist therefore describes the military strike as a mass movement of individuals who, in the final months of the war, all acted on their own initiative to seek their way back to the safety of home.

## I  The hidden military strike as a mass movement of soldiers

Deist attributes the mass flight of soldiers to the worsening morale and material situation of the troops (see Chapter 6). He also postulates that the 'only aim of the refusal... was an end to the war'. Even so, the strike was a 'political' movement in the sense that it represented a direct 'answer to the politically motivated actions of Ludendorff and the military leadership', who had gambled all their cards on a risky offensive strategy in the West.⁶ Deist describes the hidden military strike not as an open rebellion, but as a creeping withdrawal from the front that escalated into mass absence without leave. He points to the many 'walking wounded and slightly sick' in the Western Army in the summer and autumn, growing numbers of whom chose to disobey their orders and make their way home on foot or by hospital train. These and many other healthy soldiers who absconded from their divisions were participating in a practice described by the military authorities in 1918 as *Drückbergerei* (shirking).⁷ Seeking to estimate the extent of this phenomenon, Deist draws upon calculations dating back to the 1920s by a former staff officer, Erich Otto Volkmann. Having conducted research in the Reich Archive, Volkmann summarized his findings in a report for the parliamentary committee on the 'causes of the German collapse'. His figures put the number of 'shirkers' in the final months of the war, from the beginning of the German retreat in August, in the region of 750,000 to one million men. Given the numbers of slightly wounded and the conditions in the rear area of operations, Deist finds Volkmann's estimate 'in no way excessive'. Faced with a movement on this enormous scale, he writes, 'the military command was helpless'. In effect, the German army on the Western Front thus steadily disintegrated in the months leading up to the armistice. By the autumn, wrote Ludwig Beck, who served in 1918 in the command of the Deutscher Kronprinz Army Group, the front resembled 'a spider's web of fighters'. (Beck was Chief of the General Staff of the Army from 1935 and later became one of the 20 July conspirators in 1944.) The hidden strike also had wider implications away from the front, adds Deist. The collapse of the Western Army was a fundamental prerequisite for the success of the revolution that began with the Kiel Mutiny by sailors in the German navy and quickly spread to soldiers in the replacement army on German territory.[8]

The historical significance and explosive impact of Deist's 1986 article were difficult to overlook. In just a few short pages, he had outlined one of the largest mass movements in modern German history and revealed something of fundamental importance to the history of Imperial Germany: the *Reich* had fallen neither to the enemy's superior military force nor to the supposed 'stab in the back' claimed by the nationalists, but had simply collapsed militarily from within, its own soldiers abandoning it in the final months of the war to ensure their survival. In the face of the defeat that had been looming since July 1918, the troops were no longer willing to put their own lives on the line.[9] Deist later returned to the 'hidden military strike' in a 1992 essay, apparently wanting to ensure the plausibility of the thesis he had put forward in 1986. Here, he reinforces and elaborates upon his arguments using additional sources, particularly the regimental histories published in large numbers in the 1920s. When read against the grain, these regimental histories offer considerable evidence of the scale of war-weariness and collective disobedience prevalent in late summer 1918. They also contain extensive reference to the extreme lack of fire power of units on the Western Front in the weeks leading up to the official surrender. Some regiments that had numbered more than 3,000 non-commissioned officers and soldiers at the start of the war had been worn down to just 200 or even 120 men in the line of battle.[10]

## II  The arguments of the critics: An 'ordered surrender'?

Wilhelm Deist's description of a 'covert strike' in late summer and autumn 1918 quickly found the approval of many historians of the First World War, and particularly those interested in the morale and political attitudes of soldiers on the Western Front.[11] Others, however, expressed fundamental criticism, albeit not until some time later. In 2008, the British historian Alexander Watson published perhaps the most vehement rejection of Deist's narrative in a comparative study of the fighting morale of German and British troops.[12] In essence, Watson's critique is based on two interlinked lines of reasoning.

Firstly, Watson casts doubt upon the empirical evidence for the motives, and indeed the very existence of large numbers of 'shirkers' in the rear area of operations supposedly streaming in uncontrolled fashion back towards home from July and August 1918. In the second part of his argument, Watson then argues that German soldiers on the Western Front in 1918 in fact chose to surrender en masse. In the final three months of the war, writes Watson, no fewer than 186,053 German soldiers were taken prisoner on the section of the Western Front held by the British Expeditionary Force (BEF) alone. The large majority of them, he claims, gave themselves up 'without resistance'. This compares to just 142,117 Germans taken prisoner by the BEF over the four previous years. Overall, some 385,000 German soldiers surrendered on the Western Front between 18 July 1918 and the armistice on 11 November.[13] Wilhelm Deist, for his part, was fully aware of the large number of German soldiers taken prisoner in the final stages of the war. However, he regarded it as another manifestation of the Western Army's irrevocable disintegration that he analysed primarily in the context of the 'shirkers' in the rear area of operations. Based on 1920s calculations, Deist estimated that some 340,000 German soldiers were missing or imprisoned on the Western Front between 18 July and the armistice.[14] This figure is not far removed from the 385,000 cited by Watson.[15]

Watson, however, is not content to interpret the large numbers of German prisoners as an expression of a dramatic fall in fighting morale beginning in late summer 1918. For one thing, he highlights the contribution of Allied propaganda in ensuring that German soldiers were more willing to lay down their weapons and give themselves up to the enemy in autumn 1918 than at any point in the war up to that time.[16] The Allies had been carrying out mass leaflet drops over German lines since the summer, extolling the amenities of life in captivity in bright colours and calling on soldiers to surrender with the password 'republic'.[17] However, Watson also describes another, more important explanation for the large number of German prisoners. In autumn 1918, he claims, army officers led their soldiers in large groups to capitulate in an orderly fashion. For Watson, the collapse of the German army on the Western Front was not the result of a hidden strike. The form taken by the troops' 'disintegration', he argues, was in fact 'foremost that of an ordered surrender'.[18]

At first glance, the discrepancy between these different explanations for the German collapse on the Western Front in 1918 may appear little more than a minor difference of opinion between historians. When we examine its (historical) political implications, however, the full significance becomes clear. The theory of a 'mass surrender led by junior officers' is directly connected to Watson's claim that the proponents of the stab-in-the-back legend had in fact been 'correct'. At the heart of the stab-in-the-back legend was the assertion that the field army, unlike the replacement army stationed on home territory, had never fallen into the hands of a 'revolution' or revolutionary mass movement in 1918. On the Western Front, writes Watson, 'soldiers did indeed follow their orders to the end'.[19] This raises an issue of enormous historical and historiographical relevance. If Watson's claim were correct, then it would lend at least partial truth to a historical legend that was central to the history of the Weimar Republic and aggressively defended by the far right. (It goes without saying that Watson by no means claims that revolutionaries at home had undermined the fighting spirit on the front – the second core component of the stab-in-the-back legend in its various versions.) The mass movement of German soldiers on the Western Front first highlighted by Wilhelm Deist in 1986 would be struck from the history books before it had even had a chance to fully establish itself.

Watson's idea of an 'ordered surrender' has found rapid acceptance among some First World War researchers, who regard this essentially untested theory as a more plausible explanation for the German collapse than the hidden military strike.[20] Yet there is little reason to concur with Watson that large groups of German soldiers were led to surrender by junior officers. The empirical evidence provided by Watson is flimsy at best. He points out that the German troops taken prisoner by British units in 1918 included many officers and that the ratio of officers to ordinary soldiers was similar to that found in the field army as a whole. In fact, however, this does not prove that these officers had actually 'led' their men to surrender,[21] merely that troop officers in 1918 were repeatedly ordered to accompany their units on the front line and lead by example, which simultaneously increased their risk of being taken prisoner. It is also an indication that by this late stage of the war, junior officers had lost motivation just like their battle-weary men.[22] Seeking to substantiate his argument, Watson also cites the war memoirs of a Canadian captain published in 1919. The Canadian describes how his unit took a large number of German soldiers prisoner in September 1918, most of whom had been hiding in dugouts. A German captain who had already surrendered had called upon the men in one dugout after another to give themselves up.[23]

It is true that there is no reason to doubt the veracity of this recollection. There are also plenty of indications that other, similar episodes may have taken place.[24] In the final stages of the war, the military authorities in the field did indeed suspect that officers might have had a hand in proceedings when large groups of soldiers or even entire units capitulated without struggle. This suspicion is illustrated by events in the 119th Infantry Division, for example, when parts of a regiment slipped completely from the grasp of its commanders under heavy enemy fire on 27 October. Many troops surrendered or defected and the 7th Company of I.R. 46 appears to have completely disintegrated. Following the day's events, the conduct of individual officers was 'investigated', although no 'cause for intervention' was found in this case.[25] There is no question that some officers chose to surrender in the final months of the war and that a number of them may even have led their men to do the same. The flaw in Watson's narrative, however, is that he presents only a single piece of detailed evidence to support it. This is insufficient to back up his conclusion that the form taken by the disintegration of the German army in autumn 1918 was 'foremost that of an ordered surrender'.[26] Given that the field army's actual strength on the Western Front in July 1918 amounted to 3.58 million men, it requires more than a lone source to underpin such a sweeping claim.[27] It is also worth noting that Watson's book also oversimplifies and even distorts Deist's argument.[28] Thus, this chapter will now turn to the controversial question of 'shirking' at the heart of the hidden strike and subject it to a more detailed examination.

Before tackling the question of how many soldiers were involved in such actions, it is important first to examine the options available to front-line troops seeking to evade action in the final months of the war. Fully aware of the limitations of the term 'shirking', Deist pointed out that soldiers sought and found 'a variety' of ways of avoiding service on the front line that are 'not now capable of reconstruction'.[29] Notwithstanding Deist's scepticism, one aim of this chapter is to contribute to exactly such a reconstruction with the aid of the files in the Kriegsarchiv in Munich. As in every study of the German army in the First World War, it has been necessary here to compensate for the loss of archive material on the Prussian army and Army Supreme Command using the written records of other contingents of the German army. The materials used therefore primarily relate to Bavarian divisions and army high commands and to the Heeresgruppe Kronprinz Rupprecht (the army group of Crown Prince Rupprecht of Bavaria).

## III What was 'shirking'?

Before beginning to reconstruct the German collapse on the Western Front, it is helpful first to examine the terminology used by the military authorities themselves to describe the phenomenon Deist calls the 'covert strike'. This terminological analysis also reveals the practical problems confronting the army's attempts to tackle the practices and behaviour described. The units in the field often referred to *unerlaubte Entfernung* (absence without leave), a legal term defined in the Military Penal Code. This described a soldier's deliberate absence from his unit or his failure to rejoin it after becoming separated in battle. 'Serious' absence without leave was defined as a soldier's failure to return to his unit within three days.[30] The High Command of the 6th Army addressed this issue for the first time in an order sent to its divisions and other units on 24 June 1918. This demanded detailed measures 'for the prevention of absence without leave' and raised the associated problem of 'marauding'.[31] The use of this archaic term implies that, by this stage, the authorities' concern was not only that soldiers were absenting themselves for short periods, but that they were often lurking around behind the front for considerably longer than three days and committing other disciplinary offences at the same time. Significantly, the 6th Army's 24 June order not only mentioned 'absence without leave', but sought to clarify another term, too:

> The term '*Versprengter*' [straggler] must be defined as closely as possible. In *Stellungskrieg* [trench warfare], it only applies to persons returning from leave or from commando operations whose unit has moved on and is no longer to be found in the same place. Persons moving from the front to an information point without identity papers are thus generally to be regarded and treated as '*Drückeberger*' [shirkers]. Disciplinary punishment should be sought in the event that there is no punishment for absence without leave.[32]

Neither the term 'shirker' nor 'straggler' was sufficiently established or defined in military law, which was certainly one reason why the 6th Army High Command chose to put both these words in inverted commas in the original German. However, it is abundantly clear why the High Command felt it necessary to distinguish between the two phenomena. 'Stragglers' were those soldiers – rarely encountered by June 1918 – who were actively and willingly attempting to return to their unit. 'Shirkers', on the other hand, were defined in formal terms as all soldiers roving around in the area behind the front without being in possession of military identity papers authorizing their presence there. In effect, the term covered the growing number of those actively seeking under all manner of pretexts to avoid returning to their units. Despite this strict distinction, the 6th Army generally favoured disciplinary action against the shirkers by their immediate superiors rather than full court-martial proceedings. This was evidently for the practical reason that a military tribunal for (serious) absence without leave would have committed considerable time and resources and prevented the accused's return to the front line indefinitely.

The 6th Army High Command's distinction in June 1918 between shirkers and stragglers also found similar use by other military authorities.[33] However, the proposed measures for responding to these phenomena began to take an increasingly hard line. The General Command of the XXVI Reserve Corps, for example, ordered on 15 October under the heading 'Dealing with Shirkers' that 'all stragglers unable to properly justify their absence' were to be immediately 'arrested'. Any resistance was 'to be overcome ruthlessly with the use of weapons'.[34] Nevertheless, the authorities in the field appear initially to have retained a formal distinction between 'shirkers' and 'deserters', and were not prepared automatically to apply the latter category to all soldiers encountered in the rear area of operations without the correct identity papers. This is indicated, for example, by the 6th Army High Command's June 1918 order quoted above, which stated that granting a 'reprieve' was not appropriate treatment for either 'deserters' or 'shirkers'.[35] The official language evidently still being applied in autumn 1918 reserved the term 'deserter', as defined in military law, for soldiers moving directly and purposefully from the battle line to the rear area of operations. On 18 October, for example, the 4th Army High Command reported that 'numerous deserters' were moving 'rearwards, especially to Ghent' because of 'inadequately secured boundaries in the Leie-Hermann position'.[36]

On 5 November, however, in the final days before the armistice, the Prussian War Ministry issued a directive that dramatically widened the definition of 'shirking', turning it into a collective term for a host of serious disciplinary offences, despite the fact that these all had their own clear definitions in the Military Penal Code:

> The present situation of the war is demanding the most drastic action against the so-called shirking (absence without leave, desertion, cowardice, self-mutilation, endangering the military in the field, insubordination in order to evade battle).[37]

The use of the term 'shirking' in this context illustrates that, at least in some quarters, it had now become a catch-all expression for all possible forms of soldiers' refusal to fight during the hidden strike. With this exception in the final days of the war, however, it was by no means true, as Watson claims, that 'shirking' was a vague concept that could include 'anything from laziness to permanently decamping'.[38] In fact, the military authorities on the Western Front had a relatively clear definition of the term 'shirker': a soldier found in the rear area of operations or rear area (*Etappe*) who was not in possession of military papers authorizing his presence and who was evidently seeking to avoid service on the front line for as long as possible.

## IV Escape routes

Having clarified the terminology, the next step is to examine which soldiers were moving around in the rear area of operations without authorization and how they were able to do so. How was it possible, in late summer and autumn 1918, for them to remain undetected for periods of days, weeks or perhaps even months? One clue to this lies in the *Versprengte* (stragglers) mentioned in the orders from army high commands. The intensifying action and resumption of mobile warfare following the German army's spring offensive quickly led increasing numbers of soldiers to become separated from their units as the combat field grew in size. In response, the 4th Army issued a directive on 27 April concerning the 'return of stragglers' to their respective units.[39] One problem, it noted, was that the 'disappearance of people' remained 'unnoticed for extended periods' and searches for those missing were therefore often only initiated with considerable delay.[40]

As we have seen from the directives issued in June, however, the problem soon involved more than just these genuine 'stragglers'. In fact, there are some indications that a growing phenomenon of 'shirking' began to emerge even before the summer. In a diary entry dated 26/27 April, Albrecht von Thaer, who until a few days earlier had been Chief of the General Staff of the IX Reserve Corps, noted a 'general increase in shirking'.[41] This took place against the backdrop of a rapidly rising number of soldiers who were either walking wounded or sick in the wake of the German offensives that began in March. Data from the German army's *Sanitätsbericht* (official medical report), which is generally considered a highly reliable source, is available up to August 1918. This puts the number of soldiers sick or wounded but still able to walk at just under one million for the period from March to July alone.[42] These men are likely to have made up the largest group of 'shirkers' to be found in the rear area of operations and Belgian rear area.

A second major group of 'shirkers' comprised the rapidly growing numbers of soldiers absconding from troop trains carrying them from Germany to the front. In late May, the Kronprinz Rupprecht Army Group was forced to report that 'increasing' numbers of non-commissioned officers and rank-and-file soldiers were going absent without leave or committing other disciplinary offences during the journey.[43] Following detailed investigations, the Army Group notified the Army Supreme Command at the end of June that 'some transports' were reaching their destination missing '20 per cent' of the men they had departed with.[44] In October, a Landwehr lieutenant responsible for a troop transport from the training ground at Warthelager near Posen – nowadays the Polish city of Poznan – to the Western Front reported an even graver loss of manpower: of the 230 NCOs and ordinary soldiers who had originally boarded the train, just 147 had arrived at journey's end. The division affected noted that 'the majority' of the soldiers who had left en route in Belgium had certainly done so 'intentionally' and did not plan to report for duty.[45] The large majority of 'shirkers' on the troop trains to the Western Front had already served on the front line earlier in the war and were being returned to battle following injury or a posting elsewhere. Army authorities in the field cited the 'long duration of the war' and 'fear of the dangers of life on the front' as the primary reasons for shirking.[46] The aim of survival thus clearly emerges as the core motivation behind the hidden strike.

## V    Patrols and raids

How were the 'shirkers' able to absent themselves from their front-line units for so long and find shelter in the rear area of operations or rear area? The relevant orders from the command authorities in the field provide us at least some clues. They also reveal that by early summer 1918, the growing scale of such shirking meant that this was an extremely pressing question for the military itself. Army high commands ordered that every soldier apprehended 'without satisfactory ID' was to be questioned by a military prosecutor on 'where he had been since his escape, what he had lived off, where he had slept' and if he had already been 'stopped by the police' at an earlier stage.[47] To escape detection by the numerous checkpoints and patrols within the rear area of operations, on the roads in and out, and in towns and railway stations, shirkers obtained forged identity papers. Already in late April, the Army Supreme Command noted that 'a vast number of soldiers both with and without forged IDs are hanging around on the railways' waiting to 'get home across the border' using fake identity papers. Sedan and other towns in the rear area had a 'flourishing trade' in forged military IDs available from tear-off pads for between three and twenty Marks.[48]

Even without fake identity papers, it was still possible for soldiers to elude capture by the network of control posts manned by the military police and civilian police. Complaints came in the spring that the older Landsturm soldiers sent to guard stations were being extremely negligent in their duties and that it had been 'proven' that soldiers were 'evading platform barriers and checks' to board trains home.[49] In July, the Army Supreme Command felt compelled to declare once again that 'checking' identity papers was the most important measure to 'control the increase in absence without leave' and 'prevent deserters milling around behind the front and at home'.[50] Increasing numbers of ordinary soldiers had evidently succeeded in reaching Germany by obtaining forged identity papers or evading checks at the station. In August, the 214th Infantry

Division noted that such individuals had 'repeatedly' reported themselves to their home unit in Germany, claiming to have been 'separated from their troop', and had then been granted home leave on top' of their existing absence.⁵¹ To make themselves harder to identify, other soldiers covered the epaulettes indicating their army corps and regiment number. The authorities responded by banning this practice, although to what extent this was successful remains an open question.⁵²

As the retreat and heavy battles continued into the autumn, the number of soldiers absconding from the front line and making their way through the rear area of operations to the rear area continued to grow. One problem for the military command was that the frequent engagements and troop movements often resulted in soldiers' absence going 'unnoticed for a long time'. In the summer, the field police intensified its events to prevent such shirking. It visited *Soldatenheime* – soldiers' homes established some distance behind the front to help the troops relax – and performed identity checks. Such duties, the 6th Army High Command noted, were only to be performed by 'tactful individuals' so as not to upset those there legitimately. Roads leading rearwards away from the front were routinely closed to individual soldiers. In addition, the field police now introduced 'mobile traffic patrols' where rivers or canals helped to form a natural barrier.⁵³ There were ways around even these measures, however, as soldiers obtained forged identity papers or hitched a ride with trucks or convoys. In mid-October, to prevent 'shirkers crossing the blockade', a Bavarian army corps ordered routine searches of all trucks coming from the front. Drivers carrying unauthorized passengers were to be reported immediately for court-martial proceedings.⁵⁴ Finally, it is likely that many soldiers attempted to find their way around the blockades and patrols under cover of night. The numbers reaching the rear area through the rear area of operations continued to increase into the autumn.

Once soldiers arrived in the *Etappe* (rear area), they then had various opportunities for evading the military control apparatus not just for a matter of days, but for periods of weeks or months. 'Extensive protection for shirkers' existed in the French town of St. Quentin, for example. Apparently aware that many soldiers were hiding there unbeknown to the residents, a Bavarian army corps ordered a 'thorough search of the houses and particularly the cellars' to take place on 14 September. Twenty military policemen, twenty private soldiers from two divisions and two companies of a Landsturm battalion conducted the operation under the command of four officers. Even after this raid was completed, both companies remained in St. Quentin to prevent shirkers hiding in the town again, and all 'side roads and entrances' in the town not used by army traffic were blocked with barbed wire.[55]

This one-off action evidently failed to deliver anything like the decisive success desired. Just a few days later on 19 September, the army corps therefore ordered that such searches must take place 'repeatedly' and 'systematically'. It also took measures to better seal off and monitor the rear area in the corps sector. This included setting up a blockade manned by sentries at the rear of the front area and intensifying checks on road traffic. In the area controlled by the 6th Army High Command, setting up checkpoints at 'important locations' in towns and villages, as had been the practice since June, would no longer suffice; instead, patrols were to monitor the 'entire road network'. 'Areas in between' such routes were 'to be scoured for shirkers as often as possible by patrols on horseback'.[56] This was an open admission that many soldiers had evaded detection by avoiding the roads and making their escape from the front via tracks and open country.

It is clear from these reports and countermeasures that by summer 1918, substantial numbers of soldiers were absconding from the front line and moving into the rear area of operations and onward to the rear area. Many soldiers had already made it home, either using forged identity papers or, in more extreme cases, by working in large groups to storm trains carrying lightly wounded soldiers and direct them back to Germany to their own timetable.[57] In October, the most significant change in the hidden strike since the summer appears to have been the increasing number of soldiers involved. Late that month, a Bavarian infantry regiment commander forced on an odyssey from one information point to the next in search of his troops reported seeing 'masses of soldiers looking for their units' in the city of Mons. He was only too aware, however, of the large numbers of the 'unwilling' who had no intention of finding their unit. Given the general lack of organization in the rear area of operations and the overstretched information points, he concluded resignedly, these individuals would have no difficulty 'roaming around for weeks behind the front'.[58] Such men could obtain food and drink not only from businesses in the Belgian and French rear areas, but also from the army itself. This led the authorities to issue decrees against the widespread practice in many army kitchens of feeding unfamiliar soldiers or even offering them accommodation.[59] Belgian and French inhabitants of the occupied territories also sheltered many of the so-called 'shirkers'.[60] In the course of October, the number of soldiers leaving the front by train and 'particularly on foot along the roads back towards the city of Brussels' appears to have risen.[61] This indicates that blocking roads with sentries in the rear area of operations had by now lost all effectiveness in the face of the growing volume of shirking.

## VI The chronology of the military strike

The chronology of the reports and official orders we have seen above on the measures used to combat 'shirking' already provide us with a relatively clear picture of the sequence of events between spring and autumn 1918. The increase in absence without leave began in April and May in the wake of the repeated German offensives. By the end of June, the number of soldiers who had no intention of returning to their front-line units had risen considerably. By July, some 8,500 military personnel were arriving unauthorized in the Charleville *Etappenkommandantur* (rear area sub-command) each day, unable to provide a valid reason for their presence.[62] With the beginning of the German retreat in August, shirking developed into a mass phenomenon. It may be accurate to say that a 'truly comprehensive disintegration of command authority' on the front did not take place until 'the very last weeks of the war' after 3 October, when the German government under Prince Max von Baden requested discussions with the Allies on an armistice on the basis of Wilson's Fourteen Points.[63] However, it should be remembered that the military apparatus only disintegrated so comprehensively in October because its effectiveness had already been declining at an increasing pace since June.

This chronology is further corroborated by a series of decrees from the Prussian War Ministry that enjoined the authorities in the field to make extensive and ruthless use of disciplinary measures and court-martial proceedings. The last of these, notable for the definition of 'shirking' we cited above, was issued on 5 November just a few days before the armistice. Here, the Ministry described it as a matter 'of specific importance that the military police units not only in the area of operations, but also in the *Etappe* and the other occupied areas are most accurately informed about these authorizations [to impose punishments and use weapons in case of danger] in order to be able to take drastic action against those who are in breach of their duty and roaming behind the front'.[64] This was a relatively unveiled reference to the reality of the military strike as a mass movement. 'Leaving the position against orders' was one of the examples of misconduct for which the 5 November decree explicitly urged superiors to make use of their weapons to enforce obedience. This is further evidence, then, that the hidden strike originated with soldiers on the front.[65] It is also important to note that the 5 November decree was only the last in a long series explicitly mentioned by the Prussian War Ministry. The first such edict was issued on 22 July, which is an additional indication that the hidden strike began in summer 1918.[66]

Front-line soldiers numbering in their thousands and, before long, in their tens of thousands and more, began to move to the rear area of operations from late summer 1918, intending to avoid a return to their units for as long as possible. The blocking and patrolling of roads leading to the rear area of operations was powerless to stop this movement, as was tighter surveillance of towns and cities in the rear area. In September, the Army Supreme Command ordered a further measure aimed at controlling and containing the hidden strike. Military units in the field from the divisional level upwards were to establish *Versprengten-Sammelstellen*, 'assembly points for stragglers'. For the group commands, armies and army groups, these were to consist of 'basic', 'solidly built facilities'.[67] Essentially, as the Kronprinz Rupprecht Army Group explained, these were 'hutted camps'.[68]

A number of armies had already established such collection points in the summer. The practices of these facilities make it clear that their real task was not to help genuine stragglers attempting to return to their units as quickly as possible, but to round up all non-commissioned officers and rank-and-file soldiers arrested after being found 'without satisfactory identity papers'. The individuals brought to these institutions against their will were 'not to be permitted to leave the collection point under any circumstances' and were normally only transferred elsewhere 'under guard'.[69] The military authorities thus used the *Versprengten-Sammelstellen* to capture the soldiers described as 'shirkers' since the spring. The authorities in the field explicitly sought not to give these facilities the 'appearance of prison camps', advising, for example, that the use of barbed wire be avoided.[70] In reality, however, this was exactly what they were: temporary prisons for incarcerating soldiers actively participating in the hidden strike. Given the dramatic decline in fighting strength of the field regiments in September and October, the *Versprengten-Sammelstellen* also had another practical purpose, namely, to return shirkers captured by the military authorities back to their front-line units. To assist in this process, the military made use of one of the most remarkable train services in the German railways' all too extensive history of facilitating organized violence: the 'Lier (near Antwerp)–Colmar military local train 1801/1802'. The timetable shows a daily train in each direction from around 20 October 1918. Travelling south-eastwards from the town of Lier near the coast of northern Belgium all the way to Colmar in Alsace, the train linked the armies at each end of the Western Front. At each calling point, it collected 'stragglers' from the local *Versprengten-Sammelstelle* before dropping them off at their destination along the route. Each of these trains was intended to carry 1,000 men, enabling the service to return up to an estimated 40,000 soldiers to their units in the final weeks before the armistice on 11 November.[71]

## VII  Quantifying levels of 'shirking'

This brings us to the most difficult and disputed aspect of any examination of the hidden strike: quantifying its extent. It is impossible to determine the numbers of soldiers who absconded from duty and made their way to the rear area of operations or even all the way back to Germany with any precision. Wilhelm Deist made use of an estimate by Erich Otto Volkmann of the Reich Archive, who put the number at between 750,000 and one million. Volkmann's report for the Reichstag, in which he published this figure in 1929, was a direct response to criticism of the military by the republican historian Martin Hobohm, who largely blamed the collapse on the Wilhelmine elites and especially the officers. This meant that Volkmann had an interest in emphasizing and exaggerating the responsibility of individual soldiers.[72] A closer analysis reveals that Volkmann's figures did indeed rely on a highly questionable arithmetical shortcut. Taking Hobohm's estimate of approximately 300,000 shirkers, Volkmann simply doubled the number, adding a generous margin for those who had only temporarily left the front line.[73] This approach cannot constitute a reliable method of 'calculation'.

This does not mean, however, that the scale of 'shirking' suggested by Volkmann should be rejected out of hand. Alexander Watson infers from the high number of prisoners and soldiers giving themselves up voluntarily between July and November that there were only 'very few deserters or "shirkers" escaping rearwards'.[74] Such a conclusion is neither justified nor backed up by the sources. The 3rd Army's wanted lists for deserters provide evidence that contradicts Watson's claim. These lists contain the names not of soldiers who were thought to be 'stragglers' or who were expected to return to the ranks after a period of 'shirking', but of those assumed by their units from the outset to have left permanently. From July, the 3rd Army added the names of one hundred new deserters to the wanted list each day, and this number continued to increase all the way into November. If we assume similar figures for each of the ten constituent armies in the Western Army, we arrive at an estimate of some 120,000 soldiers absconding from the front line between July and the armistice. Assuming a degree of escalation towards the end of the war, this figure could have reached as high as 185,000.[75]

Even this figure probably represents an absolute minimum estimate of the number of soldiers leaving their unit to move rearwards from July until the armistice. To obtain a realistic picture of the Western Army's disintegration, however, we also need to consider absolute troop numbers. Deist put the number of men actually fighting on the Western Front in the German field army in July 1918 at 3.58 million.[76] Given the dwindling number of reserve troops and large losses, we can assume that this figure fell dramatically in the months that followed. On the basis of the last official figures available on the number of losses (soldiers killed in action, missing, taken prisoner, injured or sick) for the months from May to August, Deist calculated that the Western Army's real strength declined sharply in the final three months of the war and amounted to no more than 2.6 million men by the time of the armistice.[77] Of particular importance is the fact that the number of men reported sick (more than 900,000 men from August until the armistice) far exceeded the numbers wounded, killed in action or taken prisoner. It was these soldiers, together with the walking wounded, who were most likely to participate in the hidden strike as 'shirkers'.

Reports sent in October by a number of divisions in the Kronprinz Rupprecht Army Group give a further illustration of the enormous scale of the hidden strike. These describe the fighting strength of the army group's regiments.[78] The 8th Infantry Division provides a particularly dramatic example. On 27 October, the division reported that the 'remains' of the 153rd Infantry Regiment had 'refused' to follow orders when instructed 'to take up position to relieve' another unit. Court-martial proceedings had been instigated but offered little prospect of resolving the situation given their long duration. The division commander, General Lieutenant Arthur Hamann, was convinced that 'a large number of the rank and file would go absent without leave' if his division was sent straight back to the front. 'Exhaustion, depression' and 'lack of cohesion' had 'shattered discipline' and reduced the division's effectiveness practically to zero. The commander was only too aware that he no longer had control of his troops. Even more dramatic than this admission, however, was the battalions' 'field strength', which Hamann reported to the army group command in writing and then again by telephone. With a field strength of 250 men at most, remarked Hamann, the actual 'fighting strength' on the front line was down to no more than 'thirty men'. The staff officer handling this report in the army group command on 28 October clearly struggled to comprehend the enormity of what he had been told.

Alongside Hamann's 'thirty men', he scribbled a handwritten note: 'pro Kp.?' (per company).[79] This was not what Hamann had meant. The effective fighting strength of thirty men did not refer to a single company, but to an entire battalion of four companies. With three battalions of three regiments each, calculated Hamann, the 'division's total fighting strength was 300 men at most'.[80] These were the paltry active remains of a fighting force that had numbered more than 12,000 men at the start of the war, whom US Army intelligence had ranked until that time, with the aid of data from the British and French, as a top-category ('A') unit, excellently suited to all offensive and defensive combat.[81]

## VIII  A strike outside the public gaze

The scribbled note by the staff officer leads us to a final point worthy of a brief discussion: the military leaders' perception of the hidden strike. Noting that the diaries of high-ranking army figures give no mention to mass absconding of soldiers, some historians have concluded that no such mass movement existed.[82] However, it is not entirely true that these written sources contain no evidence of the phenomenon, nor is it surprising that they do not give it greater attention. In fact, a series of high-ranking officers noted the army's disintegration relatively overtly, including Karl von Einem, Commander of the 3rd Army, and Albrecht von Thaer. Yet the general lack of such references should not surprise us. The failure to recognise the symptoms of the hidden strike was an important element of the collective denial with which aristocratic and bourgeois staff officers spared themselves from the truth of the military defeat.[83] Both leading officers and civilian politicians in Imperial Germany – the most prominent among them including Walther Rathenau – conducted a hectic and far-reaching debate in October 1918 on the need for a 'levée en masse', a total mobilization of the nation inspired by the Jacobin campaign of 1793 that had rescued the French nation from the counter-revolutionary forces. No small number of participants in this debate bought into the vision of a defensive struggle to be fought to the bitter end on German soil.[84] That the leaders of the German military apparatus should have engaged in such debates in autumn 1918 as the fighting troops crumbled before their eyes reveals the deep socio-cultural divide and dissociation that still existed within the army.

For Wilhelm Deist, the 'covert' nature of the strike did not refer to any lack of open protest by soldiers.[85] Evidence exists of plenty of instances when troops openly refused to carry out orders from their superiors, although these incidents pale into relative insignificance in the context of mass absconding from the front line. Rather, the strike was a hidden phenomenon in the sense that it developed practically 'in isolation from the general public'. Together with the deliberate misinformation of the public by the Army Supreme Command and the 'stab-in-the-back' mythology created in the aftermath of defeat, this meant that the actual circumstances and the true scale of the German field army's disintegration never became the subject of public debate.[86] One of only very few eye witnesses who would later go on to reflect on the extent and significance of the events in writing was Fritz Einert, whose unit was in action on the Western Front in 1918.[87] Writing in 1926, the Social Democrat and enthusiastic member of the socialist veterans' association Reichsbanner (see Chapter 8) from Schmalkalden, remembered his experiences in the Thuringian 71st Infantry Regiment:

> The long suffering of the war brought the men to despair and it was said many times that we would be willing to walk home even half naked if the war would finish at long last. From mid-1918 onwards it was over; everyone was completely shattered and tried as hard as possible to save his life after the long ordeal. Troops were hardly ever replaced, the [enemy] artillery became more terrifying by the minute, and the aircraft squadrons arrived in their droves. Whole divisions' worth of German soldiers were taken captive. Replacements who arrived at the front were totally exhausted and had already been shot to pieces; many were just a penny's worth and could hardly walk more than a few kilometres. The Americans went into battle in full marching columns. Thus, the end had to come if we should not totally collapse. Even before the armistice everyone was heading at full pace in a backward direction, sometimes six marching columns next to each other; nothing could stop this. The armistice was the hour of liberation from the yoke of the terrible sufferings and privations, but also from the yoke of Prussian militarism. If anyone claims that we could have battled on, this only goes to prove that he has seen absolutely nothing of the front line. Had the armistice not come – and the Army Supreme Command knew this full well – we would have been driven across the Rhine, and the Entente would have transformed our beautiful Rhineland into a wasteland, in order to make us feel the same suffering as those who lived in the occupied territory, since what the people living in the occupied territories of the enemy countries had to endure, those [Germans] who stayed at home do not know.[88]

It would be difficult to express more clearly the interplay between the various factors behind the hidden strike. War weariness turned into mass refusal to fight at precisely the moment when the Allies' superior manpower and fire power destroyed any hope that the Germans could bring a successful end to the war.

The mass capture of German prisoners of war, the complete lack of replacement troops fit for action and the soldiers streaming at 'full speed' away from the front were all part of one and the same process. This began not in October, but already in June. From mid-1918, the hidden strike continued to escalate until the armistice. The strikers' aim: 'to save their own lives if possible'. In the final weeks and months of the war, resistance to postpone the defeat was only provided by machine gun companies, whose deadly long-distance weaponry protected the German retreat.[89]

## IX Conclusion

Controversies among historians often have a somewhat self-referential nature. As this chapter has aimed to demonstrate, however, the findings of Wilhelm Deist and the arguments of his critics represent more than just a minor dispute between researchers. Up for debate is nothing less than a whole series of events that were of fundamental importance not only to the outcome of the First World War but also to the history of violence and the German military in the years up to 1945. The organizational approach taken by the Reichswehr and Wehrmacht after the war for the *Wehrhaftmachung* (military preparation) of the German population and armed forces emerged from the experience of the army's collapse on the Western Front in 1918. This in turn laid the foundations for the enormous mobilization of violence in the Second World War.[90]

It has not been possible within the scope of this chapter to offer a comprehensive picture of the hidden strike. Given the enormous size of the German field army on the Western Front, that would require analysis of records from other non-Prussian contingents of the German army, particularly those of Saxony and Württemberg. Only then would it be possible to answer some of the important questions that remain. For example, did officers responsible for troops and transports use or threaten to use their weapons to prevent soldiers from absconding either individually or in groups? There is nothing in what we know so far to suggest that they did so in significant numbers. This was despite the fact that important passages in directives issued by the Army Supreme Command and other command authorities had been pushing since July for all officers to be instructed 'repeatedly about their right and duty to use their weapons in order to enforce obedience to their orders in cases of urgent need and extreme danger'. This would usually apply to soldiers 'leaving the position against orders' – the mass phenomenon that constituted the hidden strike.[91]

It is not yet possible to say with certainty why officers in the field and rear area were seemingly unprepared to enforce obedience using their weapons, despite explicit orders from their commanders to do so.[92] It seems likely that, at some point, they sensed that this could easily provoke their troops into open mutiny and rebellion.[93] It is probably no coincidence that in August 1918, according to a letter from the Army Supreme Command, there were growing calls to bring back the punishment of *Anbinden* (tying-up) or 'Field Punishment no. 1' as it was known in the British army.[94] This was a particularly humiliating form of arrest, which involved tying soldiers to a tree for several hours a day within sight of their colleagues. After ongoing complaints and petitions by soldiers' relatives and members of the Reichstag, the army had abolished the practice in May 1917.[95] By summer 1918, however, it appears that many commanders in the field believed that by reinstating *Anbinden*, they could create an effective deterrent without risking an open rebellion by simply shooting down shirkers.

It further remains to be clarified whether the soldiers were also pursuing political objectives with the hidden strike. There are some indications that many of the rank and file in the field army and rear area in 1918 explicitly placed their hopes in the SPD both to push through a peace agreement and to contribute to an overdue democratization of politics and society. At the end of September, for example, the 3rd Army's rear area inspectorate (*Etappeninspektion*) concluded from its reports:

> Many people are placing their hopes in international social democracy, which they believe will be the only thing capable of bringing peace; they do not expect any success from diplomatic notes; official diplomacy is finished.[96]

Whatever the answer to this question, however, it appears that, with an end to the war imminent, the decision to 'shirk' was ultimately driven by the hope of reaching home unscathed. Soldiers' determination to survive and protect themselves from the destructive violence of war was the most important cause and the primary motivation behind the mass movement of German front-line soldiers in autumn 1918. There are broader reasons, too, why the hidden strike deserves at last to take a more prominent place in the history of the First World War. The mass flight of soldiers from the front was not attributable, as some have claimed, to an 'invisible hand of war' that limited 'death and destruction' and averted the most extreme excesses of violence as if by some natural process.[97] This is a misleading metaphor. Rather, the events of 1918 were the result of collective action by the soldiers, best summed up by Deist's preferred metaphor of the military strike, despite its somewhat misleading connotations. And this metaphor also reflects the language used by the soldiers themselves. From August 1918, groups of soldiers retreating from the front line repeatedly shouted contemptuously at the reserve troops moving into position, dubbing them 'war prolongers' or 'strike breakers'.[98]

Part Three

# Processing Violence

8

# The Weimar Republic: A Brutalized Society?

The war gave millions of men across Europe first-hand experience of the practice of killing. This confronted all the combatant nations with a series of urgent questions after the armistice: What would be the legacy of the conflict? Could civilized society contain the deadly violence unleashed by the war? And would the returning veterans be able to regain their place in the communities they had left years earlier to serve on the front line? In Germany and elsewhere, violent demonstrations, strikes and disturbances became major features of the post-1918 political landscape.

## I Great Britain: A 'peaceable kingdom'?

In the first two years after the armistice, many people in Great Britain shared the fear that returning veterans could destabilize the social order. The months from January 1919 until the summer of that year saw riots, arson attacks and episodes of looting in various British cities, typically involving war veterans. In July 1919, for example, veterans in their 'khaki' uniforms participated in 'the destruction of civic buildings, the looting of shops, and the stoning of police and firefighters' in the town of Luton. As a local veterans' association was forced to admit, 'the trouble had grown out of grievances between themselves and local council officials'. A more positive picture emerged a few weeks later, when the local newspaper reported that other veterans had in fact attempted to curb the violent protest by their wartime comrades.[1] Nevertheless, the incident fuelled the fears among the British public that the front-line experience had left the country's servicemen irreparably brutalized. This led to apprehensive discussions about the implications for peaceful social coexistence. In 1920, for example, a debate in the Westminster Parliament saw cross-party agreement that veterans across the country were displaying a frightening 'callousness with regard to life'. The proceedings in Parliament followed reports of numerous robberies perpetrated by 'men who had become used to violence in the War'. In this instance, the debate concluded with the passing of the first legislation to control handguns.²

However, these public debates on the brutalization of society and political culture in Great Britain soon triggered another reaction, too. Amid the alarm at the violence, there quickly emerged a consensus across the political spectrum that Great Britain needed to remember its true values of civility and peaceableness. Over the months and years that followed, the British nation successfully revived its own self-mythology. Britain, this held, was a 'peaceable kingdom'.³ So robust was this consensual idealization of a peace-loving nation that even the violent excesses of British soldiers in Ireland left it largely unshaken. In early 1920, the government in Whitehall stepped up its fight against the IRA (Irish Republican Army) by drafting British soldiers into the Royal Irish Constabulary, the militarized police force tasked with combating the Republicans. The majority of the men were war veterans, whose uniforms earned them the moniker 'Black and Tans'. News soon reached England that the Black and Tans were indiscriminately killing civilians and committing revenge executions and other atrocities. Yet despite the seemingly obvious link between the brutality in Ireland and the perpetrators' wartime experiences, British political debate succeeded in externalizing the problem. In the eyes of observers in London, the events in Ireland did not disprove the idea of Britain as a peaceable kingdom, but were the symptom of a specifically Irish tradition of political violence that had developed since the Easter Uprising.⁴

This brief excursion into British history raises a number of issues that are also relevant to the discussion of violence and brutalization in German society after the war. Firstly, it enables us to put events in Germany into a broader European context.⁵ Notwithstanding the actions of the Black and Tans, the brutalization of European societies post-1918 tended to be greatest in the east of the continent and lowest in the west. The different histories of nation-building in each region of Europe offer a plausible explanation for this pattern. In areas of Eastern Europe such as Ukraine and the Baltic, secessionist nationalist movements attempted to form their own nation states from the fragments of the Russian Empire. Here, the intensity of political violence was much higher and the brutalization of the political culture far more extensive than in Central Europe, where countries such as Germany and Italy were relatively established national constructs despite isolated border conflicts. Western Europe, with its long-established, stable nation states such as France and Great Britain, was least affected by the violent aftermath of the war. Even here, however, the example of the Black and Tans shows that the aggression built up during the war had the potential to develop and intensify further post-1918 where questions of sovereignty and independence arose.⁶

## II  Polarization or cooperation between political camps

The British example also provides a second insight. It suggests that the way in which societies came to terms with and interpreted the experience of violence depended to a large degree on how successfully they were able to integrate various political groups, parties and camps into an overall frame of reference. In the British case, this frame of reference came in the image of the peace-loving, civilizing nation. France offers another vivid and distinctive example of such a unifying framework. There, veterans' associations made a particularly important contribution to the political culture of the Third Republic in the 1920s.⁷ Servicemen formed political camps during the war and in its immediate aftermath, resulting in high levels of political engagement. No fewer than half of all surviving veterans were politically organized. The Union Fédérale, founded during the conflict, was closely affiliated with the radicals and the Socialist Party. Meanwhile, bourgeois Catholic veterans were organized in the Union Nationale des Combattants. A Communist association of war veterans – the ARAC – completed the landscape, though it had little significance in numerical terms. The competing organizational structures reflected specific forms of sociability and patterns of social recruitment, particularly among the associations' elites. Yet despite their considerable political differences, the willingness of the *anciens combattants* to cooperate was so extensive that they came together to form an umbrella organization in 1927. On an ideological level, too, the veterans shared a relatively coherent self-image. They stood for strict anti-militarism and pacifism, condemnation of war, international understanding and disarmament and a republican patriotism that sacralized France as a land of humanity and rectitude. In their public discourse, the organized veterans summoned up a sense of unity, which they pitched against the turmoil of political life.⁸ In the face of the dramatic political conflicts and opposing interests that characterized the Third Republic in the 1920s, the veterans thus provided an element of stability that strengthened the 'republican synthesis'.⁹

In Great Britain and France, then, a cultural frame of reference transcended political camps, helping the veterans to come to terms with the violence prior to 1918 and reintegrate into civil society. In Germany, meanwhile, precisely such a common frame of reference was lacking. Since the *Kulturkampf* against the Catholic minority and the anti-socialist laws in the Bismarck era, a fundamental tension had shaped the political culture of the German nation: the opposition between a hegemonic Protestant national idea and the marginalized subcultures of the socialists (and communists from 1918) and Catholics. This did not preclude all political agreement. In 1919, moderate socialists and the Catholics of the Centre Party reached consensus with left-wing liberals on the foundation of the Weimar Republic. Nevertheless, these groups differed markedly in the ways in which they interpreted, remembered and represented the experience of wartime violence. A process of radicalization in Germany deeply polarized debate on the violence of the First World War and the legacy and memory of the war dead. This began with the armistice on 11 November 1918 and gathered momentum when the terms of the Treaty of Versailles were announced on 7 May 1919.

The Social Democrats and Centre Party campaigned publicly in protest at the harsh conditions imposed by the Allies.[10] However, it was primarily the nationalist camp that refused to accept the realities resulting from the German defeat and had a consistent tendency to 'escape into myth'.[11] Right-wing radicals and *völkisch* groups led the way along with the conservatives of the German National People's Party (DNVP). Yet even liberals of all political stripes largely agreed that, in the shadow of Versailles, the heroism on the front and soldiers' sacrifices for the nation should define German memory of the war. The front experience of the years 1914–18 therefore increasingly developed into a political mythology that glorified aggression. For the nationalist camp, it became a catalyst that would radically change bourgeois sociability from the mid-1920s. The glorification of the German army and its wartime heroism, the offensive justification of state and paramilitary violence against left-wing workers, the legitimization of *Wehrhaftigkeit* (readiness for defence), and the broad cult of violence offered no room for critical voices. On the contrary, the process of casting domestic political enemies was an important component of nationalist efforts to glorify violence and remilitarize society following defeat in the war. The most important example of this phenomenon was the denunciation of socialists and Jews as the architects of an alleged 'stab in the back' that had supposedly stolen victory from an undefeated army.[12]

## III Radicalization in the nationalist camp

The diary entries of a German naval captain, Bogislav von Selchow (1877–1943), provide a vivid example of the disillusionment, hatred and deep-rooted notions of aggressive masculinity that fed into the brutalization of the nationalist camp from late 1918.[13] Von Selchow kept his diary without interruption from the 1890s onwards. Running into several volumes, it provides a unique account of the mentality of the Wilhelmine navy officer corps. Von Selchow's emphatic affirmation of the aims of the radical nationalist Vaterlandspartei, founded in 1917 to support an annexationist agenda, and his involvement in the 'patriotic instruction' (*Vaterländischer Unterricht*) of the military from 1917 reveal his radical nationalist and anti-Semitic political standpoint. The revolution and, to an even greater extent, the Allied terms for a peace treaty, reduced von Selchow, he admits in his diary, to endless floods of tears.

Von Selchow did not confine himself to the written word in expressing his feelings. A diary entry from late 1918 features a sketch of a woman with a sly expression and long nose, intended to connote a stereotypical Jew. It is possible that the drawing was supposed to call to mind Rosa Luxemburg, the leader of the radical left-wing Spartacus Group.[14] This woman, drawn to symbolize treachery, is administering a fatal stab in the back to a German soldier. A clearer illustration of the stab-in-the-back legend would be hard to find. Yet the sketch long predates the first peak in the myth's political exploitation: the joint statement on the stab in the back made by Hindenburg and Ludendorff to a parliamentary committee of investigation on 18 November 1919.[15] What is more, von Selchow's drawing of the 'stab in the back' is no standard-issue weaponry in the battle of political interpretation. The German soldier under the steel helmet, whose iron cross and impeccable uniform represent bravery and readiness for action, is not killed by a simple dagger; since the 1789 French revolution the symbol of assassination and mob rule in the thinking of counterrevolutionaries. Instead, the murder weapon is the classical Teutonic spear of the Nibelung mythology.[16] The woman's appearance is intended to connote Judaism. The serpents upon her head identify her as Medusa, one of the Gorgons of Greek mythology. Her cunning expression signals the supposed betrayal perpetrated against the heroic German nation by a home front connotated with effeminacy and Jewishness. For the classically educated von Selchow, this was an image of sheer horror. Though von Selchow described Germany's left-wing revolutionaries as a 'human beast' following a visit to the *Vollzugsrat* (executive committee) of the Workers' and Soldiers' Councils in Berlin, the drawing symbolized more than simply this political threat. For von Selchow, far more was at stake. The revolution and, to an even greater extent, the peace terms of Versailles, were an attack on the very ideas of honour and masculinity that shaped his entire identity. In the grip of this crisis, which engulfed the existing gender, moral and political order, von Selchow even pinned his hopes on the 'masculine' demeanour of Social Democrat Friedrich

Ebert, a figure widely attacked by proponents of the stab-in-the-back myth for his work in the revolutionary Rat der Volksbeauftragten (Council of People's Representatives).[17]

Von Selchow's diary is a vivid example of the radicalization of nationalist attitudes in the wake of war and defeat. It is also exemplary for the escalation of the conflict between the nationalist and socialist camps over the interpretation of the war, and for the increasingly brutal recriminations from both sides. Germany lacked a liberal culture that could have functioned as a shared point of reference. Instead, polarization between political camps set the scene for a tendency towards brutalization in Weimar society and for the particular ways in which Germans interpreted the violence of the war.[18] Yet brutalization is also a concept that has attracted substantial controversy. Before returning to the question of whether in fact Weimar was a brutalized society, it is important to outline the contours of the debate so far.

## IV 'Brutalization': The argument of George L. Mosse

The traditional reference point for the history of brutalization in the Weimar Republic is the work by historian George Mosse (1918–1999) on Germany's political culture and special path to fascism. Born in Berlin, Mosse fled into exile from the Nazis in 1933. His dual perspective as both insider and emigrant shaped and sharpened his interpretation of German history. Like his work in many other fields, Mosse's studies on the First World War were pioneering. In 1990, he published a study entitled *Fallen Soldiers*.[19] The strength of this book lies not primarily in its empirical analysis, but in the innovative and eclectic insights and quotations it collates into a loose collage. More important, however, than the often somewhat haphazardly presented empirical sources are the topics Mosse covers. These include the mythological ideas, images and representations that concealed the 'true' – that is, extremely violent – nature of the front-line experience and reinterpreted it as a pure, idealistic and selfless sacrifice for the fatherland. Mosse notes that such idealizations and mythologies were present in all the countries involved in the war. Yet Germany, he argues, was nevertheless a unique case. Unlike in other countries, aggressive, nationalist mythologies prevailed in Germany, which portrayed an idealized notion of front-line camaraderie as a general model for social relations. This led Germans to interpret defeat as a spur to resurrect the nation by essentially continuing the wartime struggle and turning it both inwards and outwards. For Mosse, the 'brutalization' of politics after 1918 manifested itself in a series of unsettling developments: the indifference with which the public treated the wave of 324 murders against left-wing figures in the period from 1919 to 1923 alone, the work of the Freikorps and their anti-revolutionary violence, the cultivation of a highly aggressive soldierly ideal of masculinity, and even the distribution of postcards depicting atrocities by Germany's wartime enemies.[20]

These examples already indicate the limits to the insights that Mosse's argument can offer us. Few would dispute that the wave of political murders by right-wing extremists post-1918 signalled an alarming indifference to the lives of political opponents. The pacifist Emil Julius Gumbel denounced precisely this apathy towards right-wing violence in his book, *Vier Jahre politischer Mord* (Four Years of Political Murder), in 1922.[21] Few would deny either that the members of the Freikorps contributed to the brutalization of the political culture in Germany, though the social reach of this brutalization remained limited (see Chapter 9). In the case of the postcards, another limitation in Mosse's argument becomes evident. Thorough empirical sampling of the postcards sold in Germany during the war shows that Allied atrocities were generally a marginal theme. With their sentimental, often kitsch scenes, most postcards instead summoned escapist images of a peaceful world, designed to help people forget the violent reality of war.[22]

Proponents of Mosse's argument have therefore cited other indicators of the disintegrating norms of civil society in the aftermath of the war. For example, they point to the sharp rise in divorces after 1918. Men's absence during the war caused the divorce rate – measured as the number of separations per 100,000 marriages in a given year – to decline from 26.6 in 1913 to 15.9 in 1915. A sudden upturn followed the end of the conflict, and by 1920 the divorce rate had reached 59.1. This was more than twice as high as the pre-war figure and more than three times as high as in 1915.[23] One could read this development as an indication that the 'moral consequences of the war weighed heavily on the will to return to a normal life', in other words, that the men brutalized by the front no longer desired to return to the intimacy of their family.[24] This would be a plausible explanation if there were evidence of a concomitant increase in the frequency or intensity of domestic violence. The studies on divorce, however, offer no indication that this was the case.[25] It is also significant that as many as a third of the divorces that occurred after 1918 involved marriages made during or shortly after the war. There were doubtless many different reasons for these separations. These ranged from marital infidelity to the simple realization that a marriage concluded purely for financial reasons, in order to obtain family support payments during the war, could not withstand the test of everyday life in peacetime.[26]

The increased number of separations therefore did not necessarily reflect the general brutalization of gender and family relations in Germany, but was first and foremost the product of what Richard Bessel has described as 'hasty wartime or post-war marriages'.[27] However, this critical counterargument is itself unsatisfactory in an important respect. While historians are able to relativize the significance of the divorce rate by comparing the strength of marriages concluded during the war with those dating from before 1914, contemporary observers perceived the situation quite differently. As Bessel rightly emphasizes, 'this point was lost on those who viewed the rising divorce-rate, and the fact that it was far higher than in other European countries, as clear evidence of moral decline'.[28] After 1918, increasing divorce rates, rising criminality and other troubling indicators all formed part of a public discourse that believed Germany was experiencing a crisis or even complete collapse of moral norms. This belief had a strong conservative streak. After four years of privations during the war, its proponents now denounced the 'pleasure-frenzy' of many Germans in peacetime. They regarded people's legitimate interest in returning to ordinary pastimes as incompatible with the country's grave situation following the defeat.[29]

There is therefore a clear methodological necessity for a more differentiated analysis of brutalization. On the one hand, there is the question as to whether participants in the war were themselves brutalized and whether the violence they suffered and perpetrated during the conflict was directly related to violent tendencies in German society post-1918. On the other hand, there is a need to examine the extent to which brutalizing myths and ideas also spread after 1918 among those who had not actively participated in the war themselves. This indirect transmission of violence-affirming interpretations, images and myths is an important dimension of Mosse's argument that his critics have not always given full recognition.[30] It is important to bear this distinction in mind as this chapter looks briefly at some possible indicators of the scale of brutalization as a result of the war. The remainder of the chapter begins by asking whether soldiers were brutalized on the front, before using selected examples to examine the reintegration of veterans and the importance of war mythology in the Weimar Republic.

## V  Brutalization on the front?

Fears of brutalization began to grow long before the conclusion of the war. In many cases, it was soldiers themselves who began to reflect on the implications of their daily confrontation with the sight of badly wounded men and dead bodies. In their letters and diaries, some men expressed a concern that they would gradually become inured to the suffering of others, developing 'a deplorable callousness, almost barbarity'.[31] Others, meanwhile, were untroubled by such concerns. In their letters, they instead deliberately portrayed themselves as aggressive warriors, describing the ruthlessness with which they battled the enemy and the great pleasure they took in killing. One such example comes from the ranks of a squad at the renowned Hamburg gymnastics club, Hamburger Turnerschaft von 1816. Many of the squad's members signed up voluntarily for war in 1914. This was typical of many predominantly young, middle-class associations close to organized nationalism. One of the volunteers was Hans Tiemann, who became a vice-sergeant major. In a series of letters to his fellow-gymnasts in Hamburg, Tiemann described in detail his thoughts as he killed British soldiers. On one occasion, evidently aware of the limits of socially acceptable comment, he wrote two different descriptions of the same battle. One, addressed to his civilian employers, offered a toned-down version of events. In contrast, the letter he wrote to a friend and fellow-gymnast in October 1916 described the direct combat as follows:

> The first Englishman! Badly wounded. So they're in the trench after all! Soon we'll catch them. They have blocked the trench with wire and put a man there with hand grenades. Away with them! Now I was finally able to settle things with our dear cousins, and you can rest assured that I did my utmost! I had an incredible anger in me that went back to 14 August. I had also taken an Englishman's iron trench club from him. The two things together meant we cleared out the trench quickly and thoroughly. Tommy had nothing to laugh about this time.[32]

This brief excerpt reveals how Tiemann, aware of his own brutality, attempted to place it in the narrative of England's 'betrayal' in going to war against Germany. He justified the killing as a necessary act of self-defence in an almost 'atavistic' close-quarter battle, which was fought using clubs.[33] It is important, however, not to overstate the significance of Tiemann's account. Philipp Münch, who has produced an innovative study of this group of Hamburg gymnasts, has found that Tiemann's letters were 'atypical', even among these athletes, 'in their tendency to glorify violence'. In fact, Tiemann himself served only for a relatively short period on the front line, and spent far more of the war as his regiment's intelligence officer.[34] Even in middle-class nationalist circles, then, such overt brutalization and habituation to violence were the exception rather than the rule.

One might object that war letters and other autobiographical forms of narration are notoriously imprecise and inconsistent media. Some have questioned the significance of generalizations drawn from what is inevitably a rather limited sample of letters and writers.[35] However, these are criticisms on which authors such as Klaus Latzel have already reflected extensively.[36] Moreover, drawing upon sources that were not intended for publication during the war helps historians to avoid the heroic self-portrayals of nationalist circles. In fact, such rigorous source selection is a base requirement for any history of the mentalities involved in a possible brutalization at the front.[37] Studies such as Aribert Reimann's work on historical semantics, which is based on a carefully selected sample of lower-middle-class soldiers, have produced similar findings to the work on the Hamburg gymnasts. Reimann's analysis shows that only German soldiers on the Eastern Front denigrated the enemy in biologistic, racist terms. For the generally 'invisible enemies' – the Allied soldiers on the Western Front – Reimann finds that 'nationalist thinking' played an 'unexpectedly minor role', particularly among soldiers 'with a low level of education' from the lower middle and working classes.[38]

This is not to suggest that working-class soldiers were immune to brutalization from the outset. In fact, some on the radical left wing of the socialist workers' movement interpreted the First World War as a positive learning process. They believed that the war was providing the masses with the very weapons they would need to fight their class enemy at home: the bourgeoisie. An example of such rhetoric, which threatened a 'day of retribution' when workers returned from the front, is found in a war letter by a working-class soldier from Hamburg in August 1916:

> Men will return who will have no fear of sabres, who will have been taught to murder. A time will come when bodies will hang from the lamp posts, naturally those of the police. The blood of the workers will be avenged with that of the patriots.[39]

It is still impossible to say how widespread such revolutionary fantasies of violence were among members of the USPD or the far smaller Spartacus Group. However, it does not seem implausible to draw a line of continuity between such wartime letters and the second phase of the revolution, which began with the 1920 March Uprising in the Ruhr region following the defeat of the Kapp Putsch. The Red Ruhr Army recruited organized workers in the USPD and KPD, as well as among anarcho-syndicalists and non-organized labour. It waged fierce battles against the Reichswehr troops and Freikorps, whom the government had sent to defeat the uprising. The increasingly desperate fighting by left-wing workers has been interpreted, not without justification, as a continuation of the struggle against the 'hated army hierarchy of the First World War'. This hierarchy was embodied in the Ruhr by the former imperial officers facing them from the ranks of the Reichswehr and Freikorps.[40] However, it would be wrong to assume that all social democratic working-class soldiers shared the same outlook. During the war, the dominant sentiment among such men was their longing for peace. Informed by social democratic principles of anti-militarism, they were highly critical of the conflict. This left little room for brutalization even in the broadest sense of the word.[41]

All in all, it appears unlikely that the experience of war resulted in extensive brutalization among German soldiers. Another reason for this may have been that the average German soldier, at least in the second half of the conflict, fought 'without any understanding of a war aim' defined in either territorial or political terms. This, at least, was the view of Eugen Neter, who, in 1925, published an essay looking back at the final months of the war on the Western Front.[42] Neter had served during the war as a battalion doctor in a regiment from Baden. In his essay, he reflected on the reasons for soldiers' unwillingness to endure the fighting in 1918, which was manifested in the 'military strike' during the autumn of that year (see Chapter 7). One factor, he concluded, was that 'our people lacked any sense of enmity towards the enemy'. For Neter, it was telling that German soldiers did not refer to their enemies on the Western Front using any 'swear word' that 'would have indicated their contempt or anger'.[43] Neter's argument is, admittedly, a gross generalization ill-suited to the complexity of the topic at hand. However, on renewed reading today, the correspondence to recent French research is striking. Neter writes that the French soldiers were driven by an 'intense, almost savage hatred'.[44] Recent work, too, has identified the French 'war culture' and its aggressive images of the enemy as an important factor in the mobilization of French society. Hatred of the Germans, which was expressed in biologistic terms and ascribed dehumanising, animal-like qualities to the German soldiers, was a significant source of motivation for some of the French *poilus*.[45] This suggests that any tendencies towards brutalization among front-line soldiers during the war were a wider European occurrence rather than a uniquely or even primarily German phenomenon.

## VI The reintegration of the veterans

How did veterans reintegrate into German society after 1918? Did they find their way back to the structures of civil society, or did they hold the power to destabilize German society, playing a major role in the paramilitary violence post-1918?

The only way reliably to answer these questions is to closely examine the social contexts in which the reintegration of specific groups of veterans took place. The same applies to the participation of war veterans in paramilitary organizations such as the Freikorps and *Einwohnerwehren* (citizens' militias). My study of the largely rural and agrarian region of southern Bavaria attempts precisely such a contextualization.[46] The results of this work on parts of Bavaria – more precisely the districts of Upper Bavaria, Lower Bavaria and Bavarian Swabia – are briefly covered here. They are relevant not least because the foothills of the Alps in Upper Bavaria have long figured in research as a particularly fertile recruiting ground for the wave of counter-revolutionary violence after 1918. In May 1919, the Freikorps troops recruited from Upper Bavaria and elsewhere inflicted a bloody defeat on the communist Munich Council Republic. Historians have often regarded this 'White Terror' as a continuation of the 'total mobilization' of the First World War.[47] However, this impression does not withstand more detailed empirical study. The evidence shows that soldiers from Bavaria with farming backgrounds were not brutalized by the killing on the front line. Farmers and farmers' sons serving as soldiers were able to alleviate the psychological stress wrought by physical violence. They did so by resorting to traditional anchors of rural life, such as Catholic piety, the farming family and – particularly importantly at a time of severe food shortages – agrarian subsistence.[48] There was certainly some willingness among war veterans in southern Bavaria to participate in counter-revolutionary violence against the communists in Munich in spring 1919. However, this was limited to a small number of farmers' sons and agricultural servants. For these men, the likely short duration of the fighting and good pay made such military service appear lucrative.[49]

In rural Bavarian society after 1918, violence – both real and imagined – was ignited less by the war veterans' return than by the increasingly politically and emotionally charged conflict between town and countryside. From 1916 until the easing of hyperinflation at the end of 1923, many farmers in Bavaria developed what at times amounted to extraordinarily malicious fantasies of violence directed at urban-dwelling food consumers. The opposition between urban dwellers and farmers was a persistent feature of this decade of inflation. It fed on farmers' anger at wartime controls on their production and the aggressive behaviour of hoarders and profiteers from the cities. Confrontations and scuffles on fields and farmyards were a common occurrence.[50] However, this conflict did not give rise to any form of successful offensive military organization, despite the desire of leading figures in Bavarian military circles and militias to mobilize village folk against the socialist working class.

In theory, this mobilization was the task of the citizens' militias, which were formed in early 1919 in rural and urban areas alike. These paramilitary organizations equipped men with rifles and other small arms to enable them to defend private property and the public order. The citizens' militias have often been regarded as an important link between the violence of the war and the political violence after 1918.[51] However, a close empirical study tells a different story. Farmers in southern Bavaria welcomed the citizens' militias for their local task of protecting property. Militia members could patrol the land, for example, in order to prevent theft by visitors from the cities getting out of hand. But offensive action against the political left was another matter. In the wake of the Kapp Putsch of 1920, for instance, it proved impossible to motivate the militias to fight. Farmers had a passive outlook and were interested in nothing more than a defensive role. This was partly for simple practical reasons. So intensive was the work involved in running a farm that men were unwilling to leave home for even just a few days in order to fight socialist workers in the nearest town. However, another important motive was directly linked to the men's wartime experience. Farmers informed the leadership of the citizens' militias and local officials in no uncertain terms that, after years on the front, they had no intention of returning to armed (para)military service.[52] In July 1919, an official tasked with establishing the militias wrote the following report following a visit to various districts of Bavarian Swabia:

> The people are ready to defend their village and home area, the district, against all threats, but very few are prepared to take part in expeditions further afield. The aversion to even the slightest hint of a military organization is tremendous, most of the relevant men having already been in the field for a lengthy period. They want to be left in peace.[53]

At least in rural Bavaria, then, the history of the citizens' militias cannot be cited as evidence of a wartime brutalization that persisted into the Weimar Republic. A study of the Prussian province of Saxony, a more industrialized region, has reached similar conclusions. In the province's urban centres, the formation of the militias met with firm opposition from the socialist working class. The militias' presence was strongest in rural areas of the province in the Magdeburger Börde. Even there, however, farmers were sceptical about any form of mobilization that aspired to more than simply defending their property. The citizens' militias, formed in 1919 and dissolved in 1921, thus did not help to accustom the property-owning classes in town and country to the exercise of 'extralegal violence against the left'.[54] Such a hypothesis, while implied by the aggressive ideological self-portrayal of the organizations' heads, does not reflect the social and organizational practice of the militias at local level.[55]

## VII  Pacifist veterans' associations

The limits of brutalization evident in the paramilitary mobilization post-1918 also applied to the complex landscape of veterans' associations in which former servicemen gathered after the war. Here, too, nothing could be further from the truth than the idea that an entire generation of young men 'sought refuge in a life of violence in paramilitary uniform' or at least glorified violence. As Richard Bessel has pointed out, this assumption is 'inconsistent with the fact that the largest interest group formed by veterans' was not a radical nationalist grouping, but an association organized by Social Democrats committed to democratic pacifism.[56] The Reichsbund der Kriegsbeschädigten, Kriegsteilnehmer und Kriegshinterbliebenen (Reich Association of Disabled Soldiers, Veterans and War Dependants) numbered 830,000 members in 1922 and was by far the largest organization of war disabled in the Weimar Republic. Founded in 1917, the Reichsbund appealed to the memory of the war dead in advocating a moderate pacifism focused on international disarmament and non-use of force. It also established intensive contact with equivalent veterans' groups in France. Through the exchange of speakers and other symbolic gestures of reconciliation, the association sought to foster understanding between the two former war enemies.[57] The Reichsbund thus contributed to a 'cultural demobilization', in which social discourses distanced themselves from the wartime demonization of the enemy and rejected the glorification of violence.[58] These gestures of reconciliation were all the more important given that they contrasted with developments outside the socialist camp. In July 1930, Germany marked the early withdrawal of French troops from the Rhineland. The celebrations held to celebrate this 'victory' were orchestrated as a moment of national liberation. By now, aggression towards the French from nationalist circles had regained the upper hand, throwing the earlier reconciliation efforts into sharp relief.[59]

The Reichsbund was not only the most important force representing disabled veterans in Germany, but also a prominent supporter of the pacifist *Nie wieder Krieg* (No More War) movement. At its height in 1920 and 1921, No More War commemorated 1 August 1914, the date on which Germany had entered the First World War, with mass events in towns and cities across the country (see Chapter 9). From February 1924, many other war veterans from the Social

Democratic working class came together in the Reichsbanner Schwarz-Rot-Gold (Reichsbanner Black-Red-Gold). This association, explicitly founded as a League of Republican War Veterans, soon reached a membership in the region of one million men, some two-thirds of whom were ex-servicemen. This meant that the Reichsbanner boasted considerably more veterans of the front line than the self-proclaimed 'League of Front-Line Soldiers' known as Stahlhelm (Steel Helmet). The latter organization pursued an increasingly aggressive nationalist politics of remembrance. From the mid-1920s, it became an important focus of sociability in the nationalist camp, although it probably never numbered more than 350,000 men. In formal terms, the Reichsbanner was organized as a defence formation. It insisted – not always successfully – that its members wear uniforms, and marched in closed formation at demonstrations. Nevertheless, even high-profile radical pacifists like the former captain at sea, Lothar Persius, were convinced that neither members nor functionaries had any inclination towards a militaristic culture or 'playing at soldiers'. In private and public remembrance of the war experience, the Reichsbanner cultivated a discourse of victimization that treated the soldiers as proletarian victims of the wartime violence and the Wilhelmine power apparatus.[60]

In an article published in the Social Democratic *Vorwärts* newspaper just a few weeks after the election of Paul von Hindenburg as Reich President on 26 April 1925, Hermann Schützinger compared the framework of veterans' organizations in France and Germany. Schützinger was a leading member of the Reichsbanner and one of the small but important group of former career officers to find their way into the republican veterans' association (see Chapter 9). Despite the election of the ageing former field marshal, argued Schützinger in defiant tone, there were grounds for republican optimism. While some 70 per cent of French veterans were in the camp of 'war refusal and reconciliation between the peoples', membership of the Reichsbund and Reichsbanner ran at 60 per cent of German veterans and was thus not much lower. Admittedly, however, this was not an entirely fair comparison, he added, for 'even the leaders of the [generally right-wing] Union nationale would not dare to deviate from the gospel of all French war veterans, namely support for the League of Nations in order to prevent another war.'[61] Schützinger hereby addressed a decisive difference between the two countries, and one that is also significant with regard to the issue of brutalization. Like their counterparts in France, many veterans in Germany campaigned for pacifist aims and peaceful means of coming to terms with their experiences of violence. Unlike France, however, the Weimar Republic lacked a national reference culture focused on international understanding and cultural demobilization. This meant that the battle to commemorate the war and interpret its legacy led to a deep polarization between the political camps. It also encouraged the radicalization and brutalization of the rhetoric used by the nationalist right to glorify the violence of the war and reaffirm its value for the present. This culminated in the aggressive denunciation of Erich Maria Remarque's novel, *All Quiet on the Western Front*. Deeming Remarque's portrayal of the wartime experience to be emasculating and dishonouring, the National Socialists campaigned vigorously from 1929 to 1931 against the book and American film adaptation.[62] Their ultimate aim was already to discredit and destroy the republican system.

## VIII Engaging with war violence through the media

Such tendencies towards radicalization are also evident in another area that Mosse examined with his theory of brutalization: Weimar Germany's habit of subtly steering its young generation towards an interpretation of the war experience that regarded the heroic deaths on the front as a personal guide and compass for the moral renewal of society.[63] This appealed especially to the war generation socialized between 1914 and 1918. Boys and young men born between 1900 and 1910 had experienced the Great War as an adventure told through books, popular literature and maps of the front lines, all designed to illustrate German military successes. A participatory form of pedagogy had also ensured that wartime learning was fun. It had encouraged young people to collect recyclable materials and take part in other activities, fostering belief in nationalist war aims without overtly explaining them.[64]

It therefore comes as no surprise that nationalist youth associations in the Weimar Republic placed themselves at the service of those seeking to glorify war. The Bündische Jugend – small groups of middle-class youth such as the Wandervogel, who sought romanticism by hiking in the forests – aggressively referenced front-line soldiers' heroic deaths to compensate for the unalterable but, in their view, regrettable fact that they had been too young to fight. This tendency to instrumentalize war remembrance for the purposes of generational politics was especially pronounced in the Hitler Youth. Baldur von Schirach, initially as the head of the Hitler Youth from 1931 and later as *Reichsjugendführer* (Reich Youth Leader) from 1933, committed the organization to glorifying the sacrifices of the soldiers killed in the First World War. The Hitler Youth pledged their allegiance to the 'Geist der Feldgrauen' (the spirit of the field soldiers) rather than the surviving war veterans. This was in no small respect a rebellion against the conservative soldiers' associations, such as Stahlhelm and the Kyffhäuserbund that dominated war remembrance in the nationalist camp until 1933.[65]

It has been argued that if we wish to understand the loyalty inspired by the war myths in the Hitler Youth, we must take into account the broad consensus across youth groups in the Weimar Republic on the need to glorify the heroism of the war dead. This consensus encompassed not only the Wandervogel, Bündische Jugend and other middle-class youth groups, but also Catholic youth associations and the Jungbanner, the youth organization of Reichsbanner Black-Red-Gold. Such a consensus supposedly meant that contemporaries did not perceive anything specifically National Socialist or 'abnormal' about the Hitler Youth's discourse of remembrance.[66] This argument contradicts the idea that Weimar society was polarized by the different attitudes to the war among its subcultures. It is true that, from the late 1920s, war remembrance in the form mediated by war films and novels played a major role in importing nationalist mythologies into the milieu of the socialist working-class youth. For this demographic, watching war films in the cinema was a great adventure that was only ostensibly apolitical. However, it would be wrong to conclude from this that the members of the Jungbanner fully adopted the nationalist camp's mythology of sacrifice as their own. The sacrifice of the war dead for the fatherland was not at the heart of the socialist war narrative in the Jungbanner or in other youth organizations like the SPD-affiliated SAJ (Sozialistische Arbeiterjugend or Socialist Workers' Youth). Instead, young Social Democrats celebrated the positive example that those who gave their lives had set for the integration and mobilization of the working class.[67]

## IX Conclusion

This brief sketch was not intended to provide a comprehensive picture of the many aspects of brutalization in Weimar society. That is a task for a more extensive general study of the Weimar Republic.[68] Rather, my aim was to show why it is now possible to offer a more differentiated view of the brutalization of German society after 1918 than was provided by George Mosse. As the first historian to put these issues on the research agenda, Mosse opened up important new perspectives. After a long focus on the origins of National Socialism, the implications of wartime violence for developments post-1918 is now being critically examined for other European countries, too.[69] It is now clear that the question of brutalization in the Weimar Republic can no longer simply be answered by pointing to the murderous activities of the Freikorps and the continuities with National Socialism. That is a far too limited, rigid and linear form of continuity. It also overlooks the fact that developments often attributed directly to the war in fact grew out of social ruptures that only emerged after 1918.[70] This essential point is illustrated by none other than Adolf Hitler himself. As Thomas Weber has rightly concluded, there is no convincing evidence that the man who would become responsible for the deaths of millions of people was brutalized by his own experience of the First World War. Though he constantly cited the experience of the front as the major turning point in his life, his deep radicalization began only in 1919 with his involvement in the counter-revolutionary activities of the Reichswehr.[71] Hitler was surely the most brutal war veteran of the First World War. But he had not been brutalized by it.[72]

# 9

# The Delayed Rejection of Violence: Hermann Schützinger's Conversion to Pacifism

For some First World War veterans, the violence did not end with the armistice. This was truest of all for those wartime soldiers who found a political and military home, at least temporarily, in the Freikorps movement in the immediate aftermath of the conflict. In Bavaria and Berlin, in the Baltic and in Upper Silesia, these paramilitary units were involved in the brutal suppression of communist uprisings and the struggle against Bolshevism and Polish nationalists. This made them part of a transnational network of anti-Bolshevist violence. The Freikorps had direct links to paramilitary groups in Bavaria, Austria and Hungary, as well as other contacts as far away as Italy and Finland.[1] Some 250,000 men, many of whom had previously served in the German wartime army, were active in the militias. For the historian looking for a direct line of continuity from the violence of the First World War to that of the Weimar Republic, the anti-republican and anti-Bolshevist campaigns waged by the Freikorps should, without doubt, be the first port of call.[2] The direct link between the practice of violence on the front and the brutalization of the Freikorps after the war has long been recognized. It prompted the American historian Robert G.L. Waite to describe the Freikorps with a fitting military metaphor in a 1952 book as the 'vanguard of Nazism'.[3] This is something of an overstatement, though. Only some of the Freikorps members went on to become National Socialists, and the men's reasons for participating cannot be reduced to ideological motivations.[4] In the light of recent comparative research, it is also important to emphasize that paramilitary mobilization was a feature of many European countries between 1918 and 1923.[5]

Moreover, with the focus on the Freikorps, there is a risk of overlooking another reaction to the violence of the First World War, and one which was diametrically opposed to the actions of paramilitary groups: the turn to pacifism and the rejection of violence. While war became a way of life for some soldiers, motivating them to continue its violence after 1918, others greeted the wartime destruction with revulsion. This persuaded them to campaign instead for pacifist aims. What were the motives and historical contexts in which men made such life-changing commitments to pacifism after 1918? Did front-line soldiers turn to pacifism as a direct response to the practice of wartime killing, or was their rejection of violence contingent on other experiences? In what organizational forms were pacifist veterans engaged, and how did their pacifism relate to their other political beliefs? These are questions best explored in detail with individual case studies, as no two people shared identical stories. The scope for such biographical studies, however, is generally limited by a lack of sufficiently comprehensive source material. A closer insight into what motivated the First World War soldiers who turned to pacifism is thus only possible in a handful of cases.

The following biographical case study based on the life of Hermann Schützinger (1888–1962) attempts to provide at least some rudimentary answers to these questions. Schützinger himself is a somewhat unusual example of the conversion to pacifism, having served both before and during the war as a career officer in the Bavarian army. He therefore belonged to a group whose ranks were small but highly influential in terms of the public promotion of pacifist aims: the professional German officers who decided at various stages in their careers to quit the army and become pacifists.[6] The most important representatives of this group in the years that followed the First World War were Paul Freiherr von Schoenaich (1866–1954) and Berthold von Deimling (1853–1944). As the commanding general of the 15th Army Corps in Strasbourg, the latter had achieved notoriety in the Zabern Affair shortly before the war. Rather than placating the local Alsatian population, who were outraged at the disparaging comments directed at them by a German officer, Deimling instead confronted them as a stubborn defender of the German military. The shock waves of the incident in Zabern reached all the way to the Reichstag and developed into one of the greatest constitutional crises in the history of Imperial Germany.[7] Schützinger, Schoenaich and Deimling all found their political home and most important sphere of influence in the republican veterans' association Reichsbanner Schwarz-Rot-Gold (Reichsbanner Black-Red-Gold). Schützinger differed from the other two men both in terms of his age (he was twenty-two years younger than Schoenaich) and his relative avoidance of the limelight. Despite working tirelessly as a speaker until 1933, he has thus been largely forgotten. The biographical literature available on Schützinger to date is strewn with errors and reveals little in relation to his conversion to pacifism.[8]

Before examining Schützinger's turn to pacifism in more detail, it is important first to recall the organizational forms in which veterans became politically active in Germany post-1918.[9] The pacifist response to the experience of war rapidly took organizational shape in the form of the Friedensbund der Kriegsteilnehmer (Peace League of Ex-Servicemen). The League owed its existence to the initiative of Karl Vetter. The son of a bricklayer, Vetter had a working-class background in Berlin's Neukölln district and had already been involved with the socialist youth movement before the outbreak of war. The experience of the front left him badly shaken. He returned to Berlin in 1918, now a radical pacifist. There, he worked on the city's *Berliner Volks-Zeitung* newspaper, which was published by the liberal proprietor Georg Lachmann-Mosse, and joined a forum for the discussion of radical democratic and left-liberal ideas.[10]

Vetter quickly began to use the *Berliner Volks-Zeitung* to disseminate ideas critical of warfare and the military. From March 1919, Vetter published a series of articles on his own recollections of the final months on the Western Front. These met with a positive response from many readers, who praised the clear words he had found to express the hopeless situation of the German troops and inevitability of defeat. Encouraged, Vetter compiled his texts in a booklet published in late 1919: *Ludendorff ist schuld! Die Anklage der Feldgrauen* (Ludendorff is to Blame! The Indictment of the *Feldgrauen*). The booklet's title, which referenced the field-grey uniforms of the ordinary soldiers (*Feldgrauen*), was unambiguous. Vetter argued that the Army Supreme Command under Ludendorff had sacrificed these men in a pointless campaign. Instead of conceding defeat after the failure of the spring offensive, it had decided to persist with the war. This made the Supreme Command the true culprit for the German military collapse in November 1918. Vetter concluded his indictment with an appeal: The 'spirit of brute force' manifested in the Army Supreme Command's military machine should never be allowed 'to turn Europe into a graveyard again'.[11]

In October 1919, Vetter invited a series of pacifist luminaries to the editorial offices of *Berliner Volks-Zeitung*. They included Kurt Tucholsky, Carl von Ossietzky and Georg Friedrich Nicolai, physician and professor at the University of Berlin. In 1918, Nicolai had spectacularly escaped persecution for his 1917 pacifist pamphlet, *Biologie des Krieges* (The Biology of War), by flying to Denmark. The outcome of this meeting was the founding of the Friedensbund der Kriegsteilnehmer (Peace League of Ex-Servicemen). The League was aimed at veterans of all political persuasions provided they supported peace, international reconciliation and the Weimar Republic. Alongside radical pacifist aims such as conscientious objection and the abolition of standing armies, the League also issued demands that more moderate bourgeois pacifists could back. These included peace education and the creation of international tribunals to resolve conflicts. Membership was limited to veterans of the First World War, which excluded women by definition. An official surveillance report on radical activities noted that, in the view of the League's founders, ex-servicemen were the only people to have 'experienced the full horror of war first-hand'.[12] Therefore, only they could campaign for the pacifist cause with the necessary vigour and credibility.

Even at its height in 1920/1, the Peace League of Ex-Servicemen never numbered more than between approximately 25,000 and 30,000 members. This was a vanishingly small minority of the potential reservoir of 13.2 million German war veterans and did not come anywhere close to the numbers mobilized by the Freikorps. However, it appears far more impressive when compared against more established pacifist organizations such as the Deutsche Friedensgesellschaft (German Peace Society), the organizational core of moderate bourgeois pacifism. Even at the peak of its appeal in 1926/27, the Society mobilized no more than 30,000 members.[13] The Peace League of Ex-Servicemen achieved the same figure from what was effectively a standing start. This suggests that the experience of First World War violence had created a new and substantial recruitment potential for pacifist politics. The Peace League did not share the restrained political style of the bourgeois dignitaries in the German Peace Society and other organizations, which had made it almost impossible to attract working-class members prior to 1918. Instead, the League pursued its own approach to political action. It essentially provided an organizational platform for short-lived cycles of mobilization in which veterans could become involved in public campaigning. In this sense, the League anticipated the forms of protest and mobilization that would later come to typify the peace movement post-1945.[14]

At the League's founding meeting in Berlin, Karl Vetter proposed that pacifists should mark 1 August – the anniversary of the outbreak of war – with a major gathering. He pointed to the importance of decisively rejecting the nationalist interpretation of the war as a 'time of greatness'. Anti-militarist feeling was still running high among the veterans. To translate this effectively into political action, the League needed an appropriate slogan. Vetter suggested that it adopt *Nie wieder Krieg!* (No More War!).[15] The *Berliner Volks-Zeitung* had already run a special edition on 3 August 1919 with precisely that headline. Contributors had included Vetter and the newspaper's editor-in-chief, Otto Nuschke, a co-founder of the left-liberal Deutsche Demokratische Partei (German Democratic Party), who also represented the party in the Weimar National Assembly.[16] The first major demonstration under the slogan 'No More War' took place at the Lustgarten in Berlin on 1 August 1920 and attracted more than 50,000 people. Additional support for the event came from the Social Democratic organization Reichsbund der Kriegsbeschädigten (Reich Association of War Disabled) and the Reichsvereinigung ehemaliger Kriegsgefangener (Reich Association of Former Prisoners of War), which also included many Social Democrats in its ranks.[17]

The two social democratic parties – the majority wing (MSPD) and the break-away USPD formed in 1917 – held separate events in 1920. However, in 1921 and 1922, both parties supported the rallies organized by the Peace League of Ex-Servicemen. During these two years, some half a million people attended events in more than two hundred cities. This wave of mobilization for the pacifist cause rapidly ebbed away again in the months that followed. Two developments contributed to this rapid decline. In September 1922, the remaining USPD members re-joined the MSPD after the party's left wing had merged with the communist KPD in December 1920. The left-wing USPD had been the driving force behind the 'No More War' movement. Secondly, the political environment changed rapidly in 1923 following the French occupation of the Ruhr. A wave of nationalist outrage swept through Germany and left its mark on the 1 August rallies, not least because the speakers had repeatedly expressed either direct or implicit understanding for the tough peace terms of the Treaty of Versailles. Events under the 'No More War' slogan now took place only behind closed doors and encountered sharp criticism both from radical nationalists and the KPD.[18]

Nevertheless, the 'No More War' movement's achievements should not be understated. In the first four years after the end of the First World War, it succeeded in mobilizing hundreds of thousands of people, most of them war veterans, for pacifist aims: non-violence, disarmament and the outlawing of war. There is little doubt that the experience of wartime violence was the driving motivation for the former front-line soldiers who actively supported the movement.

Hermann Schützinger was one such soldier. In 1922, a poster by the Munich 'No More War' committee invited local citizens to attend a 'commemoration ceremony for the dead' in the city's Kindlkeller beer hall on 31 July. The speakers listed for the event clearly illustrated the No More War movement's international connections. They included the British suffragette Emmeline Pethick-Lawrence (1867–1954) and John Haynes Holmes (1879–1964) from New York, a minister in the Unitarian church and well-known American pacifist who championed Gandhi's principle of non-violence. Holmes brought 'greetings from a former enemy country', highlighting the potential of international reconciliation under the banner of pacifism. Also at the event was Hermann Schützinger, who gave a

**Figure 3** 'No More War': Commemoration Ceremony for the Dead in Munich on 31 July 1922.

'speech in memory of the fallen'.[19] Who was this man who moved with such apparent ease in the pacifist and left-wing socialist circles of Munich?

Schützinger, born in Bayreuth in 1888, hailed from a respectable bourgeois family.[20] His father, Heinrich Schützinger (1857–1920), was a member of the

Bavarian judiciary. In 1894, Heinrich was elected mayor of Lindau, a town on Lake Constance, prompting the family to move to the region of Bavarian Swabia. One of Lindau's bourgeois notables, he had a leading role in the local museum association and Bodenseegeschichtsverein, an association devoted to the history of Lake Constance.[21] Hermann attended a *humanistisches Gymnasium* (classical grammar school) in Kempten until 1908. In October of the same year, he joined the Bavarian 11th Infantry Regiment 'von der Tann' as an officer candidate. The regiment was stationed in Regensburg. This was the beginning of Schützinger's career as an active military officer. In 1910, he achieved promotion to lieutenant. A qualification report compiled in 1913 describes him as a decisive, 'very capable, energetic officer with clear independent judgement' and as a promising and 'very assured worker'. His 'irritable temperament' sometimes aggravated comrades and superiors. However, this proved no impediment to his military career.[22] Schützinger provoked a minor scandal in 1914 when he published a novel entitled *Die Waffen hoch!* (To Arms!) under the pseudonym Hermann Pfeiler. The title – a riposte to the successful 1889 book *Die Waffen nieder* (Lay Down Your Arms!) by the Austrian pacifist and 1905 Nobel Peace Prize laureate, Bertha von Suttner – was unambiguous about the book's anti-pacifist thrust. Against the backdrop of the second Moroccan crisis of 1911, and probably influenced by the Balkan wars of 1912–13, the book portrays war as a 'law of nature' in the relationship between people and states. In the spirit of the Social Darwinism popular in bourgeois circles after the turn of the century, the novel suggests that war is a form of 'natural selection' in which only the superior civilized nations can survive.[23]

Schützinger conceived the novel not only in response to political events, but to a personal one too, namely an unsuccessful love affair. The book is a *roman à clef*, a novel featuring real people in a different guise. It features clearly identifiable officers in Schützinger's regiment and real women from Regensburg's bourgeois circles. In what was only a small city, this created a furore,[24] albeit not on the same scale as the 'Bilse case' in 1903. In that incident, an officer writing under the pseudonym Oswald Bilse had described life in the Alsatian garrison town of Forbach in a book entitled *Aus einer kleinen Garnison* (Life in a Garrison Town). The detailed portrayal quickly led to the revealing of the author's identity and the initiation of court-martial proceedings. However, even the court had to admit that there was 'a great deal of truth' in the novel.[25] Though Schützinger's book did not have the same impact, he nevertheless felt himself compelled to withdraw it from sale only a short time after publication.[26]

When war began in August 1914, Schützinger went straight into action with the 11th Bavarian Reserve Infantry Regiment. Having initially served as the battalion adjutant, he soon took command of one of the regiment's companies and was posted to the Vosges region close to the hill of Ban de Sapt as part of the Bavarian 30th Reserve Division. Schützinger wrote regular letters to his parents on his impressions of the front line. In total, 162 of these letters have survived. The early correspondence followed the conventions of the patriotic wartime discourse commonly found in field post letters, and particularly those written by career officers.[27] Schützinger described his service on the front in detail and reflected on the reasons why the soldiers in his company followed him with 'great loyalty'. This despite the fact that, as he freely admitted, he treated them 'very roughly' during drills. He noted that he meted out the 'barbaric' punishment of 'locking [soldiers] in a cellar' for every minor infringement, such as taking a brief nap while on sentry duty. Schützinger attributed the men's conformism both to his qualities as a military leader and his paternalistic, benevolent attitude to subordinates. A letter in October 1914, for example, described how he had celebrated All Souls' Day with his company close to a mass grave. There, he had emphasized to the men, evidently without a trace of irony, that 'the company was now our family and I as the father wanted to celebrate the old German custom of All Souls' Day with them'.[28]

Schützinger also reflected on the dangers of life on the front. During the early weeks of the war, the German army suffered enormous losses. On 24 August 1914, for example, Schützinger wrote that two 'very dear' comrades had fallen 'in the fiercest grenade fire', one of them just 'ten paces' away from him. He also described his belief in 'an invisible guardian angel, who has protected me so far in even the most perilous situations'.[29] A few weeks later in early October, a 'temporary calm' descended on his section of the front, with just a 'bang of artillery fire now and then'. Facing off across no-man's land, the French and German troops 'wanted nothing from each other for the time being'. With both sides having decided to live and let live, one patrol from his company went as far as to call a friendly 'good morning' to the French sentry.[30] However, the peace did not last long. Even on such quiet sections of the front, the army needed regular information on the enemy's troop strength and fortifications on the other side of no-man's land. This meant dispatching a patrol or lone soldier to gather intelligence.

As a dutiful officer and commander, Schützinger took on such missions himself, albeit through gritted teeth. On 31 October 1914, he wrote to his parents that he never knew 'whether one would survive the evening'. He went on to recount a recent incident:

> The major annoyed me terribly, swore down the phone – no superior dared to come and see me here at the front – that *Festungsgruppe Schützinger* was not sending any reports. In my anger, I ran out there myself and crawled around on my stomach for two hours to reconnoitre the enemy obstacles myself. I was shot at in the gorge 30–40 times at least.[31]

This reconnaissance mission not only put Schützinger's own life at risk. It also forced him to endure a nightmarish encounter with the remnants of the killing, the bodies of fallen soldiers that could not be recovered from no-man's land.

> On the way back, I had to crawl along the edge of the forest through the field of the dead; they had already cut me off in the forest itself. The smell of death was awful; the corpses were bloated to twice their usual size. As I crept through, the ravens who come every day to peck the flesh off the dead bodies flew up and gave me away. The reply was a dozen bullets, but the fellows all fired too high and I came back full of cheer.[32]

It is questionable how cheerful Schützinger's return was in reality. The relief at having survived the mission unscathed perhaps partially offset the deep anxiety induced by the sight of the decaying corpses. Nonetheless, this 'cheer' is typical of the vocabulary that front-line soldiers often deployed in their letters. The aim of such phrases was to dispel their relatives' concerns and project an air of optimism. For a soldier to continue writing such reassurances, however, relied on him finding them at least partially plausible himself. Their credibility could also become more problematic when other evidence – such as the photographs many men sent from the front line – contradicted the image the author wanted to convey in his letter. Relatives could immediately recognize weight loss and other suggestions of the hardships of the trenches. In January 1915, Schützinger openly admitted that the conflict had worn him down: 'I'm coming to the end of my strength now; you can see in any case from the photographs that the war has put years on me.'[33] For a career officer like Schützinger, however, physical exhaustion alone did not diminish enthusiasm for the war. In the same letter, he proudly reported on a visit to his position by the battalion commander, who had praised the depth of his *Angriffssappen*, the slit trenches leading towards the enemy fortifications. What was more, Schützinger had even convinced the commander to modify an attack plan in line with his suggestions. He thus demonstrated precisely the leadership qualities and professional commitment the army expected from an ambitious young officer.[34]

Schützinger's letters reveal that some six months after the outbreak of war, his nationalist, military mindset remained intact. In spring and early summer 1915, however, this began to change. 'Do not publicize.'³⁵ These words, written at the beginning of a letter dated 14 April 1915, made it unmistakably clear that what followed was about to cross the boundaries of jingoistic wartime discourse. Many bourgeois families had adopted the habit of forwarding letters from their sons, which contained embellished reports of heroism at the front, for publication in newspapers.³⁶ On no account were they to do so in this case. Schützinger's letter read as follows:

> I have just had another terrible night. I had the mission of taking a section of trench near my part of the front. I succeeded. My lieutenant Königer did the job impeccably. As I jumped into the right-hand side of the trench, the entire left-hand side exploded. Three dead are still lying under the rubble. We dug out several wounded, including my lieutenant. And then there began a hail of hand grenades that made the air tremor. I was thrown to the ground several times myself; a blast ripped the cap from my head. After three hours, I had nineteen wounded who looked terrible. Stink bombs made it hard to breathe. I ordered the clearing of the trench. My three best grenade throwers, magnificent, dear, good men are dead. How much longer?³⁷

This was a 'terrible night' but, as Schützinger would discover just a few weeks later, far from the worst he would experience during his time at the front. The letter's most immediately striking feature is the extraordinary mixture of unconcealed delight at the initial success of the operation and dismay at the subsequent deadly consequences. Writing with the air of the paternalistic troop officer, Schützinger mourns the death of his 'magnificent' men, the three grenade throwers. The letter concludes with a question asked by a rapidly growing number of front-line soldiers: when would the war end?³⁸ Gone was the atmosphere of gung-ho nationalism that had characterized the initial weeks and months of the conflict, a time when few had questioned the war's meaning or duration.

As is apparent from his war letters, this also soon changed the language Schützinger used to describe his experiences of violence on the front and its deadly consequences. In a letter dated 5 May 1915, he told his parents that another close encounter with death had left him unable to enjoy the food parcel they had sent for his 27th birthday just a few days earlier. 'I will say it honestly', he added, 'this brutal and beastly murdering is becoming unbearable.'³⁹ The wording hints at the effort it cost Schützinger finally to break free of the nationalist discourse and describe the killing as other soldiers increasingly perceived it: a criminal act of murder exercised with senseless brutality. Yet it was a murder without murderers. Schützinger was far from the only soldier who was struck by the automation and anonymity of this form of murder in the First World War, where it was impossible to attribute deaths even to groups of enemy soldiers, let alone individual perpetrators.[40] As the rest of the letter reveals, however, his use of the term 'murder' appears to have been triggered less by the act of killing itself than by the sometimes agonizingly slow deaths of fatally wounded soldiers. While Schützinger was away from his dugout, a shell had hit it, burying both an orderly and an on-duty NCO, a vice-sergeant major by the name of Hagen. Having been dug out of the debris, Hagen was brought to a communication trench. Schützinger described the sight as follows:

> The left leg shot off above the knee, the right punctured three times and twisted on each occasion, three punctures in his left arm, the left-hand side of his face torn; the horrific stump of a body full of blood. And – just imagine – the man still lives and holds my hand and remains conscious for another two hours. His last words were: 'Send my love to my mother, she shouldn't grieve.' I have seen a great deal already, but this slow, conscious death was actually the most awful thing I have seen in this war.[41]

Schützinger's description of Hagen's death closes with the superlative, 'most awful'. His subsequent letters reveal how quickly the sustained fighting on his section of the front could exhaust the descriptive power of this grammatical form. Even its repeated use was soon unable to convey experiences that Schützinger himself found almost incomprehensible. One event in late June 1915 stands out in this regard. On this occasion, the 'most dreadful night', as he described it, owed its harrowing nature not principally to the violent killing of enemy soldiers, though Schützinger's account of this is dramatic enough. Nor was the death toll on his own side the most shocking aspect, though this deeply shook him too. What made this night such a pivotal moment in Schützinger's war experience was instead the premonition of his own death, which revealed its nightmarish quality only through the confounding and incomprehensible fact of his own survival.[42]

From late 1914, German units had attempted to take the hill of Ban de Sapt in the Vosges, which was held by French troops. In sustained battles at close quarters, they succeeded step by step in taking parts of the hillside. Schützinger's regiment was among those involved in the fighting. His letters from mid-April and early May 1915 cover these extremely costly battles. On 1 June 1915, Schützinger received a promotion to first lieutenant.[43] A few weeks later, on 22 June, the Germans commenced an attack designed finally to take the summit of

Ban de Sapt. This was carried out by the Bavarian 30th Reserve Division, which included Schützinger's 11th Reserve Infantry Regiment and the 14th Reserve Infantry Regiment.[44] At 3.00 pm, the Germans launched an artillery bombardment of the hill and the nearby village of Fontenelle. In an official announcement published on 1 July, the German news agency Wolffs Telegraphisches Büro described the infantry assault that began at 6.30 pm: 'The brave Bavarian reserve troops stormed forwards in an unstoppable advance, supported by the Prussian infantry and riflemen.'[45] The hill was taken at approximately 8.00 pm and the German troops readied themselves for the French counterattack. This began immediately and continued throughout the night. The following morning of 23 June saw the artillery fire reach a peak.

The reports from German headquarters described the attack as an exercise in clinical precision. This was in sharp contrast to the impressions of the young company leader Schützinger, who needed two attempts to put the events at Ban de Sapt into words and thereby at least begin to process its emotional toll. Two days after the battle of 22 June 1915, he wrote his first letter about the day's events to his parents:

> Dearest Parents, My most terrible experience of the war so far is over; I think the horror has aged me 50 years. The attack on the hill of Ban de Sapt, which cost us the majority of our officers and certainly 500 of our men, is over; my entire company staff, my sergeant, my orderly, my hand-grenade throwers, who were standing right beside me, were killed and horribly mutilated by a shell. I myself crawled back out of the dirt unscathed. Oh, this maddening luck is almost uncanny. Live well! I have still to come back to my senses, your Hermann.[46]

Despite the horror still fresh in his mind and the miraculous escape from death, Schützinger expressed his satisfaction, at least in the letter's margins, that the costly attack had succeeded: 'But at least we took it, the damned hill.'[47] The letter once again uses the superlative to appraise the day's events, though at this stage Schützinger had not yet rationally processed the experience. In a letter written on 28 June, his second attempt at putting the battle into words, he embarks on a more detailed description of the assault on Ban de Sapt. This letter reveals the real reasons for his emotional shock. It also vividly reveals how the killing of enemy troops, the deaths of German soldiers and their survival were entwined. Schützinger wrote:

> Dearest Parents, ... The storming of the hill of Ban de Sapt, which I can feel in my bones since the 22nd and which hasn't let me get a wink of sleep, seems to me increasingly like a distant, confused dream....

## The Delayed Rejection of Violence

My old Kempten friend and acquaintance Captain of the reserve Sturm said to me, half-jokingly, half-seriously, 'I should get another picture taken of myself; listen, it's my last photograph; I've got a feeling about it!' Later, as I was up on the conquered hill amid the heaviest shelling and felt the same premonition of death as my friend Sturm, my runner approached breathless from the left: 'The company on the left can't advance, the front line have been shot to bits, Captain Sturm is lying dead up there.' I was convinced: now you're going to die; if *his* premonition came true, so will *yours*.

The night from 22 to 23 June, Papa's birthday, was the most terrible of my life. I awaited my certain death from minute to minute, shell to shell.... The 11th Regiment was an assault regiment; all in all, 1,000 men will have been lost.

At the beginning of the attack, as I charged up the steps at the head of my company and worked my way forwards with the foremost men from shell crater to shell crater, we received murderous machine gun fire from the right-hand flank and some from behind – the hill of Ban de Sapt is like a wedge pushed forward into the enemy positions.

Major Schaaf, who has shown tremendous pluck, put one of our machine guns in position to keep the French one down – the French machine gun salvo was landing right in the middle of us; platoon leader, gun commander, the three gunners lay motionless, their bodies riddled with bullets; that warm rush of air I'm so familiar with passed over me again.

Followed by parts of my company and a motley crew of men, I jumped over the high parapet of the enemy's main position. Major Schaaf and his adjutant – a good, brave, flaxen-haired young reserve lieutenant (Holzgrebe), my favourite one-year volunteer [young men with a high school diploma could sign up for military service as a one-year volunteer, thus benefiting from reduced service time and other privileges] – gave me a target for the assault, the gap between the two battalions, and then I charged forwards with my men.

We charged like crazy along the trenches, over the dugouts. Our foremost line encountered almost no resistance as we had simply overrun everything; the second line and the reserves had to fight man on man, one dugout after another with hand grenades, bayonets and the good old Bavarian knives. Don't believe that the French are cowards; despite shells, hand grenades and flamethrowers, one French dugout held on for *three days*; only hunger forced the brave men out. The first lieutenant, who was sitting in there with half a platoon, got past the trench sentry and fled through our lines towards Fontenelle. He was not shot dead until he reached our foremost outpost. Respect to the brave officer! We buried him in Laitre with full honours.

My assault detachment and I had barely reached the edge of the forest on the summit opposite, and had only just found and decided on the defensive line based on tactical considerations, when we began to receive fiendish close-range artillery fire in the shallow and open communication trench.

Almost every shot hit its mark! Here we suffered by far the most losses. My right-hand platoon leader in the company section in front of me had his head blown off by one of the first shots; only his blond wartime beard hung on the grisly stump.

Night fell, the most dreadful night of my life; I constantly expected to die; I certainly thought of papa's birthday, especially at midnight. We dug ourselves in like crazy, as if we were moles gone mad; we threw the dead over the parapet because they obstructed our digging; anyone who stood upright was soon hit.

Then came the barrage before the counterattack. I knew they were coming now and shouted my order to fire. My company staff were all around me: my plucky sergeant, my best hand-grenade thrower, my most dependable orderly. I gave the order to throw two hand grenades. The first exploded. As the second took flight, we were suddenly plunged into bright fire, the pressure wave threw me to the ground and buried me in soil; my three companions who were standing right by me: one made a wild cry, the other two quiet sighs; my sergeant had his head ripped off, the second man his chest smashed in, the third his side ripped open; all three dead instantly – *I* was completely unhurt.

It was too creepy for me among the dead. I jumped 50 metres to the right and crouched in the trench between two riflemen – *the same* flash and bang; the men to the left and right of me died in a few minutes, groaning terribly; *I* remained unhurt. Even with my whole body shaking, I encouraged my men. I sat down with my Lieutenant v. Stockar and waited for the third shot and my death; but it didn't come.

It gradually became light and I was relieved from duty.

I'll tell you the rest soon in person.[48]

This is a particularly harrowing account of the physical and psychological damage wrought by the violence of the First World War. Hermann Schützinger's son Heinrich, a professor of Oriental studies in Bonn, wrote in 2003 that repeated readings of his father's letter had not lessened its emotional impact. He donated it with many other letters to Walter Kempowski's collection of self-testimonies.[49] Heinrich Schützinger was convinced that the 'slaughter of static warfare' at the Ban de Sapt was the main reason why his father had joined the peace movement after the war.[50] In his view, the events of 22 June 1915 were decisive in Hermann Schützinger's conversion to pacifism. There is little doubt that the experiences of that day were indeed a turning point in Schützinger's life. But ascribing to them the primary motive for his conversion to pacifism is inconsistent with his accounts of the remainder of the war, as will become clear later in this chapter.

The letter begins with Captain Sturm's premonition of death, which was soon fulfilled. It was not unusual before major attacking battles for soldiers and officers to express a belief that they were certain to die. This was often accompanied by preparations such as the last photograph considered by Sturm. Others wrote farewell letters to wives or family.[51] To some extent, this was a form of superstition cultivated by life on the front.[52] However, there was also a rational, empirical dimension to such thoughts. Soldiers knew only too well from their experiences of previous attacks that such missions caused a spike in casualty rates. Studies on the psychology of war have examined the origins and impacts of premonitions of death. They have found that this mentality had a 'paralyzing effect' on other soldiers in the field, which long outlasted the initial grief at the deaths themselves. When a soldier died in battle following such a premonition, he bore 'silent witness' to the truth of these superstitions.[53] This explains why Schützinger experienced the battle at Ban de Sapt as an agonizing wait for death in the certainty that his premonition, too, was about to be fulfilled.

However, the day brought other impressions, too. The assault began with intense close-quarter combat in a battle that Schützinger interpreted through the prism of collective honour and recognition. The French troops deserved respect for the bravery they had demonstrated in action. The letter gives special mention to a French officer who fiercely resisted for three days before attempting an escape. Awarding him an honourable burial after he was shot dead by a German outpost was part of the officer corps' code of honour, which we also repeatedly encounter in Ernst Jünger's diaries.[54]

So forceful was the subsequent artillery bombardment that there was little room for these deeper reflections in the second half of the letter. Schützinger's letter notes, like the official medical report discussed in Chapter 2, that the vast majority of deaths were attributable to artillery fire. Schützinger and his men were forced to endure the onslaught in the makeshift defensive position they had improvised on the Ban de Sapt hill. For all the horrific scenes described in Schützinger's letter, neither the severed limbs and decapitations inflicted by enemy fire, nor the near-constant belief that he was about to die, appear to have been the most disturbing element of his experience. Rather, what seems to have unsettled Schützinger most of all about the battle was the way his expectation of death was repeatedly confounded. Having twice witnessed the killing of close comrades standing beside him, he awaited the 'third shot' and the certain death that never came. In his letter on 24 June, Schützinger emphasized that this 'maddening luck' was 'almost uncanny'. Though he does not repeat this remark in the letter of 28

June, he suggests at least indirectly that the fact of his own survival had deeply shaken him.

In the absence of further evidence, there is no way of knowing whether Schützinger's emotional anguish crystallized into a feeling of guilt at his own survival. However, the affective language with which he describes the military qualities of his company staff certainly suggests that their violent deaths caused him lasting pain. With 'ideological warriors' like Ernst Jünger in mind, it has been argued that a 'feeling of invincibility' and belief in their own survival skills gripped soldiers who had survived several battles. These men, it is claimed, developed a form of 'hubris', believing they were 'invulnerable'.[55] Whatever its plausibility more widely, this theory does not apply to Schützinger's response to his own survival. This is clear not only from his war letters, but also from a novel he later published in 1918: *Das Lied vom jungen Sterben. Kriegsroman aus dem Ban de Sapt* (The Song of Dying Young: A War Novel from the Ban de Sapt).[56] This literary work was also an attempt to tell his parents of his experiences in a more expressive form than that permitted by his war letters.[57] Schärting, the novel's central character, bears unmistakable similarities with Schützinger and is essentially his alter ego. The plot culminates in a reconstruction of the battle at Ban de Sapt, with Schärting awaiting his certain death:

> Schärting is sure there is no escape from him now. Tired, he stretches himself out between the dead bodies and waits for the end. Left and right, the metallic thuds pound the gloom of the trenches with a flare of bright yellow light, casting dark shadows that fall to the ground, never to rise again. It is then that he notices he has lost his ring, Claire's talisman, in the fierce fighting. That seems only fitting, for sooner or later the end would come. It must be lying there with all the others: Mohsmann, Holzgrebe, Sturm, Schmitt, Naegelsbach.... Why did the wretched shot not come?[58]

Written three years after the Ban de Sapt attack, this literary text does not convey a soldier's belief in his own invincibility. Rather, the sense that Schützinger, or Schärting, faced an inevitable fate figures as the main experience of June 1915. The book ends by invoking 'German love and faithfulness' and reveals throughout that, even as late autumn 1918, Schützinger still held fast to a romanticized idealization of war.[59] For Schützinger himself, the novel served primarily to reinforce his memory of what he had witnessed at Ban de Sapt. In a letter in May 1918, he commented that the process of writing the book gave him a 'feeling of strength' that he could 'meet life's challenges'.[60]

Schützinger's descriptions of the battle in his letters and the decision to give his experiences a literary treatment show that the Ban de Sapt attack on 22 June 1915 was a momentous event in his life. However, it would be a mistake to interpret it as the direct trigger for his turn to pacifism. Schützinger's letters show that he continued to pursue his military career with undisguised ambition and enthusiasm for more than three years after the Ban de Sapt attack. This was despite setbacks. In early summer 1916, he faced an inquiry by a military court. It related to two incidents in October and December 1915 when NCOs in his company had made contact with the French troops opposite them. In the first case, the men had followed an order from Schützinger, who wanted to identify the enemy regiment. In the second instance, the NCO in question had acted on his own initiative. In all likelihood, this was an example of the practice of 'live and let live' seen on many parts of the front especially during bad weather. Schützinger described the proceedings as follows:

> The scene was observed; the NCO hauled in front of the court martial, the entire battalion relieved at a moment's notice. Everyone has it in for us; except for those who have experienced trench warfare for themselves. Our well-fed divisional staff rage and swear and insult their best, most loyal, most self-sacrificing regiment, their worthiest company. To jubilation, the NCO is acquitted. But in spite of that, I'm still fuming at the injustice perpetrated against us by these arrogant Prussians.[61]

What Schützinger omitted to tell his parents was that he was also being investigated for perjury. His testimony in the proceedings against the NCO, where he stated that he had never seen the men openly interacting with the French, contradicted other accounts of the first incident. The court suspended its proceedings against Schützinger in July 1916.[62] In January 1916, with the legal case against the NCO ongoing, Schützinger requested a transfer to another battalion. The battalion commander complied with this wish and reassigned him to the replacement battalion of the 11th Reserve Infantry Regiment from 15 May to 18 August 1916. Following his return to the field, Schützinger then served initially in the active 11th Infantry Regiment 'von der Tann', the very unit in which he had begun his career as an officer.[63] The return to his old company was a deeply depressing experience. At Verdun, the regiment had 'suffered the worst losses it is possible for a unit to bear'. In a letter to his parents, he described the sad moment when he 'greeted the single remaining comrade from my time as a lieutenant'.[64] The remainder of the 'von der Tann' officers whom Schützinger remembered from before the war were either dead or too severely injured to serve.

Neither the court martial nor the shock at the death of so many of his regimental comrades diminished Schützinger's enthusiasm for his military role. In 1917, he served as a company leader in the 32nd Infantry Regiment. He used this period to advance his military training and, in June 1917, participated in a machine gun course with a replacement unit in Ingolstadt.[65] Schützinger now turned all his ambition to improving the effectiveness of machine guns in the German army. He experimented with a new target-finding device for machine gun operators and proposed a new procedure for indirect machine gun fire.[66] A publication on machine gun training intended for official use was in print by spring 1918 and later followed by a second on 'Indirect Machine Gun Fire'.[67] Schützinger could report to his parents with pride, and perhaps more than a touch of exaggeration, that his firing procedure had earned 'great recognition from everyone'. He regarded it as 'an extraordinary personal achievement' that he had enjoyed the opportunity to become acquainted 'with leading figures behind our weapons technology'.[68]

Schützinger's intensive work to improve machine gun tactics soon brought highly visible successes in his military career. In April 1918, he was transferred to the staff of the 13th Bavarian Infantry Regiment as a machine gun officer, enabling him to further pursue his specialist interest. More recognition followed in August 1918 with a promotion to captain.[69] In autumn 1918, as the German army on the Western Front was already disintegrating, Schützinger took yet another 'step' up the military career ladder. On 15 October 1918, he wrote to his parents full of pride at his achievements and satisfaction with his new duties. His choice of language reveals the personal ambition and deliberate planning he had invested in this career:

> Dear Parents, Another step further! I have become machine gun officer in the staff of the 5th Army Head Construction and Fortification Unit. A top-notch job with enormous responsibility and reporting directly to the Chief of the General Staff. I look after the whole machine gun set-up along the army front-line zone (16 divisional sections, 45 kilometres of front) and dash by car from one position to another, one construction unit to another. Many of the positions are already under heavy flat-trajectory fire, but I find it more enjoyable than painful compared with what I used to have to deal with. In my position, I am equal to a colonel from an artillery unit and an engineering unit and have an enormous range of activities, working together with all the other weaponry. My headquarters is a château near Montmedy, but usually I spend the night up front with the troops in forest camps.[70]

Schützinger drew obvious satisfaction from his new responsibilities for the German war machine. Part of his role's appeal lay in coordinating the different types of weaponry. Now that he was an active participant in the organization of violence, he was also prepared to forget the 'painful' impact of the Allied artillery fire. In fact, he even found it 'enjoyable' to visit positions under enemy bombardment. Schützinger clearly remained the 'very capable' and keen officer described in his qualification report in 1913. He was not motivated in autumn 1918 by the pleasure of actively perpetrating violence, but by his pride at his prominent role in the German army's enormous military apparatus on the Western Front. In a letter written on 20 October 1918, less than three weeks before the armistice on 11 November, Schützinger again reached for the superlative. This time it was not to express his horror at the deaths of fellow soldiers, but satisfaction at his standing in the army:

> Yesterday and the day before were perhaps the most interesting days of my military life. In my new position, I was brought into the most important discussions of the Army High Command due to radical orders that had arrived from the Army Supreme Command. I then went out in the car and on horseback to explore the whole army area with some generals and general staff officers. Now I have been put in charge of setting up machine guns for these new positions. I started my work on a steep hilltop on the Meuse (looks like Hohentwiel [a hill created by an extinct volcano near Lake Constance]), the American long projectiles howling over my head.[71]

It was only in his final wartime letter to his parents, on 2 November 1918, that a melancholy tone returned. Schützinger now expressed his doubts about the purpose of sacrificing any more men: 'When will this pitiful existence end? I feel doubly sorry for every cartload of the wounded – why are we still letting each other be crippled?'[72]

After his regiment's return to the garrison in Regensburg at the end of November 1918, Schützinger decided to continue his military career. From mid-January until June 1919 he commanded the Stadtkompanie Regensburg, a local unit of the Volkswehr (people's militia). Like other units of its type, it gathered volunteers – mostly working-class Social Democrats – around the surviving core of a unit of the Imperial Army. Its aim was to ensure security in the city and counter the radicalization of the revolutionary *Rätebewegung* (council movement).[73] Schützinger later recalled using socialist texts for the purposes of 'civic education' in this unit, and clearly already had a close affinity with social democracy.[74] In April 1919, the Regensburg Volkswehr unit marched to Munich on behalf of the government led by the Majority Social Democrat prime minister of Bavaria, Johannes Hoffmann. Its mission was to help suppress the communist Council Republic. Schützinger initially prevailed against the soldiers' council within the unit, which opposed the deployment to the Bavarian capital. On the way to Munich, however, while Schützinger's unit were seeking billets in the town of Freising, the men were approached by an 'angry mob', who attempted to seize their weapons. Following the mediation of the local soldiers' council, it was agreed that the troops should abandon their journey and return to the garrison in Regensburg. Describing this incident in the socialist journal *Sozialistische Monatshefte* two years later, Schützinger was still seething with anger at the disgraceful 'failure' of the Volkswehr troops. As he rightly recognized, this had cleared the path for the 'White Terror' of the Freikorps under Franz Epp, which 'drowned' the Munich Council Republic 'in blood'.[75] Schützinger concluded from the episode that discipline was essential to the success of republican defence organizations, a lesson he would later apply in his police career and in the Social Democratic Reichsbanner.

His willingness to lead a unit on behalf of the SPD government reveals that Schützinger's politics were already closely aligned with the Social Democrats by spring 1919, though he was not yet a member of the party. After the defeat of the Council Republic, Schützinger initially joined the *Wehrregiment* in Munich. Numbering approximately 3,000 men, this was a militarily organized unit of the Bavarian police. It brought together various parts of the security police (*Sicherheitspolizei*) and was designed to compensate for the reduction in army troop strength.[76] It was only in November 1919, having been discharged from this unit and put on leave from active service, that Schützinger formally joined the SPD.[77] His strengthening leftist political conviction resulted partly from the Kapp Putsch, which unfolded from 13 to 17 March 1920. In Munich, the commander of the Reichswehr – as the armed forces of the Weimar Republic were called – in Bavaria, General Arnold Ritter von Möhl, demanded the transfer of executive power to the military, a clearly 'unconstitutional' act. General von Möhl thereby forced the resignation of the Social Democratic prime minister Hoffmann, whose backing consisted only of a minority cabinet tolerated by bourgeois parties. With the election of Gustav Ritter von Kahr as the new prime minister of Bavaria on 16 March, the state's transformation into the so-called *Ordnungszelle Bayern*, a right-wing, anti-republican Bavarian 'cell of order' was complete.[78]

Schützinger's reaction to these developments was twofold. Firstly, he wrote to the *Reichswehrminister* (defence minister), Gustav Noske, a Majority Social

Democrat. He reminded Noske, who had evidently encountered Schützinger before, that he had been forced to take his leave from the Reichswehr as a result of his 'cooperation with the Regensburg Majority Socialists' in leading a Volkswehr unit. But now, he added, the Kapp Putsch meant there was more at stake than his own career. Schützinger therefore offered Noske his services as an 'upstanding democrat' and expressed his wish to serve in an army conscious of its 'duty to the state'. His aim was to prevent the sort of 'desperado politics' witnessed in the Kapp Putsch and create an officer corps loyal to the Weimar Republic.[79] The letter was in vain. Just a few days later, Otto Geßler of the German Democratic Party (DDP) became the new defence minister, replacing Noske.

Undeterred, Schützinger took a second public step, effectively sealing his departure from the Reichswehr. In the *Münchener Post*, the SPD's daily newspaper in Munich, he published an article on 23 March entitled 'The Reaction in the Army'. This was an indictment of the 'political bankruptcy of the old Prussian officer corps' that the Kapp Putsch had revealed. Its fateful consequences in the events of recent days, he wrote, would be 'to the ruin of the people'.[80] This was the first of many political commentaries that Schützinger published in the *Münchener Post*. As an internal letter within the Reichswehr concluded, political engagement in this form was unacceptable from a 'still active officer' and could not go unpunished. On 31 March 1920, barely more than a week after the article was published, the Reichswehr dismissed Schützinger.[81] Soon afterwards, the Deutsche Offiziers-Bund, a right-leaning association of professional officers, excluded him from its ranks.[82]

While still on leave from active service, Schützinger had begun an economics degree in Munich, which he completed with a doctorate in 1922.[83] He was also active as a writer and, from the mid-1920s, turned professional by issuing Social Democratic press bulletins. During his time in Munich until autumn 1922, Schützinger was also closely associated with the local leadership of the MSPD around Erhard Auer, the equally energetic and authoritarian head of the Bavarian SPD. Following a demonstration by the radical right-wing *Vaterländische Verbände* (nationalist associations) on 28 June 1922, Schützinger sent the Munich SPD an extensive memorandum on how to improve the training and organization of their defence formation, the Auer Guard. As we have seen, he was also active in the 'No More War' movement. In addition, Schützinger participated actively in the 1920s in the pacifist Deutsche Liga für Menschenrechte (German League for Human Rights), the successor organization to the Bund Neues Vaterland (New

Fatherland League), which existed from 1914 until 1922 and opposed the First World War mobilization from the outset.[84]

There is insufficient space here for more than the briefest outline of the remaining years of Schützinger's life and his varied political work. Schützinger worked in the Hamburg police force in 1922, then in Saxony as a *Polizeioberst* (police colonel) in 1923. After the fall of the government of the Socialist prime minister Erich Zeigner in Saxony, he was suspended from duty. From 1924, his political work took place largely in the Reichsbanner Black-Red-Gold. He was a member of the organization's main board, the *Reichsausschuss*, and also worked for it as a speaker. His activities in the mass organization brought him a degree of prominence as is illustrated by a special portrait postcard, probably from the late 1920s. It depicts Schützinger in his Reichsbanner uniform and explicitly introduces him as a *Reichsausschuss* member.

In the Reichsbanner, Schützinger enjoyed a constructive dialogue with other pacifist officers including the former captain at sea Lothar Persius, as well as with the radical pacifist and left-wing socialist critic of the Reichsbanner, Kurt Tucholsky. Schützinger was particularly interested in the republican interpretation of the war experience in the Reichsbanner. During the Third Reich, he initially worked in publishing and later, from 1942, in statistical departments of the state organizations responsible for steering the economy. In the autumn of 1945, Schützinger became the lead business editor at the *Berliner Zeitung*. He left the divided city in 1948 and settled in Bonn in 1950. There, he was an accredited member of the Bundespressekonferenz (Federal Press Conference) and wrote articles on politics in the West German capital until his death in May 1962.[85]

## Conclusion

Hermann Schützinger was one of hundreds of thousands of former front-line soldiers who supported the 'No More War' movement and its pacifist aims after 1918. He was also part of a small circle of war veterans who, as active members of pacifist groups, condemned war and campaigned for disarmament and a 'cultural demobilization' in order to contain and overcome the hatred and aggression in the political culture.[86] Schützinger's background as a career officer was unusual for a pacifist war veteran. Efficient deployment of weaponry and the exercise of violence were a self-evident part of his chosen profession both before and after 1914. By contrast, the journalists at Berlin daily newspapers who formed the organizational core of the 'No More War' movement had served only

**Figure 4** Former Colonel of Police Dr Hermann Schützinger, member of the Reichsausschuss: postcard, no date (approx. 1927–30).

as conscripts. Artur Zickler, for example, an editor of *Vorwärts* in Berlin and another leading member of the 'No More War' movement, described the military in a 1919 brochure as a 'madhouse' full of corrupt and sadistic officers.[87]

Such rhetoric was alien to Schützinger. He did not regard the military as an institution defined by exploitation or repression, but rather as a place in which to prove himself. Neither his occasional complaints about incompetent superiors, nor the court-martial proceedings against him, lessened his ambition in developing new machine gun firing techniques until just a few weeks before the armistice. Nothing suggests that he had any moral scruples about the fact that he, his company and machine gun tactics were killing other people. However, this is not to suggest that Schützinger was completely unmoved by the killing. Shortly before the armistice in November 1918, he commented on the senselessness of further violence. In letters to, and conversations with, his parents, and later in his 1918 war novel, he had already expressed his deep emotional shock at the deaths of comrades. Feelings of guilt at the miracle of his own survival perhaps plagued him even more than the horror of witnessing death at close quarters. It seems that this empathy with the pain of others was in fact the very moral compass that almost predestined his path to pacifism. It certainly distinguished him fundamentally from Ernst Jünger, who was unable to develop any sensibility for the suffering of others. In March 1918, Jünger watched as a soldier, wounded in the trench by a shot to the head, entered his death throes. 'During the final twitches', wrote Jünger in his diary, 'he let go of his fluids. I crouched beside him and registered these events with objectivity.'[88] This was the 'aesthetic of terror', which deliberately held moral questions at a distance and which Jünger later cultivated in his war literature.[89] It could barely be further removed from the tone of Schützinger's war letters.

However, it would be incorrect to see the experience of death and survival on the Western Front as the direct motivation for Schützinger's commitment to pacifism. Not only did Schützinger continue to serve enthusiastically until almost the very end of the war, but he also established a new military unit immediately after his return home to Germany, this time under the political auspices of the Majority Social Democrats. His support of the MSPD and the republic gave Schützinger a political framework within which he would later draw lasting conclusions from important aspects of his wartime experience. It was only as he observed the fateful actions of the radical right-wing 'desperados' during the Kapp Putsch in 1920 that Schützinger decided publicly to draw a line under his military career.[90] Schützinger's pacifism was thus not a direct consequence of his experience of violence in the First World War. He became a pacifist only when the Kapp Putsch revealed the destructive political influence of the remnants of the old imperial officer corps. In this delayed decision to distance himself from the violence of the war, Schützinger had much in common with the other veterans who campaigned for pacifist aims in the 'No More War' movement and in the Reichsbanner Black-Red-Gold.

# 10

# 'Rear Area Militarism': Discussing the War in Anti-military Bestsellers in the Weimar Republic

Literature in the Weimar Republic was an important medium for exploring the experience of violence in the Great War. The publication in 1929 of what is now perhaps the best known German war novel of the interwar years – Erich Maria Remarque's *Im Westen nichts Neues* (All Quiet on the Western Front) – triggered a controversy that raged in literary and political circles alike. Remarque's book brought the author world renown and made him an enemy of the Nazis, forcing him to emigrate from Germany in 1933. It became the catalyst for a public debate on the significance of the front-line experience in the political culture of the Weimar Republic.[1] However, it would be incorrect to regard the furore around *All Quiet on the Western Front* as a sign that literature was only now catching up with the First World War.[2] In fact, the war had prompted all manner of literary representations from the very birth of the Weimar Republic. These formed their own subsegment of the literary field, in which criteria for the critical assessment and appreciation of specific types of fiction writing took shape.[3] A clever, targeted marketing campaign for *Im Westen nichts Neues* by the Ullstein publishing house had some success in influencing the book's reception by the press and critics, thus shifting the boundaries of the literary sub-field of texts on the war more generally and the rules by which it operated.[4]

Despite the enormous readership of Remarque's book, nationalist, violence-affirming war literature dominated the Weimar Republic, at least as far as sales figures were concerned. This is all the more reason here to present two lesser-known titles that tackled the war from a decidedly more critical perspective. In so doing, this chapter will also illustrate the difficulties faced by socialist and pacifist writers in thematising wartime violence. Both the authors examined here found a specific topic that enabled them to criticize the injustices of the war without discussing the violence perpetrated by ordinary German soldiers.

This chapter will examine *Charleville. Dunkle Punkte aus dem Etappenleben* (Charleville: Dark Episodes of Life in the Rear Area) by Wilhelm Appens and *Etappe Gent* by Heinrich Wandt. The two texts appeared shortly after the end of the First World War and soon became popular and widely read examples of German war literature. Both works share common themes: mismanagement, embezzlement, corruption and the exploitation of the civilian population by the German occupation force in the rear areas of Belgium and France: a set of phenomena that Appens succinctly described as 'rear area militarism'. Both authors wrote their *chroniques scandaleuses* in the form of a report, combining autobiographical elements with narration and documentation. This fits one of the premises of recent research on 1920s and 1930s war literature, which argues that the 'distinction between fiction and documentation, between "first-hand reports" and "novels" ceased to apply' during this period.[5] Furthermore, both authors attracted the attention of the Weimar authorities, who wanted to suppress their work. This makes *Charleville* and *Etappe Gent* important examples of the censorship of pacifist, anti-war literature in the Weimar Republic and of the repressive measures that the state used against left-wing authors.[6]

Their popularity, determined criticism of the war and controversial reception make both texts worthy of a closer examination and historical contextualization.[7] The chapter will attempt this using previously unexplored source material on the life and work of both authors and the measures taken against them. It begins by identifying the components of the critical discourse on the German military in the Belgian and French rear areas, which began to take shape before the end of the war. This forms the historical context for both texts (I). The second part of the chapter analyses the texts themselves, their published editions and narrative perspective (II). The chapter concludes with a closer look at the authors and their politics, as well as the reception of the two works and the state's attempts to suppress them (III).

## I The rear area as the scene of civilian life and 'shirking'

With the mobilization of mass armies during the First World War, the rear areas in Belgium, France, North Africa and occupied Russian Poland became the 'connecting zone between the fighting troops and the home front'. The military apparatus in the rear area (*Etappe*) was divided into inspectorates (*Etappeninspektionen*) and commands (*Etappenkommandanturen*), and was responsible for replenishment of manpower and supplies at the front and for managing the occupied territories.[8]

Common themes soon emerged in perceptions of life in the rear area. By 1916, these crystallized into a relatively fixed picture in the minds of both ordinary soldiers and the military authorities themselves. This was reflected in various decrees from authorities high up the command chain, which aimed to tackle a range of unwelcome phenomena. One such source of concern was the growing number of extra-marital relationships between officers and the *Etappenhelferinnen*, German non-uniformed women with civilian status, who were employed as secretaries or kitchen staff to free up men for armed duty.[9] The existence of brothels for German military personnel – including separate brothels for officers – was the subject of critical remarks in soldiers' war letters and internal military discussions.[10] The perceived abuses also included the requisitioning of food, household goods and luxury items by officers and NCOs in order to send them to Germany.[11]

These and other phenomena fostered a distinctive 'psychology of the rear area' as Hermann Hefele warned, from a nationalist perspective, in a 1918 edition of the *Tat-Flugschriften*. Its most important aspect, he argued, was the consistent absence of physical danger for the units posted there, which afforded them a 'comfortable life far removed from the line of fire'.[12] The rear area enabled military personnel of all ranks to enjoy a civilian lifestyle in stark contrast to the dangers faced by the men posted at the front. For Appens, the common expression in Charleville, 'If only peace doesn't break out!' perfectly encapsulated the 'spongers' who worked in formations and administrative roles that were entirely 'redundant'. The officers of these units 'visibly turned pale when peace was mentioned' and earned 'nothing but the scorn and derision of the front troops'.[13] The expression also captured the fundamental issue underlying these perceptions: the fact that, despite the war, the men posted to the rear area were still living in peace.

The potential set-pieces and rhetorical elements of a discourse criticizing the war were thus already in place before November 1918. After the war, the rear area would figure in this discourse as an example for the systemic corruption of the Wilhelmine military and its disconnect from reality. Yet to draw a direct line of continuity from the critical wartime perceptions circulating among front-line soldiers on the one hand, to the criticism of the military post-1918 on the other, would be to misunderstand the rear area's symbolic place in discourses on the legitimacy and memory of the war. The openness and ambiguity of the rear area as a set of symbols meant that it was not only ordinary soldiers, but also members of the military elite and radical nationalist camp who regarded the moral degradation and corruption of the wider area behind the front line as one of the main causes of the Wilhelmine system's disintegration. As Boris Barth has rightly pointed out in his study of the stab-in-the-back myth, there was a 'twofold perception' of conditions in the rear area: 'The officer corps interpreted the rear area as a hotbed of moral decay that was spreading beneath them and for which deserters, agitators, rabble-rousers and Jews were to blame. For other observers, meanwhile, it was precisely the officers who were to blame for declining moral standards.'[14] The war memoirs of Colonel Max Bauer, Erich Ludendorff's right-hand man and head of Operational Department II at the Army Supreme Command, provide a clear example of the perception of moral degradation held by the military top brass. Like many staff officers before and after him, Bauer related the problem of moral decay in the rear area primarily to the months that followed the failure of the first German offensive in spring 1918. By this stage, the defeat of the German army was looming ever more clearly into view and, as Bauer wrote, 'countless shirkers' were milling around 'at home and in the rear area'.[15]

Max Bauer thus placed the rear area firmly in the context of the radical nationalist discourse on the supposed 'stab in the back' that had betrayed the victorious army. This did not go unchallenged, however. Immediately after the war, pacifist and socialist authors published a multitude of pamphlets and essays that used the worm's-eye view of the ordinary soldier as means of indicting the arrogance and bullying behaviour of officers in the Wilhelmine army.[16] These left-wing pamphlets had a quasi-documentary nature. Their authors published them anonymously and gave them the appearance of diaries, thus reinforcing the credibility of their criticisms through the prosaic style of the daily notebook.[17] This literature included a publication entitled *Der Etappensumpf* (The Quagmire of the Rear Area), which offered 'documents about the collapse of the German army in 1916/1918' taken from the 'war diary of a common man'. The 'preface by the publisher' introduces the 'pamphlet' as a collection of excerpts from the 'diary of a medical orderly' who experienced life in the rear area from 1915 to 1918 in various military hospitals behind the Western Front. The introduction reprints a song popular among front-line soldiers, underlining the text's semi-documentary character. The lyrics to *Die Etappensäue* (the rear area swine) express some of the most important complaints about the debauchery far from the front:

> Who walks around all spick and span,
> Who finds it hard to greet his fellow man,
> Who squanders so much of the unit's dough,
> Yet speaks and writes as if he were a hero,
> Who drinks his way through all our best wine?
> That would be the rear area swine![18]

**Figure 5** Cover image from *Der Etappensumpf. Dokumente des Zusammenbruchs des deutschen Heeres aus den Jahren 1916/1918. Aus dem Kriegstagebuch eines Gemeinen* (Jena: Verlag der Volksbuchhandlung, 1920).

The illustration on the pamphlet's cover emphasizes another aspect of the anti-military discourse on the rear area, which is also raised elsewhere in the song: the licentiousness of the officer caste, whose favourite pastime was to embark on amorous adventures with local women while at the same time advocating an ideology of national purity to their men.[19] Beneath the cavorting officers, the illustration vividly depicts the rear area as a quagmire engulfing the ordinary soldiers and civilians, who are unable to escape.

## II  Charleville and Etappe Gent

In terms of their timing and subject matter, *Charleville* and *Etappe Gent* were thus part of a wider current of publications immediately after the war on the misbehaviour, corruption and moral degradation of the occupying German forces in the rear area behind the Western Front. Yet there were some important differences between the publications by Appens and Wandt and the multitude of pamphlets that presented an 'indictment by the tormented', training their sights on the abuses in the rear area. The first and perhaps most important difference was the enormous popularity achieved by Appens und Wandt. As bestsellers, *Charleville* and *Etappe Gent* took the same complaints and rhetorical techniques that already featured in existing publications and brought these criticisms of the army's role in the rear area to a much larger readership. Sales of both titles remained strong until the end of the Weimar Republic. By way of comparison, the publisher Verlag der Volksbuchhandlung distributed 10,000 copies of *Der Etappensumpf*. This figure, stated on the publication's front cover, was highly respectable for an anti-military pamphlet, but pales into insignificance compared with the figures achieved by Appens and Wandt.

Before its publication as a pamphlet, the publishing house Gerisch & Co in Dortmund serialized *Charleville* in its newspaper, the *Westfälische Allgemeine Volks-Zeitung* in August 1919. The exact date of publication for the complete 38-page-long pamphlet is unclear, but is likely to have been later the same year.[20] The text was an immediate sales success. In 1930, Appens claimed that 100,000 copies had already been printed by the peak of the hyperinflation in 1923.[21] Assuming that each print-run amounted to approximately 3,000 copies, this roughly corresponds to the numbers quoted in the *Deutsches Bücherverzeichnis*, which states that 1921 to 1923 saw the production of the 21st to 29th editions.[22] In 1927, a new version appeared containing an identical text but a new subtitle. An altered format meant that it numbered fifty-five pages. This edition indicated that 170,000 copies had been printed, a figure that probably understates the true number distributed.[23] In 1930, Appens's employer, the Prussian Ministry for Science and Education, carried out an investigation into *Charleville*. It noted that the text was available in French translation and remained on sale in its 'current form', which probably referred to the German 1927 edition.[24] By 1923, the title was already one of the bestsellers in German literary history pre-1945.[25]

A second important difference from many pamphlets written in 1919/20 was that Appens and Wandt did not publish anonymously. The title page of *Charleville* bore the name, 'Dr. Wilhelm Appens, Dortmund.'[26] The first pages briefly explained the administrative structures in which life in the rear area unfolded. This covered Charleville and neighbouring Mézières in the French Ardennes with their 40,000 inhabitants. From 25 September 1914 until January 1916, Charleville was home to the *Große Hauptquartier* (General Headquarters) with its organizational 'core' (3), the General Staff. In March 1916, two military authorities moved to Charleville: the General Staff of the Deutscher Kronprinz Army Group under the command of Crown Prince Wilhelm and the *Etappeninspektion* of the 1st Army. Administration of the town was the responsibility of the *Ortskommandant* (local commander), who reported to the *Etappeninspektion*. Appens, the first-person narrator, was an NCO assigned to the commander's mess officer (6). In the pamphlet, Appens describes himself as a philosopher 'by nature' (10) and mentions that his job as a 'teacher' had stirred his interest in troop propaganda and the 'patriotic instruction' introduced in 1917.

Appens matter-of-factly relates his impressions of the German occupation from his time as a mess officer and criticizes the state of affairs in Charleville. In places, he tells openly of his feelings of shame and moral disgust that struck him particularly when the German occupiers requisitioned the property of the French with no regard for the rights and hardships of the civilian population. On one occasion for example, having reported a captain who had stolen furniture from his French host, he was informed by the man's unit that the requisitioning had been legitimate: 'That evening, for the first time, I cried tears of anger in my quarters. Contempt and disgust prevailed over willpower' (23). Like almost all the officers in Charleville, the captain in this incident remains anonymous. Unlike Wandt, Appens generally does not name names; he denounces the system rather than individuals.

Three of the rare exceptions are General von Mudra, Chief of the 1st Army High Command; von Mudra's successor, General Below; and Below's adjutant, Major von Hatten. The 1st Army found itself in Charleville while on the retreat in October 1918. Appens recounts that he was required to requisition the home of an elderly, recently widowed woman for the benefit of the three men. Worse still, he also had orders to eject her from the spacious property within a matter of hours, even though there would have been plenty of room for her on the upper floor. Having imparted the news to Madame Noizet, writes Appens, he crept away in the manner of 'someone who had just committed a murder' (37). Appens not only expresses his moral disgust at his colleagues' actions, but presents himself as a positive exception. It was an 'open secret' in the town that 'I had connections to the crown prince', he writes. This gave him opportunities to address a number of French civilians' concerns by raising them with the royal (24).

Appens's subheadings for the short vignettes of everyday life in Charleville give little indication of why the text became a bestseller: 'Officers' housing' (18), 'The assistants' (19), 'The vegetable garden' (20), 'The bicycles' (25). The latter chapter describes the army's failure to requisition the town's bicycles in an orderly fashion. This is not great literature, but a deliberately prosaic account of the wrongs perpetrated by a thoroughly dysfunctional and cruel occupation regime. In Appens's portrayal, the system serves solely to enrich the men of the officer caste, who hold the levers of power. The text's explosive power lay in Appens's portrayal of corruption and mismanagement as manifestations of a systemic problem. He repeatedly cites 'rear area militarism' (25, 30, 33, 34) as their ultimate cause, denouncing it as a 'system of exploitation' (27). Appens, who was a member of the SPD from February 1919 until the party's outlawing in 1933, thus writes in the Wilhelmine-era tradition of Social Democratic military criticism, which denounced the social and political influence of the military as a core component of class rule.[27] By the final months of the war, however, the demise of this military system was unstoppable and the 'court life with all its trappings' surrounding the Emperor in the General Headquarters 'reminiscent of life in Ancient Rome before the fall' (7).

'Es lebe Deutschland! Vive la France!' This heading introduces the political message intended to reinforce Appens's text (37–8). It is a call to the 'proletariat of all the peoples', and especially of France and Germany, to ignore the false 'victory fanfares' and calls for revenge that followed the war. Instead, he writes, the workers should 'build a landmark for international socialism' that both respects and transcends their different nations. 'We want to hold out the hand of friendship to one another and we must do so. We are innocent of the blood of the fallen comrades' (38). However, this impassioned call, an expression of the revolutionary hopes immediately after the war, also points to the propensity of the discourse on 'rear area militarism' to distract attention from another, even more problematic history. Focusing, like Appens, on the military's excesses in the 'vegetable gardens' and 'officers' housing' meant avoiding discussion of the mass killing on the front line and of the trail of violence and physical destruction that German troops had left behind in northern France. It overlooks the fact that the rear area remained a relative idyll despite the pillaging of the German 'barbarians'. Though 'rear area militarism' enslaved the French with 'forced labour' (33), it at least spared their lives. Appens notes that when German troops first conquered Charleville in September 1914, the commanding general of the army corps promised to punish 'infringements by officers who had forgotten their duty' (33). In recalling this promise, *Charleville* reproduces a dichotomy that also typified the memoirs of First World War generals. These contrasted the virtue of the front-line troops with the depravity of the rear area.

The history of *Etappe Gent* is more complex altogether. Heinrich Wandt published the first volume in spring 1920 with the USPD-affiliated Verlag der Freien Presse in Berlin.[28] Here he also worked as the editor of the *Freie Presse* daily newspaper, which serialized the text ahead of its publication as a book.[29] Wandt originally planned to document the material in two volumes and therefore labelled the 1920 book as 'Volume one'. Before he could complete the second volume, however, a series of trials and prison sentences between September 1921 and February 1926 interrupted his work. In the summer of 1926, Wandt published a slightly abridged version of the first volume with a new publisher, the communist Agis-Verlag. According to the author, upwards of 100,000 copies of this edition were printed.[30] Wandt considered it to be his 'patriotic duty', as he noted with gentle irony, to catch up on the delayed work. In 1928 he therefore published the second volume of *Etappe Gent*, again with Agis-Verlag, under the title *Erotik und Spionage in der Etappe Gent* (Eroticism and Espionage in the Ghent Rear Area).[31] Within a year, the publisher had produced 31,000 to 40,000 copies. It is therefore reasonable to assume that up to 200,000 copies of *Etappe Gent* volumes one and two were printed in total. Hippoliet Janssens, a socialist publisher and bookseller from Ledeberg near Ghent, issued a two-volume Dutch-language edition in 1921 and 1922. The company also published a two-volume French translation at around the same time.[32]

Wandt had first-hand wartime experience of the city where the book is set. He initially served in France on the Western Front. In spring 1915, judged no longer fit for combat, he was transferred to the staff of the *Etappeninspektion* of the 4th Army in Ghent, Flanders.[33] The preface to the first volume makes the author's intentions clear. The book's aim, Wandt writes, is to provide a reminder for everyone who has 'already forgotten' of the 'shamefulness of the old militarism'.

The city of Ghent serves here as a microcosm of the rear area as a whole. He attacks those accusing him of treachery or 'dirtying his own nest', insisting that it was precisely the sort of 'thieves and murderers' portrayed in *Etappe Gent* who had first created the extreme anti-German sentiment manifested in the Treaty of Versailles (I/preface). This radical left-wing author thus swims against the current of popular nationalist, anti-Versailles feeling in 1919/20 by pointing to the causal link between the German occupation regime in Belgium and the terms of the peace treaty.[34] As Wandt explains in the preface, his book was part of the effort to prepare the ground for a new republican beginning by 'first purging all the dregs of the criminal system' that had 'brought Germany to its most terrible collapse' (ibid.).

Wandt shared Appens's socialist and anti-militarist thrust, but chose other areas of focus and a different presentational form. Like *Charleville*, Wandt's *Etappe Gent* is structured in kaleidoscopic fashion. Short passages, tied only loosely together, present the most important abuses and introduce representatives of the German occupation regime. The book begins with a brief outline of the scene of the action and the history of the German invasion on 12 October 1914. Unlike Appens, Wandt then introduces the main players by name. He records their individual contributions to the corruption and exploitation in the rear area. The first volume alone includes dedicated sections for a total of twenty-six officers, military prosecutors and military chaplains, providing a brief introduction and, in many cases, information on their post-war careers. Special mention goes to five 'blue-blooded heroes of the rear area': aristocratic officers whose indolence and lack of achievement struck Wandt as archetypal of the 'caste' of authoritarian types who had brought Germany to disaster (I/164–70, quote 166). Wandt not only parodies and criticizes the hypocrisy of the rear area, but also combines his narrative with original documents, clearly in the hope that these would unmask the nature of the Prussian military system to an even greater extent than his own words. In the second volume of *Etappe Gent*, Wandt includes a series of official military documents that fell into his hands during his time in the staff of the *Etappeninspektion*. Among them are 'authentic testimonies about officers' orgies' as well as a series of reports and orders from more senior military command authorities, such as the 2nd Army High Command and the Prussian War Ministry. These date from 1915 and 1916. For Wandt, they provide 'proof' that the 'most senior military officials had to deal with' such matters 'from a very early stage' (I/195–8, quote 195). The author's use of such evidence in the book does even more than his own eyewitness accounts to blur the boundaries between narrative fiction and objective documentation.

In addition to personalizing the narrative and incorporating historical documents, Wandt's indictment also takes an analytical tone. In the second volume in particular, he introduces various aspects of the occupation regime in more systematic form so as to demonstrate its brutality towards the Belgian civilian population.[35] These include the two-metre-high electric fence erected in late 1914 along the boundary between the Belgian rear area and the Netherlands. The Germans designed this death-trap to prevent the movement of people and information across the border. There were just three places where the barrier could be crossed on foot. Nevertheless, a growing number of Belgian military-aged men attempted to traverse the border into the Netherlands. They were joined particularly in the second half of the war by German deserters (II/76–80). Wandt also cites the numerous legal cases against Belgians accused of so-called *Kriegsverrat* ('treason' against the German war effort) for espionage or the passing-on of military secrets. These could result in death sentences (II/87–91). In addition, he mentions the 'atrocities' perpetrated on Belgian civilians during the German advance in August 1914, when 'entire communities' were set ablaze and 'hundreds of peaceful and innocent civilians, men, women and children put against the wall' (II/20).[36]

Overall, however, Wandt's text is less concerned with espionage and treason than with 'eroticism', though the two topics combine in the figure of Mademoiselle Yvonne Ingels. Ingels was the mistress of Max Henz, a captain from Berlin and adjutant to the command of the Ghent rear area. Wandt describes how she could move freely throughout the rear area under her admirer's protective wing and proved 'extremely useful to the Belgian intelligence service'. The importance of this theme is highlighted on the cover of the first volume, which depicts a scantily clad mistress sitting, champagne glass in hand, on the lap of a German officer. The image sums up the life of debauchery that officers, to quote *Etappe Gent*, preferred to describe as 'extremely urgent official business' (I/89). Wandt describes the officers with a broad rhetorical repertoire, ranging from this gentle subversion of military turns of phrase to biting ridicule that pillories their moral depravity and false gung-ho nationalism. John Heartfield's dust jacket for the second volume published in 1928 was even more explicit. In the words of the public prosecutor at District Court I in Berlin, it depicted 'an officer and a girl in a state of partial undress'.[37] Following complaints from officers named by Wandt in the book as well as from the Deutscher Offiziers-Bund (League of German Officers), a criminal investigation took place in 1929. In October of that year, a court in Berlin ordered the confiscation of all copies of the cover for offending public morality.[38]

**Figure 6** Cover image from Heinrich Wandt, *Etappe Gent. Streiflichter zum Zusammenbruch. I. Band* (Berlin: Freie Presse, 1920).

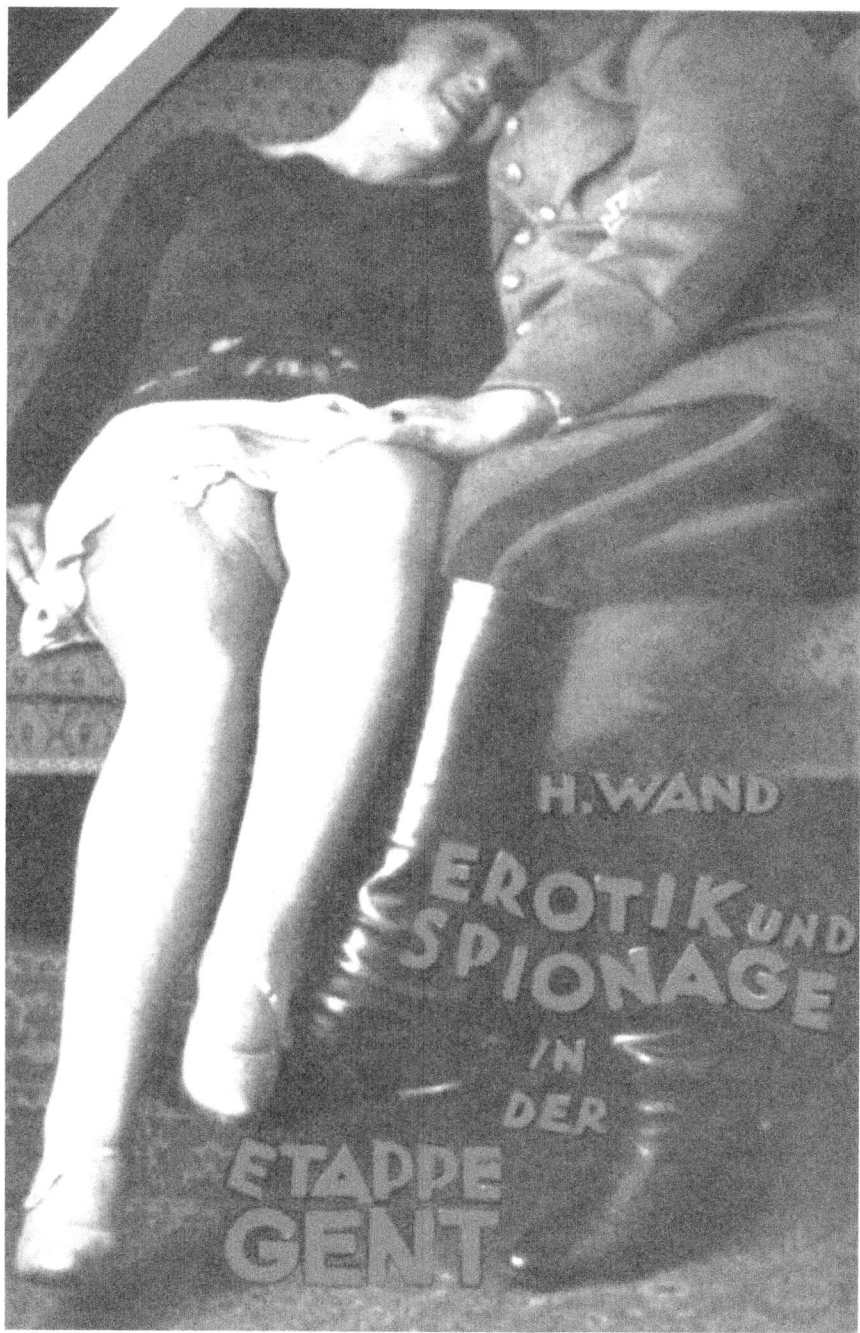

**Figure 7** John Heartfield, cover montage for Heinrich Wandt, *Erotik und Spionage in der Etappe Gent* (Vienna: Agis-Verlag, 1928).

In his critical exploration of 'eroticism' and prostitution, Wandt shares Appens's tendency to distance ordinary soldiers from complicity in the system of rear area militarism and instead to portray them as its innocent victims. Wandt describes in detail how the class divide between the rulers and the ruled was reflected in the system of 'officers' brothels'. In autumn 1917, he notes, money from the 'very poorest' Belgian civilians was used to build a further such institution (I/157ff., 161). The accusatory tone gives way to a kinder, more humorous portrayal when Wandt explains how German soldiers availed themselves of the services of 'unmarried casual prostitutes', usually local, unemployed women whom they met in small cafes or *estaminets* (I/142, 144). Wandt explains with empathy and discretely coded words that the 'decent soldiers in field grey [*biedere Feldgrauen*] had often been away from their mothers for far too long'. They wanted to have '"een groote pint Bier" or "een warm pottje koffie"', he adds, and 'also something for their heart and soul' (I/144). In Wandt's description, an order from the Army High Command in spring 1916, which put an end to this cosy practice and banned soldiers from visiting *estaminets*, appears almost as another injustice of rear area militarism. As Wandt puts it euphemistically, this was all the more 'incomprehensible' given that German soldiers 'had made themselves at home everywhere' (I/145). Wandt sums up this section with a reflection on the wretched position in which these Belgian women found themselves. This passage, too, makes clear that he absolved ordinary soldiers of any active role in the exploitative system of 'militarism', even when they contributed to the 'suffering' of the young women:

> The German soldiers were surprised by the very large numbers of women and girls who prostituted themselves. They did not take into account how militarism with its systemic brutality had disgraced these unfortunates and did not leave them any other choice, if they did not want to starve to death, for the long war had robbed them of any other way of earning a living. (I/147)[39]

Like Appens, Wandt intended his work to be a tool in the socialist attack on militarism and the glorification of war. In the preface to the first volume, he formulates this goal in slogan form: 'Down with militarism in all countries! Make way for the reconciliation of peoples!' (I/preface). In the 1926 edition, Wandt directs the thrust of his argument even more clearly at the nationalist circles that formed the *Vaterländische Verbände* (radical nationalist associations), often headed by 'the old top brass of the rear area'.[40] He also positions his text as a weapon in the battle against the stab-in-the-back legend, which radical nationalist circles were using to undermine the unpopular Weimar Republic:

'Take a closer look at those crying for revanche today, look into their German eyes and you will recognize them as the "rear area swine" of old, whose shameless life of debauchery demoralized the brave front-line troops and who were the real stab in the back of the German front.'[41] Despite this reference to the soldiers' bravery, Wandt and Appens both remain wedded to the logic of victimization inherent in the anti-war discourse on the rear area. Like many pamphlets critical of the military that were published about the rear area at this time, *Charleville* and *Etappe Gent* both emphasize the systemic nature of 'rear area militarism' so resolutely that the soldiers appear simply as harmless victims, despite their direct involvement in the German occupation of Belgium and northern France. Such a narrative perspective certainly helped both authors to instrumentalize the history of the rear area for a socialist politics of international reconciliation. However, the focus on life in the rear area far from the front line also avoided questions of the complicity or active participation of German soldiers in the violence of the first total war.

## III  Two pacifist authors and the battle against their texts

In his *Militaria* essays, in which he discussed both apologetic and critical pamphlet literature on the German army, the leftist journalist and tireless critic of right-wing politics in the Weimar Republic Kurt Tucholsky described *Charleville* in 1920 as an 'inexhaustible text', a piece of writing 'that I simply want to reproduce here from end to end and that I ask each of my readers to procure themselves and absorb thoroughly. After reading it, one grasps why we lost the war and why the world's hatred of Germany still burns.'[42] The USPD-affiliated paper *Die freie Welt*, which was distributed as a supplement in party-supporting daily newspapers, was similarly effusive. Its reviewer regarded the pamphlet as an indictment of the Wilhelmine officer corps based on 'authentic information from an impartial witness'. Citing the counter-argument often put forward by nationalist circles to refute such allegations, the article asked if the corrupt officers of Charleville were perhaps just 'exceptions'. 'No,' came the reviewer's emphatic answer. If this had been the case, 'the German officer corps would have stood up like real men to eject from their ranks such fellows who had abused their tunic, insignia and power, as soon they became aware of these atrocious acts. They all joined in.' The reviewer followed this categorical verdict with long excerpts from the pamphlet, which, he believed, deserved a place on school curriculums.[43]

But who was the 'Doctor Wilhelm Appens' who authored *Charleville*? Bernard Heinrich Wilhelm Appens was born on 7 July 1877 in Lengede, a small town near Peine, now part of Lower Saxony. He was the son of a farmer.[44] He qualified as a teacher with two entry exams in 1897 and 1902. From 1897 to 1908, Appens worked as a primary school teacher near Hildesheim, and from 1909 to 1920 at a girls' school in Dortmund. From 1912 to 1914, he took temporary leave to attend university in Grenoble and Jena and completed a PhD on 'The Educational Movements of 1848'. During the war, Appens served as an NCO of the Landwehr, initially in the 92nd Infantry Regiment. This was the very same unit in which he had performed his military service in 1898.

After the war, Appens qualified as a secondary school teacher. He was then appointed to the post of district school inspector in Hörde near Dortmund. This office, created in the Weimar Republic, shifted responsibility for school inspection from the church to the state. Appens's area of responsibility covered some 350 teachers. It remains an open question to what extent his political involvement in the SPD, which he joined in February 1919, played a role in his career. In 1921, the *Regierungspräsidium* (regional administrative authority) in Arnsberg indicated that Appens's party membership had earned him substantial support in the schools he inspected and among the local population, and that a refusal to give him a permanent position would be regarded as politically motivated.[45] Around the turn of the century, Appens had, for a time, been a member of the National-Sozialer Verein (National Social Association), the party with which the Protestant pastor Friedrich Naumann attempted to commit the liberal bourgeoisie to active social policy and integrate the working class into the Wilhelmine state.

After the war, Appens's left-wing political credentials were unambiguous. He was a member not only of the SPD, but also the Deutsche Liga für Menschenrechte (German League for Human Rights) from 1920 to 1932. The organization, which prior to 1922 called itself the Bund Neues Vaterland (New Fatherland League), promoted radical pacifism and opposed all war. These committed pacifists had drawn lessons from the established Deutsche Friedensgesellschaft (German Peace Society), which was only lukewarm in its criticism of German war policy between 1914 and 1918. Pacifist ideas also shaped the Reichsbanner Schwarz-Rot-Gold (Reichsbanner Black-Red-Gold), the nominally cross-party association of republican war veterans, of which Appens was a member between 1930 and 1933, as well as the Bund entschiedener Schulreformer (Association of Determined School Reformers). Founded in 1919, the latter consisted predominantly of teachers who were also SPD members. It campaigned for extensive reform of the school system and particularly against the existence of denominational schools. Appens participated in the association's 1922 conference together with radical pacifist Kurt Hiller, the Jewish philosopher Eugen Rosenstock and socialist Theodor Haubach. Various working groups at the event discussed ideas presented by intellectuals such as Martin Buber, René Schickele and others.[46]

In 1929, a publishing house in Charleville produced a French translation of the 1919 pamphlet, which also prompted an article in the *Echo de Paris* newspaper.[47] For the Prussian Ministry for Science, Culture and Education in Berlin, this was reason enough to demand that Appens be subjected to an official interrogation to find out whether he had authorized the translation himself. The ministry was clearly also perturbed by the German version and the fact that it had been 'repeatedly printed and distributed for over ten years'.[48] In the interrogation by the *Regierungspräsidium*, Appens first stated that he had compiled the text based on the notes in his war diary. He claimed that he had not considered the possible impact on Germany's image abroad. With his career at stake, Appens expressed himself willing to ask the publisher not to produce any more copies of the pamphlet. The interrogation found that he had not authorized the translation, but that he had probably been aware for some time that the French press were publishing excerpts from his text.[49] The ministry complained that Appens had produced such a text in the first place, given that it 'would inevitably damage Germany's reputation'.[50] Appens reacted immediately and succeeded in stopping further printing of *Charleville*. He also arranged for the publisher to destroy its remaining copies. Nevertheless, his work as a school inspector was transferred – supposedly for organizational reasons – to a new district, Stendal I, with effect from 1 April 1930, forcing him to move to Magdeburg.[51] This transfer against his wishes and so soon after the interrogation was, in Appens's view, nothing less than a 'punishment for the publication of my text, Charleville'. The author insisted at length, but ultimately in vain, that he had intended the pamphlet only as an indictment of the old regime. He protested that he had also written articles in the *Berliner Volkszeitung* criticizing the militarism of the French forces occupying the Ruhr in 1923.[52]

This was not to be the end of the matter. When the National Socialists seized power in 1933, Appens was immediately sent into retirement on a provisional basis. In July 1933, the government in Münster requested his dismissal from public service on the basis of Section 4 of the Law for the Restoration of the Professional Civil Service, the key piece of Nazi legislation that regulated the removal of Jews and committed democrats from the civil service. They cited his 'active' membership in the SPD and the League for Human Rights. Following approval from the ministry, the dismissal came in August 1933. Appens received three-quarters of the retirement pension to which he was entitled.[53] A report by the district head of the NS Lehrerbund (National Socialist League of Teachers) claimed that the dismissal had reprimanded a Social Democrat and pacifist known widely in Dortmund and beyond, whose pamphlet about Charleville had brought upon him the hatred of the nationalist camp. The report described the pamphlet's content as 'plain treason' and suggested that the author of such 'lies' had no right to receive a pension. Charleville, it stated, was 'an egregious smear on Germany and the Prussian soldiers in the world war'.[54] Following his dismissal, Appens returned to his home town of Lengede, where he lived with his mother and elder brother. He had married in 1909 but by now was long separated, though his request for a divorce in 1921 had been unsuccessful. He had no children. In 1941, Appens applied for readmission to the teaching profession, but to no avail. He passed the time after 1933 by working on a local history of Lengede, where he died in 1947.[55]

Unlike Appens, Heinrich Wandt was already firmly rooted in the socialist workers' movement prior to the war. Wandt has produced various versions of his own biographical trajectory, but all of them include erroneous details. The main outlines have only been recently established using the records of his various court cases.[56] Born in Stuttgart on 13 May 1890, the son of a master bookbinder, Wandt made his first forays into writing while still at school, publishing articles in youth magazines. In 1906, he joined the SPD. In 1912, Wandt worked briefly as an editorial secretary for the Social Democratic women's magazine, *Die Gleichheit*. The title was published by Clara Zetkin, who stood on the left wing of the party. Following his call-up to military service in 1912, Wandt deserted to Paris the next year. In March 1914, however, he turned himself in to the military authorities and spent eight months in a military prison as punishment. After his release, he served in Reserve Infantry Regiment 247 on the Western Front. In spring 1915, judged no longer fit for front-line service, Wandt was transferred to the staff of *Etappeninspektion* 4 in Ghent, where he worked until 1918 on the newspaper of the 4th Army.

Following the printing of excerpts from *Etappe Gent* in the *Freie Presse* newspaper prior to the book's publication, Wandt faced numerous libel suits from officers mentioned by name. Only two of these cases resulted in convictions as Wandt was usually able to provide evidence to substantiate his claims. A complaint by Prince Heinrich XXXVII of Reuß led to a six-month prison sentence in 1920.[57] Soon after his release, an administrative clerk at the Reich

Archive in Potsdam supplied him with a number of the archive's documents from the Ghent rear area command, which Wandt intended to use in a further criminal case against him. The clerk was subsequently arrested, as was Wandt, who was detained in October 1921 and accused of misappropriating documents. In late January 1922, with the allegations still unproven, the authorities eventually released him from custody.[58]

These episodes were just the prelude to a further trial, the form and outcome of which Wandt rightly described as a 'judicial crime'.[59] Even by the standards of the Weimar judiciary's persecution of pacifist left-wingers – the cases of the statistician Emil Julius Gumbel and the pacifist journalist Carl von Ossietzky are only the two most prominent – the Wandt case stands out as a particularly egregious example of the bending of the law for political ends.[60] There is only room for a brief outline of events here. Following his release from custody in January 1922, Wandt fled initially to Aachen, which was occupied by Belgian troops, then to Belgium itself to escape further persecution by the German authorities. However, he still returned occasionally to Germany. On one such visit in January 1923, he was arrested in Düsseldorf and promptly accused of treason. The prosecutors alleged that he had supplied the Belgian authorities with a document dating from 1918 that proved the contact between a Flemish nationalist and the German military authorities in the autumn of that year. This, they argued, constituted treason. The trial before the 5. Strafsenat des Reichsgerichts (5th Criminal Division of the Supreme Court) in Leipzig took place on 13 December 1923. The public were excluded from the proceedings. The trial began by hearing long excerpts from *Etappe Gent*, read aloud by the presiding judge. This already indicated the real reason why Wandt had been hauled before the court. In fact, the trial never heard conclusive evidence in relation to the original allegations. The defendant's presence in the dock had far more to do with his extremely popular book and its aggressive attacks on the honour and status of the officer corps.[61]

Wandt's account of the trial states that Erich Müsebeck, director of the archive department in the Reich Archive in Potsdam, and a Major Staehle from the Reichswehr Ministry both acted as key witnesses for the prosecution. Staehle also intervened in the court proceedings several times.[62] There are some indications that the Reichswehr was a driving force behind the prosecution. After a brief trial, the court sentenced Wandt to six years' imprisonment and stripped him of his civil rights for a ten-year period. Even before the court reached its verdict, Belgian, American and French newspapers began to refer to the case as a 'German Dreyfus trial'. The historical analogy with the case of Alfred

Dreyfus, a French officer wrongly convicted of espionage in 1894, illustrates the political significance of the proceedings in the eyes of foreign observers. The Dreyfus affair had shaken the Third French Republic to its core.[63] While Wandt was serving his time in prison, the Reichstag deputy Paul Levi, who was on the left of the SPD, publicized the judicial scandal in parliament in March 1925 and demanded a retrial. In May of that year, the pacifist lawyer Arnold Freymuth gave details of the case against Wandt at an event of the German League for Human Rights. The Reichsgericht resisted efforts by the defence team to call a retrial. Eventually, public pressure persuaded Reich President Hindenburg to pardon Wandt on 6 February 1926 at the suggestion of the Reich Minister of Justice, Wilhelm Marx.[64] Little is known about Wandt's political activities following his release in 1926. In May 1933, after the National Socialists had taken power, the authorities briefly detained Wandt and his partner Alice Stenger, whom he later married in 1950. Surprisingly, the regime did not imprison Wandt for any sustained period. Robbed of his profession as a political writer, however, he was left unemployed. In the years that followed, it appears that he received support primarily from the Stenger family. From 1940, he wrote articles on distilling for the *Deutsche Distillateur-Zeitung* under the pseudonym Heinrich Stenger. Immediately after the war, the US occupiers employed Wandt as a press officer in Berlin-Schöneberg. However, he soon returned to writing articles freely for Berlin daily newspapers. After suffering from dementia in the final years of his life, Wandt passed away in West Berlin in March 1965.[65]

## IV Conclusion

*Charleville* and *Etappe Gent* have a special place in the literary representation of the First World War in the Weimar Republic. Their unambiguous anti-military, socialist perspective made them exceptions in several respects. At least where sales figures were concerned, other interpretations dominated the field. These portrayed the war as a series of 'adventure stories' or, in the case of right-wing authors, amounted to a 'reinterpretation and instrumentalization of the war' for anti-republican ends.[66] Despite this, both *Charleville* and *Etappe Gent* reached a wide readership, combining documentary reporting with character-driven narratives. Together, the two titles sold somewhere between 400,000 and half a million copies, if both volumes of *Etappe Gent* are included in the total. *Charleville* and *Etappe Gent* are also exceptions within the context of the wave of anti-war and anti-military pamphlets published in 1919 and 1920, which used the perspective of ordinary soldiers to indict the Wilhelmine military apparatus.[67] Like these pamphlets, Appens and Wandt launched a political and moral attack on an obsolete regime, in which the officer corps stood for the inhumanity and corruption of the entire Wilhelmine elite. Unlike other titles with a similar thrust, however, the two publications enjoyed lasting popularity among the reading public. While most pamphlets only reached a relatively small readership and disappeared from the printing presses after 1920, *Charleville* and *Etappe Gent* remained on the market until at least the late 1920s.

This was, at best, only marginally attributable to the literary quality of the texts, which was particularly notable in the case of *Etappe Gent*. It is more plausible to assume that the publications owed their long success to the narrative of victimization they provided. Set in the rear area, far away from the killing on the front line, both texts emphasize the passive role of the ordinary soldier in the context of the German army. They thus portray German soldiers as innocent victims of a mighty military machine, an apparatus that embodied the injustice and brutality of the war even where it was not directly engaged in the destruction of human life. This idea of the soldiers as victims of the Wilhelmine military found considerable echo among socialist working class veterans, whose two most important associations – the Reichsbanner Black-Red-Gold and the Reichsbund der Kriegsbeschädigten, Kriegsteilnehmer und Kriegshinterbliebenen (Reich Association of Disabled Soldiers, Veterans and War Dependants) – created extensive space for such memories.[68] These organizations also borrowed directly from both texts. From November 1931 to February 1932, for example, the Reich Association's journal serialized a story that Heinrich Wandt had first presented in the second volume of *Etappe Gent*. It described the fate of the young Vice-Sergeant major Niederländer from Lorraine, who, in the heat of the moment, shot dead a lieutenant, his superior, in 1917. The commander of the 39th Infantry Division twice refused to accept the prison sentence handed down by the court martial and instead demanded Niederländer be sentenced to death. On the third occasion, his wish was granted. Niederländer was executed in Ghent in February 1918.[69]

Appens and Wandt are exceptions in a third respect, too.[70] To a greater degree than other, mainly socialist Weimar writers critical of the war, they found themselves subjected to political censorship and judicial persecution. In Wandt's case, these measures amounted to nothing less than an official attempt to muzzle his voice altogether. Private actions by former officers drove this policy of persecuting pacifist authors, as did the Reichswehr. Appens's case reveals that the ministerial bureaucracy played an active role in these efforts even in a state like

Prussia, which was governed by pro-republican parties. The interplay between the Reichswehr and the conservative judiciary meant that pacifist and socialist critics of the military faced some 10,000 charges of treason and high treason between 1924 and 1927 alone, leading to the conviction of 1,071 people.[71] Most of these trials involved pacifist individuals or directly political comments and publications. Nevertheless, censorship and judicial persecution were an important part of the context in which anti-war literature arose in the Weimar Republic.

Finally, it is worth mentioning a fourth distinctive feature of Appens's and Wandt's works, despite the lack of space here to explore it in full. The authors combined their analyses of the German military's brutal occupation with a detailed and, particularly in Appens's case, empathetic portrayal of the suffering among French and Belgian civilians. Appens and Wandt explicitly regarded their texts as a form of moral reparations for the injustices Germany had perpetrated during the war. In pointing out the historical background to the Allies' tough treatment of Germany after the armistice, they thus also attempted to disarm the nationalist propaganda directed at the Treaty of Versailles. Among the German public, this historical context was largely taboo. The texts' perspective and choice of topic led to French and Dutch translations of both texts, which continued to find readers in Belgium, the Netherlands and France long after the war. Wandt's trial and later pardon also spurred further interest in his work.[72]

# Notes

## 1 The First World War as a Laboratory of Violence

1. *Sanitätsbericht über das deutsche Heer im Weltkriege 1914/1918*, 3 vols. (Berlin: Mittler, 1934), vol. 3, 12, 31.
2. Wolfgang U. Eckart, 'Invalidität', in *Enzyklopädie Erster Weltkrieg*, ed. Gerhard Hirschfeld, Gerd Krumeich and Irina Renz (Paderborn: Schöningh, 2003), 584–6, figures p. 584.
3. Andrew Donson, *Youth in the Fatherless Land: War Pedagogy, Nationalism, and Authority, 1914–1918* (Cambridge, Mass: Harvard University Press, 2010).
4. Roger Chickering and Stig Förster (eds), *Great War, Total War: Combat and Mobilization on the Western Front, 1914–1918* (Cambridge: Cambridge University Press, 2000). For a self-critical discussion of the limits of this concept, see Roger Chickering, 'Total War: The Use and Abuse of a Concept', in *Anticipating Total War: The German and American Experiences, 1871–1914*, ed. Manfred Boemeke, Roger Chickering and Stig Förster (Cambridge: Cambridge University Press, 1999), 13–28.
5. See the special issue of the *Journal of Contemporary History* 48, no. 2 (2013): 'The Fischer Controversy after 50 Years', especially the important contribution by Stephan Petzold, 'The Social Making of a Historian: Fritz Fischer's Distancing From Bourgeois-Conservative Historiography, 1930–60', *Journal of Contemporary History* 48, no. 2 (2013): 271–89; Jürgen Kocka, *Facing Total War: German Society 1914–1918* (Leamington Spa: Berg, 1984); Gunther Mai, *Kriegswirtschaft und Arbeiterbewegung in Württemberg 1914–1918* (Stuttgart: Klett-Cotta, 1983). A pioneering study by Ute Daniel examines the war from a history of mentalities perspective: Ute Daniel, *The War from Within: German Working-class Women in the First World War*, trans. Margaret Ries (Oxford: Berg, 1997).
6. See Paul Fussell, *The Great War and Modern Memory* (Oxford: Oxford University Press, 1975); Bernd Hüppauf, 'Experiences of Modern Warfare and the Crisis of Representation', *New German Critique* 59 (1993): 41–76; Bernd Hüppauf, '"Der Tod ist verschlungen in den Sieg". Todesbilder aus dem Ersten Weltkrieg und der Nachkriegszeit', in *Ansichten vom Krieg*, ed. Bernd Hüppauf (Königstein: Forum Academicum, 1984) 55–91. An initial, though in many respects problematic attempt to answer these questions can be found in Modris Eksteins, *Rites of Spring: The Great War and the Birth of the Modern Age* (London: Bantam Press, 1989).

7 See Bernd Ulrich, *Die Augenzeugen. Deutsche Feldpostbriefe in Kriegs- und Nachkriegszeit 1914–1933* (Essen: Klartext, 1997); Barbara Duden, 'Der Kodak und der Stellungskrieg. Versuch einer Situierung von Weltkriegsfotografien', *Bios* 7, no. 1 (1994): 64–82; Christine Brocks, *Die bunte Welt der Krieges. Bildpostkarten aus dem Ersten Weltkrieg 1914–1918* (Essen: Klartext, 2008); Dietmar Molthagen, *Das Ende der Bürgerlichkeit? Liverpooler und Hamburger Bürgerfamilien im Ersten Weltkrieg* (Göttingen: Vandenhoeck & Ruprecht, 2007); Birthe Kundrus, *Kriegerfrauen. Familienpolitik und Geschlechterverhältnisse im Ersten und Zweiten Weltkrieg* (Hamburg: Christians, 1995); important case studies in Gerhard Hirschfeld, Dieter Langewiesche and Hans-Peter Ullmann (eds), *Kriegserfahrungen. Studien zur Sozial- und Mentalitätsgeschichte des Ersten Weltkrieges* (Essen: Klartext, 1997); on soldiers, see Anne Lipp, *Meinungslenkung im Krieg. Kriegserfahrungen deutscher Soldaten und ihre Deutung 1914–1918* (Göttingen: Vandenhoeck & Ruprecht, 2003); and my own efforts: Benjamin Ziemann, *War Experiences in Rural Germany 1914–1923*, trans. Alex Skinner (Oxford: Berg, 2007).

8 Roger Chickering, *The Great War and Urban Life in Germany: Freiburg, 1914–1918* (Cambridge: Cambridge University Press, 2007).

9 The best comparative overview of this is offered by Jay Winter and Antoine Prost, *The Great War in History: Debates and Controversies, 1914 to the Present* (Cambridge: Cambridge University Press, 2005); recent important discussions can be found in: Wencke Meteling, 'Neue Forschungen zum Ersten Weltkrieg. Englisch- und französischsprachige Studien über Deutschland, Frankreich und Großbritannien', *Geschichte und Gesellschaft* 37 (2011): 615–48; Heather Jones, 'As the Centenary Approaches: The Regeneration of First World War Historiography', *Historical Journal* 56 (2013): 857–78.

10 See Markus Pöhlmann, *Kriegsgeschichte und Geschichtspolitik: Der Erste Weltkrieg. Die amtliche deutsche Militärgeschichtsschreibung 1914–1956* (Paderborn: Schöningh, 2002), although Pöhlmann does tend to overestimate the innovative potential of this approach.

11 See Bernd Ulrich, '"Militärgeschichte von unten". Anmerkungen zu ihren Ursprüngen, Quellen und Perspektiven im 20. Jahrhundert', *Geschichte und Gesellschaft* 22 (1996): 473–503.

12 Bernd Hüppauf, 'Langemarck, Verdun and the Myth of a New Man in Germany after the First World War', *War & Society* 6, no. 2 (1988): 70–103.

13 See Karl Heinz Roth, 'Die Modernisierung der Folter in den beiden Weltkriegen. Der Konflikt der Psychotherapeuten und Schulpsychiater um die deutschen "Kriegsneurotiker" 1914–1945', *1999. Zeitschrift für Sozialgeschichte des 20. und 21. Jahrhunderts* 2, no. 3 (1987): 8–75; Peter Riedesser and Axel Verderber, *'Maschinengewehre hinter der Front'. Zur Geschichte der deutschen Militärpsychiatrie* (Frankfurt am Main: Fischer, 1996); Günter Komo, *'Für Volk und Vaterland'. Die Militärpsychiatrie in den Weltkriegen* (Münster: Lit, 1992).

14 See the ground-breaking work by Esther Fischer-Homberger, *Die traumatische Neurose* (Bern: Huber, 1975); cf. Bernd Ulrich, 'Nerven und Krieg. Skizzierung einer Beziehung', in *Geschichte und Psychologie. Annäherungsversuche*, ed. Bedrich Loewenstein (Pfaffenweiler: Centaurus, 1992), 163–92; and Bernd Ulrich, 'Kampfmotivationen und Mobilisierungsstrategien: Das Beispiel Erster Weltkrieg', in *Töten im Krieg*, ed. Heinrich von Stietencron and Jörg Rüpke (Freiburg: Alber, 1995), 399–419; Peter Leese, 'Problems Returning Home: The British Psychological Casualties of the Great War', *Historical Journal* 40 (1997): 1055–67; Paul Lerner, *Hysterical Men: War, Psychiatry and the Politics of Trauma in Germany, 1890–1939* (Ithaca: Cornell University Press, 2003); Paul Lerner, 'Psychiatry and Casualties of War in Germany, 1914–1918', *Journal of Contemporary History* 35 (2000): 13–28. See the detailed study based on medical records by Maria Hermes, *Krankheit: Krieg. Psychiatrische Deutungen des Ersten Weltkrieges* (Essen: Klartext, 2012).

15 See Bernd Ulrich, 'Paul Plaut – Psychologe zwischen den Kriegen', in *Die Weimarer Republik zwischen Metropole und Provinz. Intellektuellendiskurse zur politischen Kultur*, ed. Wolfgang Bialas and Burkhard Stenzel (Weimar: Bohlau, 1996), 97–109.

16 Paul Plaut, 'Psychographie des Kriegers', in *Beihefte zur Zeitschrift für angewandte Psychologie. 21. Beiträge zur Psychologie des Krieges*, ed. William Stern and Otto Lipmann, (Leipzig: Johann Ambrosius Barth, 1920), 1–123, quotes 68.

17 Omer Bartov, *Hitler's Army: Soldiers, Nazis and the War in the Third Reich* (New York: Oxford University Press, 1991).

18 Michael Geyer, 'Eine Kriegsgeschichte, die vom Tod spricht' in *Physische Gewalt. Studien zur Geschichte der Neuzeit*, ed. Thomas Lindenberger and Alf Lüdtke (Frankfurt am Main: Suhrkamp, 1995), 136–61, quotes 136.

19 Trutz von Trotha, 'Zur Soziologie der Gewalt' in *Soziologie der Gewalt*, ed. Trutz von Trotha (Opladen: Westdeutscher Verlag, 1997), 9–56, often serves as an important reference point; for a far broader research agenda, see Jörg Baberowski, 'Gewalt verstehen', *Zeithistorische Forschungen* 5, no. 1 (2008): 5–17. Available online: www.zeithistorische-forschungen.de/16126041-Baberowski-1-2008 (accessed 30 June 2016).

20 Wolfgang Sofsky, *Zeiten des Schreckens. Amok, Terror, Krieg* (Frankfurt am Main: Fischer, 2002), 130–46. Cf. John Keegan, *The Face of Battle: A Study of Agincourt, Waterloo, and the Somme* (London: Johnathan Cape, 1976).

21 See the justified criticism in Thomas Kühne, 'Massen-Töten. Diskurse und Praktiken der kriegerischen und genozidalen Gewalt im 20. Jahrhundert', in *Massenhaftes Töten. Kriege und Genozide im 20. Jahrhundert*, ed. Thomas Kühne and Peter Gleichmann (Essen: Klartext, 2004), 11–52, 22–4, quote 23.

22 Sofsky, *Zeiten des Schreckens*, 132.

23 For more detail, see Thomas Kühne and Benjamin Ziemann, 'Militärgeschichte in der Erweiterung. Konjunkturen, Interpretationen, Konzepte', in *Was ist Militärgeschichte?*, ed. Thomas Kühne and Benjamin Ziemann (Paderborn:

Schöningh, 2000), 9–46; also see Benjamin Ziemann, '"Vergesellschaftung der Gewalt" als Thema der Kriegsgeschichte seit 1914. Perspektiven und Desiderate eines Konzeptes', in *Erster Weltkrieg, Zweiter Weltkrieg: Ein Vergleich. Krieg, Kriegserlebnis, Kriegserfahrung in Deutschland*, ed. Bruno Thoß and Hans-Erich Volkmann (Paderborn: Schöningh, 2002), 735–58.

24 Steven Pinker, *The Better Angels of our Nature: A History of Violence and Humanity* (London: Allen Lane, 2011).

25 Ibid., 194, 196.

26 Dieter Langewiesche, 'Eskalierte die Kriegsgewalt im Laufe der Geschichte?', in *Moderne Zeiten? Krieg, Revolution und Gewalt im 20. Jahrhundert*, ed. Jörg Baberowski (Göttingen: Vandenhoeck & Ruprecht, 2006), 12–36.

27 Jay Winter, 'Britain's Lost Generation of the First World War', *Population Studies* 31 (1977): 449–66.

28 For more details, see my critique of Pinker's interpretation: Benjamin Ziemann, 'Eine "neue Geschichte der Menschheit"? Zur Kritik von Steven Pinkers Deutung der Evolution der Gewalt', *Mittelweg 36* 22, no. 3 (2012): 45–56. An English version is available online: www.history.ac.uk/reviews/review/1232 (accessed 30 October 2016).

29 Heinrich Popitz, *Phänomene der Macht*, 2nd edn (Tübingen: Mohr, 1992), 48. The best explanation of the implications of this approach is still offered by Birgitta Nedelmann, 'Gewaltsoziologie am Scheideweg. Die Auseinandersetzungen in der gegenwärtigen und Wege der zukünftigen Gewaltforschung', in *Soziologie der Gewalt*, ed. Trutz von Trotha (Opladen: Westdeutscher Verlag, 1997), 59–85.

30 Popitz, *Phänomene der Macht*, 52.

31 The blurred distinction between violence against things and violence against people is also a shortcoming of the important research by Dirk Schumann, 'Gewalt als Grenzüberschreitung. Überlegungen zur Sozialgeschichte der Gewalt im 19. und 20. Jahrhundert', *Archiv für Sozialgeschichte* 37 (1997): 366–86.

32 On Leuven, see Wolfgang Schivelbusch, *Eine Ruine im Krieg der Geister. Die Bibliothek von Löwen August 1914 bis Mai 1940* (Frankfurt am Main: Fischer,1993); cf. Alan Kramer, *Dynamic of Destruction: Culture and Mass Killing in the First World War* (Oxford: Oxford University Press, 2007), 6–19.

33 Kramer, *Dynamic of Destruction*, 10.

34 Popitz, *Phänomene der Macht*, 48.

35 Heather Jones, *Violence against Prisoners of War in the First World War: Britain, France and Germany, 1914–1920* (Cambridge: Cambridge University Press, 2011), this definition pp. 3–4, quote and examples from Torgau ibid., p. 52. On the terminological imprecisions of this work, also see the highly critical review by Reinhard Nachtigal, *Historische Zeitschrift* 296 (2013), 244–7.

36 Jones, *Violence against Prisoners of War*, 56.

37 Ibid., 39.

38 Popitz, *Phänomene der Macht*, 44.
39 Sofsky, *Zeiten des Schreckens*, 131.
40 Figures in Jones, *Violence against Prisoners of War*, 23–4. However, Jones makes considerable efforts to relativize this important finding by pointing to fluctuations over time.
41 See Bernd Ulrich and Benjamin Ziemann (eds), *German Soldiers in the Great War: Letters and Eyewitness Accounts*, trans. Christine Brocks (Barnsley: Pen & Sword, 2010), 150. Numerous examples of such perceptions can also be found in letters from German POWs in the Bavarian State Library: Bayerische Staatsbibliothek Munich, Handschriftenabteilung, Schinnereriana.
42 Joanna Bourke, *An Intimate History of Killing: Face-to-Face-Killing in Twentieth-Century Warfare* (London: Granta, 1999).
43 Ibid., 215–305. On military chaplains in the First World War, see the comparative study by Patrick J. Houlihan, 'Imperial Frameworks of Religion: Catholic Military Chaplains of Germany and Austria-Hungary during the First World War', *First World War Studies* 3, no. 2 (2012): 165–82.
44 Bourke, *Intimate History of Killing* 13–43, quote 30.
45 Ibid., 6–7.
46 Niall Ferguson, *The Pity of War* (London: Allen Lane, 1998), 363.
47 Ibid., 358.
48 Ibid., 358–9.
49 As described by Volker R. Berghahn, 'Zur Frage individueller und kollektiver Lernfähigkeit. Ernst Jünger: "Der Kampf als Inneres Erlebnis" (1922)', in *Gewalt und Gesellschaft. Klassiker modernen Denkens neu gelesen*, ed. Uffa Jensen et al. (Göttingen: Wallstein, 2011) 122–32, quote 122.
50 See Michael Geyer, 'Das Stigma der Gewalt und das Problem der nationalen Identität in Deutschland', in *Von der Aufgabe der Freiheit. Politische Verantwortung und bürgerliche Gesellschaft im 19. und 20. Jahrhundert*, ed. Christian Jansen, Lutz Niethammer and Bernd Weisbrod (Berlin: Akademie, 1995), 673–98.
51 For the following, compare the important article by Christoph Nübel, 'Neuvermessungen der Gewaltgeschichte. Über den "langen Ersten Weltkrieg" (1900–1930)', *Mittelweg 36* 25, no. 1–2 (2015): 225–48.
52 For an initial overview, see Stéphane Audoin-Rouzeau, 'Combat', in *A Companion to World War I*, ed. John Horne (Chichester: Wiley-Blackwell, 2010), 173–87. The best short analysis of German strategy in the Great War remains Hew Strachan, 'German Strategy in the First World War', in *Internationale Beziehungen im 19. und 20. Jahrhundert. Festschrift für Winfried Baumgart zum 65. Geburtstag*, ed. Wolfgang Elz and Sönke Neitzel (Paderborn: Ferdinand Schöningh, 2003), 127–44.
53 John Keegan, as cited in the important book by Matthias Strohn, *The German Army and the Defence of the Reich: Military Doctrine and the Conduct of the Defensive Battle, 1918–1939* (Cambridge: Cambridge University Press, 2010), 6.

54 Omer Bartov, *Murder in Our Midst: The Holocaust, Industrial Killing, and Representation* (New York: Oxford University Press, 1996), 48–9.
55 Ibid., 50.
56 An important study examines this question using field post letters: Klaus Latzel, *Deutsche Soldaten – nationalsozialistischer Krieg? Kriegserlebnis-Kriegserfahrung 1939–1945* (Paderborn: Schöningh, 1998); group culture in the military is examined by Thomas Kühne, *Belonging and Genocide: Hitler's Community, 1918–1945* (New Haven: Yale University Press, 2010).
57 Another, more complex version of the continuity and special path theory is put forward by Isabel V. Hull, *Absolute Destruction: Military Culture and the Practices of War in Imperial Germany* (Ithaca: Cornell University Press, 2005). Hull argues that a tendency to pursue final, radical solutions was widespread in the organizational culture of the German military in the period 1870–71, which turned violence from a means into an end in itself and facilitated genocidal practices. There is not space to offer a detailed critique of this argument here (see among others: Thomas Kühne, 'Honour and Violence', *History Workshop Journal* 62 (2006): 304–10; Roger Chickering's review of Hull's book, *German History* 24 (2006): 138–9). Chickering points out that Hull presents little new empirical material for the First World War and instead primarily reproduces the findings of John Horne and Alan Kramer on the atrocities of 1914, making additional generalizations. In fact, Kramer himself was sceptical of the idea of a line of continuity between 1914 and 1941: Alan Kramer, 'Deutsche Kriegsverbrechen 1914/1941. Kontinuität oder Bruch', in *Das Deutsche Kaiserreich in der Kontroverse*, ed. Sven Oliver Müller and Cornelius Torp (Göttingen: Vandenhoeck & Ruprecht, 2009), 341–56. Empirical objections to Hull's theory are made by Winson Chu, Jesse Kauffman and Michael Meng, 'A "Sonderweg" through Eastern Europe? The Varieties of German Rule in Poland during the World Wars', *German History* 31 (2013): 318–44, especially 325.
58 The best comparative study is Kramer, *Dynamic of Destruction*.
59 Overcoming the misleading, abstract divide between military history 'from above' and 'from below' is the aim of a study by Wencke Meteling, *Ehre, Einheit und Ordnung. Preußische und französische Städte und Regimenter im Krieg, 1870/71 und 1914/19* (Baden-Baden: Nomos, 2010). The fact that the sources used reveal only aspects of the soldiers' perspective is another matter. See my review online: http://hsozkult.geschichte.hu-berlin.de/rezensionen/2011-3-097 (accessed 30 June 2016).
60 On the spatial dimension of fighting in the West, see now in much detail the path-breaking study by Christoph Nübel, *Durchhalten und Überleben an der Westfront. Raum und Körper im Ersten Weltkrieg* (Paderborn: Ferdinand Schöningh, 2014). The pioneering study by Vejas Gabriel Liulevicius, *War Land on the Eastern Front: Culture, National Identity, and German Occupation in World War I* (Cambridge: Cambridge University Press, 2000) focuses more on occupation plans and violent fantasies than on the practice of violence. See however Gerhard P. Groß

(ed.), *Die vergessene Front. Der Osten 1914/15. Ereignis, Wirkung, Nachwirkung* (Paderborn: Schöningh, 2006).

61 Jochen Böhler, Włodzimierz Borodziej and Joachim von Puttkamer, introduction to *Legacies of Violence: Eastern Europe's First World War* (Munich: De Gruyter Oldenbourg, 2014), 1–6, quotes 1, and the other chapters in this important volume. See also Jochen Böhler, 'Enduring Violence: The Postwar Struggles in East-Central Europe, 1917–1921', *Journal of Contemporary History* 50 (2015): 58–77; an important case study is Wolfram Dornik and Peter Lieb, 'Misconceived Realpolitik in a Failing State: The Political and Economical Fiasco of the Central Powers in the Ukraine, 1918', *First World War Studies* 4 (2013): 111–24.

62 Geyer, 'Eine Kriegsgeschichte, die vom Tod spricht', 145; on the German wartime volunteers, see Alexander Watson, 'For Kaiser and Reich: The Identity and Fate of the German Volunteers, 1914–1918', *War in History* 12 (2005): 44–74.

63 See for example the brief remarks by Ferguson, *The Pity of War*, 343–6, which were insufficient even given the state of research at that time. See also Stéphane Audoin-Rouzeau and Annette Becker, *14–18: Understanding the Great War* (New York: Hill and Wang, 2003), 106, for whom the mutinies in the French army in 1917 were the 'only concrete example of a profound decline in support of the war' by soldiers. Cf. Chapter 7 of this book.

64 An excellent overview is provided by Leonard V. Smith, 'Mutiny', in *The Cambridge History of the First World War*, ed. Jay Winter, 3 vols. (Cambridge: Cambridge University Press, 2014), vol. 2, 196–217.

65 Geyer, 'Eine Kriegsgeschichte, die vom Tod spricht', 145.

66 See Benjamin Ziemann, 'Resistance to War in Germany 1914–1918: The Traces of the German "Schwejkiade"', *Český Časopis Historický* 114 (2016): 717–34.

67 Geyer, 'Eine Kriegsgeschichte, die vom Tod spricht', quote 147.

68 See Dominik Richert, *Beste Gelegenheit zum Sterben. Meine Erlebnisse im Kriege 1914–1918*, ed. Bernd Ulrich and Angelika Tramitz (Munich: Knesebeck und Schuler, 1989). The English translation appeared as Dominik Richert, *The Kaiser's Reluctant Conscript: My Experiences in the War 1914–1918*, trans. D.C. Sutherland (Barnsley: Pen & Sword, 2012).

69 The account by Nick Howard, 'Shirkers in Revolt: Mass Desertion, Defeat and Revolution in the German Army, 1917–1920', in *To Make another World: Studies in Protest and Collective Action*, ed. Colin Barker (Aldershot: Ashgate, 1996), 113–38, does not take note of Deist's work on shirking in 1918.

70 For a brief outline of central questions and research positions, see Benjamin Ziemann and Claus-Christian W. Szejnmann, '"Machtergreifung": The Nazi Seizure of Power in 1933', *Politics, Religion & Ideology* 14 (2013): 321–37.

71 See the special issue of First World War Studies 'Military Occupations in First World War Europe', *First World War Studies* 4, no. 1 (2013); for an overview: Sophie De Schaepdrijver, 'Belgium', in Horne, *Companion*, 386–402; on one particular aspect

see: Benoît Majerus, 'La prostitution à Bruxelles pendant la Grande Guerre: contrôle et pratique', *Crime, Histoire & Sociétés* 7, no. 1 (2003): 5–42.

72 Michael Pesek, *Das Ende eines Kolonialreiches. Ostafrika im Ersten Weltkrieg* (Frankfurt am Main: Campus, 2010); Susanne Kuß, *Deutsches Militär auf kolonialen Kriegsschauplätzen. Eskalation von Gewalt zu Beginn des 20. Jahrhunderts* (Berlin: Links, 2010).

73 See the comparative study by Jay Winter, *Remembering War: The Great War between Memory and History in the Twentieth Century* (New Haven: Yale University Press, 2006); Anton Kaes, *Shell Shock Cinema: Weimar Culture and the Wounds of War* (Princeton: Princeton University Press, 2009) (and my critical review of the latter in *German History* 29 (2011): 328–9; Barbara Korte, Sylvia Paletschek and Wolfgang Hochbruck (eds), *Der Erste Weltkrieg in der populären Erinnerungskultur* (Essen: Klartext, 2008).

74 See now, in comparative perspective, Christa Hämmerle, Oswald Überegger and Birgitta Baader Zaar (eds), *Gender and the First World War* (Basingstoke: Palgrave, 2014). Compare also Thomas Kühne, *Kameradschaft. Die Soldaten des nationalsozialistischen Krieges und das 20. Jahrhundert* (Göttingen: Vandenhoeck & Ruprecht, 2006); on the United Kingdom, see Michael Roper, *The Secret Battle: Emotional Survival in the Great War* (Manchester: Manchester University Press, 2009); Jessica Meyer, *Men of War: Masculinity and the First World War in Britain* (Basingstoke: Palgrave Macmillan, 2009).

## 2 Soldiers of the First World War: Killing, Surviving, Discourses of Violence

1 See the discussion in Jay Winter (ed.), *The Legacy of the Great War: Ninety Years On* (Columbia: University of Missouri Press, 2009), 91–122; an excellent overview of the French debate is provided by Benoît Majerus, 'Kriegserfahrung als Gewalterfahrung. Perspektiven der neuesten internationalen Forschung zum Ersten Weltkrieg', in *Der Bürger als Soldat. Die Militarisierung europäischer Gesellschaften im langen 19. Jahrhundert*, ed. Christian Jansen (Essen: Klartext, 2003), 271–97.

2 This chapter will primarily look at figures for the German army, for which detailed data is available. All figures, unless otherwise indicated, in: Benjamin Ziemann, *War Experiences in Rural Germany 1914–1923*, trans. Alex Skinner (Oxford: Berg, 2007), 30–41; *Sanitätsbericht über das deutsche Heer im Weltkriege 1914/1918*, 3 vols (Berlin: Mittler, 1934), vol. 3, 25, 71, 73, 177.

3 Wolfgang Sofsky, *Zeiten des Schreckens. Amok, Terror, Krieg* (Frankfurt am Main: S. Fischer, 2002), 131. See the similarly exaggerated figures in Ute Frevert, 'Männer und Heroen. Vom Aufstieg und Niedergang des Heroismus im 19. und 20.

Jahrhundert', in *Erfindung des Menschen. Schöpfungsträume und Körperbilder 1500–2000*, ed. Richard van Dülmen (Vienna: Böhlau, 1998), 323–44, 339; Volker R. Berghahn, *Sarajewo, 28. Juni 1914. Der Untergang des alten Europa* (Munich: Deutscher Taschenbuch Verlag, 1997), 110.

4 *Sanitätsbericht über das deutsche Heer*, vol. 3, 49–50.
5 For a French division, see Leonard V. Smith, *Between Mutiny and Obedience: The Case of the French Fifth Infantry Division during World War I* (Princeton: Princeton University Press, 1994), 39ff.
6 On the British army, see Jay Winter, *The Great War and the British People* (Basingstoke: Palgrave Macmillan, 1986), 81.
7 Alexander Watson, *Enduring the Great War: Combat, Morale and Collapse in the German and British Armies, 1914–1918* (Cambridge: Cambridge University Press, 2008), 15. The figures are arranged somewhat differently in *Sanitätsbericht über das deutsche Heer*, vol. 3, 73.
8 *Sanitätsbericht über das deutsche Heer*, vol. 3, 71, 73.
9 Rolf-Dieter Müller, 'Gaskrieg', in *Enzyklopädie Erster Weltkrieg*, ed. Gerhard Hirschfeld, Gerd Krumeich and Irina Renz (Paderborn: Schöningh, 2003), 519–22, 521.
10 Olaf Groehler, *Der lautlose Tod. Einsatz und Entwicklung deutscher Giftgase von 1914 bis 1945* (Reinbek: Rowohlt, 1989), 16–60.
11 Jay Winter, '1914 bis 1918: Eine Entartung des Krieges?', in *Zeitalter der Gewalt: Zur Geopolitik und Psychopolitik des Ersten Weltkriegs*, ed. Michael Geyer, Helmut Lethen and Lutz Musner (Frankfurt: Campus, 2015), 117–33, quotes 120. For the British press coverage, see Wolfgang Wietzker, 'Giftgas im Ersten Weltkrieg. Was konnte die deutsche Öffentlichkeit wissen?' (PhD diss., University of Düsseldorf, 2006), 122–3, 307. On the legal position see Isabel Hull, *A Scrap of Paper. Breaking and Making International Law during the Great War* (Ithaca: Cornell University Press, 2014), 231–8.
12 Boris Z. Urlanis, *Bilanz der Kriege. Die Menschenverluste Europas vom 17. Jahrhundert bis zur Gegenwart* (Berlin: Deutscher Verlag der Wissenschaften, 1965), 267–74.
13 Richard Bessel, *Germany after the First World War* (Oxford: Clarendon Press, 1993), 6.
14 *Sanitätsbericht über das deutsche Heer*, vol. 3, 70.
15 Ibid., 70–1.
16 Victor Klemperer, *Curriculum Vitae*, 2. vols. (Berlin: Aufbau, 1996), vol. 2, 347.
17 Stefan Kaufmann, 'Technisiertes Militär. Methodische Überlegungen zu einem symbiotischen Verhältnis', in *Was ist Militärgeschichte?*, ed. Thomas Kühne and Benjamin Ziemann (Paderborn: Schöningh, 2000), 195–209. On Anders, see the concise analysis by Jason Dawsey, 'After Hiroshima: Günther Anders and the History of Anti-Nuclear Critique', in *Understanding the Imaginary War: Culture, Thought and*

*Nuclear Conflict, 1945–90*, ed. Matthew Grant and Benjamin Ziemann (Manchester: Manchester University Press 2016), 140–64.

18 Klaus Latzel, 'Die mißlungene Flucht vor dem Tod. Töten und Sterben vor und nach 1918', in *Kriegsende 1918. Ereignis – Wirkung – Nachwirkung*, ed. Jörg Duppler and Gerhard P. Groß (Munich: R. Oldenbourg, 1999), 183–99.

19 See Christoph Nübel, *Durchhalten und Überleben an der Westfront. Raum und Körper im Ersten Weltkrieg* (Paderborn: Ferdinand Schöningh, 2014).

20 Latzel, 'Die mißlungene Flucht', 196 (quotes); cf. Peter J. Leese, *Shell Shock: Traumatic Neurosis and the British Soldiers of the First World War* (New York: Palgrave, 2002).

21 Bruce I. Gudmundsson, *Stormtroop Tactics: Innovation in the German Army 1914–1918* (New York: Praeger, 1989).

22 See also Benjamin Ziemann, 'Freikorps', in Hirschfeld, Krumeich and Renz, *Enzyklopädie Erster Weltkrieg*, 503–5.

23 Isabel V. Hull, *Absolute Destruction: Military Culture and the Practices of War in Imperial Germany* (Ithaca: Cornell University Press, 2005).

24 Michael Geyer, 'Vom Massenhaften Tötungshandeln oder: Wie die Deutschen das Krieg-Machen lernten', in *Massenhaftes Töten. Kriege und Genozide im 20. Jahrhundert*, ed. Thomas Kühne and Peter Gleichmann (Essen: Klartext, 2004), 105–42, 111. Figures in *Sanitätsbericht über das deutsche Heer*, vol. 3, 65–6.

25 Geyer, 'Vom Massenhaften Tötungshandeln', 122–40, quote 140.

26 Michael Geyer, 'Gewalt und Gewalterfahrung im 20. Jahrhundert – Der Erste Weltkrieg', in *Der Tod als Maschinist. Der industrialisierte Krieg 1914–1918*, ed. Rolf Spilker and Bernd Ulrich (Bramsche: Rasch, 1998), 241–57, 247ff.

27 Jonathan Gumz, *The Resurrection and Collapse of Empire in Habsburg Serbia, 1914–1918* (Cambridge: Cambridge University Press 2009), 27–61, figure p. 58; see also M. Christian Ortner, 'Die Feldzüge gegen Serbien in den Jahren 1914 und 1915', in *Der Erste Weltkrieg auf dem Balkan*, ed. Jürgen Angelow (Berlin: Be.Bra Wissenschaft, 2011), 123–42.

28 Alan Kramer, *Dynamic of Destruction: Culture and Mass Killing in the First World War* (Oxford: Oxford University Press, 2007), 140–4, quote 144, claims that this was 'by intention a war of annihilation to destroy the Serb state'.

29 Gumz, *The Resurrection and Collapse of Empire*, 105–41, 193–230, see p. 198 on the bombardment.

30 J.G. Fuller, *Troop Morale and Popular Culture in the British and Dominion Armies, 1914–1918* (Oxford: Clarendon Press, 1990), 58–71.

31 David Gill and Gloden Dallas, *The Unknown Army: Mutinies in the British Army in World War I* (London: Verso, 1985).

32 Emmanuelle Cronier, 'Leave and Schizophrenia: Permissionaires in Paris during the First World War', in *Uncovered Fields: Perspectives in First World War Studies*, ed. Jenny Macleod and Pierre Purseigle (Leiden: Brill, 2004), 143–58.

33 Gerard Canini (ed.), *Les fronts invisibles: nourrir – fournir – soigner* (Nancy: Presses Universitaires de Nancy, 1984).
34 Dominik Richert, *The Kaiser's Reluctant Conscript: My Experiences in the War 1914–1918*, trans. D.C. Sutherland (Barnsley: Pen & Sword, 2012).
35 Norbert Elias, *Über sich selbst* (Frankfurt am Main: Suhrkamp, 1990), 32, 35.
36 Deborah Cohen, *The War Come Home: Disabled Veterans in Britain and Germany, 1914–1939* (Berkeley: University of California Press, 2001).
37 Tony Ashworth, *Trench Warfare 1914–1918: The Live and Let Live System* (London: Macmillan, 1980); Smith, *Mutiny*, 157–62.
38 Oswald Überegger, 'Auf der Flucht vor dem Krieg. Tiroler und Trentiner Deserteure im Ersten Weltkrieg', *Militärgeschichtliche Zeitschrift* 62 (2003): 355–93, especially 366–7 on the social and age profile.
39 On desertion in the British Expeditionary Force, compare Christoph Jahr, *Gewöhnliche Soldaten. Desertion und Deserteure im deutschen und britischen Heer 1914–1918* (Göttingen: Vandenhoeck & Ruprecht, 1998).
40 Mark Cornwall, 'Morale and Patriotism in the Austro-Hungarian Army, 1914–1918', in *State, Society and Mobilization in Europe during the First World War*, ed. John Horne (Cambridge: Cambridge University Press, 1997), 173–91; Reinhard Nachtigal, 'Privilegiensystem und Zwangsrekrutierung. Russische Nationalitätenpolitik gegenüber Kriegsgefangenen aus Österreich-Ungarn', in *Kriegsgefangene im Europa des Ersten Weltkriegs*, ed. Jochen Oltmer (Paderborn: Schöningh, 2006), 167–93; Richard G. Plaschka, Horst Haselsteiner and Arnold Suppan, *Innere Front. Militärassistenz, Widerstand und Umsturz in der Donaumonarchie 1918*, 2 vols. (Munich: Oldenbourg, 1974).
41 Gumz, *The Resurrection and Collapse of Empire*, 227.
42 Vanda Wilcox, 'Discipline in the Italian Army 1915–1918', in *Warfare and Belligerence: Perspectives in First World War Studies*, ed. Pierre Purseigle (Leiden: Brill, 2005), 73–100, 74–6, 82–3.
43 Figures in ibid., 80–1, 87, 90; David Stevenson, *With Our Backs to the Wall: Victory and Defeat in 1918* (London: Penguin, 2011), 295; for a general account, see Giovanna Procacci, *Soldati e prigionieri italiani nella grande guerra* (Rome: Editori Riuniti, 1993).
44 Niall Ferguson, *The Pity of War* (London: Allen Lane, 1998), 367–94; see also Brian K. Feltman, 'Tolerance as a Crime? The British Treatment of German Prisoners of War on the Western Front, 1914–1918', *War in History* 17 (2010), 435–58, and now his *The Stigma of Surrender: German Prisoners, British Captors, and Manhood in the Great War and Beyond* (Chapel Hill, NC: University of North Carolina Press, 2015).
45 Benjamin Ziemann, *Front und Heimat. Ländliche Kriegserfahrungen im südlichen Bayern 1914–1923* (Essen: Klartext, 1997); Feltman, *The Stigma of Surrender*, ignores ample evidence that private soldiers actually liked the prospect of being taken prisoner.

46 Annette Becker, 'Paradoxien in der Situation der Kriegsgefangenen 1914–1918', in Oltmer, *Kriegsgefangene*, 24–31, quote 27, though Becker immediately infers from this exceptional case that 'many' soldiers felt the same way.
47 Jochen Oltmer, 'Einführung. Funktionen und Erfahrungen von Kriegsgefangenschaft im Europa des Ersten Weltkriegs', in Oltmer, *Kriegsgefangene*, 11–23, figures on p. 11; also see the other contributions to this excellent volume.
48 Uta Hinz, 'Kriegsgefangene', in Hirschfeld, Krumeich and Renz, *Enzyklopädie Erster Weltkrieg*, 641–6, 646.
49 Alan Kramer, 'Italienische Kriegsgefangene im Ersten Weltkrieg', in *Der Erste Weltkrieg im Alpenraum. Erfahrung, Deutung, Erinnerung*, ed. Hermann J.W. Kuprian and Oswald Überegger (Innsbruck: Universitätsverlag Wagner, 2006), 247–58.
50 Klaus Latzel, *Deutsche Soldaten – nationalsozialistischer Krieg? Kriegserlebnis-Kriegserfahrung 1939–1945* (Paderborn: Schöningh, 1998); Aribert Reimann, *Der große Krieg der Sprachen. Untersuchungen zur historischen Semantik in Deutschland und England zur Zeit des Ersten Weltkrieges* (Essen: Klartext, 2000).
51 Smith, *Mutiny*, 84ff.
52 Bernd Ulrich, *Die Augenzeugen. Deutsche Feldpostbriefe in Kriegs- und Nachkriegszeit 1914–1933* (Essen: Klartext, 1997).
53 Also on the following, see Annick Cochet, 'L'opinion et le moral des soldats en 1916 d'après les archives du contrôle postal', 2 vols. (PhD diss., Université de Paris X-Nanterre, Paris, 1986); Stéphane Audoin-Rouzeau, *Men at War 1914–1918: National Sentiment and Trench Journalism in France during the First World War* (Oxford: Berg, 1992).
54 The term *language* or *discourse* is apt since, for all the important differences between the individual speakers, their ability to describe the war was strictly circumscribed by the limitations of the discourses in which they were able to express themselves.
55 Claudia Schlager, 'Waffenbrüderschaft im heiligsten Herzen Jesu. Die deutsche und österreichische Herz-Jesu-Verehrung im Ersten Weltkrieg und die Propagierung des Tiroler Vorbildes', in Kuprian and Überegger, *Der Erste Weltkrieg im Alpenraum*, 165–78, 178.
56 Patrick J. Houlihan, *Catholicism and the Great War: Religion and Everyday Life in Germany and Austria-Hungary, 1914–1922* (Cambridge: Cambridge University Press, 2015); Annette Becker, *War and Faith: The Religious Imagination in France, 1914–1930*, trans. Helen McPhail (Oxford: Berg, 1998).
57 Patrick Porter, 'New Jerusalems: Sacrifice and Redemption in the War Experiences of English and German Military Chaplains', in Purseigle, *Warfare and Belligerence*, 101–32.
58 Benjamin Ziemann, 'Katholische Religiosität und die Bewältigung des Krieges. Soldaten und Militärseelsorger in der deutschen Armee 1914–1918', in *Volksreligiosität und Kriegserleben*, ed. Friedhelm Boll (Münster: Lit, 1997), 116–36.

59 Smith, *Mutiny*; Leonard V. Smith, 'War and Politics: The French Army Mutinies of 1917', *War in History* 2 (1995): 180–201.
60 Benjamin Ziemann, 'Geschlechterbeziehungen in deutschen Feldpostbriefen des Ersten Weltkrieges', in *Briefkulturen und ihr Geschlecht. Zur Geschichte der privaten Korrespondenz vom 16. Jahrhundert bis heute*, ed. Christa Hämmerle and Edith Saurer (Vienna: Böhlau, 2003), 261–82.
61 Dietmar Molthagen, *Das Ende der Bürgerlichkeit? Liverpooler und Hamburger Bürgerfamilien im Ersten Weltkrieg* (Göttingen: Wallstein, 2007), 187–262, 327–38.
62 Many examples for its use by both committed socialists and other soldiers in Bernd Ulrich and Benjamin Ziemann (eds), *German Soldiers in the Great War: Letters and Eyewitness Accounts*, trans. Christine Brocks (Barnsley: Pen & Sword, 2010).
63 Ziemann, *War Experiences*, 111–54; Cochet, *L'opinion et le moral des soldats*, 450–72; Angelo Bazzanella, 'Die Stimme der Illiteraten. Volk und Krieg in Italien 1915–1918', in *Kriegserlebnis*, ed. Klaus Vondung (Göttingen: Vandenhoeck & Ruprecht, 1980), 334–51. On the context of agrarian societies, see Benjamin Ziemann, 'Agrarian Society', in *The Cambridge History of the First World War*, ed. Jay Winter, 3 vols. (Cambridge: Cambridge University Press, 2014), vol. 2. 382–407.
64 For example by Modris Eksteins, *Rites of Spring: The Great War and the Birth of the Modern Age* (London: Bantam Press, 1989).
65 Nicolas Offenstadt, *Les fusillés de la Grande Guerre et la mémoire collective (1914–1999)* (Paris: Odile Jacob, 1999). On the wider context of victimization narratives in interwar France see the pathbreaking study by Leonard V. Smith, *The Embattled Self: French Soldiers' Testimony of the Great War* (Ithaca: Cornell University Press, 2007).

# 3 German Soldiers and their Conduct of War in 1914

1 Figures in Wilhelm Deist, 'Streitkräfte (Deutsches Reich)', in *Enzyklopädie Erster Weltkrieg*, ed. Gerhard Hirschfeld, Gerd Krumeich and Irina Renz (Paderborn: Schöningh, 2003), 870–6, 870.
2 Bayerisches Kriegsarchiv, *Die Bayern im Großen Kriege 1914–18*, 2 vols. (Munich: Verlag des bayerischen Kriegsarchivs, 1923), vol. 1, 7.
3 Figures in: *Sanitätsbericht über das deutsche Heer im Weltkriege 1914/1918*, 3 vols. (Berlin: Mittler, 1934), vol. 3, 31–2.
4 Jeffrey T. Verhey, *The Myth of the 'Spirit of 1914' in Germany, 1914–1945* (Cambridge: Cambridge University Press, 2000); Christian Geinitz, *Kriegsfurcht und Kampfbereitschaft. Das Augusterlebnis in Freiburg. Eine Studie zum Kriegsbeginn 1914* (Essen: Klartext, 1998).
5 Ute Frevert, *A Nation in Barracks. Modern Germany, Military Conscription and Civil Society*, trans. Andrew Boreham with Daniel Brückenhaus (Oxford: Berg, 2004).

6 On the German wartime volunteers, see Alexander Watson, 'For Kaiser and Reich: The Identity and Fate of the German Volunteers, 1914–1918', *War in History* 12 (2005): 44–74.
7 Bernd Ulrich, 'Die Desillusionierung der Kriegsfreiwilligen von 1914', in *Der Krieg des kleinen Mannes. Eine Militärgeschichte von unten*, ed. Wolfram Wette (Munich: Piper, 1992), 110–26.
8 Philipp Münch, *Bürger in Uniform. Kriegserfahrungen von Hamburger Turnern 1914 bis 1918* (Freiburg im Breisgau: Rombach, 2009), 27–56, 85–101. Wencke Meteling, *Ehre, Einheit und Ordnung. Preußische und französische Städte und Regimenter im Krieg, 1870/71 und 1914/19* (Baden-Baden: Nomos, 2010), 205–20. Meteling's text is based on regimental histories. Such sources are, however, of limited value in analysing the German army's willingness to fight. On the atrocities, see John Horne and Alan Kramer, *German Atrocities, 1914: A History of Denial* (New Haven: Yale University Press, 2001).
9 All figures in *Sanitätsbericht über das deutsche Heer*, vol. 3, 140*–3*.
10 Michael Geyer, 'Vom Massenhaften Tötungshandeln oder: Wie die Deutschen das Krieg-Machen lernten', in *Massenhaftes Töten. Kriege und Genozide im 20. Jahrhundert*, ed. Thomas Kühne and Peter Gleichmann (Essen: Klartext, 2004), 105–42, 113.
11 War diary of Georg Schenk: Bayerisches Hauptstaatsarchiv München, Abt. IV (BHStA/IV), HS 3410.
12 Benjamin Ziemann, 'Katholische Religiosität und die Bewältigung des Krieges. Soldaten und Militärseelsorger in der deutschen Armee 1914–1918', in *Volksreligiosität und Kriegserleben*, ed. Friedhelm Boll (Münster: Lit, 1997), 116–36.
13 Horne and Kramer, *German Atrocities*, 71.
14 Ibid., 71, 111.
15 For a comprehensive account, see ibid., 9–86; for a list of the gravest incidents, see ibid., 435–43; for a concise summary of the argument, see Alan Kramer, 'The War of Atrocities: Murderous Scares and Extreme Combat', in *No Man's Land of Violence: Extreme Wars in the 20th Century*, ed. Alf Lüdtke and Bernd Weisbrod (Göttingen: Wallstein, 2006), 11–33.
16 Horne and Kramer, *German Atrocities*, 474, note 99. It should be noted that Kramer has used the Schenk diary in another context: Alan Kramer, '"Greueltaten". Zum Problem der deutschen Kriegsverbrechen in Belgien und Frankreich 1914', in *'Keiner fühlt sich hier mehr als Mensch . . .' Erlebnis und Wirkung des Ersten Weltkriegs*, ed. Gerhard Hirschfeld and Gerd Krumeich (Frankfurt am Main: Fischer Taschenbuch Verlag, 1996), 104–39, 124. It is thus surprising that he did not use it with regard to events in Réméréville.
17 On death by friendly fire, see generally Horne and Kramer, *German Atrocities*, 120. However, Horne and Kramer interpret this as an example of lack of discipline among

the troops and as a trigger for further scares about *francs-tireurs*. The occurrence of friendly fire and the ensuing panic at Réméréville are confirmed by Ludwig Gebsattel, *Von Nancy bis zum Camp des Romains 1914: nach amtlichen Unterlagen des Reichsarchivs, des Münchener Kriegsarchivs und Berichten von Mitkämpfern*, 2nd edn. (Oldenburg: Stalling, 1924), 60–2.

18 For this interpretation, see Klaus Latzel, *Deutsche Soldaten – nationalsozialistischer Krieg? Kriegserlebnis-Kriegserfahrung 1939–1945* (Paderborn: Schöningh, 1998), 31ff., 129ff.

19 War diary of Georg Schenk: BHStA/IV, HS 3410.

20 Walter Bartel, 'Unbekannte Briefe an Karl Liebknecht anläßlich seiner Ablehnung der Kriegskredite im Deutschen Reichstag am 2. Dezember 1914', *Zeitschrift für Geschichtswissenschaft* 7 (1959), 597–629.

21 War diary David Pfaff, 80th Fusilier Regiment; this section of Pfaff's diary is also available in English in: Bernd Ulrich and Benjamin Ziemann (eds), *German Soldiers in the Great War: Letters and Eyewitness Accounts*, trans. Christine Brocks (Barnsley: Pen & Sword, 2010), 35.

22 See also the letter by a German soldier dated 27 September 1914, quoted in Peter Knoch, 'Erleben und Nacherleben. Das Kriegserlebnis im Augenzeugenbericht und im Geschichtsunterricht', in Hirschfeld, Krumeich and Renz, *'Keiner fühlt sich hier mehr als Mensch. . .'*, 235–59, 246.

23 Horne and Kramer, *German Atrocities*, 56.

24 Isabel V. Hull, *Absolute Destruction: Military Culture and the Practices of War in Imperial Germany* (Ithaca: Cornell University Press, 2005).

25 For a subtle biographical interpretation of these letters, see Peter Knoch, 'Kriegserlebnis als biographische Krise', in *Biographie – sozialgeschichtlich*, ed. Andreas Gestrich, Peter Knoch and Helga Merkel (Göttingen: Vandenhoeck & Ruprecht, 1988), 86–108.

26 Letters by Stefan Schimmer to his wife: BHStA/IV, Amtsbibliothek 9584.

27 On the reporting of German military operations in the press in the early months of the war, see Thomas Raithel, *Das 'Wunder' der inneren Einheit. Studien zur deutschen und französischen Öffentlichkeit bei Beginn der Ersten Weltkrieges* (Bonn: Bouvier, 1996), 311ff.

28 On the destruction of Leuven, see Horne and Kramer, *German Atrocities*, 38–42.

29 Patrick J. Houlihan, 'Local Catholicism as Transnational War Experience: Everyday Religious Practice in Occupied Northern France, 1914–1918', *Central European History* 45 (2012), 233–67, quote 267.

30 Horne and Kramer, *German Atrocities*, 104–7, Beseler quote, 104.

31 Ibid., 94–113.

32 See the concise summary of this argument in Kramer, 'The War of Atrocities', 20–3.

33 Thomas Weber, *Hitler's First War: Adolf Hitler, the Men of the List Regiment and the First World War* (Oxford: Oxford University Press, 2010), 37–8.
34 Ibid., 40–1, quotes 40.
35 Gunter Spraul, *Der Franktireurkrieg 1914. Untersuchungen zum Verfall einer Wissenschaft und zum Umgang mit nationalen Mythen* (Berlin: Frank & Timme, 2016), 169–322.
36 Ibid., 25–54, 101–15, 161–7, 639–45. Spraul's own source criticism of German regimental histories, however, is wanting. Cf. ibid., 68–80.
37 For a general argument along these lines see Jörg Baberowski, *Räume der Gewalt* (Frankfurt am Main: S. Fischer, 2015).
38 Horne and Kramer, *German Atrocities*, 172–4.
39 Nicholas Stargardt, *The German Idea of Militarism: Radical and Socialist Critics, 1866–1914* (Cambridge: Cambridge University Press, 1994).
40 Horne and Kramer, *German Atrocities*, 196–200; see also Weber, *Hitler's First War*.
41 Otto Rümmler, R.I.R. 36, to the Alter Verband in Bochum, 7 October 1914: BArch, R 9350, 271, fol. 212–3. (transcript). Rümmler located this incident in 'Ergunnites', Belgium. No such place exists. It is likely that there was an error in transcription.
42 Laura Engelstein, '"A Belgium of Our Own": The Sack of Russian Kalisz, August 1914', *Kritika* 10 (2009): 441–73, citing the official investigation, quote 458.
43 Engelstein, '"A Belgium of Our Own"'.
44 Latzel, *Deutsche Soldaten*, 166–71, quotes 167.
45 Cited in Peter Knoch, 'Die Kriegsverarbeitung der "kleinen Leute" – eine empirische Gegenprobe', in *Der Geist von 1914. Zerstörung des universalen Humanismus?*, ed. Wolfgang Greive (Loccum: Evangelische Akademie Loccum, 1990), 151–93, 188–9.
46 On the operational aspects of this battle, see Dennis E. Showalter, *Tannenberg: Clash of Empires* (Hamden, CT: Archon Books, 1991); on the remembrance of the battle see Robert Traba, 'Kriegssyndrom in Ostpreußen. Ein Beitrag zum kollektiven Bewußtsein der Weimarer Zeit', in *Kriegserlebnis und Legendenbildung. Das Bild des 'modernen' Krieges in Literatur, Theater, Photographie und Film*, ed. Thomas F. Schneider, 3 vols. (Osnabrück: Universitätsverlag Rasch, 1999), vol. 1, 399–412.
47 Peter Jahn, '"Zarendreck, Barbarendreck – Peitscht sie weg!" Die russische Besetzung Ostpreußens und die deutsche Öffentlichkeit', in *August 1914. Ein Volk zieht in den Krieg*, ed. Berliner Geschichtswerkstatt (Berlin: Nishen, 1989), 147–55.
48 Alan Kramer, 'Kriegsrecht und Kriegsverbrechen', in *Enzyklopädie Erster Weltkrieg*, ed. Gerhard Hirschfeld, Gerd Krumeich and Irina Renz (Paderborn: Schöningh, 2003), 281–92, 284; see now Alexander Watson, '"Unheard-of Brutality": Russian Atrocities against Civilians in East Prussia, 1914–1915', *Journal of Modern History* 86 (2014): 780–825.
49 August Balke, 75. Res.-Div. to Hermann Sachse, 8 August 1915: BArch, R 9350, 271, fol. 98–9. A full version of the letter is available in English in Ziemann and Ulrich, *German Soldiers*, 63–4.

50 See Michael Geyer, 'Krieg als Gesellschaftspolitik. Anmerkungen zu neueren Arbeiten über das Dritte Reich im Zweiten Weltkrieg', *Archiv für Sozialgeschichte* 26 (1986): 557–601. For the military leadership's perspective on this reorganization in Russia, see Vejas Gabriel Liulevicius, *War Land on the Eastern Front: Culture, National Identity, and German Occupation in World War I* (Cambridge: Cambridge University Press, 2000).

51 Thus the explanation by Hull, *Absolute Destruction*, 209–11, who claims that they 'had been long prepared' in terms of ideology and culture (209); see also the critique of Horne and Kramer, *German Atrocities*, by Margaret L. Anderson, 'How German is it?', *German History* 24 (2006): 122–6; Margaret L. Anderson, 'A German Way of War?', *German History* 22 (2004): 254–8.

## 4 Ernst Jünger: Practitioner and Observer of Killing

1 Nikolaus Wachsmann, 'Marching under the Swastika? Ernst Jünger and National Socialism, 1918–1933', *Journal of Contemporary History* 33 (1998): 573–89, 576.

2 Bernd Hüppauf, 'Schlachtenmythen und die Konstruktion des "Neuen Menschen"', in *"Keiner fühlt sich hier mehr als Mensch ..." Erlebnis und Wirkung des Ersten Weltkriegs*, ed. Gerhard Hirschfeld and Gerd Krumeich (Essen: Klartext, 1993), 43–84.

3 The original English translation by Basil Creighton was published by Chatto & Windus in 1929. For the more recent translation, see: Ernst Jünger, *Storm of Steel*, trans. Michael Hofmann (London: Penguin, 2004). The definitive edition of the German text is now: Ernst Jünger, *In Stahlgewittern. Historisch-kritische Ausgabe*, ed. Helmuth Kiesel, 2 vols. (Stuttgart: Klett-Cotta, 2014). This edition allows detailed comparison of the – often quite substantial – differences between the seven separate editions Jünger published during his lifetime, from 1920 to 1978.

4 Ernst Jünger, 'Der Kampf als inneres Erlebnis', in *Sämtliche Werke* (Stuttgart: Klett-Cotta, 1980), vol. 7, 7–103.

5 Klaus Theweleit, *Männerphantasien*, 2 vols. (Reinbek: Rowohlt 1980), vol. 1, 47–8, 244, 250, vol. 2, 185, 189, 195, 206–7. For an English translation, see Klaus Theweleit, *Male Fantasies*, trans. Stephen Conway, Chris Turner and Erica Carter, 2 vols. (Minneapolis: University of Minnesota Press, 1987, 1989).

6 Bernd Weisbrod, 'Military Violence and Male Fundamentalism: Ernst Jünger's Contribution to the Conservative Revolution', *History Workshop Journal* 49 (2000): 69–94, quotes 75.

7 Weisbrod, Military Violence, 83–88, quote 83. Omer Bartov, '"Fields of Glory": War, Genocide, and the Glorification of Violence', in *Catastrophe and Meaning: The Holocaust and the Twentieth Century*, ed. Moishe Postone and Eric Santner (Chicago:

University of Chicago Press, 2003), 117–35, 125, sees Jünger's warrior as 'the embodiment of the Nazi ideal'.

8 Weisbrod, 'Military Violence', 74–5. There has been extensive research on Ernst Jünger's war literature. See, among others, Gerda Liebchen, *Ernst Jünger. Seine literarischen Arbeiten in den zwanziger Jahren. Eine Untersuchung zur gesellschaftlichen Funktion von Literatur* (Bonn: Bouvier, 1977); Reinhard Benneke, *Militanter Modernismus. Vergleichende Studien zum Frühwerk Ernst Jüngers* (Stuttgart: M&P, 1992); Roger Woods, *Ernst Jünger and the Nature of Political Commitment* (Stuttgart: Akademischer Verlag Heinz, 1992); Thomas Nevin, *Ernst Jünger and Germany: Into the Abyss, 1914–1945* (London: Constable, 1997), especially 39–74; Volker Berghahn, 'Zur Frage individueller und kollektiver Lernfähigkeit. Ernst Jünger: "Der Kampf als Inneres Erlebnis" (1922)', in *Gewalt und Gesellschaft. Klassiker modernen Denkens neu gelesen*, ed. Uffa Jensen et al. (Göttingen: Wallstein, 2011) 122–32.

9 Weisbrod, 'Military Violence', 71. Also see Anton Kaes, 'The Cold Gaze: Notes on Mobilization and Modernity', *New German Critique* 59 (1993), 105–17. On p. 106, Kraes describes Jünger's war literature without qualification as 'war diaries'.

10 Matthias Prangel, 'Das Geschäft mit der Wahrheit. Zu einer zentralen Kategorie der Rezeption von Kriegsromanen in der Weimarer Republik', in *Ideologie und Literaturwissenschaft*, ed. Jos Hoogeveen and Hans Würzner (Amsterdam: Rodopi, 1986), 47–78; on the example of Remarque, see Thomas F. Schneider, *Erich Maria Remarques Roman "Im Westen nichts Neues". Text, Edition, Entstehung, Distribution und Rezeption* (Tübingen: M. Niemeyer, 2004), especially 262–3, 265–76, 359–64.

11 Helmuth Kiesel (ed.), *Ernst Jünger. Kriegstagebuch 1914–1918* (Stuttgart: Klett-Cotta, 2010).

12 Thomas Nevin, 'Ernst Jünger. German Stormtrooper Chronicler', in *Facing Armageddon. The First World War Experienced*, ed. Hugh Cecil and Peter Liddle (London: Leo Cooper, 1996), 269–77. Nevin bases his chapter entirely on *Storm of Steel*. The same applies to an essay by Peter Burschel, 'Zur Anthropologie des Krieges bei Ernst Jünger', *Freiburger Universitätsblätter* 186 (2009): 27–36, which covers many of the same issues we examine here. In a less incisive chapter, Helmut Lethen has referred to the original diaries: Helmut Lethen, 'Die Nerven und das Phantom der Stahlgestalt. Ernst Jüngers Kriegserfahrungen', in *Zeitalter der Gewalt. Zur Geopolitik und Psychopolitik des Ersten Weltkrieges*, ed. Michael Geyer, Helmut Lethen and Lutz Musner (Frankfurt am Main: Campus, 2015), 239–54.

13 Kiesel (ed.), *Kriegstagebuch*, 616–47; see also Helmuth Kiesel, *Ernst Jünger. Die Biographie* (Munich: Siedler, 2009), 112–33, which is particularly useful for further information on Jünger's life story during the war.

14 John King, 'Writing and Rewriting the First World War: Ernst Jünger and the Crisis of the Conservative Imagination, 1914–25' (PhD diss., St John's College, Oxford, 1999), 152.

15 Kiesel (ed.), *Kriegstagebuch*, 616.
16 Ibid., 618.
17 Kiesel, *Ernst Jünger. Die Biographie*, 118.
18 Ibid., 180–86.
19 As noted by Kiesel in his afterword to Jünger's diaries: Kiesel, *Kriegstagebuch*, 626.
20 All page numbers quoted in the text in brackets refer to the edition (in German) of Jünger's diaries in Kiesel (ed.), *Kriegstagebuch*.
21 Bernd Hüppauf, 'Räume der Destruktion und Konstruktion von Raum. Landschaft, Sehen, Raum und der Erste Weltkrieg/Space of Destruction and Construction of Space: Landscape, Seeing, Space and the First World War', *Krieg und Literatur/War and Literature* 3, no.5/6 (1991): 105–23; Christoph Nübel, 'Das Niemandsland als Grenze. Raumerfahrungen an der Westfront im Ersten Weltkrieg', *Zeitschrift für Kulturwissenschaften* 2 (2008): 41–52.
22 Elsewhere, Jünger refers to the infantry soldiers as 'squirrels' (37) and describes his own 'weasel'-like skill in dodging heavy shells (96).
23 See the illuminating analysis by Julia Encke, 'War Noises on the Battlefield: On Fighting Underground and Learning to Listen in the Great War', *Bulletin of the German Historical Institute London* 37 (2015): 7–21.
24 See the letter by Emil Herbst, a sick-leave inspector from Sinsheim (Alsace), born 1877 in Bingen am Rhein, who served during the war as a sapper: 2./Armierungs-Btl. 76, Armee-Abteilung Gaede to his parents, 7 April 1916: BHStA/IV, Militärgericht 6. bayer. Landwehr-Division, H 15; see also Heinrich Wandt, *Erotik und Spionage in der Etappe Gent* (Berlin: Agis, 1929), 207.
25 Kiesel, *Ernst Jünger*, 121.
26 Joanna Bourke, *An Intimate History of Killing: Face-to-Face-Killing in Twentieth-Century Warfare* (London: Granta, 1999), 182.
27 Niall Ferguson, *The Pity of War* (London: Allen Lane, 1998), 369. A similarly blunt theory is presented without evidence in Jean-Jacques Becker and Gerd Krumeich, *Der Große Krieg. Deutschland und Frankreich im Ersten Weltkrieg 1914–1918* (Essen: Klartext, 2010), 168.
28 Ferguson, *The Pity of War*, 373.
29 Dominik Richert, *The Kaiser's Reluctant Conscript: My Experiences in the War 1914–1918*, trans. D.C. Sutherland (Barnsley: Pen & Sword, 2012), 15; cf. Heather Jones, *Violence against Prisoners of War in the First World War: Britain, France and Germany, 1914–1920* (Cambridge: Cambridge University Press, 2011), 78.
30 Ferguson, *The Pity of War*, 373.
31 Ibid. Ferguson quotes from pp. 262–3 of the 1929 English edition of *Storm of Steel*.
32 Kiesel (ed.), *Kriegstagebuch*, 373–95.
33 Ferguson, *The Pity of War*, 374–9. Ferguson bases his argument on a polemic published in the right-wing nationalist *Süddeutsche Monatshefte* in 1921, whose unsubstantiated claims should be seen in the context of the attempt to prevent the

extradition of German war criminals. Cf. August Gallinger, 'Gegenrechnung. Die Verbrechen an den deutschen Kriegsgefangenen', *Süddeutsche Monatshefte* 18, no. 9 (1921): 146–244, and especially p. 146 on the motivation in relation to extradition attempts; see also my review of Ferguson's book: *Militärgeschichtliche Zeitschrift* 59 (2000): 501–3. Ferguson later presented this theory again without providing substantial new evidence: Niall Ferguson, *The War of the World: History's Age of Hatred* (London: Allen Lane, 2006), 125–30.

34 Alan Kramer, 'Surrender of Soldiers in World War I', in *How Fighting Ends: A History of Surrender*, ed. Holger Afflerbach and Hew Strachan (Oxford: Oxford University Press, 2012), 265–78, 277; see also Thomas Weber's conclusions on this issue: Thomas Weber, *Hitler's First War: Adolf Hitler, the Men of the List Regiment, and the First World War* (Oxford: Oxford University Press, 2010), 110–11, 147–8.

35 Alan Kramer, Kriegsrecht und Kriegsverbrechen, in *Enzyklopädie Erster Weltkrieg*, ed. Gerhard Hirschfeld, Gerd Krumeich and Irina Renz (Paderborn: Schöningh, 2003), 281–92.

36 Jones, *Violence*, 78.

37 Ferguson, *The Pity of War*, 371–2.

38 Michael Riekenberg, 'Über die Gewalttheorie von Georges Bataille und ihren Nutzen für die Gewaltsoziologie', *Comparativ* 21, no. 1 (2011): 105–28, especially 111, 117.

39 On German soldiers' perception of the battle, see the documentation and analysis in Gerhard Hirschfeld, Gerd Krumeich and Irina Renz (eds), *Scorched Earth. The Germans on the Somme 1914–18* (Barnsley: Pen & Sword, 2009).

40 Brian K. Feltman, 'Tolerance As a Crime? The British Treatment of German Prisoners of War on the Western Front, 1914–1918', *War in History* 17 (2010): 435–58, 446–57. Similarly to Ferguson (*The Pity of War*), Feltman bases his conclusions on questionable and often tendentious statements made by German soldiers immediately after the war.

41 Kramer, 'Surrender of Soldiers', 376.

42 Kramer, 'Surrender of Soldiers', 277.

43 See for example Jünger's sobering remarks on 20 March 1918 in Kiesel, *Kriegstagebuch*, 374.

44 Kiesel, *Ernst Jünger. Die Biographie*, 124.

45 Benjamin Ziemann, *War Experiences in Rural Germany 1914–1923*, trans. Alex Skinner (Oxford: Berg, 2007), 55–6.

46 On the genocidal nature of 'Operation Barbarossa', see Michael Geyer, 'Krieg als Gesellschaftspolitik. Anmerkungen zu neueren Arbeiten über das Dritte Reich im Zweiten Weltkrieg', *Archiv für Sozialgeschichte* 26 (1986): 557–601. The best overview of recent research is provided by Thomas Kühne, 'Der nationalsozialistische Vernichtungskrieg und die "ganz normalen" Deutschen. Forschungsprobleme und Forschungstendenzen der Gesellschaftsgeschichte des Zweiten Weltkrieges. Erster Teil', *Archiv für Sozialgeschichte* 39 (1999): 580–662.

47 Hellmuth Gruss, 'Aufbau und Verwendung der deutschen Sturmbataillone im Weltkrieg' (PhD diss., University of Berlin, 1939), especially 13ff., 21ff., 35ff., 73-4. More recent literature adds little to Gruss's thesis. See Bruce I. Gudmundsson, *Stormtroop Tactics: Innovation in the German Army 1914–1918* (New York: Praeger, 1989); Norman L. Kincaide, 'Sturmbteilungen to Freikorps: German army tactical and organizational development, 1914–1918' (PhD diss., Arizona State University, Phoenix, 1989).
48 Decree by Falkenhayn, 15 May 1916: Gruss, 'Aufbau', Annex 4, 152.
49 Ibid., 43ff., 62, 87–8, 133, 139–40.
50 Kincaide, 'Sturmabteilungen', 77, 91.
51 Brendan Murphy, 'Killing in the German Army: Organising and Surviving Combat in the Great War' (PhD diss., University of Sheffield, 2014), covers this topic extensively.
52 Kiesel, *Ernst Jünger. Die Biographie*, 131.
53 Weber, *Hitler's First War*, 108–9, quote 109; figure in: Dieter Storz, 'Handgranate', in Hirschfeld, Krumeich and Renz, *Enzyklopädie Erster Weltkrieg*, 542.
54 Michael Geyer, 'Vom Massenhaften Tötungshandeln oder: Wie die Deutschen das Krieg-Machen lernten', in *Massenhaftes Töten. Kriege und Genozide im 20. Jahrhundert*, ed. Thomas Kühne and Peter Gleichmann (Essen: Klartext, 2004), 105–42, 121. In English, see also Michael Geyer, 'How the Germans Learned to Wage War: On the Question of Killing in the First and Second World Wars', in *Between Mass Death and Individual Loss: The Place of the Dead in Twentieth-Century*, ed. Paul Betts, Alan Confino, and Dirk Schuman (New York: Berghahn, 2008), 25–50. I am grateful to Brendan Murphy for discussing his valuable insights on this essay with me.
55 Ibid., 123.
56 This qualification refers primarily to the analysis of German army trench newspapers, which were strictly controlled by the authorities. See Robert Nelson, *German Soldier Newspapers of the First World War* (Cambridge: Cambridge University Press, 2011), 88–152. Nelson does not always take this problem into account.
57 Ziemann, *War Experiences*, 111–16.
58 Thomas Kühne, *Kameradschaft. Die Soldaten des nationalsozialistischen Krieges und das 20. Jahrhundert* (Göttingen: Vandenhoeck & Ruprecht, 2006), 27–51, quotes 45–6.
59 Geyer, 'Vom Massenhaften Tötungshandeln', 131.
60 Ibid., note 104.
61 Jünger, *Storm of Steel*, 231–2.
62 Burschel, 'Anthropologie des Krieges', 36.
63 Ibid., 35–6.; cf. Weisbrod, 'Military Violence'.
64 See Dieter Langewiesche, 'Reich, Nation und Staat in der neueren deutschen Geschichte', *Historische Zeitschrift* 254 (1992): 341–81, 374.

65 There has so far been extraordinarily little research into the social structure and collective mentality of the German officer corps during the war. For a comparison with the British Expeditionary Force, see Alexander Watson, *Enduring the Great War: Combat, Morale and Collapse in the German and British Armies, 1914–1918* (Cambridge: Cambridge University Press, 2008), 108–39. However, Watson's theory that officers' 'Standesbewußtsein' (their sense of caste identity) heavily shaped their leadership is unconvincing. There is no trace of such Standesbewußtsein in Jünger's diaries, for example.

66 See, for example, with respect to the concept of honour: Ute Frevert, *Ehrenmänner. Das Duell in der bürgerlichen Gesellschaft* (Munich: C.H. Beck, 1991).

67 MacGregor Knox, 'Erster Weltkrieg und "military culture". Kontinuität und Wandel im deutsch-italienischen Vergleich' in *Das Deutsche Kaiserreich in der Kontroverse*, ed. Sven Oliver Müller and Cornelius Torp (Göttingen: Vandenhoeck & Ruprecht, 2009), 290–307, 300. For a more balanced view, see Wencke Meteling, 'Adel und Aristokratismus im preußisch–deutschen Weltkriegsoffizierkorps', in *Aristokratismus und Moderne. Adel als politisches und kulturelles Konzept 1890–1945*, ed. Eckart Conze et al. (Cologne: Böhlau Verlag, 2013), 215–38, 237–8.

68 See Michael Geyer, 'The Past as Future: The German Officer Corps as Profession', in *German Professions 1800–1950*, ed. Geoffrey Cocks and Konrad H. Jarausch (New York: Oxford University Press, 1990), 183–212.

# 5 Desertion in the German Army 1914–1918

1 See the research overview in Benjamin Ziemann, 'Fluchten aus dem Konsens zum Durchhalten. Ergebnisse, Probleme und Perspektiven der Erforschung soldatischer Verweigerungsformen in der Wehrmacht 1939–1945', in *Die Wehrmacht – Mythos und Realität*, ed. Rolf-Dieter Müller and Hans-Erich Volkmann (Munich: Oldenbourg, 1999), 589–613. The best monograph on the topic is Magnus Koch, *Fahnenfluchten. Deserteure der Wehrmacht im Zweiten Weltkrieg. Lebenswege und Entscheidungen* (Paderborn: Schöningh, 2008). On the First World War, see also the study by Christoph Jahr, *Gewöhnliche Soldaten. Desertion und Deserteure im deutschen und britischen Heer 1914–1918* (Göttingen: Vandenhoeck & Ruprecht, 1998). Some problematic aspects of Jahr's text are noted in this chapter.

2 See the report by 7./I.R. 102, 1 June 1917: Sächsisches Hauptstaatsarchiv Dresden (SHStAD), Kriegsarchiv (P) 20534, fol. 29.

3 Dominik Richert, *The Kaiser's Reluctant Conscript: My Experiences in the War 1914–1918*, trans. D.C. Sutherland (Barnsley: Pen & Sword, 2012), 245.

4 Various cases in: SHStAD, Kriegsarchiv (P) 20533, *passim*.

5  See AOK 3 to Heeresgruppe Deutscher Kronprinz, 5 May 1918: SHStAD, Kriegsarchiv (P), 20566, fol. 81. In this instance, the perpetrator was an Alsatian soldier. His victim was injured, but survived.
6  See the case of Uffz. Haffner, 11/1. I.R. in the night of 21 to 22 September 1917: SHStAD, Kriegsarchiv (P) 20534, fol. 86–7. Haffner revealed his extensive local knowledge in a conversation just a few days before his defection. In another case, prior patrols served to familiarize the deserter with the terrain: BHStA/IV, Militärgerichte 6479.
7  On the former, see: Richert, *Reluctant Conscript*, 248; Bayerisches Hauptstaatsarchiv, Abt. IV: Kriegsarchiv (BHStA/IV), Militärgerichte 6211; report by GK VII. AK dated 22 February 1917: SHStAD, Kriegsarchiv (P) 20533, fol. 113.
8  A group of six men was already relatively large; see telegram from GK II. AK to AOK 3, 12 September 1916: SHStAD, Kriegsarchiv (P) 20533, fol. 18–19.
9  On Polish soldiers, see Armee-Abt. v. Strantz to Prussian War Ministry, 17 May 1915 (copy); GK V. AK 22 June 1915 to stv. GK V. AK (copy): Geheimes Staatsarchiv Preußischer Kulturbesitz Berlin-Dahlem (GStA), I. HA, Rep. 77, Tit. 863a, no. 2b, fol. 339–40, 344–5.
10  United States War Department, *Histories of Two Hundred and Fifty-One Divisions of the German Army which participated in the War (1914–1918)* (Washington: Government Printing Office, 1920), 302, 480–1. This work is based on generally highly reliable material from Allied reconnaissance, on captured German documents and statements by German prisoners.
11  The lance-corporal in question was convicted under Section 73 of the *Militärstrafgesetzbuch* (Military Penal Code); see Kriegsrichtsrat Zschorn, 'Zu § 73 MStGB', *Archiv für Militärrecht* 8 (1919/20): 174–7.
12  Max von Gallwitz, *Erleben im Westen 1916–1918* (Berlin: Mittler, 1932), 235.
13  Benjamin Ziemann, *War Experiences in Rural Germany 1914–1923*, trans. Alex Skinner (Oxford: Berg, 2007), 56.
14  9. Res.-Div. to GK V. Res.-Korps, 16 September 1916 (copy): SHStAD, Kriegsarchiv (P) 20533, fol. 20; cf. 55. Inf.-Brigade to 28. Inf.-Div, 8 November 1916: ibid., fol. 34. In another, similar case, witnesses were unable to determine if the soldier in question had defected or if the French had pulled him forcefully into their trenches; GK V. Res.-Korps to AOK 3, 6 September 1916: SHStAD, Kriegsarchiv (P) 20533, fol. 17.
15  A tacit agreement involving the 6th Company of the 1st Bavarian Infantry Regiment was only put on record after an NCO defected: BHStA/IV, Militärgerichte 3361.
16  In another incident of this kind, such an order was only issued after the act: BHStA/IV, Militärgericht 6. Ldw.-Div. K 12.
17  GK XII. AK to AOK 3, 22 February 1917: SHStAD, Kriegsarchiv (P) 20533, fol. 109.

18 II./I.R. 467 to the regiment, 18 April 1917: SHStAD, Kriegsarchiv (P) 20533, fol. 127–32, 2. Badisches Grenadier-Rgt. to 56. Inf.-Brigade, 9 December 1916: ibid., fol. 72–4.
19 Richert, *Reluctant Conscript*, 250–1; II./I.R. 467 to the regiment, 18 April 1917: SHStAD, Kriegsarchiv (P) 20533, fol. 127.
20 Bernd Ulrich and Benjamin Ziemann (eds), *German Soldiers in the Great War: Letters and Eyewitness Accounts*, trans. Christine Brocks (Barnsley: Pen & Sword, 2010), 177; war diary of Wilhelm Pieck, entry dated 16 August 1916: BArch, SAPMO, NL 36, 12, fol. 115.
21 A translation of the letter found on 5 September 1915 was enclosed with a report from I.R. 155 to 77. Inf.-Brigade (copy), 11 September 1915: GStA, I. HA, Rep. 77, Tit. 863a, no. 2b., fol. 347–8.
22 See the materials in: Landesarchiv Schleswig, 301/1713. The district administrator of Hadersleben (Danish: Haderslev) had raised this issue in a letter to the Schleswig district president on 12 May 1917, which was evidently not acted upon: ibid.
23 District administrator Hadersleben to the district president in Schleswig, 13 December 1917: Leo Stern (ed.), *Die Auswirkungen der Großen Sozialistischen Oktoberrevolution auf Deutschland*, 4 vols. (Berlin: Rütten & Loening, 1959), vol. 2, 825–6 (document 265).
24 Letter from the Prussian War Ministry to Chief of the General Staff of the Field Army and others (copy), 9 February 1917: GStA, I. HA, Rep. 84a, 7802, fol. 147.
25 Ulrich and Ziemann, *German Soldiers*, 141–2. Some did so in order to escape the draft. See Gendarmeriestation Kellmünz (BA Memmingen) to stv. GK I. bayer. AK, 13 February 1918: BHStA/IV, stv. GK I. AK 1584.
26 A. Geisser of Brunnen (Switzerland) to A. Bücheler of Stuttgart, 25 August 1918: HStA Stuttgart/MA, M 77/1, Büschel 716.
27 Monitoring of postal and telegraph traffic stv. GK XIII. AK to Bezirks-Kommando Horb, 23 September 1917, copy of a letter dated 11 September 1917 from Ms Gertiser-Andres of Aarau to A. Schneider of Waldmössingen (Oberamt Oberndorf): HStA Stuttgart/MA, M 77/1, Büschel 715.
28 See the materials in: BHStA/IV, Militärgerichte 6402; Olaf Klose and Eva Rudolph (eds), *Schleswig-Holsteinisches Biographisches Lexikon*, 12 vols. (Neumünster: Karl Wachholtz Verlag, 1974), vol. 3, 223–5.
29 Jahr, *Gewöhnliche Soldaten*, 118.
30 For the Bavarian Army, see: 6. bayer. Ldw.-Div. to Bavarian War Ministry, 30 November 1917: BHStA/IV, MKr 11066; ibid., Militärgerichte 6415, 6477.
31 Five of these twenty-one men had done so in December 1917, while the other cases were spread over 1916 and 1917. L.I.R. 125 to 54. Ldw.-Brigade, 6 January 1918: SHStAD, Kriegsarchiv (P) 20566, fol. 9.
32 AOK 3 to Generalquartiermeister des Heeres, 8 February 1918: SHStAD, Kriegsarchiv (P) 20566, fol. 56.

33 Quote: Letter from the Zurich-born tinsmith Ernst Dreher, Uffz. der Reserve, 2. Feldpionier-Kompanie I. bayer. AK, sent from Zurich to his old unit, 24 February 1916: BHStA/IV, Militärgerichte 6237; C. Schmidt from Olten sent a similar letter to his parents and siblings (his wife and children lived in Switzerland) on 11 December 1917: SHStAD, Kriegsarchiv (P) 20566, fol. 16. See the report based on information from a deputy officer who had returned from Switzerland in: L.I.R. 125 to 54. Ldw.-Brigade, 6 January 1918: ibid., fol. 9.

34 GK XVI. AK to AOK 3, 4 January 1918: SHStAD, Kriegsarchiv (P) 20566, fol. 4. Leave from the field army to a neutral country required the approval of the Generalquartiermeister (Quartermaster General) in each case. Generalquartiermeister des Heeres to all army high commands, 22 January 1918: ibid., fol. 30.

35 Stv. GK I. bayer. AK 5 to Sanitätsamt I. bayer. AK, 5 December 1917: BHStA/IV, stv. GK I. AK 1327; Deputy General Staff of the Army to the deputy general commands, 27 June 1918: SHStAD, Kriegsarchiv (P) 10915, fol. 157; 'Geheime Rundverfügung des stv. Generalstabs', Abt. IIIb, sent to deputy general commands, 15 July 1918: Institut für Deutsche Militärgeschichte, *Militarismus gegen Sowjetmacht 1917 bis 1919. Das Fiasko der ersten antisowjetischen Aggression des deutschen Imperialismus* (Berlin: Deutscher Militärverlag, 1967), 237–8 (document 26). Numerous individual cases in: BHStA/IV, stv. GK I. AK 1351.

36 Chief of the Deputy General Staff to the deputy general commands and war ministries, 5 November 1917: SHStAD, Kriegsarchiv (P) 24137, fol. 15; Stv. Generalstab, Abt. IIIb., to Bavarian War Ministry, 27 February 1918: BHStA/IV, stv. GK I. AK 1335.

37 Chief of the Deputy General Staff of the Army to the deputy general commands and war ministries, 5 November 1917: SHStAD, Kriegsarchiv (P) 24137, fol. 14.

38 Chef des stv. Generalstabes, Abt. IIIb, 'Denkschrift über die Bestrafung des Personenschmmuggels' (copy), 3 October 1917: GStA, I. HA, Rep. 84a, no. 8211, fol. 393–97. Individual cases in: SAPMO, NL 36, 14, fol. 1. It was, of course, also possible to reach the Netherlands without such help. See for example 1. E./I.R. 106 in Leipzig to stv. GK XIX. AK, 6 September 1917: SHStAD, Kriegsarchiv (P) 24179, fol. 91.

39 We can reconstruct this process based on a confirmation from the Depot voor Diutsche deserteurs en andere Buitenlanders in Bergen dated 16 February 1918. SHStAD, Kriegsarchiv (P) 22694, fol. 4; interrogation log for the returned deserters A. Freier and R. Seidel in Emmerich, 17 February 1918: SHStAD, Kriegsarchiv (P) 22694, fol. 5ff., 29ff.; letter from the deserter Ferdinand Groß of Saargemünd (Lorraine) from Venlo to his mother and siblings, 6 February 1918; letter from Ms Kleinbeck to her nephew Ferdinand Groß in Bergen, 15 May 1918; both in: BHStA/IV, Militärgericht 6. Ldw.-Div. G 23. Statement by the retired Major Karl von Roeder: Ewald Beckmann, *Der Dolchstoß-Prozeß in München vom 19. Oktober bis 20. November 1925. Verhandlungsberichte und Stimmungsbilder* (Munich: Süddeutsche

Monatshefte-Verlag, 1925), 22, 209; WUA, vol. 10/1, *Gutachten der Sachverständigen Alboldt, Stumpf, v. Trotha zu den Marinevorgängen 1917 und 1918* (Berlin: Deutsche Verlagsgesellschaft für Politik und Geschichte, 1928), 255; Susanne Wolf, 'Guarded Neutrality: The Internment of Foreign Military Personnel in the Netherlands during the First World War' (PhD diss., University of Sheffield, 2008), 200–6.

40 Hans Rudolf Kurz, *Dokumente der Grenzbesetzung 1914–1918* (Frauenfeld: Verlag Huber, 1970), 100ff.

41 BHStA/IV, Militärgerichte 6337.

42 Carl Herrmann, *Geheimkrieg. Dokumente und Untersuchungen eines Polizeichefs an der Westfront* (Hamburg: Hanseatische Verlagsanstalt, 1930), 198. During the war, the author was head of the department for counter-espionage in the 6th Army's Secret Field Police.

43 Abba Strazhas, *Deutsche Ostpolitik im Ersten Weltkrieg. Der Fall Ober Ost 1915–1917* (Wiesbaden: Harrassowitz, 1993), 55–6, 218–19 (quote).

44 'Merkblatt für Behandlung von Fahnenfluchtfällen', sent by the Prussian War Ministry on 16 April 1918: SHStAD, Kriegsarchiv (P) 24179, fol. 206. On 24 February 1917, the Deputy General Command of the 10th Army Corps issued a decree that enabled prosecution of civilians – including relatives – who knew a deserter's whereabouts and failed to report it to the military authorities. GStA, I. HA, Rep. 77, Tit. 332y, no. 20, fol. II.

45 Weekly report of the district president of Lower Bavaria, 16 September 1918: Staatsarchiv Landshut, Rep. 168/5, 1116.

46 See the statement by Major von Röder in: Beckmann, *Der Dolchstoß-Prozeß*, 207.

47 Chief of the Deputy General Staff of the Army to the deputy general commands and war ministries of the German states on 5 November 1917: SHStAD, Kriegsarchiv (P) 24137, fol. 13.

48 Albrecht von Thaer, *Generalstabsdienst an der Front und in der O.H.L. Aus Briefen und Tagebuchaufzeichnungen 1915–1919*, ed. Siegfried A. Kaehler (Göttingen: Vandenhoeck & Ruprecht, 1958), 146; Heinz Hürten and Georg Meyer (eds), *Adjutant im preußischen Kriegsministerium Juni 1918 bis Oktober 1919. Aufzeichnungen des Hauptmanns Gustav Böhm* (Stuttgart: Deutsche Verlags-Anstalt, 1977), 52 (entry dated 1 November 1918).

49 Ziemann, *War Experiences*, 45–50.

50 Quote: Victor Klemperer, *Curriculum Vitae. Erinnerungen 1881–1918*, 2. vols. (Berlin: Aufbau, 1996), vol. 2, 345; Ferdinand Groß wrote to his mother from Venlo on 6 February 1918: 'It will probably be several years before we see each other again.' BHStA/IV, Militärgericht 6. Ldw.-Div. G 23.

51 *Armee-Verordnungsblatt* 51 (1917): 307. The deadline was later extended due to a lack of awareness of the decree: ibid., 457. The measure was intended to draw the deserters away from Dutch propaganda: WUA, vol. 10/1, 277.

52 1. E./I.R. 106 to stv. GK XIX. AK, 6 September 1917: SHStAD, Kriegsarchiv (P) 24179, fol. 91; cf. WUA, vol. 10/1, 278.
53 Max Gotthardt to his wife Meta in Burgstädt, 13 November 1917; Burgstädt police to stv. GK XII. AK, 22 December 1917: ibid., fol. 162–3. Those returning appear to have come largely from Denmark and the Netherlands. In the area under the responsibility of the Deputy General Command of the 1st Bavarian Army Corps, only one deserter turned himself in. Aktenvermerk K.M.-Abt. R, 21 June 1918: BHStA/IV, MKr 11066.
54 A defector from the 4th Company of the 20th Bavarian Infantry Reserve repeatedly told comrades before his defection in April 1915 that he was convinced this was the case. BHStA/IV, Militärgerichte 6410.
55 Hans Spieß to his sister, 12 February 1918: BHStA/IV, Kriegsbriefe 340.
56 Stv. Generalstab der Armee IIIb to the deputy general commands, 30 January 1917: SHStAD, Kriegsarchiv (P) 24179, fol. 1.
57 Copy of the letter dated 6 June 1915; GK VI. AK to AOK 3, 14 June 1915: SHStAD, Kriegsarchiv (P) 20533, fol. 1–2.
58 The punishment for desertion in the field of battle was a prison sentence of five to ten years. Soldiers defecting or deserting from their post in front of the enemy faced the death penalty (sections 71 and 73 of the Military Penal Code): *Militärstrafgerichtsordnung vom 1. Dezember 1898 und Militärstrafgesetzbuch vom 20. Juni 1872* (Mannheim and Leipzig: Bensheimer, 1913), 191–2.
59 On the War Articles and disciplinary measures used on the front line, see Ziemann, *War Experiences*, 57–64.
60 Siegfried Pelz, 'Die Preussischen und Reichsdeutschen Kriegsartikel. Historische Entwicklung und rechtliche Einordnung' (PhD diss. in jurisprudence, University of Hamburg 1979, Appendix P (Articles of War for the army, 22 September 1902)).
61 Report by Commander Solda, I.R. 49 to 4. Inf.-Div., 24 February 1916: SHStAD, Kriegsarchiv (P) 20533, fol. 9. In the event of suspicions against a specific individual, soldiers were also asked to inform on their colleagues; see Dominik Richert, *Beste Gelegenheit zum Sterben. Meine Erlebnisse im Kriege 1914–1918*, ed. Bernd Ulrich and Angelika Tramitz (Munich: Knesebeck und Schuler, 1989), 273.
62 30. Res.-Div. to Gruppe Argonnen, 18 December 1917: SHStAD, Kriegsarchiv (P) 20534, fol. 119. The 212th Infantry Division regularly told soldiers that their families would lose financial support if they deserted; see the circular dated 22 May 1918: Albrecht Kästner (ed.), *Revolution und Heer. Auswirkungen der Großen Sozialistischen Oktoberrevolution auf das Heer des imperialistischen deutschen Kaiserreichs 1917/18. Dokumente* (Berlin: Militärverlag der DDR, 1987) 53–4 (document 20).
63 Decree by the Chief of the General Staff of the Field Army, 23 June 1918: *Militarismus gegen Sowjetmacht*, 232 (document 20). Units in the replacement army

had already been asked in a letter from the Prussian War Ministry on 16 April 1918 to 'repeatedly' emphasize these points to the troops. BHStA/IV, MKr 11066.
64 Btl.-Kommandeur II./I.R. 49 to the regiment, 24 February 1916: SHStAD, Kriegsarchiv (P) 20533, fol. 11; 13. Res.-Div. to GK VII. Res.-Korps, 21 January 1917: ibid., fol. 93.
65 I.R. 49 to 4. Inf.-Div., 24 February 1916: SHStAD, Kriegsarchiv (P) 20533, fol. 9; 30. Res.-Div. to Gruppe Argonnen, 18 December 1917: SHStAD, Kriegsarchiv (P) 20534, fol. 119; II./I.R. 467 to the regiment, 18 April 1917: ibid., 20533, fol. 127–32. In Dominik Richert's division, this measure was applied to all Alsatian soldiers following his defection: Richert, *Reluctant Conscript*, 259.
66 Bodo Scheurig, *Desertion und Deserteure* (Berlin: Selbstverlag des Verfassers, 1985), 15–16; Gerhard Hirschfeld, '"Let op, Levensgevaar". Der Elektrozaun an der belgisch-niederländischen Grenze', in *Der Erste Weltkrieg. Die Ur-Katastrophe des 20. Jahrhunderts*, ed. Stefan Burgdorff and Klaus Wiegrefe (Munich: Deutscher Taschenbuch Verlag, 2008), 97. A similar method was otherwise used only to fence off the operational area of Armee Abteilung Gaede in Upper Alsace; see Joseph Rossé et al. (eds), *Das Elsaß von 1870–1932*, 4 vols. (Colmar: Verlag Alsatia, 1936), vol. 1, 335ff.
67 Interrogation logs for the returned deserters A. Freier and R. Seidel in Emmerich, 17 February 1918: SHStAD, Kriegsarchiv (P) 22694, fol. 5ff., 29ff.
68 Karlheinz Böckle, *Feldgendarmerie-Feldjäger-Militärpolizei. Ihre Geschichte bis heute* (Stuttgart: Motorbuch Verlag, 1987), 123–8.
69 Walter Nicolai, *Nachrichtendienst, Presse und Volksstimmung im Weltkrieg* (Berlin: Mittler, 1920), 41–2; Prussian War Ministry to deputy general commands, 4 July 1915, and other materials in: SHStAD, Kriegsarchiv (P) 24139, fol. 10–11, *passim*. In Bavaria, the Munich police department monitored trains in this way from May 1915; Munich Police Department to Bavarian War Ministry, 13 September 1915: BHStA/IV, MKr 11484. The process was standardized following instructions from the Deputy General Staff on 1 October 1917: ibid., stv. GK I. AK 1327.
70 Most of the arrests included in the first figure took place during the last three months of 1917 in the areas covered by the Münster and Düsseldorf police stations. The figures for the other police stations cover a shorter or slightly longer period. Chief of the Deputy General Staff to the deputy general commands, 27 February 1918: SHStAD, Kriegsarchiv (P) 24137, fol. 180. The second figure includes thirty-two arrests in the area covered by the central police station in Württemberg, which counted desertion and absence without leave together. Decree by the Deputy General Staff to the deputy general commands, 15 July 1918: *Militarismus gegen Sowjetmacht*, 237–8 (document 26). As many deserters had switched to the military leave trains, which were barely monitored at all, the military authorities planned to extend patrols to these trains, too. Chief of the Deputy General Staff to the deputy general commands, 5 November 1917: SHStAD, Kriegsarchiv (P) 24137, fol. 15;

Chief of the Deputy General Staff to the deputy general commands, 27 February 1918: ibid., fol. 177.

71 Bernd Ulrich, 'Feldpostbriefe im Ersten Weltkrieg – Bedeutung und Zensur', in *Kriegsalltag. Die Rekonstruktion des Kriegsalltags als Aufgabe der historischen Forschung und der Friedenserziehung*, ed. Peter Knoch (Stuttgart: Metzler, 1989), 40–83, quote 59 (from a decree by the Generalquartiermeister dated 4 March 1917).

72 Report by the postal surveillance office in Lörrach dated 24 October 1918: Bernd Ulrich and Benjamin Ziemann (eds), *Krieg im Frieden. Die umkämpfte Erinnerung an den Ersten Weltkrieg* (Frankfurt am Main: Fischer Taschenbuch Verlag, 1997), document 3 c.

73 Ulrich, 'Feldpostbriefe', 55–6. However, the Alpine Corps only partially implemented this instruction from the Army Supreme Command: Günther Hebert, *Das Alpenkorps. Aufbau, Organisation und Einsatz einer Gebirgstruppe im Ersten Weltkrieg* (Boppard: Harald Boldt, 1988), 50–1. Special checks on incoming and outgoing post were performed using continually updated lists of Alsace-Lorrainers and appear to have been the practice in some divisions from as early as the beginning of 1917; GK XXVII. Reserve-Korps to 53. Res.-Div. and others, 13 January 1917: SHStAD, Kriegsarchiv (P) 20155, fol. 7.

74 Chef des stv. Generalstabes, Abt. IIIb, to the deputy general commands and war ministries of the German states, 30 January 1917: BHStA/IV, stv. GK I. AK 1582.

75 Stv. GK VII. AK to the Saxon War Ministry, 12 May 1917: SHStAD, Kriegsarchiv (P) 24179, fol. 32. The cards were forwarded to the office in Emmerich responsible for monitoring post to the Netherlands, the Deputy General Staff and interested general commands.

76 Stv. Generalstab, Abt. IIIb to the Saxon War Ministry, 11 June 1917: ibid., fol. 47.

77 Information from the Army Supreme Command on the handling of desertion cases (quote), 31 December 1917; information on the handling of desertion cases from the Prussian War Ministry, to the war ministries of the German states and the deputy general commands, 16 April 1918: BHStA/IV, MKr 11066. Also relevant for the following points.

78 The termination of family support was in accordance with section 11 of the relevant act dated 28 February 1889. The authorities generally terminated support payments if a soldier was sentenced by court martial to more than six months' imprisonment; *Armee-Verordnungsblatt* 50 (1916): 63, 51, ibid. 51 (1917): 24.

79 4. Inf.-Div. to GK VII. Reserve-Korps, 25 February 1916: SHStAD, Kriegsarchiv (P) 20533, fol. 8.

80 Füsilier-Rgt. 40 to 56. Inf.-Brigade, 23 October 1916; 56. Inf.-Brigade to GK XIV, 24 October 1916. AK: SHStAD, Kriegsarchiv (P) 20533, fol. 25ff.

81 13. Res.-Div. to GK VII. RK, 19 January 1917 and 21 January 1917; report by 9./I.R. 399, 17 February 1917: SHStAD, Kriegsarchiv (P) 20533, fol. 87, 93, 108; interrogation log of the 1. bayer. I.R., 25 September 1917: ibid., 20534, fol. 87; BHStA/IV, Militärgerichte 3348.

82 Georg Benz to his parents, 3 May 1917: BHStA/IV, Militärgerichte 3361.
83 *Militärstrafgesetzbuch*, 190.
84 'Bericht über die Tagung der Militär-Juristen der Etappen-Inspektion Nr. 11 in Uesküb am 12./13. Mai 1918', *Archiv für Militärrecht* 8 (1919/20): 196–200, 197–8. Generally: Engelbert Gnielka, 'Fahnenflucht §§ 69ff. RMStGB' (PhD diss. in jurisprudence and political science, University of Greifswald, 1918). BHStA/IV, Militärgerichte 6426. The two defendants admitted the plan to defect, which they had not gone through with.
85 BHStA/IV, Militärgerichte 6440; see also Ernst Sonntag, 'Kriminalrechtliche und kriminalpsychologische Kriegserfahrungen', *Zeitschrift für die gesamte Strafrechtswissenschaft* 40 (1919): 544–79, 709–42, 575.
86 For more detail, see Jahr, *Gewöhnliche Soldaten*, 219–36.
87 Gallwitz, *Erleben im Westen*, 349. On the shortage of personnel and the lengthy processes, see Helmuth Mayer, 'Militärjustiz im neuzeitlichen Krieg', *Zeitschrift für Wehrrecht* 2 (1937/38): 329–56, 336, 338.
88 See the figures in: BHStA/IV, HS 2348; WUA, vol. 11/2, *Gutachten des Sachverständigen Reichsarchivrat Volkmann, Soziale Heeresmißstände als Mitursache des deutschen Zusammenbruches von 1918* (Berlin: Deutsche Verlagsgesellschaft für Politik und Geschichte, 1929), 121.
89 The four Bavarian divisions for which separate figures are available on desertion and absence without leave are the 1st, 5th and 11th Infantry Divisions and the 2nd Landwehr Division. BHStA/IV, HS 2348.
90 BHStA/IV, HS 2348. Figures in Volkmann, 122, which differ slightly from the archive sources. The figures published in Volkmann are quoted here. The total figures Volkmann provides for the Bavarian divisions give a distorted picture. In the case of four divisions, the lists of criminal proceedings for the year 1917 are missing. Moreover, a number of divisions were only formed in 1915/16.
91 The number of infantry divisions in the German army on 1 January of each year was as follows: 1915: 128, 1916: 162, 1917: 207, 1918: 241. There were also ten remaining cavalry divisions at the start of 1918. These were used predominantly as infantry troops. Hermann Cron, *Geschichte des deutschen Heeres im Weltkriege 1914–1918* (1937; repr., Osnabrück: Biblio, 1990), 103–7.
92 See the manuscript 'Strafrechtspflege und Mannszucht in der zweiten Hälfte des Weltkrieges': BA/MA Freiburg, RH 61/50606, fol. 7.
93 In the 3rd Bavarian Deputy Infantry Brigade, there were eighty-six convictions for desertion and 672 for absence without leave: BHStA/IV, HS 2348. Cf. Jahr, *Gewöhnliche Soldaten*, 153–4.
94 In fourteen higher military courts of the Bavarian replacement army (no lists of criminal proceedings are available for the Landau Landwehr Inspectorate; for 1916 they are only partially available for the Munich Landwehr Inspectorate) there were

a total of 8,462 convictions for desertion and absence without leave: BHStA/IV, HS 2348. A total estimate is made more difficult by the fact that the ratio of troop strengths of the Bavarian replacement army to the German replacement army fluctuated between 1:6 and 1:10 over the course of the war. *Sanitätsbericht über das deutsche Heer im Weltkriege 1914/1918*, 3 vols. (Berlin: Mittler, 1934), vol. 3, 8*; Bayerisches Kriegsarchiv, *Die Bayern im Großen Kriege 1914-18*, 2 vols. (Munich: Verlag des bayerischen Kriegsarchivs, 1923), vol. 2, 46.

95 Only one officer in the Bavarian army was convicted of either of these crimes: BHStA/IV, HS 2348. Cases of desertion by officers from Alsace-Lorraine are documented; see Rossé, *Das Elsaß*, 306.

96 Jahr, *Gewöhnliche Soldaten*, 154-5 documents only a total number of convictions for desertion and absence without leave. This figure is of limited usefulness, however, as many cases of absence without leave involved soldiers who were missing for a few hours or days without malicious intent.

97 Of the 3,203 deaths in the 20th Bavarian Infantry Regiment, only around ten were soldiers born in Alsace-Lorraine. Hugo Höfl, *Das K.-B. 20. Infanterie-Regiment Prinz Franz* (Munich: Max Schick, 1929), 301.

98 Jahr, *Gewöhnliche Soldaten*, 155, assumes that there were many unreported cases and estimates a total of 150,000 incidents of absence without leave and desertion. He claims that the military authorities afforded desertion a disproportionately large amount of attention in relation to the scale of the problem. Regardless of the estimated figure, this view is decisively refuted here.

99 Beckmann, *Der Dolchstoß-Prozeß*, 209. The figure for Switzerland is corroborated in Bettina Durrer, 'Auf der Flucht vor dem Kriegsdienst. Deserteure und Refraktäre in der Schweiz während des Ersten Weltkrieges', in *Zuflucht Schweiz. Der Umgang mit Asylproblemen im 19. und 20. Jahrhundert*, ed. Carsten Goehrlke and Werner G. Zimmermann (Zurich: Verlag Hans Rohr, 1994), 197-216.

100 WUA, vol. 6, *Gutachten der Sachverständigen von Kuhl, Schwertfeger, Delbrück, Katzenstein, Herz, Volkmann zur "Dolchstoß"-Frage* (Berlin: Deutsche Verlagsgesellschaft für Politik und Geschichte, 1928), 171.

101 Landsturm-Inspektion Schleswig 1915 to stv. GK IX. AK, appendices, 5 October 1915: Landesarchiv Schleswig, 301/1713. The figures were collected in response to a decree by the Prussian War Ministry dated 27 August 1915, which required the Deputy General Commands of the 5th, 9th, 15th and 21st Army Corps to establish how many men from the three national minorities were evading military service. SHStAD, Kriegsarchiv (P) 20533, fol. 3.

102 Estimate by a Kriminalkommissar (chief superintendent) in a letter to the district administrator of Sonderburg dated 10 May 1917. The *Schleswigsche Grenzpost* newspaper reported on 17 June 1917 that there were some 1,500 Danish deserters in Stavanger (Norway), mostly aged from eighteen to nineteen and working on the land: Landesarchiv Schleswig, 301/1713.

103 Stv. GK IX. AK to Oberpräsident der Provinz Schleswig-Holstein, 20 September 1918: Landesarchiv Schleswig, 301/1713.
104 Jahr, *Gewöhnliche Soldaten*, 368, note 162, excludes this group from his analysis, stating that the act of desertion 'is a matter of the observer's perspective'. This is true to some extent of court martials, but not to those who unambiguously documented their intention to desert by moving to another country. Jahr does not attempt to determine the full extent of the flight to neutral countries, ibid. 118–21.
105 BHStA/IV, Militärgerichte 6201, 6211, 6237, 6402, 6410, 6415, 6477, 6479.
106 This figure excludes divisions only formed at a later stage or for which lists of criminal proceedings are unavailable for several years: BHStA/IV, HS 2348.
107 United States War Department, *Histories*, 67; see ibid., 492, which indicates that for the 50th Infantry Division, also rated as first class, the Allies did not record a single case of desertion after 1 July 1917.
108 Ziemann, *War Experiences*, 30–41, 74–82.
109 This can be inferred from figures for units belonging to the 3rd Army High Command from December 1917 to August 1918 (excluding March 1918). These show the number of soldiers found guilty or suspected of defection to the enemy or desertion to neutral countries. The total number of such soldiers was fifty-two. The inclusion in this low figure of soldiers who had reached neutral countries makes it clear that the large majority of these men had fled from the rear area and replacement army. See the monthly reports by AOK 3 to Heeresgruppe Deutscher Kronprinz: SHStAD, Kriegsarchiv (P) 20566, fol. 8, 28, 66, 81, 86, 91, 96, 100.
110 See the letter by Gustav Stresemann, 1 August 1918: Wilhelm Deist (ed.), *Militär und Innenpolitik im Weltkrieg 1914–1918*, 2 vols. (Düsseldorf: Droste Verlag, 1970), vol. 2, 1242, note 22; Report by 119. Inf.-Div., 2 November 1918: WUA, vol. 6, 327.
111 Rossé, *Das Elsaß*, 297, claims that approximately 1,300 Alsatian soldiers defected to the French. This figure is based on a comparison of prisoner numbers: ibid., 300.
112 See the calculation in WUA, vol. 11/1, *Gutachten des Sachverständigen Dr. Hobohm, Soziale Heeresmißstände als Teilursache des deutschen Zusammenbruchs von 1918* (Berlin: Deutsche Verlagsgesellschaft für Politik und Geschichte, 1929), 183–4, based on lost documents of the Generalquartiermeister from the Reich Archive in Potsdam.
113 See for example BHStA/IV, Militärgerichte 6485.
114 Based on an estimate of 15,000 convictions (taking into account the very low proportion of Alsatians etc. in the Bavarian army), approximately 30,000 soldiers in neutral countries and 43,000 wanted soldiers on the Western Front from January to July 1918, deducting those who turned themselves in. There were also several thousand defectors and an unknown number of soldiers who found hiding places in the rear area and in Germany between 1914 and the end of 1917. It should be

noted that the same individuals may have been included on both wanted lists and lists of convictions.
115 Manfred Messerschmidt and Fritz Wüllner, *Die Wehrmachtsjustiz im Dienste des Nationalsozialismus. Zerstörung einer Legende* (Baden-Baden: Nomos, 1987), 131, write of 'well over one hundred thousand' deserters up to the beginning of the final phase of the war at the end of 1944. There were around twenty million conscripts in the Second World War, compared with approximately 13.3 million in the First World War.
116 See for example Karl Pönitz, 'Psychologie und Psychopathologie der Fahnenflucht im Kriege', *Archiv für Kriminologie* 68 (1917): 260–81, 272.
117 Pönitz, 'Psychologie'; C. v. Hösslin, 'Über Fahnenflucht', *Zeitschrift für die gesamte Neurologie und Psychiatrie* 47 (1919): 344–55; Alfred Storch, 'Beiträge zur Psychopathologie der unerlaubten Entfernung und Fahnenflucht im Felde', ibid. 46 (1919): 348–67; Max Meier, 'Fahnenflucht und unerlaubte Entfernung im Kriege. Aus der Militärabteilung der psychiatrischen Klinik der Akademie für praktische Medizin Köln' (medical diss., University of Bonn, 1918).
118 Karl-Heinz Roth, 'Die Modernisierung der Folter in den beiden Weltkriegen. Der Konflikt der Psychotherapeuten und Schulpsychiater um die deutschen "Kriegsneurotiker" 1914–1945', 1999. *Zeitschrift für Sozialgeschichte des 20. und 21. Jahrhunderts* 2, no. 3 (1987): 8–75.
119 See for example Pönitz, 'Psychologie'; Hösslin, 'Über Fahnenflucht'.
120 Ziemann, *War Experiences*, 100–2.
121 Jahr, *Gewöhnliche Soldaten*, 128–35, figures p. 131.
122 Storch, 'Beiträge', 356; Pönitz, 'Psychologie', 273–4; Hösslin, 'Über Fahnenflucht', 347; BHStA/IV, Militärgerichte 6211, 6379.
123 Jahr, *Gewöhnliche Soldaten*, 136.
124 Richert, *Beste Gelegenheit*, 271, 367; Pönitz, 'Psychologie', 264–5; Hösslin, 'Über Fahnenflucht', 348; Sonntag, 'Kriminalrechtliche', 570.
125 WUA, vol. 11/1, 74; Gruppe Argonnen to AOK 3, 5 July 1917: SHStAD, Kriegsarchiv (P) 20534, fol. 25.
126 Letter by Adolf Armbrust, 11./15. bayer. I.R., 15 January 1918: BHStA/IV, Militärgerichte 6201. Armbrust successfully escaped to the Netherlands. On 16 February 1919, he acknowledged the suspension of the court-martial proceedings against him. The full letter can be found in English in Ulrich and Ziemann, *German Soldiers*, 140–1.
127 Jürgen Lampe et al., *Diesem System keinen Mann und keinen Groschen. Militärpolitik der revolutionären deutschen Arbeiterbewegung 1830 bis 1917* (Berlin: Militärverlag der DDR, 1990), 398, 415ff.; Max Albert, *Soldat und doch Revolutionär. Kriegserlebnisse aus meiner Soldatenzeit* (n.p., 1923), 20. The Spartacus Group numbered only around 2,000 members: Dieter Engelmann and Horst Naumann, *Zwischen Spaltung und Vereinigung. Die Unabhängige*

*Sozialdemokratische Partei Deutschlands in den Jahren 1917–1922* (Berlin: Edition Neue Wege, 1993), 30.

128  Friedhelm Boll, *Massenbewegungen in Niedersachsen 1906–1920. Eine sozialgeschichtliche Untersuchung zu den unterschiedlichen Entwicklungstypen Braunschweig und Hannover* (Bonn: Verlag Neue Gesellschaft, 1981), 250; Fritz Zikelsky, *Das Gewehr in meiner Hand. Erinnerungen eines Arbeiterveteranen* (Berlin: Verlag des Ministeriums für Nationale Verteidigung, 1958), 135ff.; Heinz Voßke and Gerhard Nitzsche, *Wilhelm Pieck. Biographischer Abriß* (Berlin: Dietz, 1975), 68ff.

129  See the letters from the General Staff of the Field Army, Abt. IIIb, 15 June 1917 and 17 August 1917: GStA, I. HA 2.2.1 (89), 32404, fol. 5–15, 16–22; Kurt Koszyk, 'Das abenteuerliche Leben des sozialrevolutionären Agitators Carl Minster (1873–1942)', *Archiv für Sozialgeschichte* 5 (1965): 193–225, 200ff.

130  Jeffrey T. Verhey, 'The "Spirit of 1914": The Myth of Enthusiasm and the Rhetoric of Unity in World War I Germany' (PhD diss., University of California Berkeley, 1991), 192; Rossé, *Das Elsaß*, 295; GK XV. AK to the Prussian War Ministry, 12 March 1915: SHStAD, Kriegsarchiv (P) 20533, fol. 4.

131  Rossé, *Das Elsaß*, 301–5, first quote 305; Prussian War Ministry to the Saxon War Ministry, 18 May 1917, with reference to two further decrees dated 7 September 1915 and 9 October 1915: SHStAD, Kriegsarchiv (P) 24170, fol. 64 (second quote). The decree of 18 May 1917 ordered that unreliable Alsace-Lorrainers in the armies on the Western Front be assigned directly to the armies on the Eastern Front, along with all those in the home army due to be deployed in the field.

132  Rossé, *Das Elsaß*, 306; GK V. RK 23 September 1916 to AOK 3: SHStAD, Kriegsarchiv (P) 20533, fol. 22.

133  Rossé, *Das Elsaß*, 310. Lithuanian villages offered Alsatian deserters food and hiding places: Strazhas, *Deztsche Ostpolitik*, 150.

134  Archiv des Bistums Augsburg, Nachlass Karl Lang, 'Kriegschronik Karl Lang' (1934), 50–6. Lang did not record the regiment's number. It was probably a regiment of the 86th Prussian Infantry Division, which was deployed on the 'Stochod front' near Kovel from July 1916 to April 1917. United States War Department, *Histories*, 561. The regimental history of the 343rd Infantry Regiment records that there were a number of defections during the preparation of an attack that was to take place against the Russian bridgehead near Toboly on 3 April 1917; Gerhard Neumann, *Das Infanterie-Regiment Nr. 343 im Weltkriege 1914/18* (Zeulenroda: Sporn, 1937), 256–66, 265.

135  Rossé, *Das Elsaß*, 310–11.

136  WUA, vol. 11/2, 63. Volkmann (ibid.) believed that the fact some court files and lists of criminal proceedings were missing made only a 'small, insignificant' difference to the overall figures. However, it is likely that units which had seen large numbers of executions deliberately cleaned up such files and lists in the course of the demobilization and revolution.

137 Jahr, *Gewöhnliche Soldaten*, 18 (number of death sentences carried out in the British Expeditionary Force), 234, 248-51.
138 Jahr tries to rescue the comparison by stating that the British figures may also be doubtful: ibid., 377, note 262. However, the intensive British research on the topic does not share these doubts. See for example Gerard Oram, *Military Executions During World War I* (Basingstoke: Palgrave Macmillan, 2003).
139 Jahr, *Gewöhnliche Soldaten*, 217.
140 Bavarian War Ministry to the mobile units, 22 January 1918: BHStA/IV, stv. GK I. AK 618; the relevant decree by the Prussian War Ministry had already been enacted on 12 January 1918: Rossé, *Das Elsaß*, 304.
141 United States War Department, *Histories*, 35; Stern, *Die Auswirkungen*, vol. 4, 1578-9 (document 692).
142 Gallwitz, *Erleben im Westen*, 354, 318, 442.
143 On soldiers of Polish origin, see Alexander Watson, 'Fighting for another Fatherland: The Polish Minority in the German Army, 1914-1918', *English Historical Review* 126 (2011): 1137-66.
144 Prussian War Ministry to Prussian Interior Ministry, 15 November 1915, Armee-Abt. v. Strantz to Prussian War Ministry, 17 May 1915, GK V. AK to stv. GK V. AK, 26, February 1915 and 22 June 1915 (copies): GStA, I. HA, Rep. 77, Tit. 863a, no. 2b., fol. 337-8, 62, 339-40, 342, 344-5.
145 United States War Department, *Histories*, 85, 199 (quote), 217, 302; Gallwitz, *Erleben im Westen*, 115.
146 GK V. AK to stv. GK V. AK, 26 February 1915 (quote) and 22 June 1915, stv. GK V. AK to Prussian War Ministry, 4 March 1915 (copies), with reference to the decrees of 21 January and 16 February 1915 [these decrees are unavailable]: GStA, I. HA, Rep. 77, Tit. 863a, no. 2b., fol. 342, 344-5, 341.
147 See the notes in United States War Department, *Histories*, 182, 217.
148 Prussian War Ministry to Prussian Interior Ministry, 15 November 1915: GStA, I. HA, Rep. 77, Tit. 863a, no. 2b., fol. 337-8.; Prussian Interior Ministry to the War Ministry, 25 December 1915 (draft) and the replies from the War Ministry to the Interior Ministry dated 10 February and 2 April 1916: GStA, I. HA, Rep. 77, Tit. 863a, no. 16, no fol. Watson, 'Fighting', 1165, also emphasizes these differences in integration.
149 WUA, vol. 7/1, *Entschließung und Verhandlungsbericht: Der Deutsche Reichstag im Weltkrieg* (Berlin: Deutsche Verlagsgesellschaft für Politik und Geschichte, 1928), 380-1 (quote); Rossé, *Das Elsaß*, 302.
150 See the various notes in: United States War Department, *Histories*.
151 Hans-Ulrich Wehler, *Deutsche Gesellschaftsgeschichte*, 4 vols. (Munich: C.H. Beck, 1995), vol. 3, 961-5, quote 962. Letter by a Polish solider in French captivity, a copy of which was sent by the Prussian War Ministry to the Prussian Interior Ministry on 23 May 1916: GStA, I. HA, Rep. 77, Tit. 863a, no. 16, no fol.

152 Freiherr von Vietinghoff to the Prussian War Ministry, 14 July 1915 (copy): GStA, I. HA, Rep. 77, Tit. 863a, no. 16, no fol.
153 Hans-Ulrich Wehler, 'Der Fall Zabern von 1913/14 als eine Verfassungskrise des Wilhelminischen Kaiserreichs', in *Krisenherde des Kaiserreichs* (Göttingen: Vandenhoeck und Ruprecht, 1970), 65–83; Hans-Ulrich Wehler, 'Das Reichsland Elsaß-Lothringen von 1870–1918', in ibid., 17–63; Hans-Ulrich Wehler, 'Polenpolitik im Deutschen Kaiserreich 1871–1918', in ibid., 181–99; David Schoenbaum, *Zabern 1913: Consensus Politics in Imperial Germany* (London: Allen & Unwin, 1982).
154 Alan Kramer, 'Wackes at War: Alsace-Lorraine and the Failure of German National Mobilization, 1914–1918', in *State, Society and Mobilization in Europe during the First World War*, ed. John Horne (Cambridge: Cambridge University Press, 1997), 105–21.
155 Prussian War Ministry to all army groups, army high commands, etc., 23 August 1917: BHStA/IV, stv. GK I. AK 618; Arnold Heydt, '*Elsässer-links raus!' Das Buch der Erlebnisse eines elsässischen Frontsoldaten* (Strasbourg: Dernières Nouvelles, 1932), *passim*. On the impact of the special postal surveillance, A. Schalk, 2./mobiles Ldst.-Inf.-Rgt. 13 to J. Bucher in Stuttgart, 3 November 1916: HStA/MA Stuttgart, M 77/1, Büschel 730.
156 Wolfgang Hug, 'Soldatsein im Kaiserreich. Militärischer Alltag in Zeugnissen aus der Region', *Zeitschrift des Breisgau-Geschichtsvereins "Schau-ins-Land"* 111 (1992): 141–53, 150.
157 Letter by the Prussian War Ministry, 18 March 1918: BHStA/IV, stv. GK I. AK 618. The Deputy General Command of the 1st Bavarian Army Corps put this measure into force. See also Heydt, '*Elsässer-links raus!*', 12.
158 Translation of a letter by Landsturm soldier Stanislaus Klos to his brother Josef, 29 April 1915: GStA, I. HA, Rep. 77, Tit. 863a, no. 8, no fol.; Matthias Erzberger to the Prussian interior minister, 20 May 1915: ibid.
159 Reinhard Schiffers and Manfred Koch (eds), *Der Hauptausschuß des Deutschen Reichstags 1915–1918*, 4 vols. (Düsseldorf: Droste Verlag, 1981–83), vol. 1, 110 (14 May 1915), 132 (28 May 1915).
160 Rossé, *Das Elsaß*, 307, 309, 314–5; on the following, see also: Chief of the General Staff of the Field Army to Reichskanzler, 5 February 1917 (quote): GStA, I. HA, Rep. 84a, no. 7802, fol. 146.
161 Helfferich and the Prussian War Ministry advocated criminal proceedings for incitement to desert under section 141 of the Penal Code. State Secretary of the Reich Interior to Reichskanzler (quote), 24 February 1917, Prussian War Ministry to Under Secretary of State in the Imperial Chancellery (copy), 2 April 1917: GStA, I. HA, Rep. 84a, no. 7802, fol. 143–4. Report on cases of defection by Danish and Polish soldiers: Prussian War Ministry to the Army Supreme Command, 9 February 1917: ibid., fol. 147. On the brutal practice of protective custody in Alsace-Lorraine, see Rossé, *Das Elsaß*, 241–8.

162 SPD Reichstag deputies held this opinion; see MdR Böhle, in Schiffers and Koch, *Der Hauptausschuß*, vol. 3, 1271 (23 March 1917). However, Watson, 'Fighting', 1160, claims that the tendency of members of the Polish minority to desert declined in 1917.
163 Ersatz-Reservist Josef Trommelschlager to sapper August Dantung in Thorn (copy), 1 November 1916: HStA/MA Stuttgart, M 77/1, Büschel 730.
164 Prussian War Ministry to Prussian Interior Ministry, 4 May 1915, appendix 1: GStA, I. HA, Rep. 77, Tit. 863 a, no. 16, no fol.
165 Ulrich, 'Feldpostbriefe', 71, note 62; Prussian War Ministry to Chief of the General Staff of the Field Army and others, 2 October 1917: SHStAD, Kriegsarchiv (P) 24170, fol. 105.
166 Bernd Ulrich (in collaboration with Benjamin Ziemann), 'Das soldatische Kriegserlebnis 1914-1918' (course study material of FernUniversität in Hagen: The Great War, Kurseinheit 4, Hagen, 1995), 81.
167 German Embassy in Stockholm to Reichskanzler, 22 August 1916 (copy): BArch, R 1501, 12391, fol. 31.
168 Reinhard Nachtigal, 'Privilegiensystem und Zwangsrekrutierung. Russische Nationalitätenpolitik gegenüber Kriegsgefangenen aus Österreich-Ungarn', in *Kriegsgefangene im Europa des ersten Weltkriegs*, ed. Jochen Oltmer (Paderborn: Schöningh, 2006), 167–93, 181, 192.
169 See the letters by the Obere Leitung ... to the investigation units in the individual general commands, 18 January 1918 and 16 July 1918. The figure is cited in Prussian War Ministry to deputy general commands, 1 June 1918: SHStAD, Kriegsarchiv (P) 10930, fol. 13–17, 85–90, 49.
170 As Christoph Jahr calls them in the title of his book, *Gewöhnliche Soldaten*.
171 See the table ibid., 278. Jahr hinders an understanding of his own figures by commenting that the sharp increase in the final months of the war was not attributable to the Alsatians. He does not relate the figures up to June 1918 to the percentage of Alsatians in the army as a whole.
172 Friedrich Altrichter, *Die seelischen Kräfte des deutschen Heeres im Frieden und im Weltkriege* (Berlin: Mittler & Sohn, 1933), 167–8.

# 6  Disillusionment and Collective Exhaustion among German Soldiers on the Western Front: The Path to Revolution in 1918

1 Wilhelm Deist, 'Auf dem Wege zur ideologisierten Kriegführung: Deutschland 1918–1945', in *Militär, Staat und Gesellschaft. Studien zur preußisch-deutschen Militärgeschichte* (Munich: R. Oldenbourg, 1991), 385–429, 392ff., quote 393; Wilhelm Deist, 'Die Reichswehr und der Krieg der Zukunft', *Militärgeschichtliche Mitteilungen* 45 (1989). 81–92. On the 'hidden military strike' see Chapter 7 in this volume.

2 Richard Bessel, *Germany after the First World War* (Oxford: Clarendon Press, 1993) 256–9; Benjamin Ziemann, *War Experiences in Rural Germany 1914–1923*, trans. Alex Skinner (Oxford: Berg, 2007), 227–40.
3 Bernd Ulrich and Benjamin Ziemann (eds), *Krieg im Frieden. Die umkämpfte Erinnerung an den Ersten Weltkrieg* (Frankfurt am Main: Fischer Taschenbuch Verlag, 1997); Benjamin Ziemann, *Contested Commemorations: Republican War Veterans and Weimar Political Culture* (Cambridge: Cambridge University Press, 2013), especially chapter 1.
4 For a general account, see Klaus Latzel, *Deutsche Soldaten – nationalsozialistischer Krieg? Kriegserlebnis-Kriegserfahrung 1939–1945* (Paderborn: Schöningh, 1998), 103–7, 125–32; Klaus Latzel, 'Vom Kriegserlebnis zur Kriegserfahrung. Theoretische und methodische Überlegungen zur erfahrungsgeschichtlichen Untersuchung von Feldpostbriefen', *Militärgeschichtliche Mitteilungen* 56 (1997), 1–29.
5 However, it should be noted that this source material for the German army is incomplete. As far as the author is aware, only the reports of the 5th Army are available: BA/MA, RH 61/50794. Alexander Watson also relies heavily on this source material in his analysis of the 'morale' of German soldiers during the final year of war. He comes to different conclusions, however: Alexander Watson, *Enduring the Great War: Combat, Morale and Collapse in the German and British Armies, 1914–1918* (Cambridge: Cambridge University Press, 2008), 184–200. Fragments survive from the field post surveillance offices of various divisions in the files of the Bayerisches Hauptstaatsarchiv in Munich (Abt. IV) and in the Sächsisches Hauptstaatsarchiv.
6 Bernd Ulrich, *Die Augenzeugen. Deutsche Feldpostbriefe in Kriegs- und Nachkriegszeit 1914–1933* (Essen: Klartext, 1997), 87–105.
7 As part of his work for the Weimar parliamentary committee, the historian Ludwig Bergsträsser put together an insightful collection of letter and diary excerpts from private sources, dating especially from 1918, and published some of them in the report: WUA, vol. 5, *Verhandlungsbericht: Die allgemeinen Ursachen und Hergänge des inneren Zusammenbruches, 2. Teil* (Berlin: Deutsche Verlagsgesellschaft für Politik und Geschichte, 1928), 262–335. See also Wolfgang Kruse, 'Krieg und Klassenheer. Zur Revolutionierung der deutschen Armee im Ersten Weltkrieg', *Geschichte und Gesellschaft* 22 (1996): 530–61, 549.
8 WUA, vol. 11/1, *Gutachten des Sachverständigen Dr. Hobohm, Soziale Heeresmißstände als Teilursache des deutschen Zusammenbruchs von 1918* (Berlin: Deutsche Verlagsgesellschaft für Politik und Geschichte, 1929), quote 264; for 1918 see ibid., 312–44.
9 Kruse, 'Klassenheer', *passim*.
10 In line with the more general argument by Reinhart Koselleck, 'Space of Experience and Horizon of Expectation: Two Historical Categories', in *Futures Past. On the*

Semantics of Historical Time, trans. Keith Tribe (New York: Columbia University Press, 2004), 255-75.

11 Benjamin Ziemann, *Front und Heimat. Ländliche Kriegserfahrungen im südlichen Bayern* (Essen: Klartext, 1997), 23ff., 163-97.

12 Bernd Ulrich and Benjamin Ziemann (eds), *German Soldiers in the Great War: Letters and Eyewitness Accounts*, trans. Christine Brocks (Barnsley: Pen & Sword, 2010), 149-50.

13 Fritz Klein et al. (eds), *Deutschland im Ersten Weltkrieg*, 3 vols. (Berlin: Akademie-Verlag, 1969), vol. 3, 135-78; Dieter Engelmann, 'Der Januarstreik 1918 im rheinisch-westfälischen Industriegebiet', *Jahrbuch für Regionalgeschichte* 9 (1982): 95-104; Bernhard Grau, *Der Januarstreik 1918 in München*, in *Gegenwart in Vergangenheit. Beiträge zur Kultur und Geschichte der Neueren und Neuesten Zeit. Festgabe für Friedrich Prinz zu seinem 65. Geburtstag*, ed. Georg Jenal (Munich: Oldenbourg, 1993), 277-301; Volker Ullrich, 'Der Januarstreik 1918 in Hamburg, Kiel und Bremen', *Zeitschrift des Vereins für Hamburgische Geschichte* 71 (1985): 45-74; Volker Ullrich, *Vom Augusterlebnis zur Novemberrevolution. Beiträge zur Sozialgeschichte Hamburgs und Norddeutschlands im Ersten Weltkrieg 1914-1918* (Bremen: Donat, 1999).

14 Wilhelm Deist (ed.), *Militär und Innenpolitik im Weltkrieg 1914-1918*, 2 vols. (Düsseldorf: Droste, 1970), vol. 1, 934.

15 Ulrich and Ziemann, *German Soldiers*, 172. The differences in the social outlook and mentality of industrial workers, given their dual service on the front line and on the home front, have not yet been examined systematically. Important indications are provided by works on the wartime economy and society; see for example Gunther Mai, *Kriegswirtschaft und Arbeiterbewegung in Württemberg 1914-1918* (Stuttgart: Klett Cotta, 1983), especially 363; Gerald D. Feldman, *Army, Industry and Labor in Germany 1914-1918* (Oxford: Berg, 1992); Ute Daniel, *The War from Within: German Working Class Women in the First World War*, trans. Margaret Ries (Oxford: Berg, 1997), especially chapter 3.

16 Postal surveillance reports of the 5th Army dated 10 January and 24 February 1918 and the letter excerpts in: BA/MA, RH 61/50794, fol. 35-6, 44-64; undated draft of a report by stv. GK I. bayerisches AK to the Bavarian War Ministry on reactions to the January strike on the front line and in Germany, including numerous letter excerpts: Bayerische Staatsbibliothek München, Handschriftenabteilung (BSB), Schinnereriana. This report was based on the inspection of civilian and field post letters in the surveillance office Bahnpostamt München I. Also see stv. Unterrichts-Offizier 52. Inf.-Div. to Gruppe Py: Sächsisches Hauptstaatsarchiv Dresden, Kriegsarchiv (P), 10 February 1918, 21133, fol. 82; WUA, vol. 5, 282.

17 Letter excerpts in: BA/MA, RH 61/50794, fol. 51 ('Radaubrüder'), 61 (quote).

18 Ibid., fol. 54, 47.

19 Ibid., fol. 64. See this and other letter excerpts on the strike in English translation in Ulrich and Ziemann, *German Soldiers*, 172.
20 Martin H. Geyer, *Verkehrte Welt. Revolution, Inflation und Moderne. München 1914-1924* (Göttingen: Vandenhoeck & Ruprecht, 1998), 98ff., 390; Ulrich, *Die Augenzeugen*, 156-68; Ute Planert, *Antifeminismus im Kaiserreich. Diskurs, soziale Formation und politische Mentalität* (Göttingen: Vandenhoeck & Ruprecht, 1998), 182-3, 205, 218, 229, 282-94; Christa Hämmerle, '". . . wirf ihnen alles hin und schau, daß du fort kommst." Die Feldpost eines Paares in der Geschlechter(un)ordnung des Ersten Weltkrieges', *Historische Anthropologie* 6 (1998): 431-58.
21 BA/MA, RH 61/50794, fol. 57, 55 (quote). On the links between opposition to the war and the willingness to fight in the upcoming offensive, see Hermann Cron (ed.), *Kriegsbrief-Sammlung des Deutschen Transportarbeiterverbandes* (Potsdam: Reichsarchiv, 1926), 6.
22 Klaus Schreiner, '"Wann kommt der Retter Deutschlands?" Formen und Funktionen von politischem Messianismus in der Weimarer Republik', *Saeculum* 49, no. 1 (1998): 107-60.
23 Letter from a soldier on the front (undated), enclosed with the report by stv. GK I. bayerisches AK to the War Ministry on reactions to the January strike: BSB, Schinnereriana.
24 Ulrich, *Die Augenzeugen*, 72; Franz Xaver Bergler, '"Es sieht ja mit Frieden werden gar nichts gleich". Briefe von der Front', *Allmende*, 17/18 (1987): 119-35, 129.
25 See BA/MA, RH 61/50794, fol. 62ff., quote 63; on the form and prevalence of national hatred among soldiers, see Ziemann, *War Experiences*, 137-44; Latzel, *Soldaten*, 160-71, 211-19. On the organizational preparations for the offensive see Martin Middlebrook, *The Kaiser's Battle. 21 March 1918: The First Day of the German Spring Offensive* (London: Allen Lane, 1978) 35-64, 106-130; on 'Operation Michael', see also the critical account in Holger H. Herwig, *The First World War. Germany and Austria-Hungary 1914-1918* (London: Arnold, 1997), 392-432.
26 *Gutachten des Sachverständigen Dr. Hobohm*, 312.
27 BA/MA, RH 61/50794, fol. 64.
28 Hermann Cron (ed.), *Das Archiv des Deutschen Studentendienstes von 1914* (Potsdam: Reichsarchiv, 1926), 35 (first quote); WUA, vol. 5, 288 (second quote), 296; by contrast, Martin Hobohm's report stated that the euphoria was limited to the troops involved in the offensive: *Gutachten des Sachverständigen Dr. Hobohm*, 312.
29 Ziemann, *Front und Heimat*, 137-8.
30 Quotes: BA/MA, RH 61/50794, fol. 63, 62; cf. WUA, vol. 5, 291-2.
31 WUA, vol. 5, 286.
32 Ibid., 287.
33 Ziemann, *War Experiences*, 74-77; BA/MA, RH 61/50794, fol. 72; WUA, vol. 5, 296, 325; Wilhelm Deist, 'Verdeckter Militärstreik im Kriegsjahr 1918?', in *Der Krieg des kleinen Mannes. Eine Militärgeschichte von unten*, ed. Wolfram Wette (Munich: Piper,

1992), 146–67, 152, 154; Jakob Siegler to the 'Alter Verband', 8 June 1918: Bundesarchiv Berlin (BArch), R 9350, 271, fol. 239; Herwig, *World War*, 410.
34  Letter from NCO Fiessmann, 5 May 1918: see Ulrich and Ziemann, *German Soldiers*, 173. Cf. WUA, vol. 5, 288.
35  Klaus Latzel, 'Die mißlungene Flucht vor dem Tod. Töten und Sterben vor und nach 1918', in *Kriegsende 1918. Ereignis – Wirkung – Nachwirkung*, ed. Jörg Duppler and Gerhard P. Groß (Munich: R. Oldenbourg, 1999), 183–99, 188.
36  See Ulrich and Ziemann, *German Soldiers*, 75.
37  Letter from a lance corporal dated 25 April 1918: WUA, vol. 5, 292.
38  Herwig, *World War*, 400ff.; Dieter Storz, '"Aber was hätte anders geschehen sollen?" Die deutschen Offensiven an der Westfront 1918', in Duppler and Groß, *Kriegsende*, 51–95; Wilhelm Meier-Dörnberg, 'Die große deutsche Frühjahrsoffensive 1918 zwischen Strategie und Taktik', in *Operatives Denken und Handeln in deutschen Streitkräften im 19. und 20. Jahrhundert*, ed. Militärgeschichtliches Forschungsamt (Herford: Mittler, 1988), 73–95.
39  Heinrich Aufderstrasse to Hermann Sachse, 1 May 1918: BArch, R 9350, 271, fol. 88–91.
40  Hermann Cron (ed.), *Kriegsbrief-Sammlung des Sekretariats Sozialer Studentenarbeit* (Potsdam: Reichsarchiv, 1927), 32–3. (quote); WUA, vol. 5, 295, 298ff., 303, 308–9; letter excerpts from the postal surveillance report of the 5th Army dated 31 August 1918: BA/MA, RH 61/50794, fol. 80–91, especially fol. 81, 82, 84, 87ff.
41  Report from the 6th Army's postal surveillance office dated 4 September 1918, compiled on the basis of 53,781 inspected letters: Hans Thimme, *Weltkrieg ohne Waffen. Die Propaganda der Westmächte gegen Deutschland, ihre Wirkung und ihre Abwehr* (Stuttgart: Cotta, 1932) 264–71, 268.
42  BA/MA, RH 61/50794, fol. 116; WUA, vol. 5, 303.
43  Heinrich Aufderstrasse to Hermann Sachse, 27 August 1918: BArch, R 9350, 271, fol. 101; Ulrich and Ziemann, *Krieg im Frieden*, 27–8; BA/MA, RH 61/50794, fol. 114; Carlo Schmid, *Erinnerungen* (Bern: Scherz, 1979), 66, 74.
44  Postal surveillance office report dated 28 September 1918 and accompanying letter excerpts; postal surveillance report dated 17 October 1918 (quote): BA/MA, RH 61/50794, fol. 92–105, 106.
45  Eugen Neter, *Der seelische Zusammenbruch der deutschen Kampffront. Betrachtungen eines Frontarztes*, Süddeutsche Monatshefte 22, no. 10 (1924/25): 1–47, 11, 24.
46  Kruse, 'Klassenheer', 556 and *passim*.
47  Ziemann, *War Experiences*, 153; BA/MA, RH 61/50794, fol. 115; Thimme, *Weltkrieg*, 278ff.
48  Deist, *Militär und Innenpolitik*, 1251–2.; Schmid, *Erinnerungen*, 74.
49  Letter excerpts in: BA/MA, RH 61/50794, fol. 112, 115 (quotes); WUA, vol. 5, 282, 320; Ulrich and Ziemann, *Krieg im Frieden*, 29–30.
50  Ziemann, *War Experiences*, 57–64, Ziemann, *Front und Heimat*, 148–56.

51 Quote: Fritz Einert to his parents, 11 May 1918: BArch, R 9350, 275, fol. 21–2.
52 Letter excerpt accompanying postal surveillance report of 31 August 1918: BA/MA, RH 61/50794, fol. 89. On attitudes towards the censorship of field post in summer 1918, see Ulrich and Ziemann, *German Soldiers*, 176.
53 This argument is advanced by Kruse, 'Klassenheer', 559. Kruse points to the loyalties and composition of the Soldatenräte (soldiers' councils). However, in terms of their programme and organization, the Western Army never took the initiative to a significant extent in the formation of Soldatenräte. This was primarily due to the time pressure imposed by the terms of the armistice. The councils of the Western Army – which were often installed rather than elected – were primarily 'bodies for maintaining discipline' rather than 'organizers of revolution'. Cf. Schmid, *Erinnerungen*, 77 (quote); Ulrich Kluge, *Soldatenräte und Revolution. Studien zur Militärpolitik in Deutschland 1918/19* (Göttingen: Vandenhoeck & Ruprecht, 1975), 102–25, 250; Dieter Dreetz, 'Rückführung des Westheeres und Novemberrevolution', *Zeitschrift für Militärgeschichte* 7 (1968): 578–89; Roland Grau, 'Zur Rolle der Soldatenräte der Fronttruppen in der Novemberrevolution', ibid., 550–64; Bessel, *Germany*, 76.
54 This was pointed out by Ludwig Bergsträsser based on his good knowledge of the relevant files in the *Reichsarchiv* and numerous personal accounts. See his article in the *Berliner Tageblatt*, 21 March 1928: BArch, R 72, fol. 31.
55 Ziemann, *War Experiences*, 81–2.
56 Cron, *Transportarbeiterverband*, 4.
57 Ziemann, *War Experiences*, 86–7.
58 Letter excerpts from the 5th Army's postal surveillance report, 17 October 1918: BA/MA, RH 61/50794, fol. 114, 116.
59 Geyer, *Verkehrte Welt*, especially 382–8.
60 Quotes from letters sent by military post in October 1918: Ulrich and Ziemann, *Krieg im Frieden*, 30–1. On the Vaterlandspartei, see the fundamental reinterpretation by Heinz Hagenlücke, *Deutsche Vaterlandspartei. Die nationale Rechte am Ende des Kaiserreichs* (Düsseldorf: Droste, 1997).
61 Letter by a front-line soldier, 9 July 1918: BSB, Schinnereriana.
62 WUA, vol. 5, 302 (quotes), 303, 305.
63 Reinhold Maier, *Feldpostbriefe aus dem Ersten Weltkrieg* (Stuttgart: W. Kohlhammer, 1966), 166 (letter dated 13 July 1918); *Sanitätsbericht über das deutsche Heer im Weltkriege 1914/1918*, vol. 3 (Berlin: Mittler, 1934), 121ff.
64 Christoph Jahr remarks that a 'comprehensive dissolution' of command authority, resulting especially from the mass shirking, only took place from October and was sealed to some extent by the armistice talks. Christoph Jahr, *Gewöhnliche Soldaten. Desertion und Deserteure im deutschen und britischen Heer 1914–1918* (Göttingen: Vandenhoeck & Ruprecht, 1998), 166. See also Chapter 7 of this volume.

65 Gerald D. Feldman, Eberhard Kolb and Reinhard Rürup, 'Die Massenbewegungen der Arbeiterschaft in Deutschland am Ende des Ersten Weltkrieges (1917–1920)', *Politische Vierteljahresschrift* 13 (1972): 84–105, quote 94; also Klaus Tenfelde, 'Massenbewegungen und Revolution in Deutschland 1917–1923. Ein Forschungsüberblick', in *Revolutionäres Potential in Europa am Ende des Ersten Weltkrieges*, ed. Helmut Konrad and Karin M. Schmidlechner (Vienna: Böhlau, 1991), 9–15.

66 For a first step in this direction, if not always an entirely convincing one, see Scott Stephenson, *The Final Battle: Soldiers of the Western Front in the German Revolution of 1918* (Cambridge: Cambridge University Press, 2009).

# 7 The German Army in Autumn 1918: A Hidden Military Strike?

1 Wilhelm Deist, 'The Military Collapse of the German Empire', *War in History* 3 (1996): 186–207. Originally published in German as 'Der militärische Zusammenbruch des Kaiserreiches. Zur Realität der Dolchstoßlegende', in *Das Unrechtsregime. Internationale Forschung über den Nationalsozialismus, vol. 1, Ideologie, Herrschaftssystem, Wirkung in Europa*, ed. Ursula Büttner (Hamburg: Hans Christians Verlag, 1986), 101–29.

2 See the fitting acclaim for Deist's work in Jay Winter, 'The Breaking Point: Surrender 1918', in *How Fighting Ends. A History of Surrender*, ed. Holger Afflerbach and Hew Strachan (Oxford: Oxford University Press, 2012), 299–309, 309.

3 Deist, 'The Military Collapse'.

4 Ibid., 204.

5 On the limits of the analogy see Anne Lipp, *Meinungslenkung im Krieg. Kriegserfahrungen deutscher Soldaten und ihre Deutung 1914–1918* (Göttingen: Vandenhoeck & Ruprecht, 2003), 146.

6 Deist, 'The Military Collapse', 204.

7 Ibid., 201–2.

8 Ibid., numbers of shirkers: p. 202, Beck quotation: p. 204. See WUA, vol. 11/2, *Gutachten des Sachverständigen Reichsarchivrat Volkmann, Soziale Heeresmißstände als Mitursache des deutschen Zusammenbruches von 1918* (Berlin: Deutsche Verlagsgesellschaft für Politik und Geschichte, 1929). On the Reich Archive and its revanchist and nationalist viewpoint, see Markus Pöhlmann, *Kriegsgeschichte und Geschichtspolitik: Der Erste Weltkrieg. Die amtliche deutsche Militärgeschichtsschreibung 1914–1956* (Paderborn: F. Schöningh, 2002).

9 Benjamin Ziemann, *War Experiences in Rural Germany 1914–1923*, trans. Alex Skinner (Oxford: Berg, 2007), 97–8.

10 Wilhelm Deist, 'Verdeckter Militärstreik im Kriegsjahr 1918?', in *Der Krieg des kleinen Mannes. Eine Militärgeschichte von unten*, ed. Wolfram Wette (Munich: Piper, 1992), 146–67, figures p. 159.

11 See Chapter 6 in this volume; Ziemann, *War Experiences*, 108–10; Wolfgang Kruse, 'Krieg und Klassenheer. Zur Revolutionierung der deutschen Armee im Ersten Weltkrieg', *Geschichte und Gesellschaft* 22 (1996): 530–61.

12 Alexander Watson, *Enduring the Great War: Combat, Morale and Collapse in the German and British Armies, 1914–1918* (Cambridge: Cambridge University Press, 2008).

13 Ibid., 215–16.

14 Deist, 'The Military Collapse', 203, and Wilhelm Deist, 'Verdeckter Militärstreik', 150, with reference to calculations by the former General Staff Officer Hermann von Kuhl in the 1920s. This figure is also cited by Niall Ferguson, *The Pity of War* (London: Allen Lane, 1998), 368, who was the first to point to the high numbers of prisoners as a symptom of and contributor to the German defeat.

15 Watson, *Enduring*, 216, note 131, cites as evidence Friedrich Altrichter, *Die seelischen Kräfte des deutschen Heeres im Frieden und im Weltkriege* (Berlin: Mittler & Sohn, 1933), 157. This is correct but also reveals Watson's highly selective use of sources. On this very page, Altrichter points to the rapid increase in shirkers and deserters absconding since July.

16 Watson, *Enduring*, 220.

17 See the documents in Bernd Ulrich and Benjamin Ziemann (eds), *German Soldiers in the Great War: Letters and Eyewitness Accounts*, trans. Christine Brocks (Barnsley: Pen & Sword, 2010), 176–7.

18 Watson, *Enduring*, 224–9, quote 229.

19 Ibid., 231.

20 See Wencke Meteling, Ehre, *Einheit und Ordnung. Preußische und französische Städte und Regimenter im Krieg, 1870/71 und 1914/19* (Baden-Baden: Nomos, 2010), 307–8; Scott Stephenson, *The Final Battle: Soldiers of the Western Front in the German Revolution of 1918* (Cambridge: Cambridge University Press, 2009), 14, 48–9; Jonathan Boff, *Winning and Losing on the Western Front: The British Third Army and the Defeat of Germany in 1918* (Cambridge: Cambridge University Press, 2012), 116–7. A balanced short description can be found in David Stevenson, *With Our Backs to the Wall: Victory and Defeat in 1918* (London: Penguin, 2011) 285–92.

21 Watson, *Enduring*, 224. On p. 225, Watson cites reports on Austrian units. It is unclear how this is relevant to the collapse of the German army.

22 Alan Kramer, 'Surrender of Soldiers in World War I', in *How Fighting Ends: A History of Surrender*, ed. Holger Afflerbach and Hew Strachan (Oxford: Oxford University Press, 2012), 265–78, especially 269.

23 Watson, *Enduring*, 226–9.

24 See the example in Kramer, 'Surrender', 272.

25 Report by 119. Inf.-Div., Ia 169, 2 November 1918: BHStA/IV, Heeresgruppe Kronprinz Rupprecht, 188.
26 Watson, *Enduring*, 229. A similar criticism can be found in Kramer, 'Surrender', 273, note 64.
27 Figure in Deist, 'The Military Collapse', 203.
28 Watson, *Enduring*, 207, claims for example that destroying the army was the 'purpose' of the military strike. Yet Deist makes it clear that, in his view, the main purpose of the strikers was to ensure their own survival by bringing an end to the war and that the collapse of the army was merely a consequence of their actions.
29 Deist, 'The Military Collapse', 201.
30 Sections 64–68 of the Military Penal Code; see *Militärstrafgerichtsordnung vom 1. Dezember 1898 und Militärstrafgesetzbuch vom 20. Juni 1872* (Mannheim: Bensheimer, 1913), 189–90.
31 AOK 6, Ic no. 49 605, 'Betreff: Unerlaubte Entfernung von der Truppe', 24 June 1918: BHStA/IV, 4. Inf.-Div., Bund 89.
32 Ibid. Disciplinary punishment was handled by the immediate superiors without recourse to a court-martial tribunal.
33 See the directive from AOK 4 dated 16 June 1918 (Id 9861), which is identical in large parts and appears to have served as a template for AOK 6: BHStA/IV, 4. Inf.-Div., Bund 89.
34 GK XXVI. Reserve-Korps, 15 October 1918: BHStA/IV, I. bayer. AK, Bund 31.
35 AOK 6, Ic no. 49 605, 24 June 1918, 'Betreff: Unerlaubte Entfernung von der Truppe': BHStA/IV, 4. Inf.-Div., Bund 89.
36 AOK 4, Id no. 10670, 18 October 1918: BHStA/IV, AOK 6, Bund 22.
37 Ulrich and Ziemann, *German Soldiers*, 155.
38 As claimed by Watson, *Enduring*, 208.
39 At least this was how the directive from the 6th Army High Command (Id 9861) dated 16 June 1918: BHStA/IV, 4. Inf.-Div., Bund 89 interpreted the content of AOK 4, Id 9573, 27 April 1918. The latter directive was not available.
40 AOK 6, Id 9861, 16 June 1918: BHStA/IV, 4. Inf.-Div., Bund 89.
41 Diary entry dated 26/7 April 1918. Thaer had been moved to the Army Supreme Command just a few days earlier on 24 April. Albrecht von Thaer, *Generalstabsdienst an der Front und in der O.H.L. Aus Briefen und Tagebuchaufzeichnungen 1915–1919*, ed. Siegfried A. Kaehler (Göttingen: Vandenhoeck & Ruprecht, 1958), 188.
42 Deist, 'Verdeckter Militärstreik', 157.
43 Heeresgruppe Kronprinz Rupprecht IIb 54027 to AOK 2., 4., 6. Armee, 29 May 1918: BHStA/IV, Heeresgruppe Kronprinz Rupprecht, 456.
44 Heeresgruppe Kronprinz Rupprecht IIb 56992 to OHL, 27 June 1918: ibid.
45 Report by lieutenant in the Landwehr Holzhausen, 16 October 1918 (copy), forwarded by 119. Inf.-Div.: Heeresgruppe Kronprinz Rupprecht, 188.

46 AOK 4, IIb 14982/18 to Heeresgruppe Kronprinz Rupprecht, 10 June 1918: ibid.
47 AOK 6, Ic no. 49 605, 24 June 1918, 'Betreff: Unerlaubte Entfernung von der Truppe': BHStA/IV, 4. Inf.-Div., Bund 89.
48 AOK 4, Id 9566, 27 April 1918, notification of a letter by Heeresgruppe Kronprinz Rupprecht dated 25 April 1918: BHStA/IV, 4. Inf.-Div., Bund 86.
49 Ibid., 'Zusätze' (additions) by the 4th Army High Command.
50 Chief of the General Staff of the Field Army, IIIb no. 52862, 20 July 1918: BHStA/IV, AOK 6, Bund 22.
51 214. Inf.-Div. to GK II. bayer. AK, 12 August 1918: BHStA/IV, Heeresgruppe Kronprinz Rupprecht, 456.
52 AOK 18, Ic/Ii no. 426, 13 October 1918: BHStA/IV, I. Bayer. AK, Bund 31.
53 AOK 6, Ic no. 49 605, 24 June 1918, 'Betreff: Unerlaubte Entfernung von der Truppe': BHStA/IV, 4. Inf.-Div., Bund 89.
54 Gruppe Endres, GK I. bayer. AK, Ia/Id 15710 op., 14 October 1918: BHStAIV, I. bayer. AK, Bund 31.
55 Gruppe Endres, Gen.-Kdo. I. bayer. AK, Ia/Id no. 1397 op. geh., 13 September 1918: BHStA/IV, I. Bayer. AK, Bund 31.
56 Gen.-Kdo. I. bayer. AK, Ia/Id no. 1574, 19 September 1918: BHStA/IV, I. bayer. AK, Bund 31.
57 Deist, 'Verdeckter Militärstreik', 157, based on the army's official medical report.
58 5. bayer. Inf.-Div., 26 October 1918, based on a report by the commander of the 21st Infantry Regiment: BHStA/IV, AOK 6, Bund 22.
59 AOK 6 Ia/Iv no. 84337, 29 October 1918: BHStA/IV, AOK 6, Bund 22.
60 AOK 6, Id 9861, 16 June 1918: BHStA/IV, 4. Inf.-Div., Bund 89.
61 Etappen-Inspektion 6, Ib 2076, 26 October 1918: BHStA/IV, AOK 6, Bund 22.
62 Altrichter, *Die seelischen Kräfte*, 157.
63 As described by Christoph Jahr, *Gewöhnliche Soldaten. Desertion und Deserteure im deutschen und britischen Heer 1914–1918* (Göttingen: Vandenhoeck & Ruprecht, 1998), 166.
64 Prussian War Ministry, 5 November 1918 11772/18 C 4: BHStA/IV, MKr 11232, Prod. 143, cited in Ulrich & Ziemann, *German Soldiers*, 156.
65 Ibid.
66 Prussian War Ministry M. 7385/18 C 4, 22 July 1918: BHStA/IV, 4. Inf.-Div., Bund 89. The Bavarian War Ministry issued a similar directive, no. 185911 R on 18 August 1918: ibid.
67 Chief of the General Staff of the Field Army, Ib no. 98708 geh.op./14037 E., 13 September 1918, 'Grundsätze für "Sammlung und Weiterleitung von Versprengten"': BHStA/IV, AOK 6, Bund 22.
68 Heeresgruppe Kronprinz Rupprecht to AOK 4, 6 and 17, 27 September 1918: ibid.

69 AOK 6, Id 9861, 16 June 1918: BHStA/IV, 4. Inf.-Div., Bund 89.
70 Heeresgruppe Kronprinz Rupprecht to AOK 4, 6 and 17, 27 September 1918: BHStA/IV, AOK 6, Bund 22.
71 See Chef des Feldeisenbahnwesens, Eisenbahn-Transportabteilung des Westens, 20 October 1918, and the attached 'Fahrplan für die Militärlokalzüge 1801/1802 Lier b Antwerpen-Colmar'; also Heeresgruppe Kronprinz Rupprecht, telegram to AOK 6, 16 October 1918. Both in ibid.
72 This is rightly emphasized by Watson, *Enduring*, 207. However, it is unclear why Watson, in full knowledge of this political bias, follows Volkmann's line in his examination of the officer corps during the war, emphasizing the caring, paternalistic attitude of the officers towards their subordinates. See for example p. 134. Criticism of the discrepancy between Hobohm and Volkmann can also be found in Lipp, *Meinungslenkung*, 129ff.
73 This justified criticism can be found in Watson, *Enduring*, 207–8. Cf. WUA, vol. 11/2, 66.
74 Watson, *Enduring*, 209.
75 Dieter Dreetz, 'Rückführung des Westheeres und Novemberrevolution', *Zeitschrift für Militärgeschichte* 7 (1968): 578–89, 580. The lower figure based on 100 men per day is my addition. Dreetz's estimate was based on the following source, now available in Dresden: Sächsisches Hauptstaatsarchiv Dresden (SHStA), Kriegsarchiv (P), no. 7645, Fahnenfluchtliste 3. Armee 1918.
76 Watson, *Enduring*, 209, does not take into account this declining actual strength of the Western Army.
77 Deist, 'Verdeckter Militärstreik', 151.
78 See for example 2. Garde.-Div. 16 October 1918, 52. Res.-Div. 8 October 1918, 23. Inf.-Div. 24 September 1918 all in: BHStA/IV, Heeresgruppe Kronprinz Rupprecht, 188.
79 8. Inf.-Div., Ia pers. no. 64, 'betr. Kampfwert der Division', 27 October 1918: ibid.
80 Ibid.
81 See the list at www.agw14-18.de/formgesch/formatio_div.html (accessed 9 May 1916) based on the documents in United States War Department, *Histories of Two Hundred and Fifty-One Divisions of the German Army which participated in the War (1914–1918)* (Washington: Government Printing Office, 1920).
82 Watson, *Enduring*, 209.
83 Wencke Meteling, 'Der deutsche Zusammenbruch 1918 in den Selbstzeugnissen adeliger preußischer Offiziere' in *Adel und Moderne. Deutschland im europäischen Vergleich im 19. und 20. Jahrhundert*, ed. Eckart Conze and Monika Wienfort (Cologne: Böhlau, 2004), 289–321, especially 295–6.
84 See the ground-breaking essay by Michael Geyer, 'Insurrectionary Warfare: The German Debate about a Levée en Masse in October 1918', *Journal of Modern History*, 73 (2001): 459–527.

85 As Watson claims in *Enduring*, 206. Watson misrepresents this aspect of Deist's argument.
86 Deist, 'The Military Collapse', 206–7.
87 On this discrepancy between private memory and public perception, see Richard Bessel, 'Die Heimkehr der Soldaten: Das Bild der Frontsoldaten in der Öffentlichkeit der Weimarer Republik', in '*Keiner fühlt sich hier mehr als Mensch. . . .' Erlebnis und Wirkung des Ersten Weltkriegs*, ed. Gerhard Hirschfeld and Gerd Krumeich (Essen: Klartext, 1993), 221–39.
88 Quoted in: Benjamin Ziemann, ' "Gedanken eines Reichsbannermannes auf Grund von Erlebnissen und Erfahrungen." Politische Kultur, Flaggensymbolik und Kriegserinnerung in Schmalkalden 1926. Dokumentation', *Zeitschrift des Vereins für Thüringische Geschichte* 53 (1999): 201–32, 224.
89 Kramer, 'Surrender', 272–3.
90 See the extensive overview of individual aspects of this process in Bruno Thoß and Hans-Erich Volkmann (eds), *Erster Weltkrieg – Zweiter Weltkrieg: Ein Vergleich. Krieg, Kriegserlebnis, Kriegserfahrung in Deutschland* (Paderborn: Schöningh, 2002); a particular aspect of the theoretical preparations for war is examined in a fascinating study by Frank Reichherzer: *'Alles ist Front!' Wehrwissenschaften in Deutschland und die Bellifizierung der Gesellschaft vom Ersten Weltkrieg bis in den Kalten Krieg* (Paderborn: Schöningh, 2012).
91 Quotes from Prussian War Ministry, 5 November 2018 11772/18 C 4: BHStA/IV, MKr 11232, Prod. 143, cited in Ulrich and Ziemann, *German Soldiers*, 155–6.; see the directive from the Chief of the General Staff of the Field Army, Ia no. 9191 geh. op, 9 July 1918, reprinted in Erich Otto Volkmann, *Der Marxismus und das deutsche Heer im Weltkrieg* (Berlin: Reimar Hibbing, 1925), 313. On the absconding from reserve transports, see the directive dated 15 August 1918 from the Prussian War Ministry, the aim of which was to identify the ringleaders and then enforce obedience with the use of weapons: BHStA/IV, 4. Inf.-Div. Bund 89.
92 Eugen Neter, 'Der seelische Zusammenbruch der deutschen Kampffront. Betrachtungen eines Frontarztes', *Süddeutsche Monatshefte* 22, no. 10 (1924/25): 1–47, 28, indicates that officers were also unwilling to force discipline using their weapons during the revolutionary transition period before the troops returned home.
93 See Altrichter, *Die seelischen Kräfte*, 211, for a description of just such an incident.
94 Chief of the General Staff of the Field Army, Ia no. 9845, 16 August 1918, reprinted in Volkmann, *Der Marxismus*, 314–5.
95 Ziemann, *War Experiences*, 59–60.
96 Etappen-Kommandantur 47 to Etappen-Inspektion 3, 24 September 1918: Sächsisches Hauptstaatsarchiv Dresden, Militärarchiv, Kriegsarchiv (P), 21133, fol. 6.

97 This is the metaphor used by Holger Afflerbach, *Die Kunst der Niederlage. Eine Geschichte der Kapitulation* (Munich: C.H. Beck, 2013), 10 (quote), 197. On p. 205, Afflerbach writes that the German soldiers 'capitulated' in autumn 1918. This is somewhat misleading as the soldiers' actions were not a response to their military opponent so much as their own military leadership.
98 Altrichter, *Die seelischen Kräfte*, 169.

## 8 The Weimar Republic: A Brutalized Society?

1 This and the following points from the brilliant essay by Jon Lawrence, 'Forging a Peaceable Kingdom: War, Violence, and Fear of Brutalization in Post-First World War Britain', *Journal of Modern History* 75 (2003): 557–89, 568.
2 Ibid., 562.
3 As argued by Lawrence, 'Forging a Peaceable Kingdom', *passim*; see also Adrian Gregory, 'Peculiarities of the English? War, Violence and Politics 1900–1939', *Journal of Modern European History* 1 (2003): 44–59.
4 Lawrence, 'Forging a Peaceable Kingdom', 576–87; Gregory, 'Peculiarities', 52–4; on the broader context see also Dirk Schumann, 'Einheitssehnsucht und Gewaltakzeptanz. Politische Grundpositionen des deutschen Bürgertums nach 1918 (mit vergleichenden Überlegungen zu den britischen "middle classes")', in *Der Erste Weltkrieg und die europäische Nachkriegsordnung. Sozialer Wandel und Formveränderung der Politik*, ed. Hans Mommsen (Cologne: Böhlau, 2000), 83–105.
5 See also Robert Gerwarth and John Horne (eds.), *War in Peace: Paramilitary Violence in Europe after the Great War* (Oxford: Oxford University Press, 2013); Mark Edele and Robert Gerwarth, 'The Limits of Demobilization: Global Perspectives on the Aftermath of the Great War', *Journal of Contemporary History* 50 (2015): 3–14.
6 See the important argument by Dirk Schumann, 'Europa, der Erste Weltkrieg und die Nachkriegszeit: Eine Kontinuität der Gewalt?' *Journal of Modern European History* 1 (2003): 24–43, especially 30–3; see also Piotr Wróbel, 'The Seeds of Violence: The Brutalization of an East European Region', in: ibid., 125–49.
7 On this point and the following, see Antoine Prost, *In the Wake of War: 'Les Anciens Combattants' and French Society 1914–1939*, trans. Helen McPhail (Providence: Berg, 1992); Antoine Prost, 'The Impact of War on French and German Political Cultures', *Historical Journal* 37 (1994): 209–17.
8 Chris Millington, *From Victory to Vichy: Veterans in inter-war France* (Manchester: Manchester University Press, 2012) puts greater emphasis on the anti-parliamentary and thus anti-democratic aspects of the ancients combattants' political discourse.

9 This term coined by Stanley Hoffmann, 'Paradoxes of the French Political Community', in *In Search of France*, Stanley Hoffmann et al. (Cambridge, Mass.: Harvard University Press, 1963), 1–117, especially 3–21.
10 Judith Voelker, '"Unerträglich, unerfüllbar und deshalb unannehmbar". Kollektiver Protest gegen Versailles im Rheinland in den Monaten Mai und Juni 1919', in *Der verlorene Frieden. Politik und Kriegskultur nach 1918*, ed. Jost Dülffer and Gerd Krumeich (Essen: Klartext, 2002), 229–41.
11 Anneliese Thimme, *Flucht in den Mythos. Die Deutschnationale Volkspartei und die Niederlage von 1918* (Göttingen: Vandenhoeck & Ruprecht, 1969).
12 Boris Barth, *Dolchstoßlegenden und politische Desintegration. Das Trauma der deutschen Niederlage im Ersten Weltkrieg 1914–1933* (Düsseldorf: Droste, 2003) reveals the prehistory of this myth in the radicalization of the nationalist camp during the war.
13 See the excerpts from the diary in '"Wir als deutsches Volk sind doch nicht klein zu kriegen . . .". Aus den Tagebüchern des Fregattenkapitäns Bogislav von Selchow 1918/19', *Militärgeschichtliche Mitteilungen* 55 (1996): 165–224.
14 This important point in Richard Scully, 'Hindenburg: The Cartoon Titan of the Weimar Republic, 1918–1934', *German Studies Review* 35 (2012): 541–65, 546. Scully does not refer to the diary but to a cartoon criticizing the stab in the back, which was published in the satirical magazine *Kladderadatsch* in 1919 and reproduces von Selchow's original drawing: Werner Hahmann, 'An die Kurzsichtigen', *Kladderadatsch*, 30 November 1919. It is a mystery how the magazine obtained the drawing.
15 The sketch is in Epkenhans, '"Wir als deutsches Volk"', 175. On the context of the appearance by Hindenburg and Ludendorff, see Barth, *Dolchstoßlegenden*, 302–39.
16 See Herfried Münkler and Siegfried Storch, *Siegfrieden. Politik mit einem deutschen Mythos* (Berlin: Rotbuch-Verlag, 1988), 86ff.
17 Epkenhans, '"Wir als deutsches Volk"', 205 (first quote), 213 (second quote).
18 For a more detailed version of this argument, see Benjamin Ziemann, 'Die Erinnerung an den Ersten Weltkrieg in den Milieukulturen der Weimarer Republik', in *Kriegserlebnis und Legendenbildung. Das Bild des 'modernen' Krieges in Literatur, Theater, Photographie und Film*, ed. Thomas F. Schneider, 3 vols. (Osnabrück: Universitätsverlag Rasch, 1999), vol. 1, 249–70.
19 George L. Mosse, *Fallen Soldiers* (Oxford: Oxford University Press, 1990), 159–81.
20 Ibid., 173.
21 Emil Julius Gumbel, *Vier Jahre politischer Mord* (1922; repr., Heidelberg: Verlag Das Wunderhorn, 1980).
22 Christine Brocks, *Die bunte Welt des Krieges. Bildpostkarten aus dem Ersten Weltkrieg 1914–1918* (Essen: Klartext, 2008).
23 Figures in Richard Bessel, *Germany after the First World War* (Oxford: Clarendon Press, 1993), 231; based on Bessel's figures, see also Nicolas Beaupré, *Das Trauma des großen Krieges 1918–1932/33* (Darmstadt: Wissenschaftliche Buchgesellschaft, 2009), 232.

24 Quote: Beaupré, *Das Trauma des großen Krieges*, 232.
25 This supposition about domestic violence: ibid. However, Dirk Blasius, *Ehescheidung in Deutschland im 19. und 20. Jahrhundert* (Frankfurt am Main: Fischer Taschenbuch Verlag, 1992), found no indications of such an increase in domestic violence in his qualitative evidence.
26 Bessel, *Germany after the First World War*, 232.
27 Ibid., 232 (quote); Birthe Kundrus, 'Gender Wars. The First World War and the Construction of Gender Relation in the Weimar Republic', in *Home/Front: The Military, War, and Gender in Twentieth-Century Germany*, ed. Karen Hagemann and Stefanie Schüler-Springorum (New York: Berg, 2002), 159–79, suggests that a general crisis of gender relations occurred, but does not offer convincing evidence.
28 Bessel, *Germany after the First World War*, 232.
29 See extensively on this topic, ibid., 220–53, quote 221.
30 Beaupré, *Das Trauma des großen Krieges*, 230–7, especially 233. Schumann, 'Einheitssehnsucht und Gewaltakzeptanz', differentiates along similar lines but is more critical of the brutalization argument.
31 From a letter written in October 1914 by the student F.G. Steinbrecher, quoted in Mark Hewitson, '"I Witnesses": Soldiers, Selfhood and Testimony in Modern Wars', *German History* 28 (2010): 310–25, quote 318. The letter is from the famous collection of students' war letters, edited in several versions by Philip Witkop.
32 Letter dated 2 October 1916, cited in Philipp Münch, *Bürger in Uniform. Kriegserfahrungen von Hamburger Turnern 1914 bis 1918* (Freiburg im Breisgau: Rombach, 2009), 140–1.
33 As Münch correctly argues, ibid., 141.
34 Ibid., 146–7.
35 As argued by Hewitson, 'I Witnesses', 311–12, 318–19, 324.
36 See Klaus Latzel, 'Kriegsbriefe und Kriegserfahrung. Wie können Feldpostbriefe zur erfahrungsgeschichtlichen Quelle werden?', *Werkstatt Geschichte* 22 (1999): 7–24; Klaus Latzel, 'Vom Kriegserlebnis zur Kriegserfahrung. Theoretische und methodische Überlegungen zur erfahrungsgeschichtlichen Untersuchung von Feldpostbriefen', *Militärgeschichtliche Mitteilungen* 56 (1997): 1–30; Bernd Ulrich, 'Feldpostbriefe im Ersten Weltkrieg – Bedeutung und Zensur', in *Kriegsalltag*, ed. Peter Knoch (Stuttgart: Metzler, 1989), 40–83; see also the study by Martin Humburg, *Das Gesicht des Krieges. Feldpostbriefe von Wehrmachtssoldaten aus der Sowjetunion 1941–1944* (Opladen: Westdeutscher Verlag, 1998), which proposes a quantitative analysis to solve these issues. Hewitson, 'I Witnesses', does not discuss any of these works. Further case studies and reflections can be found in: Veit Didczuneit, Jens Ebert and Thomas Jander (eds), *Schreiben im Krieg – Schreiben vom Krieg. Feldpost im Zeitalter der Weltkriege* (Essen: Klartext, 2011).
37 However, Hewitson, 'I Witnesses', bases his article solely on such collections printed during the war.

38 Aribert Reimann, *Der Große Krieg der Sprachen. Untersuchungen zur historischen Semantik in Deutschland und England zur Zeit des Ersten Weltkriegs* (Essen: Klartext, 2000), 167–222, quote 180.
39 Anonymous letter by a working-class soldier in August 1916, quoted in Volker Ullrich, *Vom Augusterlebnis zur Novemberrevolution. Beiträge zur Sozialgeschichte Hamburgs und Norddeutschlands im Ersten Weltkrieg 1914–1918* (Bremen: Donat, 1999), 61.
40 Barth, *Dolchstoßlegenden*, 279. Many vivid descriptions of radical left-wing violence can be found in the monumental work by Erhard Lucas, *Märzrevolution im Ruhrgebiet*, 3 vols. (Frankfurt am Main: März Verlag, 1970–78). An alternative interpretation, which views the violence of the workers in the wake of the Kapp Putsch essentially as an 'act of self-defence against the imminent counterrevolution' can be found for the Prussian province of Saxony (the borders of which corresponded roughly to today's federal state of Saxony-Anhalt) in Dirk Schumann, *Political Violence in the Weimar Republic, 1918–1933: Fight for the Streets and Fear of Civil War*, trans. Thomas Dunlap (Oxford: Berghahn, 2009), 35–41, quote 306.
41 See Wolfgang Kruse, 'Krieg und Klassenheer. Zur Revolutionierung der deutschen Armee im Ersten Weltkrieg', *Geschichte und Gesellschaft* 22 (1996): 530–61.
42 Eugen Neter, 'Der seelische Zusammenbruch der deutschen Kampffront. Betrachtungen eines Frontarztes', *Süddeutsche Monatshefte* 22, no. 10 (1924/25): 1–47, quote 31.
43 Ibid., 31.
44 Ibid.
45 Stéphane Audoin-Rouzeau and Annette Becker, *14–18: Understanding the Great War* (New York: Hill and Wang, 2003), 103–4. It should be noted that the exaggeration of the 'war culture' in this book has drawn strong criticism from French experts. See primarily Nicolas Offenstadt, 'Der Erste Weltkrieg im Spiegel der Gegenwart. Fragestellungen, Debatten, Forschungsanätze', in *Durchhalten! Krieg und Gesellschaft im Vergleich 1914–1918*, ed. Arnd Bauerkämper and Elise Julien (Göttingen: Vandenhoeck & Ruprecht, 2010), 54–80. The book by Audoin-Rouzeau and Becker is nevertheless important in our context as a corrective to the notion of a special German path of brutalization put forward by Mosse. See also the informative overview of this debate in Benoît Majerus, 'Kriegserfahrung als Gewalterfahrung. Perspektiven der neuesten internationalen Forschung zum Ersten Weltkrieg', in *Der Bürger als Soldat. Die Militarisierung europäischer Gesellschaften im langen 19. Jahrhundert*, ed. Christian Jansen (Essen: Klartext, 2003), 271–97.
46 Benjamin Ziemann, *War Experiences in Rural Germany 1914–1923*, trans. Alex Skinner (Oxford: Berg, 2007).
47 Bernd Weisbrod, 'Gewalt in der Politik. Zur politischen Kultur in Deutschland zwischen den beiden Weltkriegen', *Geschichte in Wissenschaft und Unterricht* 43 (1992): 391–404, quote 394.

48 See Ziemann, *War Experiences*, 73–209.
49 Ibid., 229–331.
50 Ziemann, *War Experiences*, 166–203; see also Klaus Tenfelde, 'Stadt und Land in Krisenzeiten. München und das Münchener Umland zwischen Revolution und Inflation 1918–1923', in *Soziale Räume in der Urbanisierung. Studien zur Geschichte Münchens im Vergleich 1850 bis 1933*, ed. Wolfgang Hardtwig and Klaus Tenfelde (Munich: Oldenbourg, 1990), 37–57.
51 Weisbrod, 'Gewalt in der Politik', 393; cf. James M. Diehl, *Paramilitary Politics in Weimar Germany* (Bloomington: Indiana University Press, 1977), 55ff.; Hans Mommsen, *Aufstieg und Untergang der Republik von Weimar, 1918–1933* (Berlin: Ullstein, 1998), 59.
52 Ziemann, *War Experiences*, 227–40.
53 Wehrkommissar for Schwaben und Neuburg to GK I. bayer. AK, 1 July 1919: BHStA/IV, stv. GK I. AK 3895, quoted in Ziemann, *War Experiences*, 234.
54 Schumann, *Political Violence*, 16–25, quote 307.
55 Andreas Wirsching neglects this social and organizational practice: Andreas Wirsching, *Vom Weltkrieg zum Bürgerkrieg? Politischer Extremismus in Deutschland und Frankreich 1918–1933/39. Berlin und Paris im Vergleich* (Munich: Oldenbourg, 1999), 300–4, 309–13.
56 Bessel, *Germany after the First World War*, 258.
57 Christian Weiß, '"Soldaten des Friedens". Die pazifistischen Veteranen und Kriegsopfer des "Reichsbundes" und ihre Kontakte zu den französischen *anciens combattants* 1919–1933', in *Politische Kulturgeschichte der Zwischenkriegszeit 1918–1939*, ed. Wolfgang Hardtwig (Göttingen: Vandenhoeck & Ruprecht, 2005), 183–204.
58 On this term see John Horne, 'Kulturelle Demobilmachung 1919–1939. Ein sinnvoller Begriff?', in ibid., 129–50.
59 Nadine Rossol, *Performing the Nation in Interwar Germany. Sport, Spectacle and Political Symbolism 1926–1936* (Basingstoke: Palgrave Macmillan, 2010), 90–101.
60 For a detailed study, see Benjamin Ziemann, Contested Commemorations: *Republican War Veterans and Weimar Political Culture* (Cambridge: Cambridge University Press, 2013), especially 60–164, on Persius 75–6, quote 78.
61 Hermann Schützinger, 'Frankreichs Frontsoldaten. Ihr Urteil über die Wahl Hindenburgs', *Vorwärts*, 3 June 1925.
62 See Thomas F. Schneider, *Erich Maria Remarques Roman 'Im Westen nichts Neues'. Text, Edition, Entstehung, Distribution und Rezeption* (Tübingen: M. Niemeyer, 2004); Modris Eksteins, 'War, Memory and Politics: The Fate of the Film All Quiet on the Western Front', *Central European History* 13 (1980): 60–82. On the part played by wartime brutalization in the identity of committed National Socialists, see Patrick Krassnitzer, 'Die Geburt des Nationalsozialismus im Schützengraben. Formen der Brutalisierung in den Autobiographien von nationalsozialistischen Frontsoldaten', in

*Der verlorene Frieden. Politik und Kriegskultur nach 1918*, ed. Jost Dülffer and Gerd Krumeich (Essen: Klartext, 2002), 119–48.
63 George L. Mosse, 'Two World Wars and the Myth of the War Experience', *Journal of Contemporary History* 21 (1986): 491–513; Mosse, *Fallen Soldiers*, 69–88.
64 See Andrew Donson, *Youth in the Fatherless Land: War Pedagogy, Nationalism, and Authority, 1914–1918* (Cambridge, Mass: Harvard University Press, 2010).
65 Arndt Weinrich, *Der Weltkrieg als Erzieher. Jugend zwischen Weimarer Republik und Nationalsozialismus* (Essen: Klartext, 2012).
66 Ibid., 149; specifically on the Jungbanner, see the short section based on a selective analysis of published sources: ibid., 114–19.
67 Ziemann, *Contested Commemorations*, 151–64.
68 Among the shorter comprehensive studies, the following stands out for its extensive and balanced treatment of these issues: Matthew Stibbe, *Germany 1914–1933: Politics, Society and Culture* (Harlow: Longman, 2010), 67–97.
69 For France, see the sceptical argument in Antoine Prost, 'Les limites de la brutalisation. Tuer sur le front occidental 1914–1918', *Vingtième Siecle* 81 (2000): 5–20. Generally, compare Gerwarth and Horne, *War in Peace*.
70 This applies especially to the question of the continuity of political violence, not least that perpetrated by the SA in Nazi Germany. See the regional study by Schumann, *Political Violence*; on the SA, see Sven Reichardt, *Faschistische Kampfbünde. Gewalt und Gemeinschaft im italienischen Squadrismus und in der deutschen SA* (Cologne: Böhlau, 2002) and Sven Reichardt, 'Totalitäre Gewaltpolitik? Überlegungen zum Verhältnis von nationalsozialistischer und kommunistischer Gewalt in der Weimarer Republik', in *Ordnungen in der Krise. Zur politischen Kulturgeschichte Deutschlands 1900–1933*, ed. Wolfgang Hardtwig (Munich: R. Oldenbourg, 2007), 377–402.
71 Thomas Weber, *Hitler's First War: Adolf Hitler, the Men of the List Regiment and the First World War* (Oxford: Oxford University Press, 2010).
72 For an incisive comparative analysis of the Fascist myth of the 'war veteran' see now Ángel Alcalde, 'War Veterans and the Transnational Origins of Italian Fascism (1917–1919)', *Journal of Modern Italian Studies* 21 (2016): 565–83.

# 9 The Delayed Rejection of Violence: Hermann Schützinger's Conversion to Pacifism

1 Robert Gerwarth, 'The Central European Counterrevolution: Paramilitary Violence in Germany, Austria and Hungary after the Great War', *Past & Present* 200 (2008): 175–209. The close contacts between Bavarian and Austrian paramilitaries are described in detail by Horst G.W. Nußer, *Konservative Wehrverbände in Bayern, Preußen und Österreich 1918–1933*, 2 vols. (Munich: Nusser Verlag, 1973).

2 Ian Kershaw, 'War and Political Violence in Twentieth-Century Europe', *Contemporary European History* 14 (2005): 107–23, 113.
3 Robert G.L. Waite, *Vanguard of Nazism: The Free Corps Movement in Postwar Germany 1918–1923* (Cambridge, Mass: Harvard University Press, 1952). Cf. Matthias Sprenger, *Landsknechte auf dem Weg ins Dritte Reich? Zu Genese und Wandel des Freikorpsmythos* (Paderborn: Schöningh, 2008).
4 See the critical remarks in Thomas Weber, *Hitler's First War: Adolf Hitler, the Men of the List Regiment, and the First World War* (Oxford: Oxford University Press, 2010), 244–6.
5 Robert Gerwarth and John Horne (eds), *War in Peace: Paramilitary Violence in Europe after the Great War* (Oxford: Oxford University Press, 2012).
6 Wolfram Wette and Helmut Donat (eds), *Pazifistische Offiziere in Deutschland 1871–1933* (Bremen: Donat Verlag, 1999).
7 Stefan Appelius, 'Der Friedensgeneral Paul Freiherr von Schoenaich. Demokrat und Pazifist in der Weimarer Republik', *Demokratische Geschichte* 7 (1992): 165–80; on Deimling, see the comprehensive biography by Kirsten Zirkel, *Vom Militaristen zum Pazifisten: General Berthold von Deimling – eine politische Biographie* (Essen: Klartext, 2008).
8 Dieter Riesenberger, '"Soldat der Republik". Polizeioberst Hermann Schützinger (1888– ca. 1960)', in Wette and Donat, *Pazifistische Offiziere*, 287–301. Riesenberger's pioneering study is incomplete and contains errors both with respect to Schützinger's life pre-1918 and post-1933. Riesenberger was also unable to consult the sources referred to in the following.
9 See Reinhold Lütgemeier-Davin, 'Basismobilisierung gegen den Krieg: Die Nie-wieder-Krieg-Bewegung in der Weimarer Republik', in *Pazifismus in der Weimarer Republik*, ed. Karl Holl and Wolfram Wette (Paderborn: Schöningh, 1981), 47–76.
10 Benjamin Ziemann, *Contested Commemorations: Republican War Veterans and Weimar Political Culture* (Cambridge: Cambridge University Press, 2013), 26–7.
11 Karl Vetter, *Ludendorff ist schuld! Die Anklage der Feldgrauen* (Berlin: Koch & Jürgens, n.d. [1919]), 15.
12 Quote: Report by Staatskommissar für die Überwachung der öffentlichen Ordnung, 3 December 1919: StA Bremen, 4, 65, 1157, fol. 5; Ziemann, *Contested Commemorations*, 32–4.
13 Figures in Helmut Donat and Karl Holl (eds), *Die Friedensbewegung. Organisierter Pazifismus in Deutschland, Österreich und in der Schweiz* (Düsseldorf: Econ Taschenbuch Verlag, 1983), 72, 138.
14 Karl Holl, *Pazifismus in Deutschland* (Frankfurt am Main: Suhrkamp, 1988), 144.
15 Carl von Ossietzky, 'Nie wieder Krieg. Der Rundlauf einer Parole' (1923), in *Sämtliche Schriften*, 8 vols. (Reinbek: Rowohlt, 1994), vol. 2, 267–70, 268. On the literary ideology of the 'time of greatness', see Wolfgang G. Natter, *Literature at War*,

*1914–1940: Representing the 'Time of Greatness' in Germany* (New Haven: Yale University Press, 1999).

16 'Nie wieder Krieg!', *Berliner Volks-Zeitung*, 3 August 1919.

17 'Nach sechs Jahren', *Berliner Volks-Zeitung*, 1 August 1920.

18 Lütgemeier-Davin, 'Basismobilisierung'.

19 See figure 3.

20 The most reliable outline of his biography is found in Heinrich Schützinger, 'Biographie von Dr. Hermann Schützinger', 13 August 2003: Akademie der Künste Berlin, Kempowski-Biographienarchiv (AdK, Kempowski-BIO), 6865/1. On his military career, see the materials in Schützinger's personnel file: Bayerisches Hauptstaatsarchiv München, Abt. IV: Kriegsarchiv (BHStA/IV), OP 49443.

21 Martina Steber, *Ethnische Gewissheiten: Die Ordnung des Regionalen im bayerischen Schwaben vom Kaiserreich bis zum NS-Regime* (Göttingen: Vandenhoeck & Ruprecht, 2010), 105.

22 Qualifikations-Bericht des Bataillons-Kommandeurs, 20 June 1913: BHStA/IV, OP 49443.

23 Riesenberger, '"Soldat der Republik"', 288–9; on the context provided by the Balkan wars, see the report on Schützinger's personality compiled by retired captain Albert Dunzinger as part of a libel action against the editor of the *Sachsenstimme* newspaper and sent to the lawyer Erich Scheer: BHStA/IV, OP 49443. Dunzinger compiled the regimental history of the 11th Infantry Regiment: Albert Dunzinger, *Das K.B.11. Infanterieregiment von der Tann* (Munich: Verlag Bayerische Kriegsarchiv, 1921).

24 Retired captain Albert Dunzinger to lawyer Erich Scheer, 18 November 1925: BHStA/IV, OP 49443.

25 Quoted in Hartmut John, *Das Reserveoffizierkorps im Deutschen Kaiserreich 1890–1914. Ein sozialgeschichtlicher Beitrag zur Untersuchung der gesellschaftlichen Militarisierung im Wilhelminischen Kaiserreich* (Frankfurt am Main: Campus, 1981), 30; see also Hartwig Stein, 'Der Bilse-Skandal von 1903. Zu Bild und Zerrbild des preussischen Leutnants im späten Kaiserreich' in *Eliten im Wandel. Gesellschaftliche Führungsschichten im 19. und 20. Jahrhundert*, ed. Karl Christian Führer, Karen Hagemann and Birthe Kundrus (Münster: Westfälisches Dampfboot, 2004), 259–78.

26 Statement by Schützinger's lawyer, Erich Saenger, in a trial against Klaus Eck, editor of the *Miesbacher Anzeige*, at the Munich District Court in 1920/1. Copies in: BHStA/IV, OP 49443. See also Markus Pöhlmann, 'Anonyme und pseudonyme Militärliteratur im deutschsprachigen Raum 1848–2000. Zum mediengesschichtlichen Phänomen und zur Forschungsproblematik', *Militärgeschichtliche Zeitschrift* 69 (2010): 80–95, 80.

27 Bernd Ulrich, *Die Augenzeugen. Deutsche Feldpostbriefe in Kriegs- und Nachkriegszeit 1914–1933* (Essen: Klartext, 1997), 106–42.

28 Hermann Schützinger to his parents, 31 October 1914: AdK, Kempowski-BIO, 6865/1. Except where otherwise indicated, all letters quoted from this collection in the following were addressed to Schützinger's parents.
29 Hermann Schützinger, 24 August 1914: AdK, Kempowski-BIO, 6865/1.
30 Hermann Schützinger, 3 October 1914: AdK, Kempowski-BIO, 6865/1; more generally, see also Tony Ashworth, *Trench Warfare 1914-1918: The Live and Let Live System* (London: Macmillan, 1980).
31 Hermann Schützinger, 31 October 1914: AdK, Kempowski-BIO, 6865/1.
32 Ibid.
33 Hermann Schützinger, 20 January 1915: AdK, Kempowski-BIO, 6865/1.
34 Ibid.
35 Hermann Schützinger, 14 April 1915: AdK, Kempowski-BIO, 6865/1.
36 Ulrich, *Die Augenzeugen,* 109-16.
37 Hermann Schützinger, 14 April 1915: AdK, Kempowski-BIO, 6865/1.
38 See Benjamin Ziemann, *War Experiences in Rural Germany 1914-1923*, trans. Alex Skinner (Oxford: Berg, 2007), 84-5.
39 Hermann Schützinger, 5 May 1915: AdK, Kempowski-BIO, 6865/1.
40 Klaus Latzel, *Deutsche Soldaten - nationalsozialistischer Krieg? Kriegserlebnis-Kriegserfahrung 1939-1945* (Paderborn: Schöningh, 1998), 244-63; Klaus Latzel, 'Die mißlungene Flucht vor dem Tod. Töten und Sterben vor und nach 1918', in *Kriegsende 1918. Ereignis - Wirkung - Nachwirkung*, ed. Jörg Duppler and Gerhard P. Groß (Munich: R. Oldenbourg, 1999), 183-99, 188-9.
41 Hermann Schützinger, 5 May 1915: AdK, Kempowski-BIO, 6865/1.
42 Hermann Schützinger, 28 June 1915: AdK, Kempowski-BIO, 6865/1.
43 Personalbogen Schützinger, no date: BHStA/IV, OP 49443.
44 On this and the following, see Bayerisches Kriegsarchiv, *Die Bayern im Großen Kriege 1914-18*, 2 vols. (Munich: Verlag des bayerischen Kriegsarchivs, 1923), vol. 1, 232-3.
45 'Berichte aus dem deutschen Großen Hauptquartier, veröffentlicht durch Wolffs Telegraphisches Bureau, 1. Juli 1915', www.stahlgewitter.com/weltkrieg/1915_ban_de_sapt.htm, accessed 30 September 2016.
46 Hermann Schützinger, 24 June 1915: AdK, Kempowski-BIO, 6865/1.
47 Ibid.
48 Hermann Schützinger, 28 June 1915: AdK, Kempowski-BIO, 6865/1. Emphasis in the original.
49 Heinrich Schützinger to Walter Kempowski, 4 February 2003: AdK, Kempowski-BIO, 6865/1.
50 Heinrich Schützinger to Walter Kempowski, 15 May 2003: AdK, Kempowski-BIO, 6865/1.
51 See for example the letter from Johann Baptist Blehle to his wife, 8 May 1915: StA Augsburg, Amtsgericht Immenstadt, Zivilsachen E 29/1920. Blehle did not return

from battle on 9 May 1915. His wife submitted the letter to the declaration of death proceedings in 1920 and it remains in the court files.
52 E. Schiche, 'Ueber Todesahnungen im Felde und ihre Wirkung', in *Beihefte zur Zeitschrift für angewandte Psychologie. 21. Beiträge zur Psychologie des Krieges*, ed. William Stern and Otto Lipmann (Leipzig: Johann Ambrosius Barth, 1920), 173–8, 174. On war psychology and psychiatry, see Susanne Michl and Jan Plamper, 'Soldatische Angst im Ersten Weltkrieg. Die Karriere eines Gefühls in der Kriegspsychiatrie Deutschlands, Frankreichs und Russlands', *Geschichte und Gesellschaft* 35 (2009): 209–48, 220–7.
53 Schiche, 'Todesahnungen', 175.
54 See Chapter 4 of this volume.
55 Michael Geyer, 'Vom Massenhaften Tötungshandeln oder: Wie die Deutschen das Krieg-Machen lernten', in *Massenhaftes Töten. Kriege und Genozide im 20. Jahrhundert*, ed. Thomas Kühne and Peter Gleichmann (Essen: Klartext, 2004), 105–42, 131. In English, see also Michael Geyer, 'How the Germans Learned to Wage War: On the Question of Killing in the First and Second World Wars', in *Between Mass Death and Individual Loss: The Place of the Dead in Twentieth-Century*, ed. Paul Betts, Alan Confino and Dirk Schuman (New York: Berghahn, 2008), 25–50.
56 Hermann Schützinger, *Das Lied vom jungen Sterben. Kriegsroman aus dem Ban-de-Sapt* (Dresden: Pierson, 1918).
57 Hermann Schützinger, 2 November 1918: AdK, Kempowski-BIO, 6865/1.
58 Schützinger, *Das Lied vom jungen Sterben*, 227–8.
59 Ibid., 228.
60 Hermann Schützinger to his father, 28 May 1918: AdK, Kempowski-BIO, 6865/1.
61 Hermann Schützinger to his father, 12 January 1916: AdK, Kempowski-BIO, 6865/1.
62 Gericht der stv. 12. Infanterie-Brigade Regensburg, Einstellungsverfügung, 31 July 1916: BHStA/IV, OP 49443.
63 Hermann Schützinger to Bataillonskommandeur II./R.I.R. 11, 17 February 1916, and Personalbogen Schützinger, no date: BHStA/IV, OP 49443.
64 Hermann Schützinger, 27 August 1916: AdK, Kempowski-BIO, 6865/1.
65 Hermann Schützinger, 20 June 1917: AdK, Kempowski-BIO, 6865/2.
66 Hermann Schützinger, 22 February 1918: AdK, Kempowski-BIO, 6865/2.
67 Hermann Schützinger to his father, 28 May 1918: AdK, Kempowski-BIO, 6865/1.
68 Hermann Schützinger, 22 February 1918: AdK, Kempowski-BIO, 6865/2.
69 Excerpt from the Kriegs-Rangliste, 5 May 1920, and Personalbogen Schützinger, no date: BHStA/IV, OP 49443.
70 Hermann Schützinger, 15 October 1918: AdK, Kempowski-BIO, 6865/1.
71 Hermann Schützinger, 20 October 1918: AdK, Kempowski-BIO, 6865/1.
72 Hermann Schützinger, 2 November 1918: AdK, Kempowski-BIO, 6865/1.

73 Riesenberger, 'Soldat der Republik', 290; on the timing see Abwicklungsstelle 11. I.R. in Regensburg, 'Beurteilung Schützinger', 29 July 1919: BHStA/IV, OP 49443; Hermann Schützinger, 'Die deutsche Arbeiterklasse und die Wehrfragen der Zukunft', *Sozialistische Monatshefte* 27, no. 9 (1921): 439–47, 443.

74 Schützinger, 'Die deutsche Arbeiterklasse', 443.

75 Ibid., 444.

76 Pol. Dir. Munich to Reichsarchiv-Zweigstelle Munich, 9 January 1923: BHStA/IV, OP 49443; Jose Raymund Canoy, *The Discreet Charm of the Police State: The Landpolizei and the Transformation of Bavaria 1945–1965* (Leiden: Brill, 2007), 43–4.

77 According to Schützinger's own statement in a trial against Klaus Eck, editor of the *Miesbacher Anzeiger*, at the Munich District Court in 192/21. Copies in: BHStA/IV, OP 49443. A different month is cited in Riesenberger, 'Soldat der Republik', 290.

78 Ursula Büttner, *Weimar. Die überforderte Republik 1918–1933. Leistung und Versagen in Staat, Gesellschaft, Wirtschaft und Kultur* (Stuttgart: Klett-Cotta, 2008), quote 146; Hans Fenske, *Konservativismus und Rechtsradikalismus in Bayern nach 1918* (Bad Homburg: Gehlen, 1969).

79 Hermann Schützinger to Reichswehrminister, 16 March 1920 (copy): BHStA/IV, OP 49443.

80 Hermann Schützinger, 'Die Reaktion in der Armee', *Münchener Post* 23 March 1920.

81 Heeres-Abwicklungs-Amt Bayern to Oberbefehlshaber Reichswehr-Gruppenkommando 4, 26 April 1920: BHStA/IV, OP 49443.

82 Heeres-Abwicklungs-Amt Bayern, Vormerkung zum Personalakt Schützinger, 26 February 1921: BHStA/IV, OP 49443.

83 Heinrich Schützinger, 'Biographie von Dr. Hermann Schützinger', 13 August 2003: AdK, Kempowski-BIO, 6865/1.

84 Ziemann, *Contested Commemorations*, 211–13.

85 Heinrich Schützinger, 'Biographie von Dr. Hermann Schützinger', 13 August 2003: AdK, Kempowski-BIO, 6865/1; Ziemann, Contested Commemorations, 212–15.

86 On this concept, see John Horne, 'Kulturelle Demobilmachung 1919–1939. Ein sinnvoller Begriff?', in *Politische Kulturgeschichte der Zwischenkriegszeit 1918–1939*, ed. Wolfgang Hardtwig (Göttingen: Vandenhoeck & Ruprecht, 2005), 129–50.

87 Artur Zickler, *Im Tollhause* (Berlin: P. Singer, n.d. [1919?]).

88 Helmuth Kiesel (ed.), *Ernst Jünger. Kriegstagebuch 1914–1918* (Stuttgart: Klett-Cotta, 2010), 390.

89 See the comments by Kiesel: ibid., 578–9, 634; see also Karl Heinz Bohrer, *Die Ästhetik des Schreckens. Die pessimistische Romantik und Ernst Jüngers Frühwerk* (Munich: Hanser, 1978).

90 This phrase, used by Schützinger, has also been similarly applied in historiography; see Wolfgang Sauer, 'National Socialism: Totalitarian or Fascism?', *American Historical Review* 73 (1967): 404–24, 411.

## 10 'Rear Area Militarism': Discussing the War in Anti-military Bestsellers in the Weimar Republic

1. On the marketing and reception of Im Westen nichts Neues in Germany, see Thomas F. Schneider, *Erich Maria Remarques Roman 'Im Westen nichts Neues'. Text, Edition, Entstehung, Distribution und Rezeption* (Tübingen: M. Niemeyer, 2004).
2. Cf. Michael Gollbach, *Die Wiederkehr des Weltkrieges in der Literatur. Zu den Frontromanen der späten Zwanziger Jahre* (Kronberg: Scriptor Verlag, 1978).
3. For a comprehensive account, see Jörg Vollmer, 'Imaginäre Schlachtfelder. Kriegsliteratur in der Weimarer Republik. Eine literatursoziologische Untersuchung' (PhD diss., Freie Universität Berlin, 2003).
4. See Schneider, *Erich Maria Remarques Roman*.
5. Thomas F. Schneider and Hans Wagener, 'Einleitung', in *Von Richthofen bis Remarque. Deutschsprachige Prosa zum I. Weltkrieg*, (Amsterdam: Rodopi, 2003), 11–16, quote 14.
6. Klaus Petersen, *Zensur in der Weimarer Republik* (Stuttgart: J.B. Metzler, 1995), see 178–9 on Etappe Gent.
7. *Etappe Gent* receives various brief mentions in studies on war literature in the Weimar Republic. See for example Hans Harald Müller, *Der Krieg und die Schriftsteller. Der Kriegsroman in der Weimarer Republik* (Stuttgart: J.B. Metzler, 1986), 24. Ulrich Baron and Hans-Harald Müller, 'Die Weltkriege im Roman der Nachkriegszeiten', in *Lernen aus dem Krieg? Deutsche Nachkriegszeiten 1918 und 1945*, eds Gottfried Niedhart and Dieter Riesenberger (Munich: C.H. Beck, 1992), 300–18, 303, claim inaccurately that of the 'anti-military' texts published as independent texts rather than as parts of series or as articles, only *Etappe Gent* enjoyed long-term success. See also Nicolas Beaupré, *Écrire en guerre, écrire la guerre. France, Allemagne 1914–1920* (Paris: CNRS, 2006), 120; Vanessa Ther, '"Humans are cheap and the bread is dear": Republican portrayals of the war experience in Weimar Germany', in *Untold War: New Perspectives in First World War Studies*, eds Heather Jones, Jennifer O'Brien and Christoph Schmidt-Supprian (Leiden: Brill, 2008), 357–84, 378–9; Boris Barth, *Dolchstoßlegenden und politische Desintegration. Das Trauma der deutschen Niederlage im Ersten Weltkrieg 1914–1933* (Düsseldorf: Droste, 2003), 508–9.
8. Bruno Thoss, 'Etappe', in *Enzyklopädie Erster Weltkrieg*, eds Gerhard Hirschfeld, Gerd Krumeich and Irina Renz (Paderborn: Schöningh, 2003), 465.
9. On these women army auxiliaries, see Bianca Schönberger, 'Motherly Heroines and Adventurous Girls: Red Cross Nurses and Women Army Auxiliaries in the First World War', in *Home/Front: The Military, War, and Gender in Twentieth-Century Germany*, eds Karen Hagemann and Stefanie Schüler-Springorum (New York: Berg, 2002), 87–113, especially 90–1. See also the decree by Etappen-Inspektion 1, 7 June

1918, reprinted in WUA, vol. 11/1, *Gutachten des Sachverständigen Dr. Hobohm, Soziale Heeresmißstände als Teilursache des deutschen Zusammenbruchs von 1918* (Berlin: Deutsche Verlagsgesellschaft für Politik und Geschichte, 1929), 67 (document 25).

10 Bernd Ulrich and Benjamin Ziemann (eds), *German Soldiers in the Great War: Letters and Eyewitness Accounts*, trans. Christine Brocks (Barnsley: Pen & Sword, 2010), 122–3; cf. WUA, vol. 11/1, 161.

11 See the war letter by Franz Lauterbach dating from August 1917 in Ulrich and Ziemann, *German Soldiers*, 120–21.

12 Hermann Hefele, *Zur Psychologie der Etappe*, Tat-Flugschriften 24 (Jena: Diederichs, 1918), 5.

13 Wilhelm Appens, *Charleville. Dunkle Punkte aus dem Etappenleben* (Dortmund: Gerisch & Co., n.d. [1919]), 15–16. This edition has thirty-eight pages. See the longer excerpt of this passage in English in Ulrich and Ziemann, *German Soldiers*, 121.

14 Barth, *Dolchstoßlegenden*, 72. Barth also provides examples of conservative perceptions of the rear area in contemporary accounts. See also Scott Stephenson, *The Final Battle: Soldiers of the Western Front in the German Revolution of 1918* (Cambridge: Cambridge University Press, 2009), 126.

15 Max Bauer, *Der große Krieg in Feld und Heimat. Erinnerungen und Betrachtungen* (Tübingen: Osiander, 1921), 190.

16 See Bernd Ulrich, 'Die Perspektive "von unten" und ihre Instrumentalisierung am Beispiel des Ersten Weltkrieges', *Krieg und Literatur/War and Literature* 1, no. 2 (1989): 47–64.

17 See for example *Anklage der Gepeinigten! Geschichte eines Feldlazarettes. Aus den Tagebüchern eines Sanitäts-Feldwebels* (Berlin: Firn Verlag, 1919).

18 *Der Etappensumpf. Dokumente des Zusammenbruchs des deutschen Heeres aus den Jahren 1916/1918. Aus dem Kriegstagebuch eines Gemeinen* (Jena: Verlag der Volksbuchhandlung, 1920), quotes 3 (preface), 5 (song lyrics).

19 The lines in question run as follows: 'Wer läuft, den deutschen Frauen zur Schmach/ Geputzten, verseuchten Französinnen nach': ibid., 5.

20 See *Westfälische Allgemeine Volks-Zeitung* 8 August 1919 to 18 August 1918; see the excerpts in Niedersächsisches Hauptstaatsarchiv Hannover (NHStAH), Hann. 180, Hildesheim no. 11666, vol. II, fol. 80.

21 'Vernehmung des Schulrates Dr. Appens, Hörde über den Neudruck und die Übersetzung seiner Schrift 'Charleville' in die französische Sprache', Arnsberg regional administrative authority to Prussian Ministry for Science, Culture and Education, 2 February 1930: NHStAH, Hann. 180, Hildesheim no. 11666, vol. II, fol. 251–2.

22 *Deutsches Bücherverzeichnis, 1921–1925* (Leipzig: Verlag des Börsenvereins der Deutschen Buchhändler zu Leipzig, 1926), vol. 7, 93.

23 Wilhelm Appens, *Charleville. Ein trübes Kapitel aus der Etappen-Geschichte des Weltkrieges 1914/1918* (Dortmund: Gerisch & Co., 1927).

24 Prussian Ministry for Science, Culture and Education to Arnsberg regional administrative authority, 4 March 1930: NHStAH, Hann. 180, Hildesheim no. 11666, vol. I, fol. 266.

25 For reasons I am unable to ascertain, neither Charleville nor Etappe Gent feature in the list of books selling more than 100,000 copies in Donald Day Richards, *The German Bestseller in the 20th Century: A Complete Bibliography and Analysis 1915–1940* (Bern: H. Lang, 1968), 55–93.

26 The following page numbers in parentheses refer to the 1919 edition.

27 According to Appens's own statement in 'Fragebogen zur Durchführung des Gesetzes zur Wiederherstellung des Berufsbeamtentums', 7 April 1933: NHStAH, Hann. 180, Hildesheim no. 11666, vol. III. See Nicholas Stargardt, *The German Idea of Militarism: Radical and Socialist Critics, 1866–1914* (Cambridge: Cambridge University Press, 1994).

28 Heinrich Wandt, *Etappe Gent. Streiflichter zum Zusammenbruch. I. Band* (Berlin: Freie Presse, 1920). This edition has 182 pages. It is cited in the text as follows: (I/page number).

29 Heinrich Wandt, *Das Justizverbrechen des Reichsgerichts an dem Verfasser der 'Etappe Gent'* (Berlin: Der Syndikalist, 1926), 7.

30 Heinrich Wandt, *Etappe Gent. Streiflichter zum Zusammenbruch* (Vienna: Agis-Verlag, 1926), quote 4.

31 Heinrich Wandt, *Erotik und Spionage in der Etappe Gent* (Vienna: Agis-Verlag, 1928). This edition has 208 pages. The 1929 print run states that 31,000 to 40,000 copies were published.

32 The Dutch title was: *Etappenleven te Gent: Kantteekeningen bij de Duitsche ineenstorting* (Ledeberg: Hippoliet Janssens, n.d.). No copies of this edition are shown in major multi-library catalogues. The French translation was published as: Heinrich Wandt, *Vie d'étape à Gand. En marge de l'effondrement allemand*, 2 vols. (Ledeberg: Hippoliet Janssens, n.d.). The volumes number 168 and 150 pages respectively. It was not possible to obtain a copy of this edition. See also Christian De Backer, 'Heinrich Wandt (1890–1965), auteur van het Etappenleven ete Gent. Een proeve van bio-bibliografie', *Handelingen van de Maatschappij voor Geschiedenis en Oudheidkunde te Gent* 39 (1985): 223–46, 223, 244–5. My thanks to Bernard A. Wilkin for providing me with a copy of this essay.

33 Wandt, *Das Justizverbrechen*, 7. On Wandt's life, see also De Backer, 'Heinrich Wandt', 226ff.

34 On this context, see John Horne and Alan Kramer, *German Atrocities, 1914: A History of Denial* (New Haven: Yale University Press, 2001), 329–65. Horne and Kramer do not study *Etappe Gent*, and therefore underestimate the significance of

German voices who spoke out against the denial and trivialization of German war crimes.
35 On his criticism of the forced labour and deportation of Belgian civilians, see Jens Thiel, 'Menschenbassin Belgien'. Anwerbung, Deportation und Zwangsarbeit im Ersten Weltkrieg (Essen: Klartext, 2007), 175–6.
36 On the context, see Horne and Kramer, German Atrocities, 9–86.
37 Generalstaatsanwalt beim Landgericht I Berlin, 13 April 1929: Landesarchiv Berlin (LAB), A Rep. 358-01 (Generalstaatsanwaltschaft beim Landgericht Berlin), no. 2057.
38 Deutscher Offizier-Bund to Reich Interior Ministry (copy), 22 November 1928, and verdict of the Berlin-Mitte Local Court, 1 October 1929: LAB, A Rep. 358-01, no. 2057.
39 See the English translation of a longer excerpt in Ulrich and Ziemann, German Soldiers, 123.
40 Wandt, Etappe Gent (1926), 3.
41 Ibid.
42 Kurt Tucholsky, 'Militaria', Die Weltbühne 16, no. 1 (1920): 107, also in idem, Gesammelte Werke in 10 Bänden, 10 vols. (Reinbek: Rowohlt, 1975), vol. 2, 265.
43 'Charleville. Ein unbequemes Blatt preussischer Geschichte. Mit vier Bildern die keine Karikaturen sind' Freie Welt, 20 May 1920 (see the excerpt in Bundesarchiv Berlin-Lichterfelde (BArch), R 8034 II, 7497, fol. 38).
44 The following information is primarily based on 'Personalblatt Kreisschulinspektor Dr. Appens zu Hörde', n.d.: NHStAH, Hann. 180, Hildesheim no. 11666, vol. I; the 'Fragebogen zur Durchführung des Gesetzes zur Wiederherstellung des Berufsbeamtentums', 7 April 1933: NHStAH, Hann. 180, Hildesheim no. 11666, vol. III; and other documents in Appens's personnel file.
45 Arnsberg regional administrative authority to Prussian Ministry for Science, Culture and Education, 4 June 1921: NHStAH, Hann. 180, Hildesheim no. 11666, vol. I, fol. 67–8.
46 Bund entschiedener Schulreformer, 'Einladung zum Kongreß Menschenbildung und Lebensgestaltung, Mainz, Pfingsten 1922': NHStAH, Hann. 180, Hildesheim no. 11666, vol. I, fol. 113. The best overviews of the pacifist groups mentioned here can be found in Helmut Donat and Karl Holl (eds), Die Friedensbewegung. Organisierter Pazifismus in Deutschland, Österreich und in der Schweiz (Düsseldorf: Econ Taschenbuch Verlag, 1983).
47 Wilhelm Appens, Charleville pendant l'occupation allemande, 1914–1918. Visions d'histoire de la vie d'étape (Charleville: Imprimerie R. Renvez, 1929). It was not possible to locate the article in the Echo de Paris.
48 Prussian Ministry for Science, Culture and Education to Arnsberg regional administrative authority, 24 January 1930: NHStAH, Hann. 180, Hildesheim no. 11666, vol. I, fol. 250.

49 Arnsberg regional administrative authority to Prussian Ministry for Science, Culture and Education, 2 February 1930: NHStAH, Hann. 180, Hildesheim no. 11666, vol. I, fol. 251-2.
50 Prussian Ministry for Science, Culture and Education to Arnsberg regional administrative authority, 4 March 1930: NHStAH, Hann. 180, Hildesheim no. 11666, vol. I, fol. 266.
51 Prussian Ministry for Science, Culture and Education to Wilhelm Appens, 12 April 1930: NHStAH, Hann. 180, Hildesheim no. 11666, vol. I, fol. 266.
52 Wilhelm Appens to Prussian Ministry for Science, Culture and Education, 14 May 1930 (copy): NHStAH, Hann. 180, Hildesheim no. 11666, vol. I, fol. 272-4.
53 Prussian Ministry for Science, Culture and Education to Wilhelm Appens, 27 March 1933: NHStAH, Hann. 180, Hildesheim no. 11666, vol. III, fol. 180; Prussian Ministry for Science, Culture and Education, 23 August 1933 (copy): ibid., no fol.
54 NSDAP, Kreis Gelsenkirchen, 1 July 1933, report of Kreisobmanns des NS Lehrerbundes Lobbe to Gauleitung Westfalen-Nord: ibid., no fol.
55 Wilhelm Appens to Reichsminister für Erziehung, Wissenschaft und Volksbildung, 28 March 1941: NHStAH, Hann. 180, Hildesheim no. 11666, vol. III, no fol.; 'Ortschronik Lengede an der Fuhse 1151-2001' (2001), www.lengede.de/portal/php/index.php?ID=1149 (accessed 14 October 2016).
56 See Jörn Schütrumpf, 'Nachbemerkung', in Heinrich Wandt, *Erotik und Spionage in der Etappe Gent, Deutsche Besatzungsherrschaft in Belgien während des Ersten Weltkriegs*, (Berlin: Dietz, 2014), 319-62; cf. De Backer, 'Heinrich Wandt', 226.
57 Verdict of Landgericht I in Berlin, 31 December 1920: LAB, A Rep. 358-01, no. 2032.
58 Friedrich Karl Kaul, 'Es lebe der nächste Krieg...! Das Verfahren gegen den Schriftsteller Heinrich Wandt, 13. Dezember 1923', in *Justiz wird zum Verbrechen. Der Pitaval der Weimarer Republik* (Berlin: Das Neue Berlin, 1953), 123-49, 130-4.
59 Wandt, *Das Justizverbrechen*, 6-28. Wandt documented the trial and his imprisonment in *Der Gefangene von Potsdam*, 2 vols. (Vienna: Agis-Verlag, 1927).
60 Felix Fechenbach, 'Der Fall Wandt', *Die Weltbühne* 22, no. 1 (1926): 20-2. On the Gumbel case, see Christian Jansen, 'Der Zivilist als Außenseiter', in *Emil Julius Gumbel. Portrait eines Zivilisten* (Heidelberg: Wunderhorn, 1991), 9-77, especially 35-40. On both cases see also Benjamin Ziemann, 'German Pacifism in the Nineteenth and Twentieth Centuries', *Neue Politische Literatur* 60 (2015): 415-37, 425-6.
61 Wandt, *Das Justizverbrechen*, 8-9; cf. Kaul, 'Es lebe der nächste Krieg', 139.
62 Wandt, *Das Justizverbrechen*, 13-14, 17-18.
63 Kaul, 'Es lebe der nächste Krieg', 145; De Backer, 'Heinrich Wandt', 236.
64 Wandt, *Das Justizverbrechen*, 24-26.
65 De Backer, 'Heinrich Wandt', 239-43.
66 Schneider and Wagener, 'Einleitung', 14.

67 Ulrich, 'Perspektive von unten'.
68 Benjamin Ziemann, *Contested Commemorations: Republican War Veterans and Weimar Political Culture* (Cambridge: Cambridge University Press, 2013).
69 See the serialization of Heinrich Wandt, 'Die Tragödie eines Kriegsfreiwilligen', *Reichsbund*, 20 November 1931 to 5 February 1932. Wandt first told Niederländer's story in *Erotik und Spionage in der Etappe Gent* [1928], 172–5.
70 Vollmer, 'Imaginäre Schlachtfelder', 127–207.
71 Rainer Wohlfeil, 'Reichswehr und Republik', in *Handbuch zur deutschen Militärgeschichte*, ed. Militärgeschichtliches Forschungsamt, 9 vols. (Frankfurt am Main: Bernard & Graefe, 1969), vol. 6, 162.
72 The international reception of both texts remains a subject for future research. Newspapers and archives in Belgium, France and the Netherlands would be of interest, as would the files of the German Foreign Office, which may provide information on how the German authorities monitored reactions to the texts abroad. National and international press commentaries on Wandt's pardon in 1926 can be found in: BArch, R 43/I, 556. On *Charleville*, see for instance the review in the Parisian newspaper *L'Intransigeant*, 22 October 1921, which praises the 'exceptional value' of Appens's book.

# Select Bibliography

Audoin-Rouzeau, Stéphane and Annette Becker. *14–18: Understanding the Great War.* New York: Hill and Wang, 2003.

Baberowski, Jörg. *Räume der Gewalt.* Frankfurt am Main: S. Fischer, 2015.

Bartov, Omer. *Murder in Our Midst: The Holocaust, Industrial Killing, and Representation.* New York: Oxford University Press, 1996.

Bessel, Richard. *Germany after the First World War.* Oxford: Clarendon Press, 1993.

Boff, Jonathan. *Winning and Losing on the Western Front: The British Third Army and the Defeat of Germany in 1918.* Cambridge: Cambridge University Press, 2012.

Bourke, Joanna. *An Intimate History of Killing: Face-to-Face-Killing in Twentieth-Century Warfare.* London: Granta, 1999.

Chickering, Roger and Stig Förster, eds. *Great War, Total War: Combat and Mobilization on the Western Front, 1914–1918.* Cambridge: Cambridge University Press, 2000.

Deist, Wilhelm. 'The Military Collapse of the German Empire'. *War in History* 3 (1996): 186–207.

Eichenberg, Julia and John Paul Newman, eds. *The Great War and Veterans' Internationalism.* Basingstoke: Palgrave Macmillan, 2013.

Feltman, Brian K. 'Tolerance as a Crime? The British Treatment of German Prisoners of War on the Western Front, 1914–1918'. *War in History* 17 (2010): 435–58.

Feltman, Brian K., *The Stigma of Surrender: German Prisoners, British Captors, and Manhood in the Great War and Beyond.* Chapel Hill, NC: University of North Carolina Press, 2015.

Ferguson, Niall. *The Pity of War.* London: Allen Lane, 1998.

Gerwarth, Robert and John Horne, eds. *War in Peace: Paramilitary Violence in Europe after the Great War.* Oxford: Oxford University Press, 2012.

Geyer, Michael. 'Eine Kriegsgeschichte, die vom Tod spricht'. In *Physische Gewalt. Studien zur Geschichte der Neuzeit*, edited by Thomas Lindenberger and Alf Lüdtke, 136–61. Frankfurt am Main: Suhrkamp, 1995.

Geyer, Michael. 'How the Germans Learned to Wage War: On the Question of Killing in the First and Second World Wars'. In *Between Mass Death and Individual Loss: The Place of the Dead in Twentieth-Century*, edited by Paul Betts, Alan Confino, and Dirk Schuman, 25–50. New York: Berghahn, 2008.

Gumz, Jonathan. *The Resurrection and Collapse of Empire in Habsburg Serbia, 1914–1918.* Cambridge: Cambridge University Press 2009.

Horne, John and Alan Kramer. *German Atrocities, 1914: A History of Denial.* New Haven: Yale University Press, 2001.

Houlihan, Patrick J. *Catholicism and the Great War: Religion and Everyday Life in Germany and Austria-Hungary, 1914–1922*. Cambridge: Cambridge University Press, 2015.

Hull, Isabel V. *Absolute Destruction: Military Culture and the Practices of War in Imperial Germany*. Ithaca: Cornell University Press, 2005.

Hüppauf, Bernd. 'Experiences of Modern Warfare and the Crisis of Representation'. *New German Critique* 59 (1993): 41–76.

Jahr, Christoph. *Gewöhnliche Soldaten. Desertion und Deserteure im deutschen und britischen Heer 1914–1918*. Göttingen: Vandenhoeck & Ruprecht, 1998.

Jones, Heather. *Violence against Prisoners of War in the First World War: Britain, France and Germany, 1914–1920*. Cambridge: Cambridge University Press, 2011.

Kiesel, Helmuth. *Ernst Jünger. Die Biographie*. Munich: Siedler, 2009.

Kramer, Alan. *Dynamic of Destruction: Culture and Mass Killing in the First World War*. Oxford: Oxford University Press, 2007.

Kühne, Thomas. 'Massen-Töten. Diskurse und Praktiken der kriegerischen und genozidalen Gewalt im 20. Jahrhundert', in *Massenhaftes Töten. Kriege und Genozide im 20. Jahrhundert*, edited by Thomas Kühne and Peter Gleichmann, 11–52. Essen: Klartext, 2004.

Kühne, Thomas. *Belonging and Genocide: Hitler's Community, 1918–1945*. New Haven: Yale University Press, 2010.

Latzel, Klaus. *Deutsche Soldaten – nationalsozialistischer Krieg? Kriegserlebnis-Kriegserfahrung 1939–1945*. Paderborn: Schöningh, 1998.

Lawrence, Jon. 'Forging a Peaceable Kingdom: War, Violence, and Fear of Brutalization in Post-First World War Britain'. *Journal of Modern History* 75 (2003): 557–89.

Liulevicius, Vejas Gabriel. *War Land on the Eastern Front: Culture, National Identity, and German Occupation in World War I*. Cambridge: Cambridge University Press, 2000.

Meyer, Jessica. *Men of War: Masculinity and the First World War in Britain*. Basingstoke: Palgrave Macmillan, 2009.

Murdoch, Brian. *German Literature and the First World War: The Anti-War Tradition. Collected Essays by Brian Murdoch*. Farnham: Ashgate, 2015.

Murphy, Brendan. 'Killing in the German Army: Organising and Surviving Combat in the Great War'. PhD diss., University of Sheffield, 2014.

Nübel, Christoph. *Durchhalten und Überleben an der Westfront. Raum und Körper im Ersten Weltkrieg*, Paderborn: Schöningh, 2014.

Nübel, Christoph. 'Neuvermessungen der Gewaltgeschichte. Über den "langen Ersten Weltkrieg" (1900–1930)'. *Mittelweg 36* 25, no. 1–2 (2015): 225–48.

Plaut, Paul. 'Psychographie des Kriegers'. In *Beihefte zur Zeitschrift für angewandte Psychologie. 21. Beiträge zur Psychologie des Krieges*, edited by William Stern and Otto Lipmann, 1–123. Leipzig: Johann Ambrosius Barth, 1920.

Reichardt, Sven. Violence and Community: A Micro-Study on Nazi Storm Troopers. Central European History 46 (2013), 75–97.

Schneider, Thomas F. *Erich Maria Remarques Roman 'Im Westen nicht Neues'. Text, Edition, Entstehung, Distribution und Rezeption*. Tübingen: M. Niemeyer, 2004.

Smith, Leonard V. *Between Mutiny and Obedience: The Case of the French Fifth Infantry Division during World War I*. Princeton: Princeton University Press, 1994.

Smith, Leonard V. *The Embattled Self: French Soldiers' Testimony of the Great War*. Ithaca: Cornell University Press, 2007.

Smith, Leonard V. 'Mutiny'. In *The Cambridge History of the First World War*, edited by Jay Winter, 3 vols, 2: 196–217. Cambridge: Cambridge University Press, 2014.

Stephenson, Scott. *The Final Battle: Soldiers of the Western Front in the German Revolution of 1918*. Cambridge: Cambridge University Press, 2009.

Ulrich, Bernd. 'Kampfmotivationen und Mobilisierungsstrategien: Das Beispiel Erster Weltkrieg'. In *Töten im Krieg*, edited by Heinrich von Stietencron and Jörg Rüpke, 399–419. Freiburg: Alber, 1995.

Ulrich, Bernd. *Die Augenzeugen. Deutsche Feldpostbriefe in Kriegs- und Nachkriegszeit 1914–1933*. Essen: Klartext, 1997.

Ulrich, Bernd and Benjamin Ziemann, eds. *German Soldiers in the Great War: Letters and Eyewitness Accounts*, trans. Christine Brocks. Barnsley: Pen & Sword, 2010.

Watson, Alexander. *Enduring the Great War: Combat, Morale and Collapse in the German and British Armies, 1914–1918*. Cambridge: Cambridge University Press, 2008.

Weber, Thomas. *Hitler's First War: Adolf Hitler, the Men of the List Regiment and the First World War*. Oxford: Oxford University Press, 2010.

Ziemann, Benjamin. *War Experiences in Rural Germany 1914–1923*, trans. Alex Skinner. Oxford: Berg, 2007.

Ziemann, Benjamin. *Contested Commemorations: Republican War Veterans and Weimar Political Culture*. Cambridge: Cambridge University Press, 2013.

# Index

Aachen 221
Aarau 97
absence without leave 102, 105–9, 136, 140–2, 144, 147, 252 n.70, 254 n.89, 93–4, 255 n.96, 98
Africa 118, 204
Agis-Verlag 211, 215
Air Force 71
aircraft 28, 152
*Aktionsmacht* 6, 128
Alkmar 98
*All Quiet on the Western Front* 66, 174, 203
Alldeutscher Verband 97
Allenstein (Olsztyn) 58
Alsace 12, 30, 95, 113, 117, 148, 243 n.24, 252 n.66, 253 n.73,
Alsace-Lorraine 94, 107, 112–13, 115, 117, 130, 255 n.95, 97
ammunition 28, 58
amnesty 107, 118
amputations 1
Amsterdam 112
Anders, Günther 25, 233 n.17
anger 74, 77–8, 80, 88, 119, 167, 169–70, 185, 196, 209
anti-Catholicism 47, 53–5
anti-militarism 161, 169
anti-Semitism 58, 163
anti-war literature 204, 224
Antwerp 148
anxiety 25, 43, 185
Appens, Wilhelm 15, 204–5, 208–12, 216–20, 223–4
ARAC 161
Ardennes 50, 209
Arditi units 26
Armbrust, Adolf 111–12, 257 n.126
armistice 14, 134, 138, 152
  after the 90, 121, 159, 162, 177, 224
  before the 79, 108, 135–6, 142, 147, 149–50, 153, 195, 200
  demands/hopes 51, 132

  talks 266 n.64
  terms of the 130, 266 n.53
Army Supreme Command 83, 87, 101, 103–4, 117–18, 140, 143–4, 148, 152–4, 179, 195, 206, 253 n.73
army trench newspapers 245 n.56
Arnsberg 218
Articles of War *see Kriegsartikel*
artillery 3, 25, 27, 44–5, 47, 49, 68, 72, 88, 95, 124, 152
  artillerymen 25
  bombardment 32, 70, 188, 191
  fire 6, 22–4, 28, 49, 57, 69–70, 77, 80, 83, 184, 188, 190–1, 195
  munition 30
  shells 4, 23–4
  units 28, 194
  war 71, 80, 90
  weapons 8, 40
atomic bomb 25
atrocities 5, 27, 42, 46, 50, 53–5, 57–8, 61, 73, 86, 160, 165, 213, 230 n.57, 238 n.8
attendance of mass 36
Auer, Erhard 197
Aufderstrasse, Heinrich 128–9
Austria-Hungary 3, 35, 177, 299 n.43
authenticity 66
autobiographical writings 64, 167, 204

Baden 73, 169
Baden, Prince Max von 131, 147
Balkan wars 183, 280 n.23
Balkans 27, 34
Balke, August 59–60
Baltic 160, 177
Bamberger 95
Ban de Sapt 184, 187–93
bankruptcy 126, 132, 197
baptism of fire 44–5
barbarism 6, 59
barbed wire 10–11, 75, 81, 94–5, 146, 148

Barth, Boris 205
Bartov, Omer 4, 10–11
*Battle as an Inner experience* 64
Battle of Caporetto 34
Battle of Tannenberg 58
Battle of the Somme 4, 75, 77, 104
battlefields 8–11, 20–1, 52, 54–5, 64, 68–9, 74–5, 87–9, 94
battles of matériel 3, 21, 30, 43, 80, 95
Bauer, Max 206
Bavaria 25, 107, 140, 170–1, 177, 196, 252 n.69
Bavarian Palatinate 50
Bavarian Swabia 170–1, 183
bayonets 23–4, 51–2, 85, 189
Bayreuth 182
Beck, Ludwig 136
Belgium 15, 42, 46, 48, 53–4, 56–7, 60–1, 73, 98, 100, 144, 148, 204, 212, 217, 221, 224, 240 n.41, 289 n.72
Below, Otto von 209
Bergen 98, 249 n.39
Bergsträsser, Ludwig 262 n.7, 266 n.54
Berlin 99, 102, 112, 122–4, 163–4, 177, 179–80, 198, 200, 211, 213, 219, 222, 287 n.38
*Berliner Volks-Zeitung* 179–80, 219
*Berliner Zeitung* 198
Beseler, Hans Hartwig von 54
Bessel, Richard 166, 172
Bilse, Oswald 183
*Biologie des Krieges* 179
Bismarck, Otto von 125, 161
Black and Tan 160
blockade 102, 145–6
Bochum 56
Bolshevism 177
bombardments 9, 28, 32, 68–70, 80, 188, 191, 195
Bonn 190, 198
book of heroism 67
Bosnia-Herzegovina 33
bourgeoisie 168, 218
 bourgeois families 2, 38, 132, 182, 186
 bourgeois officers 151
 bourgeois pacifists 179–80
 bourgeois society 2
 bourgeois veterans 161
Bourke, Joanna 8, 73
Braunschweig 112

British Expeditionary Force 29, 114, 138, 235 n.39, 246 n.65, 259 n.137
brothels 205, 216
Brussels 98, 146
brutalization 14, 160, 162, 164–9, 171–7, 275 n.30, 276 n.45, 277 n.62
Buber, Martin 219
Bulgaria 28
Bund entschiedener Schulreformer 218
Bund Neues Vaterland 197, 218
Bündische Jugend 174–5

Cadorna, Luigi 33
Cambrai 83
cannon fodder 70
cannons 28, 51, 68
captivity 7, 34–5, 76, 100, 119, 138, 259 n.151
caritas 53
casualties 4, 6, 20, 22–3, 26, 47, 72, 80
ceasefire 22, 30, 81, 95, 127
cemetery 114
censorship 103–4, 117, 131, 204, 223–4, 266 n.52
Central Europe 11–12, 160
Central Powers 28, 32, 35, 123, 130–1
Centre Party 162
Champagne 118
Charleville 147, 209–11, 217, 219–20
*Charleville. Dunkle Punkte aus dem Etappenleben* 204–5, 208, 211–12, 217–19, 222–3, 286 n.25, 289 n.72
Chemnitz 100
Chickering, Roger 2
citizenship 104
civil war 11, 28
civilians 11, 74, 116, 208, 250 n.44
 atrocities/violence against 5–6, 27–8, 53, 57, 61
 Belgian 46, 50, 53–5, 57, 60, 213, 216, 224, 287 n.35
 French 46–7, 49, 53, 56, 60, 209–10, 224
 German 7, 41
 killing of 53–4, 56–7, 60, 85, 160
 of occupied territories 42, 204
 Serbian 27
civility 160
civilization 19, 38

class 11, 111, 132
  army 122
  divide 216
  lower 59
  middle 38, 42, 167–8, 174–5
  officer 33
  property-owning 171
  rule 210
  society 2
  upper 7
  working 13, 134, 168–73, 175, 179–80, 195, 218, 223, 276 n.39
clergy 36, 46, 54, 113
close-quarter combat 8, 40, 83–6, 90, 167, 191
code of honour 84, 191
collapse, German/military 107, 122, 130, 134–6, 138–40, 149, 153, 179, 206, 212, 268 n.21, 269 n.28
Colmar 148
Cologne 7, 99
colonies 15
Combles 70
comradeship 38, 86–7
corruption 14, 29, 204–5, 208, 210, 212, 223
Council Republic 170, 196
counter-attack 83
court-martial 33–4, 103–4, 106, 110, 141, 145, 147, 150, 183, 200, 257 n.126, 269 n.32
cowardice 46, 102, 109, 116, 142
Croatia 33
cultural history 2–3
culture of war 19–20

daggers 23, 89, 163
*Das Lied vom jungen Sterben. Kriegsroman aus dem Ban de Sapt* 192
DDP 180, 197
deaths 1, 7, 21–4, 47, 80, 174, 176, 187–8, 191–2, 195, 200, 225 n.97
death
  heroic 35, 174
  instinct 8–9, 25
  penalty 114, 251 n.58
  rate 7, 22, 35, 43
  sentence 34, 114, 213, 259 n.137
decimation 33–4
defeat 34, 63, 79, 126, 129, 135, 137, 152–3, 164, 166, 168, 170, 179, 196

German 89, 162, 268 n.14
  military 121, 130, 133, 151, 206
defection 13, 94–5, 97, 100–1, 103–5, 107–8, 112–13, 115, 247 n.6, 251 n.54, 252 n.65, 256 n.109, 258 n.134, 260 n.161
defence 74, 84
  aggressive 27
  force 54
  formation 173, 197
  in depth 26–7, 87
  organizations 196
  readiness for 162
  technique 10
Deimling, Berthold von 178
Deist, Wilhelm 14, 135–40, 149–51, 153–4, 231 n.69, 237 n.1, 267 n.2, 269 n.28, 272 n.85
Delbrück, Hans 122
demobilization 104, 130, 134, 258 n.136
  cultural 172, 174, 198
democratization 130, 154
demonstrations 126, 159, 173, 180, 197
Denmark 96, 102–3, 107, 179, 251 n.53
depression 41, 67, 150
Deputy General Staff 98, 103, 252 n.69, 253 n.75
*Der Etappensumpf* 206–8
*Der Kampf* 112
desertion
  barriers for 99–100
  in the British Expeditionary Force 235 n.39
  combating 102–4, 114
  court-martials and 105–7, 113, 115, 142, 254 n.93–6, 256 n.104
  definition of 105, 142, 252 n.70
  extent of 13, 93, 103, 108, 254 n.89, 255 n.98, 256 n.109
  of French soldiers 40
  mass 32, 120
  motives for 109–11, 117, 119
  nationality and 32–3, 112, 115
  opportunities for 96, 101
  in the press 97
  self-mutilation and 34
destruction 8, 32, 52, 70, 84, 90, 131, 154, 177
  of buildings/towns 6, 28, 46, 58, 159, 239 n.28

of the human body 6, 223
physical 1, 25, 211
self-destruction 12, 86
total 26–7, 61
will to 64
detention 100
*Deutsche Distillateur-Zeitung* 222
Deutsche Friedensgesellschaft 180, 218
Deutsche Liga für Menschenrechte 197, 218, 220
Deutscher Offiziers-Bund 197, 213
diarrhoea 24
*Die freie Welt* 217
*Die Gleichheit* 220
disarmament 63, 161, 172, 181, 198
discrimination 117–8
disease 23, 125
disillusionment 9, 42, 128
disintegration 138, 140, 147, 150–2, 205
disobedience 103, 108, 137
Dittmann, Wilhelm 125
divorces 165–6, 220
DNVP 162
dog patrols 102
Dortmund 208–9, 218, 220
Dreyfus, Alfred 221–2
drills 29, 49, 184
dugouts 25, 68, 70, 79, 81, 113, 139, 187, 189
Düsseldorf 221, 252 n.70

East Prussia 58–9
Easter Uprising 160
Eastern Europe 11–12, 160
Eastern Front 11, 22, 27, 34, 57–61, 82, 85, 108, 112–13, 115, 168, 258 n.131
Ebert, Friedrich 163–4
*Echo de Paris* 219, 287 n.47
effeminacy 64, 163
Einem, Karl von 151
Einert, Fritz 152
*Einwohnerwehr* 121, 170
Elias, Norbert 5, 30
emotions, collective 1
enemy fire 30, 55, 68–71, 88, 94, 110, 128, 139, 191
English Channel 29
*Entente* 35, 124, 152
Epp, Franz 196
eroticism 213, 216

Erzberger, Matthias 129
espionage 102, 211, 213, 222, 250 n.42
Étaples 29
*Etappe* 142, 145, 147, 204, *see also* rear area
*Etappe Gent* 204, 208, 211–13, 217, 220–3, 284 n.6–7, 286 n.25, 34
Europe 2, 5, 7, 13, 24, 27, 30, 159–60
executions 13, 27, 33–4, 81, 113–15, 120, 160, 258 n.136
exhaustion 108, 133–4, 150, 185
experiences
    of the army's collapse 153
    of death 35, 200
    in the early days of the war 43, 48, 50
    of friendly fire 55
    front-line 20, 36, 47, 110, 123, 159, 162, 164, 176, 179, 203
    history of 123
    of hunger 127
    Jünger's wartime 9, 66, 68, 71–2, 75, 85, 88–9
    of mechanized warfare 13, 90
    Schützinger's wartime 187–8, 190–3, 200
    of smuggling food 98
    of violence 3, 14, 161–2, 178–9, 181, 200, 203, 173, 186
    of the war of attrition 63
    wartime 2, 11, 42, 47, 53, 56, 66, 97, 152, 160, 169, 171, 173–4, 178, 198, 211
    of a weapon 25
eye witnesses 8, 152

face to face combat 8, 78, 83
face to face killing 73, 81
farmers 1, 12, 29, 99, 110, 170–1
fascism 164
fatalism 133
fear of death 36
femininity 125
Ferguson, Niall 8, 73–4, 231 n.63, 243–4 n.33
field
    army 41, 99, 106–7, 134–5, 138–40, 150, 152–4, 249 n.34
    hospitals 23, *see also* military hospitals
    kitchens 28
    police 102, 108, 145, 250 n.42
    punishment no. 1 154

Finland 177
Fins 71
Fischer, Fritz 2
Flabas-Hammont 96
flamethrowers 83, 189
Flanders 6, 94, 102, 211
folklore 58
Fontenelle 188–9
food
    rations 99, 127
    shortage 7, 24, 124, 170
    supplies 24, 35, 127
Forbach 183
forced labour 211, 287 n.35
fortifications 82, 94, 184–5, 194
France 6, 19, 24, 37–8, 40, 42, 48, 50–4, 57–8, 60, 107, 112–13, 118, 160–1, 172–3, 204, 210, 224
France, northern 15, 43, 46, 53, 98, 211, 217
Franco-German War 1870/71 24, 50, 54
francs-tireurs 50, 53–5, 61, 239 n.17
fraternization 112
Free Trade Union 128
Free Workers 112
Freiburg/Breisgau 2
Freie Arbeiter 112
*Freie Presse* 211, 220
Freikorps 121, 165, 168, 170, 176–7, 180, 196
Freising 196
Freud, Sigmund 8
Freymuth, Arnold 222
Friedensbund der Kriegsteilnehmer *see* Peace League of Ex-Servicemen
friendly fire 47, 53, 55, 57, 61, 70, 238 n.17
front-line
    action 70, 135
    experiences 47, 159, 164, 203
    fighting 30, 110
    service 32, 124, 220
    soldiers 2, 15, 28–9, 81, 85, 126, 148, 185–6, 205–6
        brutalization of 169
        expectations of 123–4, 134
        fear of 46
        former 181, 198
        heroic deaths of 174
    mass movement of 134, 154
    pacifism and 178
    perseverance of 19
    politicization of 122, 130
    taking prisoners 74
    units 30, 101, 132, 140, 144, 147–8, 211, 217
    zone 194
Fussell, Paul 2

Galicia 58
Gallipoli 118
Garde Civique 54
garrisons 29, 56, 68, 96, 106, 116, 183, 195–6
gas masks 70
Gaulle, Charles de 34
GDR 112
genocide 10–11
Gerisch & Co 208
German East Africa 15
German League for Human Rights *see* Deutsche Liga für Menschenrechte
German Literature Archive 66
German Peace Society *see* Deutsche Friedensgesellschaft
Geßler, Otto 197
Geyer, Michael 4, 12, 27, 86–7
Ghent 142, 211–13, 220–1, 223
graves 52, 114–15, 179, 184
grenades 184, 186
Grenoble 218
grief 36, 67, 191
grievances 100, 122–3, 127, 131–2, 159
Gumbel, Emil Julius 165, 221
Gumbinnen (Gusev) 58

Hague Convention 7, 74
Halberstadt 31
Hamann, Arthur 150–1
Hamburg 167–8, 198
hand grenades 23, 72, 75, 79–80, 83–5, 90, 167, 186, 188–90
Hanover 66, 68, 99
Hašek, Jaroslav 12
Hatten, Major von 209
Haubach, Theodor 219
Heartfield, John 213, 215
Hefele, Hermann 205

Helfferich, Karl 117, 260 n.161
Henz, Max 213
Herbst, Emil 243 n.24
Herxheim 50, 52
Herz, Ludwig 107
Hesse 58
hidden military strike 14, 35, 93, 98, 108, 119, 121, 136–7, 139, 261 n.1
Hildesheim 218
Hiller, Kurt 219
Hindenburg Line 84
Hindenburg, Paul von 58, 163, 173, 222, 274 n.15
history of mentalities 2, 225 n.5
Hitler Youth 174–5
Hitler, Adolf 54, 176
hoarders 170
Hobohm, Martin 122, 126, 149, 264 n.28, 271 n.72
Hoffmann, Johannes 196
Hofmann, Michael 64
Hohentwiel 195
Holmes, John Haynes 181
Holocaust 10–11
Holy Communion 36
home leave 29, 96–7, 117, 119, 145
Hörhold, Berthold 31
Horne, John 46, 53–5, 230 n.57, 238 n.17, 286 n.34
hostage-taking 27–8, 57
Hungary 177
hunger 127, 189
Hüppauf, Bernd 2
hyperinflation 170, 208, *see also* inflation

ideology 86, 208, 241 n.51, 279 n.15
Imperial Penal Code 109
imperialism 28
Independent Social Democrats *see* USPD
indiscipline 33, 58
inequality 130, 132
infantry 22, 25–6, 30, 44, 69, 71, 101, 104, 128, 188, 254 n.91
  French 45, 47
  soldiers/infantrymen 19, 40, 68, 70, 80–1, 85, 98, 111, 243 n.22
inflation 132, 170, *see also* hyperinflation
influenza 24, 133
Ingels, Yvonne 213
Ingolstadt 34, 194

injuries 1, 6, 23–4, 26, 30, 47, 66, 80, 83, 86, 99, 110
injustices 111, 130, 132, 193, 203, 216, 223–4
innovations, tactical 26, 86
insubordination 132, 142
intelligence 28, 32, 76, 107, 115–16, 151, 167, 184, 213
international law 23, 46, 54, 60
interwar period 2, 14–15, 26, 121
invincibility 87–8, 192
IRA 160
Ireland 160
Italy 34–5, 38, 107, 160, 177

Janssens, Hippoliet 211
Jena 218
Jews 10, 162, 206, 219
Jones, Heather 6
Jospin, Lionel 40
Jospin, Robert 40
Judaism 163
Jungbanner 175, 278 n.66
Jünger, Ernst 3, 8, 13, 26, 63–90, 128, 191–2, 200, 241 n.3, 243 n.22

Kahr, Gustav Ritter von 196
Kalisz 57
*Kampf als inneres Erlebnis* 64
Kapp Putsch 168, 171, 196–7, 200–1, 276 n.40
Kariger, Wilhelm 100
Keegan, John 4
Kempowski, Walter 190
Kempten 183, 189
Kiel 136
Kiesel, Helmuth 66–7, 81, 83
killing
  act/practice of 3, 6, 9, 20, 67, 159, 178, 187
  anonymity of 83
  of civilians 46–7, 53–4, 56–7, 60, 82, 85, 160
  face to face 24, 73, 80, 86
  mass 4, 36, 43, 211
  pleasure of 8, 90, 167
  of surrendering/wounded soldiers 73–4, 76–8, 80
King, John 66
Klemperer, Victor 24–5

*Komitadjis* 27–8
Konstanz 97
Koworsk 113
KPD 168, 181
Kramer, Alan 46, 53–5, 230 n.57, 238 n.17, 286 n.34
*Kriegsartikel* 51, 101
Kriegsgeschichtliche Forschungsanstalt des Heeres 106
Kulturkampf 161
Kupka, Robert 100
Kyffhäuserbund 175

labourers 33, 99, 110, *see also* workers
Lachmann-Mosse, Georg 179
Lake Constance 96–7, 183, 195
*Landser* 87
Landwehr 50, 95, 97, 115, 143, 218
Lang, Karl 113–14, 258 n.134
Latzel, Klaus 168
League of Nations 173
Lechfeld 25
Ledeberg 211
Leie-Hermann position 142
Leipzig Trials 74, 221
Lengede 218, 220
Lettow-Vorbeck, Paul von 15
Leuven 6, 51, 53, 55, 228 n.32, 239 n.28
Levi, Paul 222
Liebknecht, Karl 48, 112, 239 n.20
Liège 51, 71
Lier 148
Lindau 183
listening posts 94, 101, 110
literature 3, 24, 39, 66, 70, 178, 210, 217
Lithuania 59, 98
Lodz 57
looting 57, 127, 159
Lorraine 43, 51, 223, 249 n.39
loss rate 21–2
Lower Bavaria 99, 170, 250 n.45
Lower Franconia 50
Lower Saxony 218
Ludendorff, Erich 117, 129, 136, 163, 179, 206, 274 n.15
Luton 159
Luxemburg, Rosa 163

machine guns 10, 23–4, 51, 77–8, 81, 83, 86, 128, 194–5

companies 153
fire 3, 72, 189, 194, 200
gunners 128
Magdeburg 219
Magdeburger Börde 171
Majority Social Democrats *see* MSPD
male fundamentalism 64, 66
malnutrition 7, 35
Maltese Cross 65
marauding 141
Marbach 66
March Uprising 1920 168
Marx, Wilhelm 222
masculinity 15, 64, 88, 162–3, 165
Masurian Lakes 58
Mauthausen 35
melee weapon 23–4
memoirs 12, 113–14, 139, 206, 211
memory 4, 15, 40, 73, 162, 172, 182, 192, 205, 272 n.87
metaphors 9–10, 12, 64, 67–70, 77–8, 85, 87, 125, 135, 154, 177, 273 n.97
Mézières 209
militarism 56, 152, 211, 216, 219
military
  aggression 27
  apparatus 1, 13, 19–20, 102, 132, 147, 151, 195, 204, 223
  authorities 25, 37, 93, 97, 99–100, 103, 107–9, 112–13, 115–20, 125, 136, 139–42, 148, 205, 209, 220–1, 250 n.44, 252 n.70, 255 n.98
  chaplains 8, 37, 53, 113, 212, 229 n.43
  courts 19, 105–6, 193, 254 n.94
  defeat 121, 130, 133, 151
  discipline 10, 132, 135
  elites 50, 131, 205
  history 2, 4, 8, 10, 106, 135, 230 n.59
  hospitals 26, 67, 206, *see also* field hospitals
  judges 32, 105
  justice system 114
  mobilization 41, 63
  policy 2
  psychiatrists 3, 8, 109–10
  records 2
  service 11–12, 22, 32, 37, 42, 87, 93, 97, 107, 110–11, 170–1, 189, 218, 220, 255 n.101

strike 14, 35, 79, 93, 98, 108, 119, 121, 136–7, 139, 147, 155, 261n1
technology 1, 8, 90
training 55, 194
Wilhelmine 64, 205, 223
Military Penal Code 101, 105, 140, 142
militias 121, 170–2, 177, 195
minefields 102
Minster, Carl 112
mobilization 2, 28, 97, 130, 153, 171, 175, 180–1, 198
  anti-republican 90
  French 169
  general 43
  mass 12, 204
  military 41–2, 63
  paramilitary 172, 177
  total 151, 170
modernism 39
modernity 3
Möhl, Arnold Ritter von 196
Mons 146
Montmedy 194
mortality rate 23
mortars 68, 70, 83, 94–5
Mosse, George 164, 174–5, 276 n.45
MSPD 122–3, 125, 132, 181, 196–7, 200
Mudra, Bruno von 209
Münch, Philipp 167
*Münchener Post* 197
Munich 105, 140, 170, 181–2, 196–7, 252 n.69, 254 n.94
mutinies 12, 19, 29, 33, 37, 40, 136, 154, 231 n.63
Münster 103, 219, 252 n.70
Müsebeck, Erich 221

Nancy 46
narratives 4, 40, 66, 137, 140, 175, 204, 212–13, 217, 222–3, 237 n.65
national minorities 12, 32, 93–4, 103, 105, 107, 109, 112, 115–16, 118–19, 255 n.101
National Socialism 14, 175, 210
National-Sozialer Verein 218
nationalism 37–8, 89, 116, 133, 167, 186, 213
  soldierly 63, 87

nationalist
  camp 162, 173, 175, 205, 220, 274 n.12
  discourse 38, 186, 206
  youth associations 174
nationhood 37–40, 50
Naumann, Friedrich 218
Nazi regime 14, 93
Nazis 3, 35, 164, 177, 203
NCOs 33, 41, 86, 93, 95, 101, 106, 116, 1 43, 187, 193, 205, 209, 218, 247 n.15
Neidenburg (Nidzica) 58
nervous collapse 25
Neter, Eugen 130, 169
Netherlands 96, 98, 100, 102, 107, 111–12, 213, 224, 249 n.38, 251 n.53, 253 n.75, 257 n.126, 189 n.72
Neufchâteau 50
New Fatherland League *see* Bund Neues Vaterland
Nicolai, Georg Friedrich 179
*Nie wieder Krieg* movement 172, 180
Niederländer, Major 223, 289 n.69
no man's land 72, 80, 82, 94–5, 184–5
Nobel Peace Prize 183
North Schleswig 96, 103, 107
Noske, Gustav 196–7
NS Lehrerbund 220
Nuremberg 43

occupation 15, 53, 58–9, 181, 204, 209–10, 212–13, 217, 224, 230 n.60
occupied territory 29, 146, 152, 204
Oellingen 50
offensive in spring 1918 10, 13, 21, 86, 125, 143, 179
officer
  class 33, 208, 210
  corps 89, 121, 163, 197, 201, 206, 217, 221, 223, 246 n.65, 271 n.72
officers
  behaviour of 49–50, 206
  career 14, 173, 178, 184–5, 197–8
  junior 33, 49, 138–9, 185
  NCO's and 101, 205
  pacifist 198
  soldiers and 3, 7, 27, 33, 39, 54, 67, 77, 84, 188, 191
official medical report 23, 143, 191, 270 n.57

Operation Barbarossa 244 n.46
Operation Michael 126, 264 n.25
Orainville 68
Order of Merit 65
Ossietzky, Carl von 179, 221
outbreak of war 20, 179–80, 185

pacifism 14, 161, 172, 177–8, 180–1, 190, 193, 200, 218
Pan-German League 131
paramilitary
    groups 121, 177
    mobilization 172, 177
Paris 51–3, 58, 220
parliamentarization 131
patriotic instruction 126, 163, 209
patriotism 38, 49, 161
peace 14, 37–9, 57, 81, 127, 132–3, 179, 184, 205
    agreements 51, 154
    conditions for 130, 181
    immediate 123
    longing/hope for 52, 90, 123–4, 129, 131, 169
    movement 134, 180, 190
    negotiations 52, 123
    Scheidemann 131
    treaty 163, 212
Peace League of Ex-Servicemen 179–81
perpetrators 3–4, 6, 10–11, 19, 26, 42, 55, 57, 109, 160, 187, 247 n.5
Persius, Lothar 173, 198
Pethick-Lawrence, Emmeline 181
Pfaff, David 48–50, 53
Pfeiler, Hermann *see* Schützinger, Hermann
photographs 2, 77–8, 100, 185, 189, 191
picture postcards 2
Pieck, Wilhelm 112
piety 50, 170
Pinker, Steven 5, 228 n.28
pistols 23, 49–50, 72–3, 77, 86
Plaut, Paul 3
poems 1, 15
*poilus* 19, 38, 169
poison gas 9, 23–4
police operations 28
politicization 122, 130
Popitz, Heinrich 6–7, 19, 128

Popp, Margarete 44
Posen *see* Poznan
postal surveillance 102–3, 122, 130, 260 n.155
Potsdam 221, 256 n.112
POW's 7, 34–5, 118, 229 n.41
Poznan 116, 143
prayers 36, 44, 48–9, 114
premonitions 45, 187, 189, 191
prison camps 35, 98, 100, 118, 148
prisoners of war 35, 98, 100, 118, 149, 256 n.111, 268 n.14
    British 7, 73
    capturing 7, 34, 48, 50–1, 58, 71–80, 90, 96, 138–9, 150, 235 n.45
    French 7, 97, 119
    German 7, 73, 76, 138–9, 153, 247 n.10
    Romanian 35
    Russian 97
    treatment of 6–7, 74, 84
    violence against 75
profiteers 37, 39, 170
projectiles 68–70, 195
Prokuplje 28
Promethean gap 25
propaganda 1, 37, 52, 100, 115, 126, 138, 209, 224, 250 n.51
prostitution 216
protofascism 66, 88, 90
Prussia 65, 224
Prussian Interior Ministry 116
Prussian Ministry for Science, Culture and Education 209, 219
Prussian War Ministry 100, 102, 104, 112, 115, 117, 142, 147–8, 212, 252 n.63, 260 n.161, 272 n.91
psychological damage 25, 30, 190, *see also* trauma

radio units 30
rape 56–7
Rat der Volksbeauftragten 164
*Rätebewegung* 134, 195
Rathenau, Walther 151
Ravenna 33
rear area 29, 102, 206, 208–13, 223
    Belgian 102, 143, 204, 213, 221
    conditions in the 206
    deserters in the 98–9
    discourse on the 210, 217

French 204
German rule in the 15
life in the 37, 205, 209, 211–12
militarism 14, 201, 210–11, 216–17
mutinies in the 33
officers in the 154, 216
of operations 136–8, 142–9
shirkers in the 137–8, 143–5
soldiers in the 96, 105, 108, 114, 118, 256 n.109, 114
rebellion 136, 154, 175
reciprocity 76–7, 79
reconciliation 172–3, 179, 181, 216–17
Red Ruhr Army 168
refugees 12
refusal 34, 108, 110, 120–1, 134, 136, 142, 152, 173, 218
forms of 13, 109–10
mass 13, 101
Regensburg 183, 195–7
regimental histories 55, 137, 238 n.8, 240 n.36, 258 n.134, 280 n.23
Regniéville 72
Reich Archive 2, 114, 136, 149, 221, 256 n.112, 267 n.8
Reich Interior Ministry 2
Reichsbanner Schwarz-Rot-Gold 152, 173, 175, 178, 196, 198, 201
Reichsbund der Kriegsbeschädigten, Kriegsteilnehmer und Kriegshinterbliebenen 172–3, 181, 223
Reichsmilitärgericht 105
Reichstag parliamentary subcommittee 107, 122
Reichsvereinigung ehemaliger Kriegsgefangener 181
Reichswehr 153, 168–9, 176, 196–7, 221, 223–4
Reimann, Aribert 168
Reims 6, 68
religion 36, 38–9, 53
Remarque, Erich Maria 66, 174, 203, 242 n.10
remembrance 12, 36, 58, 70, 89, 173–5, 240 n.46
Réméréville 45–7, 238 n.16, 17
replacement army 29–30, 41, 106, 124, 134, 137–8, 251 n.63, 254 n.94, 256 n.109

representations 3, 12–13, 36, 164, 203, 222
republic 37, 89, 96, 130, 138, 200
resistance 12, 34, 54–5, 80, 84, 93, 138, 142, 153, 189
Reuß of Köstritz, Prince Heinrich XXXVII 220
Reventlow, Count Ernst von 97
Reventlow, Franziska zu 97
Reventlow, Rolf 97
revolution 37–8, 89, 122, 124, 136, 138, 163, 168, 258 n.136
Rhine 96–7
Rhineland 152, 172
Richert, Dominik 12, 30, 73, 111, 252 n.65
rifles 23–4, 49, 51, 56–7, 80–3, 86, 113, 171
Roeder, Karl von 107
Rohr, Willy 82
Romania 107
Rosenstock, Eugen 219
routine 3, 34, 68, 73–4, 78, 83, 114, 145
Royal Irish Constabulary 160
Ruhr region 168–9, 181, 219
Rümmler, Otto 56–7, 240 n.41
Russia 22, 43, 49, 57, 59–60, 94, 107, 113, 118, 123, 241 n.50
Russian Poland 58–9, 204

sabres 23, 168
Sachse, Hermann 59
Sacred Heart of Jesus 36
sacrifice 37, 40, 111, 133, 162, 164, 174–5, 179
Saxony 57, 100, 153, 171, 198, 276 n.40
Saxony-Anhalt 276 n.40
Scheidemann, Philipp 129, 131
Schenk, Georg 43–50, 53, 55–6, 238 n.16
Schickele, René 219
Schimmer, Stefan 50–3, 55–6
*Schipper* 29
Schirach, Baldur von 174
Schleswig-Holstein 96
Schmalkalden 152
Schoenaich, Paul Freiherr von 178
Schützinger, Hermann 14, 173, 178, 181–8, 190–201, 279 n.8, 280 n.20, 23, 26, 283 n.90
Second International 39
Second World War 8, 10–11, 26–7, 87, 153, 257 n.115
security police 196

Sedan 144
Selchow, Bogislav von 162–4, 274 n.14
self-defence 24, 167, 276 n.40
self-destruction 12, 86
self-discipline 27
self-mutilation 32, 34, 93, 109–10, 142
self-testimonies 190
Senones 50
sentry duty 71, 83, 114, 184
Serbia 27–8, 107
sermons 37
Serres 44
sexual relationships 29
shell shock 3, 25
shellfire 68, 70
shirkers 12, 32, 99, 108, 119, 136–8, 141–6, 148–50, 154, 206, 268 n.15
shortage of labourers 99
shrapnel 23, 44, 69, 71, 83
Siegfried Position 84
slaughtering 129
snipers 26, 32
Social Darwinism 55, 183
social democracy 125, 131, 154, 195
socialism 39, 210
socialist movements 38
Socialist Party of France 161
Socialist Workers' Youth 175
Sofsky, Wolfgang 4, 7, 21
Somme 3–4, 21, 43, 75, 77, 104
Sonderweg 61
South Eastern Europe 11
Soviet Union 4, 59, 82
Sozialistische Arbeiterjugend 175
*Sozialistische Monatshefte* 196
Spartacus Group 112, 163, 168, 257 n.127
SPD 48, 131, 154, 175, 196–7, 210, 218, 220, 222, 261 n.162
spirit of 1914 126
Spraul, Gunter 55, 240 n.36
St. Quentin 145
stab-in-the-back 121, 125, 135, 138–9, 162–4, 205, 216
Staehle, Major 221
Stahlhelm 173, 175
standing army 42
Stendal 219
Stenger, Alice 222
Stenger, Heinrich 222
Stenger, Karl 73–4

stereotypes 1, 54, 59
Stokes, Lieutenant 80
*Storm of Steel* 9, 13, 64–7, 73, 87–9, 242 n.12
storm troops 10, 13, 26, 63–4, 67, 82–3, 85, 87, 89
Strasbourg 112
strike, January 123–6, 134, 263 n.16
Stuttgart 220
surrender 34, 51, 73–4, 76, 78–80, 84
    mass 138
    official 137
    ordered 137–40
survival 12, 28, 66–7, 80, 137, 144, 187–8, 192, 200, 269 n.28
    rates of 30, 32, 35
    surviving the war 4, 13, 19, 88, 93, 161, 175, 195
    survivors 20, 31
Suttner, Bertha von 183
Switzerland 96–8, 102, 107, 117, 119, 249 n.33, 255 n.99
swords 23, 96, 138

tacit agreements 30, 81, 95, 247 n.15
Tat-Flugschriften 205
telephone 150
Thaer, Albrecht von 143, 151, 269 n.41
theodicy 37
Theresienstadt 35
Theweleit, Klaus 64
thick description 4–5
Third French Republic 161, 222
Third Reich 25, 198
Thirty Years' War 5
three-class voting system 131
Tiemann, Hans 167
Tilburg 100
Torgau 7, 228 n.35
trade unions 56–7, 59–60, 132
training courses 28, 30
trains 29, 98, 102, 143–4, 146, 149, 252 n.69, 70
trauma 3, 7–9, 66, 121, *see also* psychological damage
treason 98, 118, 125, 213, 220–1, 224
Treaty of Versailles 63, 162, 181, 212, 224
trench warfare 4, 10, 25, 32, 66–8, 71, 77, 80–1, 83, 127, 141, 193
trophies 76–7

truncheons 72
Tucholsky, Kurt 179, 198, 217
tunnels 68–70
tying-up 154

U-boats 31
Ukraine 160
Ullstein publishing house 203
Ulrich, Bernd 3, 13
unconditional victory 129
Union Fédérale 161
Union Nationale des Combattants 161
United Kingdom 3, 5–6, 38, 40, 97, 115, 159–61, 232 n.74
Upper Bavaria 170
Upper Silesia 116, 177
Upper Swabia 97
USPD 112, 125, 132, 168, 181, 211, 217

*Vaterländischer Unterricht see* patriotic instruction
Vaterlandspartei 124, 133, 163, 266 n.60
Verdun 3, 21, 30, 43, 118, 193
Verlag der Freien Presse 211
Verlag der Volksbuchhandlung 208
Versprengten-Sammelstellen 102, 148–9
veterans 14, 121, 160, 166, 169, 175, 177, 179–81
   associations 159, 161, 170, 172–3, 178, 218
   bourgeois 161
   pacifist 40, 172, 178, 198, 201
   republican 173, 178, 218
   socialist 40, 152, 223
Vetter, Karl 179–80
victimhood 35, 39–40, 70
victimization 39, 70, 173, 217, 223, 237 n.65
victory 38, 42, 52, 58, 70, 79, 90, 99, 124, 126, 128–9, 135, 162, 172, 210
Vietinghoff, Hermann von 116
violence,
   absence of 15
   acts of 5, 7, 9, 20, 50, 64, 74, 82
   aestheticization of 26
   analysis of 4–5, 12, 22, 74
   anti-revolutionary 165
   collective 55
   coming to terms with 14
   counter- 13
   cycles of 20
   de-escalating the 28
   deadly 85, 159
   definition of 6
   escalation of 10–11
   exercise of 22, 64, 198
   experience of 14, 161, 200, 203
   forms of 7, 9, 11, 20, 67
   gendering of 15
   history of 5–6, 8, 11, 73, 153
   imagination of 10
   laboratory of 9
   lethal 4, 13, 21, 87
   machinery of 12
   observer of 66
   organized 1, 5, 148, 195
   orgy of 9
   paramilitary 121, 162, 169
   perpetration of 1
   physical 67, 170
   political 14, 160, 171, 278 n.70
   practice of 2–3, 14–15, 66, 75, 82, 86, 90, 177, 230 n.60
   radicalization of 13, 15
   representations of 13
   stigma of 9
   war of 1, 118, 154
   wartime 3, 5, 9, 66, 74, 162, 173, 175, 181, 203
*Völkischer Beobachter* 63
Volkmann, Erich Otto 114, 116, 136, 149
Volkswehr 195–7
volunteers 12–13, 42, 48–50, 63, 71, 83, 89, 121, 167, 189, 195, 231 n.62, 238 n.6
*Vorwärts* 173, 200
Vosges mountains 30, 50–1, 95, 184, 187

Waite, Robert G.L. 177
Wandervogel 174–5
Wandt, Heinrich 15, 204, 208–9, 211–17, 220–4, 288 n.59, 289 n.69, 72
war
   of annihilation 4, 27–8, 85, 234 n.28
   crimes 57, 74, 287 n.34
   diaries 9, 13, 26, 42, 53, 66–7, 74, 88–90, 122, 128, 206, 219, 242 n.9

effort 1–2, 5–6, 12, 22, 37, 60, 101, 132, 213
enthusiasm 41, 46, 126–7, 185, 193–4
guerrilla 15, 27–8, 55
horses 28, 58
industry 29
letters 25, 70, 125, 167, 186, 192, 200, 205, 275 n.31, 285 n.11
literature 63, 87–8, 200, 203–4, 206, 224, 242 n.8, 9, 284 n.7
loans 48, 130
logistics of 28
machine 30, 41, 70, 195
neurosis 3, 25
novels 15, 24, 174–5, 183, 192, 200, 203–4
people's 27, 46
profiteers 37, 39
total 1, 10, 217
weariness 103, 117, 123, 133, 137, 152
warfare
  future 121
  genocidal 87
  industrialized 9, 23, 28, 64
  mechanized 13, 42, 70, 89–90
  mobile 21, 34, 43, 47, 127–8, 143
  totalization of 61
Warthelager 143
wasteland 25, 152
Watson, Alexander 137–40, 142, 149, 246 n.65, 262 n.5, 268 n.15, 268 n.21, 271 n.72, 272 n.85
Weber, Thomas 54, 176
Wehrmacht 4, 26, 59, 82, 85, 87, 93, 109, 153
Weimar Republic 14–15, 58, 63, 90, 125, 139, 162, 164, 166, 171–7, 179, 196–7, 203–4, 208, 216–18, 222, 224, 284 n.7
Weisbrod, Bernd 64, 66
welfare state 3

West Prussia 112, 116
Western Europe 160
Western Front
  collapse of the 134, 138, 140, 153
  Eastern and 11, 22, 61
  final months on the 169, 179
  German troops on the 10, 21, 23, 26, 79, 83, 122–4, 133, 136–8, 150, 168, 194–5
  losses on the 43, 143
  rear area of the 206, 208
  refusal on the 13, 108, 132, 135, 139
  violence on the 67, 69, 82
*Westfälische Allgemeine Volks-Zeitung* 208
White Terror 170, 196
Wilhelm II 89, 111, 130, 210
Wilhelmshaven 31
Wilson, Woodrow 130, 147
Wolffs Telegraphisches Büro 188
workers 125, 132, 210, *see also* labourers
  councils 134, 163
  German 60, 112
  industrial 1, 27, 32, 38, 110, 123, 135, 263 n.15, 276 n.40
  munition 37
  organized 56, 168
  recalled 124
  socialist 135, 162, 168, 171, 220
  unorganized 56
worm's-eye view 52, 206
wounded 1, 20, 23, 44, 69, 73–9, 83–4, 86, 89, 102, 133, 136, 143, 146, 150, 166–7, 186–7, 195, 200
Württemberg 97, 153, 252 n.70

Ypres 23

Zabern Affair 116–17, 178
Zeigner, Erich 198
Zetkin, Clara 220
Zickler, Artur 200

Made in the USA
Coppell, TX
21 July 2022